THOSE WERE THE DAYS 2.0

the beatles and apple

STEFAN GRANADOS

This updated edition first published in Great Britain in 2021
by Cherry Red Books (a division of Cherry Red Records),
Power Road Studios, 114 Power Road, London W4 5PY

A CIP Catalogue record for this book is available from the
British Library.

ISBN: 978-1-909454-86-6

Layout by Nathan Eighty (nathan.eighty@gmail.com).

THOSE WERE THE DAYS 2.0

the beatles and apple

ONCE THERE WAS A WAY...

I climbed out of a white Rolls Royce limo, walked up a few stairs and opened the door to 3 Savile Row...it was more than 50 years ago. That day I stepped into the wonder and simple magnificence of a magical time, incredible people, and the beginning of cherished memories. When I open the pages of Stefan Granados's beautiful book, *Those Were The Days 2.0,* I once again find myself carried back to that same phenomenal place...a place where I once belonged.

There is a clarity and kindness of intent in Stefan's writing approach to a vision simply called Apple. I asked Paul McCartney why they named it Apple, and after a pause he answered with a wink, "Have you ever heard anyone say anything bad about an apple?" Because of the way Stefan visits those days and places, I have a sense of reunion to the most monumental time in my life. Within these pages I revisit old friendships with renewed insight. I am brought to a fresh wonder of what went on in both London and L.A. back then and what it was like working with the most exciting and talented four musicians I have ever known.

The reason I am writing these words is because, for me, this book makes that whole journey personal for a reader. Apple had heart; real people and real stuff going down that was unmatched in its creativity, talent and dedication to purpose!

The great reward for me in reading *Those Were The Days 2.0* is that at Apple there was so much that I was unaware of that was going on around us and within us in the frenzy of it all. Stefan artfully presents the facts, follies, and forevermore essence of an unmatched era that brought joy to so many of our lives.

I can't go back, but once again I am able to get back to those days within the pages of this excellent book.

Peace and love,

Ken Mansfield
U.S. Manager of Apple Records, 1968-1969

Ken Mansfield is the author of several books, including his most recent, *The Roof*, which details his time at Apple and the afternoon he spent as a guest of the Beatles on the roof of 3 Savile Row, watching the Beatles play their final live concert. More information is available at www.kenmansfield.com

THOSE WERE THE DAYS 2.0:
THE BEATLES AND APPLE

Originally entitled *Those Were The Days: The Unauthorized History Of The Beatles' Apple Organization 1967-2002,* the previous edition of this book was published by Cherry Red Publishing in 2002. It was the first-ever comprehensive exploration of both the music and business of Apple from its inception through to its then-current incarnation.

Much has changed since the original publication of *Those Were The Days,* particularly in how music is created, marketed, and consumed. The music of the Beatles has not been exempted from the impact of those changes. Since 2002, the Beatles – under the auspices of Apple – finally made the jump to digital music, became a Las Vegas attraction, and faced off in the court room for one final time against the now omnipresent Apple Inc., the technology company that had morphed into a major player in the music industry over the decades that had passed since the Beatles first learned of a small company in California that was trading under the name Apple Computers.

This expanded edition of *Those Were The Days* brings the still-evolving Apple saga up to date and adds a significant amount of new information and images to the original work. It hopefully reflects Apple as it was known by its former employees and by the artists who created the music that has endured for so many years. That is the spirit in which it was written.

INTRODUCTION

Just a short walk from London's bustling Piccadilly Circus is Savile Row, a street lined with handsome townhouses that have historically been home to some of England's finest tailors. Given the select clientele served by these bespoke tailors, for decades there had been only modest activity on the street, except for the small groups of people who regularly gathered in front of number three, to gaze up at the roof and to take pictures on the steps of what appeared to be nothing more than a typical – and sometimes derelict – Georgian building.

The daily arrival of visitors to number three has never really let up. The numbers may have dwindled slightly with the passing years, but individuals from all walks of life from around the world still make the pilgrimage, despite there being not much to see other than the exterior of a building. But once upon a time long ago, it was an entirely different scene. In the early seventies, busloads of tourists regularly pulled up in front of the building to take photos of the Hare Krishna devotees and long-haired young men who swarmed in and out of the building at all hours of the day. Teenage girls clad in mini-skirts could often be seen huddled at the foot of the stairs in all sorts of weather, straining to hear the muffled sounds of guitars and drums filtering out of the basement. They would remain there for hours, waiting for a chance to see an outlandishly dressed 28-year-old Paul McCartney come breezing out of the front door and to quickly disappear into a waiting car or around the corner up Vigo Street.

Today (circa 2020), there are once again crowds of young people coming and going at number three, but they now come to shop at Abercrombie and Fitch, the London outpost of an American clothing chain that opened for business at this location in 2013. There had been a spirited protest from an odd coalition of tailors and music fans who believed that a chain store did not belong on Savile Row, particularly in a building whose roof was the site of the last public performance of the Beatles. Abercrombie and Fitch ultimately prevailed, and there is now – outside of a small display of Beatles books and memorabilia – little left to link the building to its past life as the home of the Beatles' Apple organization, the company that the group established in 1967 to manage their business affairs and which would later evolve into a music publisher and record company. Yet, even in its current manifestation, 3 Savile Row continues to draw a steady flow of Beatles fans from around the world, curious to see if they can discern the slightest spark of magic in the group's old London haunt of the sixties and, perhaps, even score a bargain from the sale rack of Abercrombie and Fitch.

Apple still captures the imagination of many who fall under the powerful spell of the Beatles, which is not surprising given that the iconic Apple logo is once again featured prominently on all Beatles-related products. Apple is clearly a thriving business, yet, paradoxically, it has historically been regarded as a failure, or as an idealist sixties experiment that went horribly wrong. At best, Apple is remembered – if at all – as the ill-fated venture that the Beatles had hoped would be a corporate manifestation of sixties youth culture. From its hurried, almost haphazard inception in early 1967, Apple evolved quickly and grew to an organization that boasted close to sixty employees by late 1968. The rapid speed at which Apple developed certainly played a role in the company's ultimate undoing, yet the Beatles' plans for Apple were ambitious and showed just how quickly the group – at this point in their career – could transform their whims into action. Over the course of the eight years that Apple functioned as a record label – launching the careers of stars like Mary Hopkin, James Taylor, Badfinger, Billy Preston and Hot Chocolate – Apple blossomed, withered, and then slowly faded away, much like the free-spirited sixties pop culture that had sparked its inception. From the jubilant launch in 1968, to the subdued, almost indifferent closing of the record division in 1975, Apple's collapse symbolized not only the end of the myth of the Beatles, but also the dissolution of the ideals, forward-thinking attitudes, and positive energy of an entire era.

Yet Apple exists to this day, tucked away on a quiet side street in the heart of London. In fact, Apple never really went away. Apple has long been regarded as the Beatles' great folly, but the reality of Apple tells a different tale. Through its careful cultivation of the Beatles brand, it takes in millions of pounds a year on behalf of the surviving Beatles and their respective estates. Though Apple's hallways are no longer filled with young musicians and record executives, there are always several Beatles-related projects to keep Apple's small staff busy. In many ways, Apple has finally evolved into the streamlined business office that the four Beatles had envisaged when they set up the company all those years ago.

The story of Apple is a fascinating chapter of the Beatles' history, but it is a story that is by no means exclusive to the Beatles. Between 1968 and 1972, Apple was a leading independent record label, operating much like any of the other long-defunct independent English record labels of the day such as Pye, Track, or Immediate. The mid-to-late sixties into the early seventies was a time when seven-inch singles still ruled the music scene and a singer or pop group could literally walk into a record company office from off the street with a primitive, home-made demo recording of a song, and emerge a few hours later with a record deal. There were no lawyers, just a handshake, a hastily signed contract and a promise to have the artist booked into a recording studio in a few weeks' time.

It was an era when an independent label in England could get a record played on the BBC on a Friday afternoon and – if their distribution was sorted – have a national hit by the following week. Success was not attained through focus groups and integrated marketing campaigns but rather through creating good records that were championed by radio disc jockeys with whom record labels worked to cultivate personal relationships. Apart from the fact that Apple was owned by the most successful pop group of the sixties, it was not all that different from the other independent labels of the era and the story of Apple captures much of that special and long-gone time in pop music.

ABOUT THIS BOOK

Creating a comprehensive Apple chronicle many decades after the fact inevitably posed significant challenges. At the time of the first edition of *Those Were The Days*, several key players in the Apple story – including John Lennon, George Harrison, Bernard Brown, Derek Taylor, Pete Ham and Tom Evans of Badfinger, Billy Preston, Mal Evans, Ron Kass, George Alexander of Grapefruit, Wayne Gabriel of Elephant's Memory, and several others – had already passed away. Since then, they have been joined by Neil Aspinall, Allen Klein, Jackie Lomax, Terry Doran, Mike Gibbins of Badfinger, Paul Tennant of Focal Point, Rick Frank of Elephant's Memory, and Tom Smith and Guy Masson of Mortimer. Thankfully, many former Apple artists and staff are alive and well and have graciously agreed to be interviewed for this book.

The passage of time has, not surprisingly, dulled the memories of some of the participants.

So, while many of the individuals interviewed can still vividly recall the events that distinguished their respective associations with Apple, exact dates and certain details may have slipped beyond the grasp of memory. There were occasions when quotes from previously published interviews given by these people during the sixties and seventies were far more detailed and evocative of the era than the quotes taken from the 1996–2020 interviews conducted by the author. In such cases, decisions were made to use the previously printed material, rather than new quotes that did not do justice to the Apple story.

A special note of caution must be made about the financial figures quoted in this book. Given that Apple was – and remains – a privately held company, it is not required to disclose its financial records in any significant detail. Compounding the challenge of the limited nature of available published financial records, inflation and the fluctuation of exchange rates over the past half a century makes it difficult (if not impossible) to accurately convert sales figures and royalty rates from the sixties and early seventies into current day pounds or dollars. Because of these factors, financial details are not likely to be exact figures and they are given for illustrative purposes only.

Ultimately, it is only the Beatles' accountants who know exactly how much Apple paid for the Savile Row building, or how much Apple artist Doris Troy was given as a weekly wage. The numbers quoted in this book were typically arrived at through comparing several reliable sources and, in general, appear to be reasonable estimates that are probably close to the actual amounts.

No attempt was made to involve Apple in the creation of the first edition of *Those Were The Days*. Neil Aspinall, the long serving MD of Apple, was notoriously discrete about Apple's business and inner workings. He rarely granted interviews, and when he did, he typically forbid any efforts to record the conversations. As was the case with the first edition of *Those Were The Days, Those Were The Days 2.0* is an "unofficial history" and is not authorized by, or in any way affiliated with Apple Corps Ltd..

Finally, in the interest of avoiding libel suits (and sullying the memories of people who are no longer around to defend themselves) I have intentionally left out incidents that I considered to be dubious, mean-spirited, or simply not relevant to the central Apple story. I have endeavored to keep my editorial voice and interpretation of events to a minimum, preferring to rely on the testament of those involved to tell the story of Apple. After all, it is *their* story.

CONTENTS:

PART ONE: THE NEMS YEARS

For a young person, life in post-war England was a much different proposition than that of their parents' generation. The country had yet to fully recover from the ravages of the Second World War, yet by the early sixties, the austerity of the war years was fading and there were ample employment opportunities to be had. Those born during and immediately after the war were now teenagers and the English business community had begrudgingly come to the realization that teens now constituted an influential market segment. The entertainment industry in particular found that catering to the youth market could be quite lucrative. Most of the records and films consumed by English teens during this period were imported from America, though by the early sixties, home grown musical acts such as Billy Fury and Cliff Richard and the Shadows were giving the Americans a run for their money.

American pop culture loomed large in post-war Europe, and for the most part, professional opportunities in the entertainment business were limited for native-born talent. For an aspiring pop group of the era like the Beatles – from Liverpool of all places – a career in music typically promised little more than weekly engagements at local dances and youth clubs, and if they were lucky, perhaps a chance to cut a record that might get one or two spins on Radio Luxembourg or the BBC. Of course, fate held something quite different in store for the Beatles. Less than a year after their debut single, "Love Me Do," became a minor national hit, the Beatles suddenly found themselves engulfed by a tidal wave of fan hysteria. During the halcyon days of 1963 and 1964, Beatlemania swept unchecked across the world, and in its wake, show business, popular music and arguably the world itself would be changed forever.

Guiding the Beatles throughout the turbulent years of Beatlemania was their manager, Brian Epstein. From 1962 to 1967, the Beatles were managed exclusively by Epstein. Coming from an affluent Liverpool family, the mild-mannered Epstein bore little resemblance to a typical "pop" manager of the day. Prior to managing the Beatles, Epstein's music industry experience had been limited to running the record department of his parents' Liverpool store, NEMS (North End Music Stores). But given that he was one of the few people in Liverpool to have actually conducted business with the London-based record companies, Epstein's decision to venture into artist management was not as far-fetched as it seemed at the outset. The Beatles were impressed with Epstein's music industry connections and his genuine enthusiasm for their music, so they eagerly signed the management contract he offered them on 24 January

1962. After Ringo Starr replaced previous drummer Pete Best in August, an updated management agreement was signed on 1 October that would bind the Beatles to Epstein through to the end of September 1967.

Epstein formed a new company, NEMS Enterprises, to look after the Beatles and any other clients he might later sign. From that point onward, all of the money generated by the Beatles was funnelled directly into NEMS. In exchange, the four Beatles were each given a salary and, later, had their living expenses paid by the company, with any excess funds being deposited in banks or invested on behalf of the group.

Despite sharing a name, NEMS Enterprises was not associated with the NEMS shops. There was a family connection, however, in that NEMS Enterprises had been partially funded by Brian's younger brother, Clive, who, like Brian, worked at one of the NEMS stores. Shares of NEMS Enterprises were split between three parties, with Epstein controlling 70% of the company, Clive Epstein controlling 20% and the four Beatles each getting a 2.5% stake in the new venture.

Initially, Epstein's management duties focused on securing a recording contract for the group, polishing their professional presentation, and overseeing the group's live bookings. But once the full force of Beatlemania took hold in 1963, the relationship evolved exponentially and the Beatles became increasingly reliant on Epstein and NEMS to take care of almost every aspect of their personal and professional lives.

Receiving a 25% share of the Beatles' gross income (the management deal was tiered so that there would be a 10% commission on earnings up to £400 a week, 20% for earnings up to £800 per week and 25% for earnings in excess of £800), Epstein was certainly very well compensated for his efforts. But to his credit, Epstein served the band with a remarkable sense of care and devotion and it was obvious that he regarded the Beatles as much more than just a once-in-a-lifetime business opportunity. In the early days of Beatlemania, Epstein's name was synonymous with the Beatles. Due in large part to the remarkable success of the group, Epstein was able to build NEMS into a high-powered management company that would become the dominant force behind the Liverpool music scene.

Having seen what Epstein had done for the Beatles, artists from every corner of Liverpool and the surrounding region rushed to align themselves with NEMS. From 1963 onward, NEMS managed the careers of Cilla Black, Gerry and the Pacemakers, the Fourmost, and Billy J. Kramer, as well as several lesser-known Liverpool groups.

Under Epstein's skillful direction, NEMS developed a diverse and initially highly successful client roster. But it was clear to all of the other NEMS artists that the Beatles were Epstein's one true passion. Whether charged with finding a house for one of the Beatles, negotiating television appearances, or quietly settling such personal matters as threatened paternity suits, Epstein handled his duties in an efficient, dignified manner and all four Beatles considered him to be not only a manager, but a friend. When it came to the Beatles, no matter was too trivial to be given Epstein's full attention.

In retrospect, Epstein's principal shortcoming was his marked lack of business acumen. Still, while much of the Beatles' success can, and should, be attributed to their immense talent, it was Epstein's music industry contacts and his careful handling of the group's image and presentation that transformed the Beatles from a rough, leather-clad rock and roll group from "up North" into a polished, international show business phenomenon.

Today, Epstein's significant contributions to launching the Beatles' career are often overshadowed by the astonishingly poor business deals that he negotiated on behalf of the group. The original recording agreement Epstein signed with EMI in 1962 was a one-year contract that gave EMI the option of extending the Beatles' contract for three successive years. In return, the group would get one penny of recording royalties for each single sold and precious little more for each album sold in England. For any Beatles recordings licensed to record companies outside of England, the group would receive only half of the English royalty rate.

In Epstein's defence, the record deal that he negotiated was not unusual by music industry standards of the day. He would fare far worse with the merchandising deal that he set up on behalf of the group. Epstein's most celebrated fiasco was the 10% royalty rate that he accepted for the English and later the North American licensing rights to manufacture and sell such seemingly trivial Beatles merchandise as wigs, shampoo, trading cards and the countless other novelty items that flooded variety stores during the peak of Beatlemania. When Epstein entered into these deals in late 1963 and early 1964, the 30-year-old ex-furniture and record salesman from Liverpool was no match for the quick-talking businessmen who appeared to be offering him thousands of pounds in exchange for the simple use of the Beatles' name on what he perceived to be insignificant teen-oriented products. Due to the limited scope of his business experience, Epstein effectively gave away the rights to the Beatles' merchandising – a move that would ultimately cost the Beatles millions of dollars of lost revenue.

The underlying problem was that there was simply no precedent. Few music industry professionals in that era – let alone a novice like Epstein – ever imagined just how much money music merchandising could generate. To Epstein, any revenue from the sale of such ancillary Beatles products was just found money to supplement the Beatles' live and recording income.

Never considered to be a great negotiator, Epstein's true strengths were his well-developed organizational abilities and his conservative, reliable stewardship of the Beatles' finances. With Epstein overseeing the group's affairs, the four Beatles enjoyed a relatively carefree existence when it came to financial matters. If they wanted any item – be it a car, a house, or items as mundane as new clothes – they simply charged it to NEMS and the bill would be paid with no questions asked.

Given that NEMS was so thoroughly involved in managing their finances, the four Beatles made few personal investments during the peak years of Beatlemania. The investment activities of the individual Beatles were limited to Ringo Starr's interest in a high-end but short-lived construction company and Paul McCartney's decision (unbeknownst to the other three Beatles) to buy additional shares in Northern Songs, the music publishing company that held the rights to the Beatles' songs.

Epstein had made sure that the four Beatles held shares in the companies that were set up to handle various aspects of the Beatles' business. One such entity was Subafilms, the NEMS-run film company that controlled the group's share of the Beatles' feature film projects and was also responsible for producing Beatles promotional films (in the days before video) for television.

The four Beatles also all owned shares of Northern Songs, the company that held the publishing rights to the Beatles' original compositions.

Music publisher Dick James had been exceptionally fair to the Beatles (by standards of the day) when he set up Northern Songs in February 1963. Recommended to Brian Epstein by Beatles producer George Martin, James had a tremendous amount of respect for the Beatles and their music. The Beatles may have been little more than a talented group with one minor hit ("Love Me Do") to their credit when James first met with Brian Epstein in November 1962, but James, a failed pop singer and then-struggling music publisher, knew that the songs of Lennon and McCartney had the potential to become major hits.

In exchange for the publishing rights to the Beatles' second single, "Please Please Me," James leveraged his music industry connections to secure the Beatles a coveted spot on the BBC television program *Thank Your Lucky Stars*. Impressed by James' ability to get the Beatles on television, Epstein decided that Lennon and McCartney would sign with Dick James Music.

But Dick James had other ideas. In a highly unusual move during an era in which songwriters would often sign away their royalties for little or no money, James proposed setting up a subsidiary company, Northern Songs, for the sole purpose of publishing the songs of Lennon and McCartney (George Harrison would also sign to Northern once he started writing songs). Under this deal, the Beatles and NEMS were given shares that represented just under a 50% stake in the company. In the early sixties, a standard publishing deal would typically split royalties 50:50, with half going to the music publisher and the other half to the writer(s). The Beatles signed a traditional 50:50 deal with Northern Songs, but the innovative arrangement devised by James allowed both NEMS and the Beatles to profit from the publisher's share of the royalties in addition to the 50% writer's share that Lennon and McCartney received as songwriters. James's reason for essentially entering into a music publishing partnership with the Beatles was not driven by any sense of altruism, but rather, by his interest in ensuring that the Beatles would maintain a long-term relationship with Dick James Music if they had a significant ownership stake in Northern Songs.

Several years later, Lennon and McCartney would become co-owners (80% was owned by Lennon and McCartney, the remaining 20% by NEMS) of a company formed on 4 February 1965 known as Maclen Music Ltd. Even though Lennon and McCartney were signed to Northern Songs, Maclen "licensed" the rights to publish Lennon and McCartney songs to Northern Songs and collected the writer's share of the publishing royalties on behalf of Lennon and McCartney from Northern Songs.

In 1964, Dick James had set up a company known as Maclen Music Inc. to publish the songs of Lennon and McCartney in North America, Mexico, and the Philippines, but unlike Maclen Music Ltd., this company was owned and controlled by Northern Songs.

Outside of their passive investments in Subafilms and Northern Songs, all four Beatles – initially, at least – seemed to be perfectly willing to let their royalties pile up in their NEMS account and to simply charge any expenses they had to NEMS.

In the sixties, it was generally accepted that artists were responsible for creating the music and that professional managers took care of the business. Out of all of the English groups who sold millions of records during the "British Invasion," only Dave Clark of the Dave Clark Five had the foresight, and skill, to take full control of his group's business affairs. Not only did Clark negotiate a royalty rate with EMI that far exceeded that of the Beatles, but he also retained the rights to all of his band's master tapes (which he had only licensed to EMI for a set period of time) and music publishing. Clark was shrewd, and he would also later buy the rights to the celebrated English pop music television show *Ready Steady Go!*, giving him exclusive rights to live TV performances by the Beatles and other top groups of the era.

By the mid-sixties, both Harrison and McCartney started to take a greater interest in the finances of the Beatles, yet there was actually very little that one or even two Beatles could do to shape the direction of the group's collective business activities. Since the earliest days of the group, the Beatles made all of their decisions by consensus. Given the success of this democratic system, each Beatle was somewhat reticent to appear too domineering in the eyes of the others. In the interest of preserving harmony within the group, it was often simply easier to let Epstein or another outsider handle business matters.

Compared to many of their contemporaries, the Beatles were unusually democratic for a pop group. The way they conducted their business was largely governed by the strong personal ties between the four members of the band. Having been bound together through the non-stop recording and touring schedule that they maintained for close to five years, by 1967 the Beatles enjoyed a near family-like relationship and were quite accustomed to doing almost everything together.

Each Beatle had explored individual pursuits after the group ceased touring in 1966. These included such non-Beatles projects as John Lennon's acting role in the film *How I Won The War* and Paul McCartney composing the musical score for the film *The Family Way*. Neither of these projects were regarded as a serious attempt to establish careers outside of the group and none of the side projects seemed to detract from the band's intense sense of camaraderie. When the Beatles settled back into Abbey Road Studios in late 1966 to begin work on *Sgt. Pepper* they were still an incredibly tight-knit unit. In the summer of 1967, the Beatles even explored buying a Greek island where they could live and work together. They went as far as to visit Greece and select an island to purchase before they suddenly lost interest and dropped the whole project.

It was in this spirit that they entered into their next venture, the jointly owned business that would become Apple. Curiously, while each Beatle had at one time or another stated that the Beatles as a group would not go on forever, none of them appeared to envision the possibility that there could ever come a time when they would no longer be on speaking terms, let alone be business partners.

Since the summer of 1966, the Beatles and their NEMS-appointed financial advisors – principally Harry Pinsker and Stephen Maltz of the accounting firm Bryce, Hanmer and Isherwood – had been exploring options for setting up a new Beatles corporation that would consolidate the groups' business affairs and enable them to lessen the impact of the notoriously harsh tax system (when Apple was formed, the Beatles' income was being taxed at a rate of approximately 90%) that existed in Britain at that time. This proposed corporate entity – that would ultimately manifest itself as Apple – was not set up to replace Epstein and NEMS, but rather, to complement the NEMS organization.

The high-level plan would be to create several Beatles backed business ventures that would generate immediate income and eventually be floated as a public company.

The first step towards establishing this business structure was to form a new partnership called Beatles and Co. in April 1967. To all intents and purposes, Beatles and Co. was an updated version of the Beatles' original partnership, Beatles Ltd. Under the new arrangement, each Beatle would own 5% of Beatles and Co. and a new corporation owned collectively by the four Beatles (which would soon be known as Apple) would control the remaining 80% of Beatles and Co. On 4 December 1967, Beatles Ltd. changed its name to Apple Music Ltd., which would later be changed for the final time to Apple Corps. Ltd.

With the exception of individual songwriting royalties, which would continue to be paid directly to the composer of a particular song, all of the money earned by the Beatles as a group would to go directly to Apple and would thus be taxed at a lower corporate tax rate.

The timing of the formation of this new Beatles company had been largely driven by EMI being due to pay out approximately £1,000,000 in accumulated royalties to the Beatles in January 1967. Under the new scheme, the Beatles would receive £800,000 from Apple for their shares in Beatles and Co., paid out in two installments. These payments would be taxed as capital gains which was a lower rate than the individual tax rate. The first installment of £400,000 was paid out to the Beatles in April, with the second installment due to be paid out in April 1971, when it was anticipated that Apple would be generating the revenue needed to cover the remaining payment. In the meantime, the remaining funds from the EMI royalty payment – less taxes and NEMS' 25% commission – would be used to fund the launch of Apple.

The Beatles appeared to be so anxious to begin reaping the tax rewards offered by this plan that they entered into their new partnership agreement having given little thought to the possible future implications of their actions. John Lennon – who was taking copious amounts of LSD throughout the period that Apple was formed – would later claim that he didn't remember signing any new partnership agreement at all.

Peter Brown, a former NEMS shop employee who moved down to London in 1965 to become Brian Epstein's personal assistant, explains the origins of Apple: "When Apple was formed, which was before Brian died, it wasn't called Apple, but the structure of the buyout was there. The reason the Beatles sold 80% of themselves to this entity, which would become Apple, and to change Beatles Ltd. to Beatles and Co. was to save taxes. The reason that the 80% sale was triggered was because of the accumulated royalties at EMI that they were due to receive and the fact that if the royalties had been paid to them as individuals, it would have been taxed at 85% or something like that. This structure was set up by Clive Epstein [Brian Epstein's brother] as a tax structure. At one point it was suggested that this be a real estate company; that was the original idea for lack of anything else. They couldn't figure out what to do with all this capital. All of this was set up while Brian was alive. After Brian died, my recollection is that they then decided to take this entity and create what they did, which was Apple."

The formation of this new Beatles business entity happened to coincide with a period of marked turmoil at NEMS. By late 1966, Epstein appeared to be growing weary of running the now sprawling NEMS organization. In January 1967, he appointed Robert Stigwood, an Australian artist manager and booking agent who had been working in England for several years, to be co-Managing Director and to oversee the day-to-day operations of NEMS. Epstein would continue to have sole responsibility for the Beatles and Cilla Black, but Stigwood would be responsible for the remainder of the NEMS roster as well as the artists that he had brought over with him to NEMS, specifically Cream and the Bee Gees.

Barbara Bennett, who worked for NEMS in the small Stafford Street office that Epstein had set up as a dedicated Beatles office maintains that Stigwood was the perfect person for Epstein to bring into NEMS. "Robert Stigwood was a fabulous man. He brought in Cream, the Bee Gees and, I think, the Paramounts to NEMS. Robert was fantastic and he was gay. The problem with Brian was that he was gay, but he wasn't comfortable with women. He didn't have a rapport with women at all. He was comfortable with his secretary, Joanne, who worked from his house at Chapel Street, and I was working for him in the office. He was fine with us two, but nobody else. It was really strange. But Robert was a different sort of man. He always used to say to the girls, 'I'm doing a reception tonight for the Bee Gees. Would you mind serving the drinks?' But about a half hour in, he would come up and say, 'They can get their own drinks now,' and we could join the party. And the next morning there would be fantastic flowers on your desks to thank us for what we had done. Such a nice man."

Due in part to Epstein's personal problems that sprung from his increasingly complex gay lifestyle and escalating drug use, there had been times throughout 1966 when Epstein seemed to be losing control of his ability to effectively manage NEMS and the Beatles. To Epstein's dismay, by 1967 the Beatles had become very much aware of how NEMS' handling of the band's merchandising had cost the group millions of dollars of income. The Beatles also resented the fact that many lesser groups had secured far more lucrative record contracts than Epstein had secured with EMI for the Beatles.

Epstein would somewhat rectify matters when it was time to renegotiate the Beatles' EMI contract in January 1967. In exchange for re-signing to EMI until 1976, the Beatles would receive 10% of the wholesale price of an English album and 17.5% of the wholesale price of each album sold in America. But the new agreement also exposed a darker side of Brian Epstein. Feeling less valued and needed since the Beatles ceased touring in August 1966, Epstein was becoming increasingly preoccupied with the prospect of the Beatles not renewing his management contract, which was set to expire at the end of September 1967. Presumably driven by this fear, Epstein inserted into the new EMI contract a clause that stipulated that royalty payments would be channeled through NEMS – who would continue to deduct their 25% commission before passing the remaining funds to the Beatles – for the duration of the nine-year deal. No provision was made to address how payments would be structured if the NEMS management deal was terminated. The Beatles – who had complete trust in Epstein – would not learn about this regrettable clause until several years later.

Despite their concerns about Epstein's emotional state and displeasure with some of the business deals that NEMS had brokered early in their career, the Beatles never publicly announced any intention to leave Epstein upon the expiration of his management contract. None of the band's associates from that time – with the notable exception of Pete Shotton, a life-long friend of John Lennon who would be hired to manage one of Apple's first business ventures – believe that the Beatles would ever have left Epstein. They would have certainly renegotiated the terms of the management agreement, but once the financial terms had been adjusted to be more favorable to the Beatles, there was no other compelling reason for the group to sever their ties with Epstein and NEMS. The Beatles wanted to have more control over their creative and business activities, but that desire could certainly have been realized within the existing NEMS relationship.

Setting up Beatles & Co. had been the first step in establishing the proposed corporate structure for the Beatles that would allow the group to have more control over their finances and a significantly lower tax burden. But the next step would be of far greater interest to the group.

Having set up their new company, they now needed to create an actual business in which to invest their capital if they were going to receive any tax benefit without running afoul of Inland Revenue. Being some of the best-known, most-respected young millionaires in the world, the Beatles felt the need to invest in a business that would simultaneously complement their image and provide a good measure of financial security.

Given such an ambiguous mandate, the Beatles were decidedly unsure about what form their new business should take. But as 1967 wore on and the Beatles moved into one of the most adventurous stages of their development (both personally and musically) they began to envision their business venture as becoming something more ambitious than a simple tax shelter.

Much of the energy and idealism that would define the early development of the Beatles' new company was drawn directly from the flowering youth culture and the exciting art and music scenes that had emerged in London towards the end of 1966. By the summer of 1967

– the much heralded "Summer Of Love" – London (along with San Francisco in the United States) found itself at the epicentre of a dynamic youth movement. As winter gave way to spring, the youth of Britain (or at least London) were filled with a wonderful sense of optimism and the BBC and offshore pirate radio stations made sure that the entire nation was awash in the remarkable sounds of such colourfully named groups as Pink Floyd and the Jimi Hendrix Experience. The Beatles were quite taken with swinging London, and it was not unusual to find one or more Beatles checking out "happenings" or performances by the one of the many new groups.

It was not only music that was capturing the imagination of England's youth and the interest of the world's media. In almost every corner of London, new boutiques, art galleries, and specialty bookshops were springing up and the best and brightest young minds in England were attempting to reshape a few select London neighbourhoods in their own image. Comprising the first generation of English youth who were too young to feel the full impact of the Second World War, these fashionable teenagers and twenty-somethings felt free to pursue their interest in music, art, and leisure, and they did so with great zest. The introduction of drugs to the scene only served to bolster the generally giddy spirit of the time.

Poised at the absolute centre of all this activity was Paul McCartney. With his impressive home in the posh St. Johns Wood section of London, a beautiful, sophisticated actress girlfriend, stylish clothes, and immense musical talent, McCartney was among the best-known exponents of swinging London.

While the other three Beatles languished in the London suburbs with their wives and young children, McCartney would attend beat poetry readings, check out the new bands, go to the theatre, listen to avant-garde composers such as Karl Stockhausen, and even make his own experimental films. McCartney was fully consumed by the wave of creativity that had swept over London, and he genuinely felt that the Beatles could use their wealth and influence to help nurture this exciting new scene.

One of the early ideas for the Beatles' new company had been to set up a chain of record shops across England, the idea being that the Beatles would be able to amass sizable property holdings under the pretext of purchasing shop space. It was an interesting idea, but it never got beyond the initial planning stages. Clive Epstein put forward a suggestion that the Beatles open a chain of shops that only sold greeting cards (no such shops existed at the time), but that idea was dismissed as being too mundane a business for a group like the Beatles. Unable to reach a consensus on establishing a retail business, the Beatles ultimately decided that their first commercial venture would be a music publishing company, which would find and develop promising young songwriters.

Given the relatively low start-up cost and the Beatles' collective expertise in songwriting, establishing a music publishing company was certainly a logical option to pursue. But first, a name would be needed for their new company. It was Paul McCartney who came up with an ideal name for their venture, "Apple." Long-serving Apple Managing Director Neil Aspinall recalled: "Paul came up with the idea of calling it Apple, which he got from René Magritte. I don't know if he was a Belgian or Dutch artist... he drew a lot of green apples or painted a lot of green apples [the painting in question was Magritte's *Le Jeu de Mourre*]. I know Paul bought some of his paintings in 1966 or early 1967. I think that's where Paul got the idea for the name from." Even though it was initially not clear what form Apple would ultimately take, when the *Sergeant Pepper* album was released in June 1967, the Beatles had already mysteriously thanked "The Apple" on the back cover of the album.

The responsibility for setting up Apple Music Publishing was given to Terry Doran, a 28-year-old Liverpool native who was a friend and business associate of Brian Epstein. By 1967, Doran had also befriended the Beatles and he was particularly close to John Lennon. Prior to being tapped to head Apple Publishing, the flamboyant Doran had run a car dealership in London called Brydor Cars that he co-owned with Epstein. Doran was the first to admit that his experience in auto sales was not particularly applicable to music publishing. But to the Beatles of 1967, enthusiasm and a social familiarity were sometimes worth far more than practical experience in a given field.

Initially, Apple Publishing was closely linked with NEMS, sharing a floor with two of Robert Stigwood's companies – Abigail Music (who published the Bee Gees) and Dratleaf Music (who published Cream) – at 17 Curzon Street in Mayfair. Stigwood's companies were managed by a formidable German publishing executive, Rudi Slezak, and the three companies would share support personnel, primarily Jean Griffiths, who had been hired away from Sparta Music Publishing to handle the copyright administration.

Working out of a small one-room office, Doran spent the summer of 1967 tending to the paperwork and logistics required to launch Apple's publishing business. Apple was not yet ready to put any songwriters under contract during this early phase of the business, but they did obtain several copyrights, including a song by a group called Sands. Sands were signed to Robert Stigwood's Reaction label, and the Apple published b-side of their debut single was "Listen To The Sky," which is now considered to be one of the landmark songs of the psychedelic era.

The Sands copyright was most likely gifted to Apple by Stigwood, as songwriter Rob Tolchard has no recollection of ever signing a deal with Apple. Presumably trying to generate some goodwill with the Beatles and genuinely wanting to help get their new venture off the ground, Stigwood assigned the copyrights to "Listen To The Sky" and Cream's arrangement of the blues song "Outside Woman Blues" (which would appear on Cream's *Disraeli Gears* album in November 1967) to Apple Publishing. Brian Epstein and his American business partner, Nat Weiss, also apparently gifted a copyright to Apple, which was "Words," a song that was soon to appear as the b-side to the new single by the Cyrkle, an American group managed by Epstein and Weiss.

Sales of the Sands and Cyrkle singles were negligible, but securing the copyright for a song featured on a Cream album was a great start for Apple Publishing. But the long-term vision that Doran and the Beatles had for Apple Publishing was to develop a stable of songwriters who would write material for their own groups to perform as well as be covered by other artists. Even before Apple Publishing had been formally launched, Doran had already made contact with two aspiring songwriters from Liverpool whom he thought would be perfect for Apple.

In June 1967, Paul Tennant and Dave Rhodes were visiting London when they decided on a whim to see if they could find Paul McCartney's house. Upon reaching McCartney's Cavendish Avenue home, they saw McCartney's mini exit the driveway and they followed the car to Hyde Park where McCartney got out to walk his dog.

"We sort of abandoned our car, and Dave and I knew instinctively that we were going to go talk to Paul McCartney about our songs," explained Tennant. "We followed him into the park, and sure enough we started talking to him. We told him our story, that we had been writing songs, we needed someone to listen to them, and Paul's answer was, 'Well, what do you want me to do about it?' We told him, 'Well, we'd like you to help us,' and he replied, 'But, why should I?' and that's the way the conversation went. After about five or so minutes, he must have decided that he had enough of talking to us, so he pulled a piece of paper out of his pocket, wrote a number on the paper and said, 'Listen, if you take this and phone this guy up and tell him I sent you, he will listen to your songs.' So I said, 'OK, thanks Paul, goodbye,' and off he strutted with the dog and off we went back to our car. On the paper was just a number and a name, Terry Doran. There was no mention of Apple."

Once back in Liverpool, Tennant and Rhodes finally managed to get through to Terry Doran. True to his word, McCartney had indeed mentioned meeting Tennant and Rhodes to Doran, and after a brief phone discussion, Doran arranged for the pair to take the overnight bus down to London so that they could play him their songs at Apple's Curzon Street office. "We went upstairs to the top of the building where there were three small offices," recalled Paul Tennant. "On one door there was handwritten on a piece of cardboard paper the word "Apple." We walked in and there was Terry Doran sitting there in a lime green suit, happy as can be. So we played him four songs and he said, 'I really think these songs are good. I'll tell you what, we've got to get these recorded and get an acetate done.' After we had recorded the demo, Terry asked us if we wanted to come back and stay at his house. We jumped back in Terry's car and drove out to Esher. On the way down, we still had no idea of what Apple was, so as we're driving back on the A3 Terry starts telling us the story about Apple, how it was owned by the Beatles and it was going to be the biggest thing in the world. We were gobsmacked when we realized what Apple was."

That evening, Doran left Tennant and Rhodes at his home while he went to play the acetate to John Lennon. Upon his return a few hours later, Tennant recalled how Doran told them that "John Lennon is really knocked out by your songs. What we're going to do now is Brian (Epstein) wants to hear them," so off Terry goes again somewhere and leaves us at the house. The next morning Terry told us he had seen Brian Epstein the night before and that Brian thought our songs were really good as well. There was one song we did, "Miss Sinclair's Courtship," that Brian had thought was going to be a massive hit. But the song that John Lennon had liked had been one called "'Cept Me," which was a bit more of a psychedelic type thing."

Tennant and Rhodes returned to Liverpool only to be summoned back to London a few weeks later to record more demos for Apple. "It was at that stage that Brian Epstein told Terry that he wanted to get involved with us," remembers Tennant, "so Brian – whom we never met – told Terry that he wanted us to form a band and that he wanted it to be called Focal Point."

Epstein – who had been named one of the Directors of Apple Music – had little direct involvement with Apple, although his input certainly helped shape the formation of the company. Whatever tentative plans that the Beatles may have had for Apple, however, were dramatically altered when Brian Epstein was found dead in his London home on Sunday, 27 August 1967. Only thirty-two-years-old at the time of his death, Epstein had apparently overdosed on prescription sleeping pills. The Beatles, who were in Bangor, Wales attending a lecture on transcendental meditation, were devastated by the news. When reached in Bangor, the Beatles appeared before the news cameras to offer a statement, looking shocked and disorientated. John Lennon would later admit that it was at that moment that he first felt that the Beatles were finished.

Epstein's death was a pivotal event in the development of Apple. The Beatles collectively felt a sense of loyalty to both NEMS and the Epstein family, but with Brian Epstein now out of the picture, it was obvious that the Beatles' relationship with NEMS would not continue in the same manner as it had when Epstein was alive. In the weeks following Epstein's death, the Beatles appeared willing to remain affiliated with NEMS, yet they made it clear to all that they were now looking to get more direct control of their destiny and business affairs.

The most contentious issue that arose between the Beatles and NEMS following Epstein's death was when the Beatles learned that Robert Stigwood was angling to take control of the company. It transpired that Epstein – unbeknownst to the Beatles – had made a tentative deal to sell NEMS to Stigwood. Prior to Epstein's death, the Beatles had assumed that Stigwood was simply another NEMS employee, and they were most annoyed that Stigwood felt that he could simply pick up where Epstein left off as manager of the Beatles.

As an enticement to join NEMS, Epstein had extended an offer to Stigwood and Stigwood's business partner, David Shaw, to allow them to purchase controlling interest in NEMS for £500,000. The standing offer was valid until September 1967, and when Epstein unexpectedly died in August, Stigwood and Shaw announced their intention to secure the requisite funding and exercise their option to purchase NEMS. Stigwood's ambitions were thwarted only after the Beatles informed Stigwood that there was absolutely no way that they would accept him as their manager.

Stigwood had little interest in NEMS if it did not include the Beatles, and he abandoned his plans to purchase the company. NEMS paid Stigwood £25,000 to extract itself from the deal that Brian had entered into less than a year earlier. By the end of October, Stigwood had fully severed his associations with NEMS and – taking Cream and the Bee Gees with him – started his own company, RSO. Stigwood's RSO Records would become one of the most successful record labels of the seventies.

Following Stigwood's departure, Brian Epstein's younger brother, Clive, reluctantly assumed control of NEMS. For several months after Epstein's death, the Beatles' relationship with NEMS changed very little, with the NEMS office continuing to oversee the Beatles' day-to-day affairs. There was even a brief period when the Beatles contemplated taking a more active role in NEMS and entertained ideas of using the company as an outlet for discovering and nurturing new artists, which is exactly what they eventually did with Apple.

"We tried to form Apple with Clive Epstein, but he wouldn't have it... he didn't believe in us, I suppose... he didn't think we could do it," recalled Ringo Starr several years later. "He thought we were four wild men, and we were going to spend all his money and make him broke. But that was the original idea of Apple – to form it with NEMS... we thought, now Brian's gone, let's really amalgamate and get this thing going, let's make records and get people on our label and things like that. So we formed Apple, and they formed NEMS, which is doing exactly the same thing as we [Apple] are doing. It was a family tie and we thought it would be a good idea to keep it in, and then we saw how the land lay and we tried to get out."

Peter Brown, the NEMS employee who inherited the lion's share of the responsibility for looking after the Beatles after Epstein's death, does not think that the idea of the Beatles using NEMS to discover and develop talent was a likely proposition. "I don't remember that, and I'm sure that if that was so I would remember because there wouldn't have been anything like that being discussed without me knowing," recalls Brown, adding, "It would have been so foreign to Clive Epstein that I don't think that it would have been workable."

Whatever the situation may have been, the Beatles appeared to be willing to stick with NEMS for the time being. But with NEMS struggling to find its footing after the death of Brian Epstein, the Beatles decided to start leveraging their nascent Apple organization to undertake several creative endeavors. Only weeks after Epstein's death, the first major Apple project was already well under way. Apple's first venture would be the production of a new Beatles movie called *Magical Mystery Tour*, which was filmed and edited from September to November 1967. Cooked up by Paul McCartney on a long-haul flight back from America, *Magical Mystery Tour* was intended to be a spontaneous, arty film that would capture the free-spirited vibe of the summer of 1967.

Since Apple had yet to develop a formal staff structure, Beatles road manager Neil Aspinall and Paul McCartney assumed most of the responsibility for coordinating the various aspects of the film's production. The resulting chaos – which ranged from the "Magical Mystery Tour" bus and film crew venturing down small roads in rural England only to encounter a bridge too narrow to accommodate the bus, to not having enough hotel rooms for the entire cast – surely must have made the Beatles miss the brisk efficiency of the NEMS organization.

For the first few months of Apple's existence, the company did not even have an office. Prior to Epstein's death, most Apple business was conducted from the NEMS office, as the small Apple Publishing office on Curzon Street could not accommodate more than a few people at a time. It was only towards the end of June 1967 that Apple finally secured a proper London office, purchasing the freehold of a four-storey building at 94 Baker Street, on the corner of Baker and Paddington, for £76,500. In August, Apple Publishing – along with Robert Stigwood's Abigail and Dratleaf Publishing companies – moved into the Baker Street building.

Excited by the novelty of being businessmen and anticipating Apple to develop further business interests, the Beatles appointed Neil Aspinall to be Managing Director of the budding Apple organization. "A lot of people were nominated or put themselves forward to run it... but there didn't seem to be any unanimous choice," remembered Aspinall. "So I said to them, foolishly I guess, 'Look, I'll do it until you find somebody that you want to do it.'"

Fortunately for the Beatles, Aspinall was not a typical beat group road manager. He turned out to be qualified to do far more than book hotels, load vans, and set up musical instruments on a stage. Prior to becoming a full-time Beatles employee in 1962, Aspinall had contemplated a business career and had been working on a correspondence degree in accounting before his work with the Beatles took him away from his studies. But it was Aspinall's loyalty to the Beatles, rather than his innate business sense, that made him the natural choice to be Managing Director of Apple. After Brian Epstein died in August 1967, Aspinall and fellow road manager Mal Evans were the only non–Beatles left in the group's inner circle and the Beatles placed a high premium on trust and loyalty. The individual Beatles had complete trust in Neil Aspinall and were confident that he would be up to the task.

Mal Evans would not fit as snugly into the Apple concept as Aspinall. Though he would ultimately be given a free hand to scout talent and dabble in record production for Apple, it was agreed that Evans would probably be best suited to remain in his role as a road manager for the Beatles.

While Neil Aspinall and the Beatles busied themselves with *Magical Mystery Tour*, Terry Doran officially commenced operations at the Apple Publishing office at Baker Street. "When Brian died, we thought, shit, that's that," recalled Paul Tennant. "Terry told us that Brian had died, but that it was not a problem. He said, 'I still want you to be called Focal Point, but I want to manage you.' Once we got the band together, all of us signed five-year publishing deals with Apple. This was around the time Apple moved to Baker Street in late August. Terry told us, 'We've got a really good office now, and we're putting a studio in upstairs.' We thought that was brilliant. It was suggested to us then that the best thing to do would be for us to all move down to London. This was about September, and Apple got Focal Point a house in Highbury. Apple got us a nice house, we'd get a little retainer off of Apple, and anything we wanted we could just ask for and they would get it for us."

Joining Focal Point at Apple would be several other songwriters whom Terry Doran had taken an interest in during the summer of 1967. The Scottish songwriting duo of Benny Gallagher and Graham Lyle had come down to London in 1967 to try to make a career for themselves as songwriters. Unlike Focal Point, they were not music industry novices. They had previously been members of the group James Galt and had written the songs that comprised the two James Galt singles issued by Pye Records in 1966. Upon moving to London, they signed to Polydor Records, who issued their superb single, "Trees," as Gallagher–Lyle in July.

But the deal with Polydor was unsatisfactory, and Gallagher and Lyle spent the summer of 1967 looking for new professional opportunities.

"Benny and I had gone down to London and were living there, just trying to get a break," remembers Lyle. "While we were there, we were introduced to Terry Doran, who was just starting up Apple publishing when we met him at the Radio London offices in Curzon Street. He was so enthusiastic about how great Apple was going to be, and we were a little skeptical at first, as we had heard stories before about how things were going to be great. But he signed us to Apple. I don't think he mentioned anything about the Beatles when we met with him. But the press got hold of how the Beatles were starting their own company, so we learned about it through the press. We were both still working straight jobs to make ends meet. They paid us twenty-five pounds a week each, and we'd go in and get cheques signed by Ringo or George every week. We would go in and deliver whatever songs we had written that week. It was great for us."

Doran had also come across George Alexander, a twenty-nine-year-old songwriter (coincidentally, also from Scotland) whom he had put under contract to Apple earlier that summer. Alexander's real name was Alex Young, and he was the eldest brother of a family that included George Young of the Australian band the Easybeats (the Young family had emigrated to Australia in the early sixties) and Malcolm and Angus Young, who would go on to form the rock group AC/DC in the seventies.

Out of all the writers signed to Apple, it was George Alexander whom Terry Doran thought had the greatest potential. Alexander initially recorded solo demos for Apple, but Doran soon hit upon the idea of forming a group around Alexander to perform his songs. The new group would be comprised of Alexander and three former members of the London-based band Tony Rivers and the Castaways, a harmony pop band styled after American groups like the Four Seasons or the Beach Boys.

"One of the guys in the Castaways – Kenny Rowe – liked to go clubbing, and we'd all hop into his mini and go into town," recalls John Perry, who was a guitarist and singer in the Castaways. "I was bumping into all these people, and I met Terry Doran one night in the Speakeasy and we just got chatting about this and that. I didn't know who the hell he was. Then he bought me a drink, and that turned into a conversation. We chatted at the bar, and I said, 'Well who do you work for?' and he said, 'Apple Publishing.' Well, of course, at the time, Apple Publishing, no one knew what that was, it sounded like a fruit company or something. All the companies at the time sounded like firms of solicitors, like Campbell and Connelly and things like that. But I left it for a couple of months, as a matter of fact, and then I rang him up since nothing else was going on, so I thought, well let's go see this guy. I went up to see him and played him some of my songs. He didn't like my songs that much, but he said, 'Well we got this writer, George Alexander,' and then he played me a few of his songs, and I liked them. Then he was like, 'Well, we'd like George to join the band.' I had never met him or anything, but he had already done quite a lot of stuff in Germany, with this group the Big Six. He was a bit further down the road than us. We were all youngsters, or teenagers, and he was clearly not a teenager. I never knew what his birthday was, but I got the impression that he was possibly even five to ten years older than us. He just seemed older (Alexander was, in fact, born in 1938 and was twenty-nine years old when he signed to Apple). He didn't look like pop star material to me, but Terry seemed quite keen on it."

It was agreed that John Perry and several other members of the Castaways – drummer Geoff Swettenham and his brother, Pete, who played rhythm guitar – would meet at Apple to discuss forming a band with George Alexander. Geoff remembers: "Towards the end of November, John took us up to Apple to meet Terry Doran. We went upstairs at 94 Baker Street, and we sat there outside in the reception room waiting because Terry was late. Then, all of a sudden, there was this scrambling up the stairs. They were rickety old stairs, it wasn't like a modern flash building, then the door flies open, and Terry came through the door in mid-air and landed on his knees, with this huge afro haircut. He was apologizing for being so late and was being like Terry always was, which was energetic and happy. Eccentric, I suppose, in a really nice way. The amazing thing was that within a week of meeting Terry that day, we were in the studio doing things." The initial meeting was followed by several rehearsal sessions, after which the quartet decided that they would continue working together as a band.

Doran appointed himself manager of Apple's latest "discovery," and Apple even took it upon themselves to find a suitable name for the group. After considering and quickly discarding "The Rights Of Man" as a potential name, it was John Lennon who dubbed the quartet "Grapefruit," a name that was shared by a small book of poetry he was reading, written by a Japanese-American artist named Yoko Ono.

No expense was spared on Grapefruit. "Apple paid for our house and gave us a retainer every week," explains Geoff Swettenham. "They kept us alive, basically. They got us a great flat just off of Baker Street, except for George, who got his own flat because he was married with a kid, but the three of us lived there, and Apple paid for everything."

John Perry agrees with Swettenham, adding that, "NEMS basically put us on a retainer and also gave us a car and accounts in various restaurants and clubs, so we could just sign for stuff. It was help yourself, really. It was kind of wacky, but we didn't abuse that. We were very naive, to be honest. We were told to go to Martin Wesson at NEMS – who was the accountant – and we were told to go tell him how much we wanted. NEMS also paid for our flats. George was married and had one or two kids, and he lived near to Baker Street on Marylebone Road. The rest of us lived on the other side of Baker Street in Montagu Mews North. Lennon lived in Montagu Mews. I actually rang him up once while I was on an acid trip, and I asked him, 'John, what happens? What do I do? It's freaking me out,' and he said, 'Meditate, man, mediate.'"

Apple Publishing effectively became a production company for the group, financing all of Grapefruit's recording sessions, which Apple would then license to a record label. Since Apple had yet to launch a record division, they signed a deal for Grapefruit with RCA Records in England and to American producer Terry Melcher's Equinox label in America. Terry Doran had recently concluded a deal with Melcher for Melcher to be Apple Publishing's sub-publisher in North America, so signing Grapefruit to Melcher's label made perfect sense.

Grapefruit were sent into a studio with Melcher on 24 November 1967 to record their debut single. John Perry remembers: "Our very first session was in the basement of IBC studios in Portland Place. Terry Melcher was in the box, we were all set up in this huge studio space, and on the right-hand side the stairs came down into the studio. And on one side of the studio there was Paul McCartney and John Lennon and Mal Evans, just this plethora of pop legends hanging out and smoking Woodbines, expecting something from us!"

Perry remembers that all four members of the group were extremely nervous to be performing for two of the Beatles, but they managed to get some music down on tape. The resulting single, "Dear Delilah," was a fine, if somewhat ominous, piece of psychedelic-tinged pop that was quite accomplished for a group that had been together for only a few weeks.

Released in January 1968, "Dear Delilah" would be the first record by an Apple-backed group to be issued in England. To mark the occasion, Apple sponsored a reception to introduce the group to the press on 18 January 1968. "It was at the Hanover Grand Hotel, in Hanover Street off of Regents Street," recalls John Perry, "and I have an indelible image of my mum looking up and shaking hands with John Lennon. Talk about when two worlds collide!" Apple would also pay for press advertisements that showed a photo taken at the event of Grapefruit seated at a table, surrounded by three Beatles (Lennon, McCartney, and Starr), Rolling Stone Brian Jones, Donovan, and Cilla Black. Given the catchy nature of the song and the generous publicity that the group received for being "the Beatles' first discovery" (much to the chagrin of Focal Point), "Dear Delilah" became a minor hit, eventually reaching number 21 in the UK charts in February 1968.

Even though Terry Doran would later proclaim that he "wasn't much good at music publishing," he did manage to sign some excellent songwriters to Apple Publishing in the space of only a few months. But securing hits and cover versions of Apple copyrights would prove to be more difficult than anticipated, and Doran determined that he needed to find qualified help if he was going to make Apple Publishing a success.

To that end, twenty-seven-year-old Mike Berry – previously with Sparta Music Publishing – was hired to help scout new talent and ostensibly work to secure cover versions of Apple copyrights, although once hired Berry seemed to focus his efforts almost exclusively on finding new writers. "I joined Apple just before Christmas 1967," remembers Berry, "and I was there until about June or July 1968. It was Paul McCartney who hired me. McCartney asked Jean Griffiths – who had worked at Sparta Music before she became copyright manager at Apple – if she knew of anyone who might want to come work for Apple, and Jean rung me up and asked if I would like to talk to Paul, and I said why not." Berry – who had worked in music publishing for close to five years – was energetic and hard-working, and his presence at Apple helped make the publishing division a far more professional operation than it had previously been.

Berry remembers that, outside of Jean Griffiths and Wayne Bardell, no one at Apple knew much about the publishing business. "Paul (McCartney) came in one day, and he said, 'What's publishing?'" recalls Berry. "He didn't really know anything about anything. I just said, 'Have you got a couple of hours?' and he did. He sat with me all afternoon with his dog there, of course. He just sat there, and we went through things. In those days, it was 50:50, 50% to the publisher, 50% to the artist, and I told him I thought that was absolutely disgraceful, because things were changing at that time and that was the old school way of doing things, but McCartney said, 'No, that sounds good to me.' He was quite intrigued by it all."

Seemingly lost amongst all this activity was Focal Point. With Grapefruit now deemed to be the Apple group with the most commercial potential, Focal Point found it increasingly difficult to keep Apple focused on their career. "Around Christmas, Terry Doran came and told us he had offers for recording contracts with Liberty, MGM, EMI or Decca and that he was trying to get Terry Melcher to produce us," recalled Paul Tennant. "He also mentioned Wayne Bickerton, who was a house producer at Decca on the Deram label. Because Wayne Bickerton was another Liverpudlian, we thought, 'Well, let's go with Decca.' We recorded four tracks at Decca. The two that came out were the ones we didn't want. We thought they would be the b-sides, if anything. The track that we wanted was a track called "Never Never," which was a really psychedelic type thing. So we did the Decca recordings, then went back and signed an agency deal with NEMS. We were hanging around Apple, in and out of the shop, helping ourselves to things in the shop. They also took us and kitted us out on Kings Road. Vidal Sassoon did our hair, and the world was our oyster. We were mixing with people like Keith Moon at that Speakeasy, who told us how good he thought we were, and Gary Walker told us we were the best band that Apple had got.

"This was about the time that Grapefruit came along. We knew something was amiss, that something was happening. What happened then was something political happened, and everybody just seemed to lose interest in Focal Point and all the interest went to Grapefruit. We couldn't understand why. There was no animosity between us and Grapefruit, we were all friends. But there was something that was not quite right. When our debut single – "Love You Forever" – was released, there was a big reception when the record came out (on 20 May 1968), but Terry never came to this and we couldn't understand why. We saw him later, and he told us that something came up. I think there were a lot of political things going on with the Beatles at the time, because Yoko Ono had shown up and she was hanging around, and Paul McCartney took a listen to our record and I know he was hemming and hawing whether he thought it was right, and there was a bit of talk going on about it and then it just fizzled out."

Immersed in creating their own music, the Beatles ultimately took only a passing interest in the songwriters signed to their new publishing company, and Terry Doran was able to run Apple Publishing with little interference from either Neil Aspinall or the Beatles. Aspinall's primary concern at the time was to try to sort out the Beatles' tangled business affairs, a task that had taken on additional urgency in the wake of the death of Brian Epstein.

Setting up a Beatles business office proved to be a bigger challenge than anyone had imagined possible. "We didn't have a single piece of paper. No contracts. The lawyer, the accountants and Brian, whoever, had that," recalled Aspinall. "Maybe the Beatles had been given copies of various contracts, I don't know. I know that when Apple started I didn't have a single piece of paper. I didn't know what the contract was with EMI, or with the film people or the publishers or anything at all. So it was a case of building up the filing system, finding out what was going on while we were trying to continue doing something."

Aspinall's job was certainly not made any easier by the Beatles' lack of a unified vision for Apple. A tangible structure for Apple had only just barely been established when the Beatles started to initiate projects designed to follow through on their vague aspiration to champion new talent in such diverse fields as music, film, television, and electronics.

Since September, the Beatles had lavished a great deal of attention and money on a venture that would ultimately evolve into Apple Electronics. Yannis Alexis Mardas (dubbed "Magic Alex" by John Lennon) was a young Greek television repairman who had somehow managed to capture the Beatles' fancy with his ability to be a highly entertaining companion and his crude prototypes of clever electronic gadgets (despite them having no real practical value).

Mardas had been introduced to the Beatles in the summer of 1967 by mutual friend John Dunbar, the owner of the Indica, a small, hip London bookstore and art gallery. Fascinated by Mardas's electronic "toys," the Beatles decided to go into business with him, financing a company called Fiftyshapes Ltd. Later, when the Beatles decided to make Apple a multifaceted entertainment organization, Fiftyshapes Ltd. morphed into Apple Electronics and was brought into the Apple fold.

Apple Electronics had briefly set up a temporary office in the Baker Street building, but in September, Apple purchased a nondescript building at 34 Boston Place for £15,750 that would serve as the laboratory of Apple Electronics as well as storage for the Beatles now mothballed touring equipment. Mardas started work on the Apple Electronics lab in October, but the facility would not be fully functional until February 1968.

The opening of a retail store on the ground floor of the Baker Street building had been another idea that had captured the fancy of several of the Beatles. Setting up retail businesses had actually been what Stephen Maltz and Harry Pinsker had envisioned when they had proposed the tax scheme that they planned to lead to the eventual creation of a publicly held Beatles company.

Ultimately known as the "Apple Boutique," the Beatles' store was envisaged to be a prototype for a chain of stores to be opened across the world. The fact that Baker Street was not a well-known shopping area did not deter the Beatles from using their property as a platform for diving headfirst into retail sales.

The Beatles held lofty aspirations for their boutique, envisaging the shop as a place for "beautiful people to buy beautiful things." The reality was that the Apple Boutique was basically a "head shop," selling psychedelic trinkets and clothes, records, inflatable plastic furniture, books, and jewellery. The boutique did manage to attract a regular flow of tourists, lunchtime browsers, and shoplifters, but it proved much harder to lure paying customers into the store.

The task of managing the Apple Boutique had been given to John Lennon's childhood friend Pete Shotton. Like Terry Doran at Apple Publishing, Shotton was not an obvious choice to be put in charge of a new, high-profile Apple business. Prior to coming to London to run the Apple Boutique, Shotton had been successfully running a supermarket that John Lennon had bought for him to manage in 1965. Shotton may have had no experience with running a clothing boutique, but the fact that he had run some sort of store, combined with the fact that Lennon, Harrison, and McCartney had known Shotton since they were teenagers, made the amiable Shotton the right person for the job as far as the Beatles were concerned.

The hiring of individuals such as Terry Doran and Pete Shotton illustrated how the Beatles hoped that the open-minded business structure at Apple would provide an opportunity for young – though not necessarily traditional – businessmen to distinguish themselves in the world of commerce. Excited by the novelty of having their own company, the Beatles wanted to give friends from the same working-class Liverpool background as themselves a chance to show the world that business was not necessarily the exclusive domain of the upper classes of British society.

With great fanfare, Apple announced to the press that the Apple Boutique would open for business in November 1967. Predictably, due to several unforeseen delays, it was not until the evening of 5 December 1967 that the Apple Boutique finally opened its doors. To celebrate, Apple staged a gala grand opening where George Harrison and John Lennon mingled with invited guests who were feted with apple juice and green Granny Smith apples.

The Apple Boutique officially opened for business several days later on 7 December, and the general public seemed to be genuinely fascinated by the Beatles' new shop. Even in a sophisticated city like London, never before had such a strange collection of merchandise been collected under one roof.

A significant portion of the shop's stock was comprised of colourful psychedelic outfits and posters created by a trio of Dutch designers – and their British manager, Barry Finch – who called themselves the Fool. The boutique was also intended to serve as a retail outlet for the gadgets created by Apple Electronics. These creations were to have included a transistor radio that could be used to broadcast music directly from a record player and a small box with randomly blinking lights that was dubbed "The Nothing Box." Tellingly, by the time the boutique opened, the only contribution that Apple Electronics had made to the boutique was to install the lighting in the shop.

The Fool had come to the Beatles' attention through the design work they had done for the Saville Theatre, a London performance venue under the wing of Brian Epstein. Greatly impressed with the Fool's vibrant psychedelic style, the Beatles hired the group to work on a variety of projects, which included painting a piano and a gypsy caravan for John Lennon, decorating the interior of George Harrison's bungalow, and creating the outfit that Ringo Starr wore in the *Our World* broadcast performance of "All You Need Is Love."

When the Beatles decided to open the Apple Boutique, the Fool were naturally asked to become the shop's in-house designers. In addition to conjuring up an unusually fanciful line of clothes, they were given the task of decorating both the interior and the exterior of the boutique. With an unrestricted budget and a brief to make the Beatles' boutique stand out on the relatively staid street of shops and offices, the Fool designed a massive three-story psychedelic mural to grace the side of the building.

The resulting mural – a brightly coloured, Indian-styled goddess that took up the entire side of the building – was nothing if not striking. The Beatles were quite pleased with the painting, but other businesses in the area were less-than-enamoured by the Fool's creation. Even though they were no longer owners of the property, the Portman Estate (94 Baker Street had been purchased at auction in October 1952 by Suburban Industrial Properties Ltd., who in turn sold the building to Apple in 1967) objected to what the Beatles had done to the 16th century building, and they enforced a 1953 covenant that restricted public advertisement. The mural was found to constitute a form of advertising for the shop, and Apple was soon forced to paint the wall white with a simple "Apple" scripted in the middle.

But being compelled to paint over the Fool's mural would be the least of Apple's problems. There was often a healthy crowd of curious tourists and students browsing in the shop, but the Apple Boutique made little money. The bespoke nature of the outfits created by the Fool and the expensive raw materials used to manufacture the clothes ensured that the creations were both expensive to purchase and that those that sold had little or no margin. Even the boutique stock not created by the Fool was not as enticing to the public as Pete Shotton and the Beatles had anticipated. Outfits like designer Harold Tillman's see-through chiffon tuxedo that had seemed very hip in the psychedelic summer of 1967 looked quite out of place on the cold streets of London during the winter of 1967-68 and, for the most part, remained unsold.

Peter Brown remembers the Apple Boutique as a very unusual place of business. "Customers seemed to be there only to shoplift or to stare at Jenny Boyd [George Harrison's sister-in-law], who was working there as a salesperson along with a self-styled mystic named Caleb. Caleb slept underneath a showcase on one of his many breaks. The store was also sometimes tended by a fat lady who dressed in authentic gypsy costumes."

Reflecting further, Peter Brown admits that, "The Apple Boutique was a bit of a rip off. It was a case of the Beatles trying to be too cool for their own good. It was a beautiful shop. The merchandise looked great. I don't think it was very good quality, but you weren't looking for something to last forever, you were looking to look great next Saturday. Looking back, I suppose it's no worse than the rag industry today, where designers do what they can to take the capital they are given and run with it. But the Fool were really pretty hypocritical. They were pretending to be these cool, lovely people when they were, in fact, a bit less than scrupulous in the way they did things. The Fool would totally run rings around poor Pete

Shotton. There was always this problem of them saying, 'Don't say that to me, because we're too cool for it,' and he would be confronted with this problem of trying to be a businessman while trying to be cool at the same time."

Brown insists that, contrary to popular belief, the Beatles were quite aware that the Apple Boutique was rapidly getting out of control. In January 1968, Pete Shotton was replaced by John Lyndon, who had no retail experience but who had previously worked for NEMS as an artist manager and as Director of Theatrical Productions at Epstein's Saville Theatre. Realizing what he was up against, Lyndon immediately instituted more responsible business practices at the shop and made a valiant attempt to reign in the Fool's excessive spending. Despite Lyndon's efforts, it was estimated that the store went on to eventually lose close to £20,000. On top of the money that was lost at the shop, it is alleged that the Apple organization would also have to write-off the cost of a Jaguar sports car that Apple had purchased for Shotton's use but which it had never reclaimed after Shotton left the company.

By the end of 1967 Apple was already becoming quite an interesting little organization. Given that the Beatles had started the year with only a vague concept for starting a business to minimize their tax exposure, the fact that they managed to set up several fully functioning businesses in the space of less than a year suggested that 1968 was going to be a big year for Apple.

1968: SOMETHING NEW EVERY DAY

With the successful launch of Apple's music publishing and retail operation behind them, the Beatles ushered in 1968 with a flurry of Apple related activity. On 1 January, Stephen Maltz – formerly with Bryce, Hanmer and Isherwood, the accountancy firm used by NEMS and the Beatles – was hired to be the Business and Financial Manager of Apple. Maltz was also appointed to Apple's board of directors.

Ensconced in a makeshift office at 94 Baker Street, Maltz had a formidable list of issues to address when he started work at Apple, ranging from changing the name of Beatles Ltd. to Apple Corps. Ltd., to registering the Apple trademark in forty-seven countries. Several new Apple ventures – including a record label and films – were being planned, and efforts were already well underway to expand the publishing and boutique businesses. The Beatles may have been unable at this point in time to articulate a clearly defined concept of what Apple would be, but there was no shortage of interesting ideas that were being given serious consideration.

But if Apple were to become such a multifaceted company, they would need significantly more office space than they had at their disposal at Baker Street. To accommodate the employees that would be required to carry out the Beatles' ambitious – and sometimes still ominously vague – plans, Apple took out a one-year lease of an entire floor in an eight-storey modern office building at 95 Wigmore Street. The Apple staff, with the exception of those working for Apple Publishing and the Apple Boutique at Baker Street, moved into the fourth floor of the Wigmore Street building on 22 January 1968.

Most of the staff hired by Apple in early 1968 were old associates of the Beatles who came over directly from NEMS. Several had already spent a good part of the preceding year supporting the Beatles' preliminary efforts to set up Apple. Alistair Taylor, who had been working in various capacities for Epstein and NEMS since 1961, was hired as Apple's Office Manager. Barbara Bennett, who had been with NEMS since 1964, was hired to be Neil Aspinall's secretary. "It was a great office to work in," recalls Bennett. "The Beatles were very much in the office every day at that time. They would come in for board meetings and did all that, they were very involved."

Upon securing the office space and personnel needed to support the expansion of the company, Apple next turned its attention to developing a definitive corporate logo. This task was given to Gene Mahon, a genial Irishman who had previously served as art director on the photo shoot for the back cover of *Sgt. Pepper.* Prior to commissioning Mahon to undertake this project, Apple had been using several illustrated apples, as well as a photo of an odd-looking apple that had been provided by American designer Tom Wilkes, on their stationary and in press advertisements.

That February, whilst the Beatles were in India basking in the winter sun and gentle wisdom of the Maharishi, Neil Aspinall invited Mahon to meet with him at Wigmore Street to initiate work on a logo that would convey the style and fresh attitude of the Beatles' new company. Aspinall offered little in the way of direction, other than that they were looking for a photograph of an apple to put on the record label. It was Mahon who came up with the inspired idea of having a full apple on one side of the record, and a photo of the same apple sliced in half on the other side. Mahon envisaged that all of the song titles and credits could be printed on the sliced half of the label and that the other side of the record would be the image of a whole apple with no writing on it whatsoever.

Aspinall liked the concept and asked Mahon to provide Apple with some photos to evaluate. Working with photographer Paul Castell, Mahon shot pictures of several apples on a variety of different backgrounds and submitted them to Apple for their consideration. The photo proofs were reviewed by Aspinall and the four Beatles, and the decision was made to use a photo of a green Granny Smith apple. Once the final image was selected, English illustrator Alan Aldridge was hired to script the copyright information that was required to appear on the labels of records issued in England. Unfortunately, due to trade requirements of the day that stipulated that the contents of a record must be printed on both sides of the record, Mahon's original idea of having an unadorned full apple on one side of the label had to be abandoned. Apple had nevertheless acquired a visually attractive, very distinctive logo and were now one step closer to being able to release music on an Apple Records label.

Most of Apple's corporate activity shifted to Wigmore Street as of early 1968, but to the public, the Apple Publishing office and the Apple Boutique at Baker Street remained the most visible – and accessible – outpost of the burgeoning Apple empire. Apple Publishing was particularly active during this period, and Terry Doran had high hopes for several of the songwriters he had recently signed. Jackie Lomax, a twenty-three-year-old Liverpool native, had started writing songs for Apple in November 1967 (he would sign a five-year publishing deal with Apple Publishing on 1 January 1968). Unlike Grapefruit and Focal Point, Lomax was a hardened music business veteran by the time he made his way to Apple's Baker Street office. Between 1961 and 1966, Lomax had been the singer and bassist of the R&B influenced Merseybeat group the Undertakers, and he knew the Beatles from when both bands played the Liverpool club circuit.

In 1965, the Undertakers, along with the Pete Best Band (a Liverpool group featuring former Beatles drummer Pete Best), had been lured to the United States by a record producer who desperately wanted to cash in on the British Invasion. Expecting to find fame and fortune in America, the Undertakers instead found themselves stranded in New York City, unable to play shows due to visa problems and living on the floor of a dingy recording studio. After recording only one single, the Undertakers broke up in 1966. Lomax remained in New York City where he supported himself by playing with several semi-pro local groups in clubs in Greenwich Village.

Lomax's career was looking fairly hopeless at this juncture. But a chance encounter with Liverpool acquaintance Cilla Black would give his professional fortunes a much-needed boost. Running into Lomax at a party in New York City, Black conveyed to the down on his luck singer that Brian Epstein – who was also in New York City – had been looking for him. Lomax connected with Epstein the following day and was soon under contract to NEMS. Epstein assembled a group around Lomax and christened them the Lomax Alliance. They were signed to CBS Records and recorded a fine album that was, sadly, never released. CBS did issue one of the tracks, "Try As You May," as a single in May 1967, but it was not a commercial success.

When Epstein died, Robert Stigwood took over as Lomax's manager but only agreed to finance a new single if Lomax cut a Bee Gees song as a b-side. "Genuine Imitation Life" (backed with the Bee Gees' "One Minute Woman") was issued by CBS in November 1967, but it failed to chart. By this time, Stigwood had left NEMS, and Lomax was astute enough to realize that he had no future with the company. Lomax next decided to contact the Beatles to see if they would be interested in financing a group that he was looking to form with Chris Curtis, the former drummer of the Searchers. According to Lomax, it was John Lennon who talked him out of forming the group, telling Lomax that he would be better off as a solo artist and suggesting that Lomax go to Baker Street and talk to Terry Doran.

Lomax recalled going to Apple's Baker Street office almost every day, where he would work on demo tapes of his latest compositions. When a song was finished, he would take the tape downstairs to Terry Doran, who would listen to it, fill out the necessary paperwork, and give Lomax an advance of £20 for each completed song. Given that Apple Records was only in the earliest of planning stages, Lomax had absolutely no idea what Apple Publishing intended to do with all the material that he and the other Apple writers were composing. From what he could discern, Doran and the rest of Apple's small staff put minimal effort into getting other artists to record any of the material he was writing.

Contrary to Lomax's perception that Apple Publishing was doing little to promote the work of their songwriters, Apple Publishing did, in fact, manage to secure a few cover versions of Apple copyrights. Several English acts – including Andy Ellison and Ways And Means – recorded George Alexander songs during the early months of 1968. Ways And Means even almost had a hit with Alexander's "Breaking Up A Dream," a song that Grapefruit had only performed for a BBC radio session.

Grapefruit released their second single, "Elevator," in April 1968. "Elevator" was arguably a far more commercial single than "Dear Delilah," yet nothing Apple did – which included having Paul McCartney direct a promotional film shot in Hyde Park on 26 March – could give "Elevator" the lift it needed to become a chart hit.

Apple had naively assumed that the combined quality of Grapefruit's records and the promotional clout of the Beatles would propel Grapefruit into the charts. They were dismayed to learn that launching a successful pop group was perhaps not as simple as it seemed. In fact, the English music press quickly soured on Grapefruit. Despite Grapefruit writing their own material and performing on their records, the group were frequently dismissed as mere Beatles clones or, worse still, as a manufactured pop group along the lines of the Monkees.

Grapefruit's single was quickly followed by the long-awaited debut of Focal Point, who released their first (and only) record in May. The a-side that Deram Records had selected was the pleasant ballad "Love You Forever," but it failed to garner much airplay and the single sold only a few hundred copies. The b-side, "Sycamore Sid," would have made a far superior a-side and it remains to this day one of the great English psychedelic rock records of the sixties.

Within weeks of its release, it was obvious that "Love You Forever" was not going to chart. Apple was uncharacteristically quick to end their patronage of Focal Point. "Apple simply stopped paying the rent on the house we lived in and the retainer they were providing us with to live off," recalls Focal Point bassist Dave Slater. "It was Alan Lewis who gave us the news. Terry just made himself invisible at this time. We found ourselves a flat in another part of London and lived off social security until we were on the point of real hunger. It's at that point we moved back to Liverpool around November 1968. We never went to Apple at Savile Row"

Undaunted by the difficulties encountered in their efforts to establish Grapefruit and Focal Point as a hit making acts, Apple Publishing continued to aggressively seek out and sign new songwriters during the first half of 1968. One of the first songwriters Mike Berry signed to Apple Publishing was Dave Lambert (future member of the Strawbs), who in 1968 was the lead singer and guitarist of a North London mod-psych trio known as Fire.

Fire were already under contract to Decca Records when they came to Berry's attention. "In February 1968 I was called to go up to Baker Street for the first time," recalls Lambert. "Mike Berry had already been out to see us play live, and then they invited us up to the offices. I went to the office, and Neil Aspinall brought some contracts in for me to sign. "Father's Name Is Dad" and "Treacle Toffee World" had already been recorded. They also gave us these cards that we got when we joined. It was a reconstruction of the *Please Please Me* cover inside on a staircase and they're looking over, and it says, 'Nice to have you with us.'"

As Lambert notes, "Father's Name Is Dad" – a superb, hard-driving, freakbeat number – had already been recorded, but Decca seemed reluctant to release the record. But that all changed once Decca learned that Fire had been signed to Apple. The record was issued in March 1968. With the backing of Decca and Apple, it seemed inevitable that the record would be a hit, but that surprisingly failed to happen. "When "Fathers Name Is Dad" came out, I don't think that Apple coordinated with Decca the way they should have done, really," muses Lambert. "But there were always people on the phone, and we did a lot of press with the teen magazines like *Jackie*. Then there was the re-recording, which was most bizarre. I was up in the Apple office one day just before the single was released, and Mike Berry told me that Paul had heard it and really loved the riff. The next thing I heard was a phone call a couple of days after the record was released, telling us that we were back into the studio over the weekend. I'm not sure if it was George or Paul, but one of them had heard it on the radio and decided that it was a good record, but it could be much better."

Under pressure from Apple, Decca agreed to stop distribution of the record, brought Fire back into the studio to add more vocals and guitar overdubs to the master tape, and then repressed the single with the new version of "Father's Name Is Dad." "It's unbelievable, when you think about it now, that Decca would agree to this," says Lambert. "It could have only been their respect to the pressure of Apple. It was played pretty well on the radio, John Peel played it, but it didn't sell. But with the re-recording and the re-issue of the record and not having the record in the shops, the record was probably let down from that side."

Apple devoted considerable resources to the group, promoting Fire to the press and even getting the Fool to design stage clothes for the group, but it was not enough to secure them a hit record.

Alan Morgan, previously the bass player for the psychedelic pop group

Felius Andromeda, was another songwriter signed to Apple around this time. "Myself and a guy called Steve Webber were signed to Apple after I left Felius Andromeda," remembers Morgan. "We were there the same time as Gallagher and Lyle and Grapefruit. We used to go to the office at Baker Street and have to go through the Apple shop which was quite chaotic. I remember that the painting on the outside of the building used to cause a lot of traffic crashes, because it was such an incredible sight. You have to remember that the Beatles were still so big. You would walk in the door and walk past Paul McCartney and John Lennon, which was quite weird, really. We used to go upstairs and lay down demos on a Revox with a guy called Lionel Morton. I don't know what he did at Apple, whether he wanted to be an A&R man, a producer, or what, but whenever we recorded at Apple, we seemed to end up with him. We were signed by Terry Doran. I remember Terry Doran coming down to this studio where we used to record in London, down the old Kent Road, and liking all this stuff that we played him. He had this big Rover three-litre car, which was painted up all psychedelically like John Lennon's Rolls. I remember going into the East End of London with him – which was a rough part of London at the time – and he looked liked one of the bloody people from *Yellow Submarine* with his flared trousers and fur coat. It was quite amazing how people looked at him in this East End pub, people couldn't make out what was going on."

Terry Doran was apparently quite taken with Felius Andromeda. The group's organist, Denis Couldry, was also signed to Apple Publishing. Decca had kept Couldry under contract after Felius Andromeda split and both sides of the two singles he released in 1968 – "I Am Nearly There" and "Penny For The Wind" – were Apple copyrights.

Soon after joining Apple, Couldry formed a group, Smile, whose drummer was Roger Swallow. "I have many recollections of Apple in Baker Street," says Swallow. "The ground floor was the Beatles' clothing boutique, the 1st floor above was a dentist's office, the next the main Apple office, and the top floor was a small studio where we hung out mainly. The office was inundated with tapes from everywhere. Lionel Morton was among the screeners. I spent countless hours up there with him going through tapes – horrendous! Apple paid us a little, I think, for wading through the tapes and making some demos of the better songs. Terry Doran was our main contact. The people I most remember were Grapefruit – George Alexander was around a lot and we had some fun – and James Taylor, who was around quite a bit for a few weeks. The Beatles made rare appearances, George more than the others; he was the most charismatic, the place went very quiet when he came in. John caused a riot a couple of times on Baker Street. One time we watched from above as he approached Apple followed by hundreds of kids, the whole street was blocked off; he came in for a few minutes, left, and we watched as he walked off followed by the same crowd, shutting down Baker Street."

To assist with the influx of new writers who were being signed to Apple, Terry Doran hired Jack Oliver in January 1968. Oliver remembers: "I had a job at Chappell Music Publishing, and I was also in a group called the Chocolate Watchband (not the American garage rock band, but rather an English pop band who released two singles in 1967). We recorded for Decca and then decided to call it a day. There was a guy, Terry Oakes, who I had worked with at Chappell, and I said to him, 'Look, we're going to fold the group. Do you know of any jobs around?' and he said, 'Well, there's a new company opening up, maybe they want someone.' He gave me the guy's name and number, and it was Terry Doran, who was running Apple Publishing at the time."

"I went for this interview with him, and it was quite interesting. I went into this office on Baker Street, and it was this completely white office; everything in the office was white, and there were these two white leather Chesterfield sofas. Everything was white except for Terry Doran, who had this big 'fro and all these psychedelic clothes. I still didn't know who it was. He said, 'I don't really need anyone, but I'll talk to you anyway,' so we spoke a bit, and I told him, 'Well it looks to me like you need an assistant,' and he said, 'Well, alright, you can start tomorrow.' I started the next day, and he said, 'Oh, we're going to Midem tomorrow. Do you want to go?' I said, 'Yeah, sure.' I went, and we had a suite at the Carlton. I still didn't really know what was going on, and then from out of one of the rooms walks Paul McCartney. Then I knew, and I thought to myself, 'This is going to be a good gig.' I spent the rest of the week with Paul McCartney, basically just posing around Cannes. We worked hard there, and we did a lot of stuff. To be honest, I wasn't in publishing that long. As soon as I got there, I was involved in Mary Hopkin's management more than anything, because Mike Berry and Terry Doran were doing the publishing. I was only with Terry for a couple of months, and then I went over to Derek Taylor's office. Publishing stayed in Baker Street, and I went over to Savile Row in the press office for a while, working for Derek Taylor."

By February, Apple had been structured into five divisions. In addition to the Beatles, there was Merchandising (retail and wholesale), Music (records and publishing), Apple Electronics, and Apple Films. Apple also announced plans for further divisions, including Apple Publicity, Apple Management, and the Apple Foundation for the Arts, although these entities appeared to develop little further than the corporate registration stage. Apple Publicity was presumably intended to be part of the record division, although Apple was never involved with publicizing any non-Apple artists. Apple Management was another division that failed to materialize. Terry Doran did manage Focal Point and Grapefruit, but there never was any formal Apple Management structure. As for the Apple Foundation for the Arts, it was really nothing more than an idealistic dream that the Beatles had briefly contemplated during the exuberant early days of Apple.

It may have been the least tangible part of the Apple organization, but the essentially non-existent Apple Foundation for the Arts was the division that seemed to attract the greatest interest from the general public. Soon after the Beatles floated their vague desire to assist deserving artists through the Apple Foundation for the Arts, Apple's Wigmore Street office was overrun with would-be poets, film makers, sculptors, authors, musicians, and event organizers, each trying to secure funding for their self-described revolutionary ventures.

The Beatles would later claim that being besieged by countless people looking for hand-outs was one of the worst aspects of Apple. But they really had nobody to blame but themselves for attracting the unrelenting waves of dreamers and hustlers that descended upon the Apple office. Even though the Beatles genuinely wanted Apple to find and nurture deserving new talent in a variety of media, they completely failed to articulate their objectives in a manner that would dissuade less-than-gifted aspiring artists from camping out in Apple's waiting room in a desperate attempt to gain an audience with one of the Beatles. Derek Taylor later recalled that George Harrison was the first Beatle to notice that Apple was under siege, telling Taylor that he hated Apple and especially how Apple was attracting so many people looking for hand-outs of one sort or another.

In conjunction with the hordes of aspiring artists and crass opportunists who turned up daily at Apple, it was during Apple's early days at Wigmore Street that the staff first noticed the presence of a group of fans who would later become affectionately known as the "Apple Scruffs." The scruffs, a group comprised of mostly young women who shared an intense devotion to the Beatles, were some of the most dedicated Beatles fans ever. Positioning themselves outside of the Apple offices and the recording studios where the Beatles worked, they would remain at their collective vigil year-round and in every kind of weather, just for the chance of seeing a Beatle or getting an autograph.

The arrival of the scruffs certainly added yet another splash of colour to the proceedings at Apple. Most days throughout the spring of 1968, there always seemed to be something interesting happening at 95 Wigmore Street. As the scruffs milled around the entrance to the building, upstairs, various Apple staffers struggled to keep a semblance of order in the frequently overcrowded reception area. Somewhat sheltered from the chaos in the large communal room at the back of the office suite, Neil Aspinall and various combinations of Beatles spent hours making plans and assembling the management team that they would need to have in place in order to make Apple an international presence in the entertainment industry.

It had been decided that Apple would launch a record label in mid-1968. The Beatles had considered several of their associates, including Peter Asher and Mal Evans, to run the label, but they ultimately selected Ron Kass, a 33-year-old American, to be President of Apple Records. Prior to joining Apple, Kass had been in charge of international operations for Liberty Records. The appointment of Ron Kass was particularly significant, as Kass was the first person to join the senior management team of Apple who was not English nor had any previous association with the Beatles.

"Ron Kass was a very, very experienced international record executive," enthuses Peter Brown. "We got him from Liberty Records, which in those days was a very big thing. He was running it in Europe, and he was very successful at it. He was a very experienced man. He did a very good job at Apple. We weren't necessarily looking for an American to run the label, but we ended up with an American who knew the American record industry, but who was also experienced in Europe. In Ron we had someone who was experienced in Europe and America, which was unique, because in those days, record industry executives didn't travel that much, unlike today where you have Americans in London and Londoners in America. Apple was really one of the first international record labels as far as its international reach and view."

Supporting Kass at Apple Records would be Peter Asher, the 23-year-old older brother of Paul McCartney's fiancé, Jane Asher. Asher was appointed Apple's A&R Director and would be responsible for finding, developing, and producing talent for the Apple label. Unlike other Apple executives such as Terry Doran, who came to Apple without ever even having worked in the music business, Asher did have considerable music industry experience, albeit on the other side of the microphone. As one half of the pop duo Peter and Gordon, Asher had tasted considerable international success in the mid-sixties with such McCartney penned songs as "World Without Love" and "I Don't Want To See You Again." Asher's production experience prior to joining Apple was limited to a few unsuccessful singles, but he had spent the four preceding years touring the world and making records, and he had developed very strong opinions of how a record company should function and how records should be made.

Asher recalls that it seemed very natural for him to end up at Apple: "Paul was a friend of mine, and I spent lot of time hanging out with him at his house when he had the original idea for Apple. I was in on a lot of the planning, or maybe even more dreaming than planning, of having a record label. Paul was the most actively involved with the record label. They had this thing that they wanted to bring in an American business guy, which ended up being Ron Kass. Paul asked if I would be interested in producing some records for Apple. He liked some of the stuff I had been doing. I had produced a couple of records, so I said, 'Sure,' and later on he said, 'Well, why don't you run the label? We're going to get an American business guy to be the boss, but you can run the artist aspect of it.'"

"At that point, none of us really knew what we were doing," Asher stresses. "We were filled with a general sense of optimism and thought, how hard could this be? I had already decided that I had pretty much had it with performing. Gordon and I were fading out and weren't working together much. I had enjoyed being in the studio more, so I had produced a couple of records, of which Paul had played on (a single by former Manfred Mann vocalist Paul Jones that featured McCartney, Jeff Beck, and ex-Yardbird Paul Samwell-Smith backing Jones on "And The Sun Will Shine" and "The Dog Presides"), so I had a feeling that what I wanted to do was more in the production area. So, when Paul talked about it, he had his ideas for the label, I made some suggestions, and as the company developed, that's when he said, 'Say, why don't you come and do it?'"

Apple Films was another line of business that took root in early 1968. Apple had self-produced the *Magical Mystery Tour* film the previous year, but there was no formal organization to handle the Beatles' film projects. To lead the new film division, the Beatles appointed 45-year-old Denis O'Dell to be Director of Apple Films. O'Dell had previously worked with the Beatles on *A Hard Day's Night* and had also assisted with the *Magical Mystery Tour* project. Though several decades older than his new employers, O'Dell had embraced modern filmmaking and was highly regarded in the film industry and within the Beatles' circle. In addition to O'Dell, Apple brought in 44-year-old Brian Lewis to assist in the film department and to be Apple's contracts expert.

O'Dell was primarily a film producer and would focus most of his effort on developing a slate of inaugural projects for the film division. The day-to-day activities at Apple Films, such as filming promo clips and sifting through scripts and books for film ideas, were delegated to former NEMS employee Tony Bramwell.

Like so many of Apple's early employees, Bramwell was one of the original NEMS staff that had come down to London from Liverpool. Bramwell had first crossed paths with the Beatles while he was a schoolboy. "When I was a kid, I used to carry Gerry (Gerry and the

Pacemakers) Marsden's guitar to gigs for him, so I could get in free," he remembers. "When Gerry went off to Hamburg, and the Beatles came back from Hamburg, I started doing the same thing for George, who was actually a childhood friend of mine. I started to travel around with them until about the time of "Love Me Do," and then they asked me to help out with the equipment full time, which I did until around November 1963, around the time of "I Want To Hold Your Hand," when they needed a driver. I was too young for a licence, so they got Mal. I carried on working in the NEMS office and handling the presentation side of it, the stage shows, the tours for all the NEMS acts. Then I ran the Saville Theatre until Brian's death. I was also very involved with Subafilms. We did all the Beatles' video clips.

"After Brian died, there was a day when we all moved out of NEMS and went to Apple. I was hired to work for Apple Films. I had a brief training course in TV direction in the mid-sixties. I directed a couple of editions of *Ready Steady Go!*, a few quiz shows. Brian sent me out to learn how television worked. He thought it would be a good idea to have somebody at NEMS who knew TV, film speeds, lighting and all that. So when it came to Apple, I did all of the Apple videos. I can't remember all of them. They were usually something along the lines of taking a camera out for a day and shooting people running around in Hyde Park. I remember filming Mary Hopkin in Paul's garden, Paul playing his guitar in the studio. I was at Apple Films for about a year until we started up Apple Records. The problem with Apple Films was that United Artists, who had the rights to finance and distribute Apple Films, didn't think it was such a great idea, so that was a bit of a disaster. We actually bought the rights to *Lord Of The Rings,* which the Beatles would have starred in. We were in pre-production. We actually did basic location shooting for a film called *Walkabout*. We sent a couple of guys down to Australia to shoot locations. We ended up selling the rights to *Walkabout* to Nicholas Roeg, and it was very successful."

To complete the raid of NEMS personnel, Peter Brown was brought over to become Apple's Administrative Director and to sit on Apple's Board of Directors. Although Peter Brown would work out of the Apple office and had the appearance of being an Apple executive, Brown was actually employed by Beatles and Co, the corporate manifestation of the Beatles partnership.

Ever since the death of Brian Epstein, the Beatles had increasingly turned to the embryonic Apple organization to provide them with the same sort of personal and professional services that had been typically handled by NEMS. The Apple staff – particularly Neil Aspinall – could provide much of the office support that was once the exclusive domain of NEMS, but within Apple there developed a distinct need for someone to look after the Beatles' personal affairs.

The most obvious person to assume this responsibility was Peter Brown. It was Brown who assumed many of Epstein's duties at NEMS, both as social and personal coordinator for the individual Beatles, in the months that followed Epstein's death. Bill Oakes, Peter Brown's personal assistant from 1969 to 1970, believes that the Beatles viewed Brown as "the spirit of Brian Epstein. He was Epstein's assistant. He was the person who discovered Epstein's body, and he was keeper of the Epstein flame."

"What happened was that when Brian died, Peter simply went and sat in Brian's chair, it's as simple as that. I don't think anyone ever appointed him manager. When Stigwood made his run for NEMS and then split off with the Bee Gees, the Beatles started Apple. Peter Brown certainly had nothing to do with the business set up of Apple, because he was not a businessman, he was the front man, the Beatles' spokesman, he was the man who got on with marrying them off and who John sings about in "The Ballad Of John And Yoko." Peter Brown was very involved with the Beatles' personal lives. I mean, the Beatles' room in Apple's Savile Row office, his room, it was never 'the office.' It was 'Peter Brown's room,' which was the Beatles' room. There was a red–light system outside of the office, and when the red light was on, it meant that there was a Beatle in residence and that you couldn't come in, unless it was me or Peter. So we would put on the red light even if there wasn't a Beatle in there!"

The four Beatles were reasonably comfortable entrusting their personal business to Peter Brown, but it was Paul McCartney with whom Brown had the closest relationship. George Harrison was apparently not particularly fond of Brown, nor does Brown claim to have been close to Harrison. Harrison went along with having Brown installed as the Beatles' "personal manager," but he also wanted to ensure that there would be a few people that he personally respected and enjoyed working with on Apple's staff.

It was Harrison who was most responsible for bringing former Beatles press officer Derek Taylor to Apple. At the time he joined Apple in 1968, Taylor already had a long history with the Beatles. Having come to the band's attention after writing several glowing reviews of the group for the Northern edition of *The Daily Express*, Taylor was hired by Brian Epstein to ghostwrite Epstein's 1964 "autobiography," *A Cellar Full Of Noise,* and to ghostwrite a column by George Harrison that appeared in one of the weekly English music papers. Taylor would work as the Beatles' press officer for most of 1964, before moving to America in 1965 after falling out with Epstein. Setting up an office in Los Angeles, Taylor became a very successful independent publicist for groups such as the Byrds, Paul Revere and the Raiders, the Beach Boys, and several other artists. Taylor was also one of the principal organizers of the now-fabled 1967 Monterey Pop Festival.

Derek Taylor was still in bed one warm spring morning when he received a phone call at 8am from all four Beatles, who were calling together from the Apple office in London. He would later recount that the Beatles appeared to each have different ideas of what role he would assume at Apple, but that they were unified in their desire to have Taylor join their new company. Within days of the conversation, Derek Taylor was already making plans to move his family back to England.

Settling his wife, Joan, and their children into a rustic home in the Surrey countryside, Taylor reported to work at Apple on 8 April 1968. Despite having just moved his entire family across the Atlantic Ocean, Taylor stepped into the Wigmore Street office that day with absolutely no idea of what he would be doing for Apple. Taylor had hoped that he might be put in charge of Apple Records, but neither Taylor, Peter Asher, nor Mal Evans would be asked to run Apple Records. When it was clear that he would not be given the job of running the label, Taylor discussed being given the title of "Office Eccentric" with Paul McCartney. Quite to Taylor's surprise, McCartney agreed to his quixotic request and instructed Taylor to have a sign made for his office door. Sadly, like so many of the ideas that were bounced around the Apple office, nothing ever came of the idea of having an "Office Eccentric" on the Apple payroll.

Taylor was ultimately coaxed into accepting the role of Apple's press officer, and he quickly became a staunch and devoted champion of the idealist goals of Apple. To assist him in the press office, Taylor hired Richard DiLello, a 23-year-old American originally from New York City who had found himself in London after making a hippie pilgrimage to North Africa. Needing to assign DiLello a formal title so that the young American could register to work in England, Taylor dubbed the afro-sporting DiLello the "house hippie" and put him to work sorting out a massive pile of Beatles press cuttings.

Considering that Taylor was at the time one of the premier publicists in the music industry, the salary Apple gave him – £115 a week – was not overly generous. There was a widely-held public perception that anyone associated with the Beatles or Apple was earning a fabulous salary, yet only Peter Brown and Ron Kass received any special compensation. "The most I ever made was £30 a week," laughs Bill Oakes. "They were cheap bastards. I was always short of money, and I was always getting stuck with the bill because my friends thought, he works for "them," he's got money! Peter Brown had a marvelous deal. He made around £100 a week, but he had everything paid for, his mews apartment, his restaurant bills, his groceries. Jimmy, the Apple doorman, used to get Peter Brown's groceries." In addition to paying for Peter Brown's apartment, Apple also rented a London townhouse for Ron Kass.

The pay for a typical Apple employee may have been modest, but there was no shortage of people who wanted to work for the company. Given the influx of new staff, the Wigmore Street office was soon no longer sufficient in size to contain the ever-expanding Apple organization. On top of the cramped working conditions, the Apple staff were further challenged by having to work in an office that was not particularly well-suited to a music company. Matters came to a head on 10 July when Stephen Maltz circulated a memo to the staff informing them that the management of the Wigmore Street building had decreed that Apple employees were not allowed to play music in the office during business hours due to several complaints from other tenants.

Finding a more suitable office was yet another critical task that Apple's management team now needed to resolve in short order. Of particular importance that spring was the need to finalise an international distribution arrangement for the Apple label. Starting in February, Neil Aspinall – later joined by Ron Kass – began visiting the United States to engage in talks with five major American labels. Although the Beatles, as a group, were under contract to EMI, they were free to align Apple with any label they wanted. If EMI wanted to distribute the Beatles' new record label, they would need to make their case to Apple and ultimately present a better offer than the competition.

Since the start of the year, Apple had been actively seeking talent. Apple Publishing had close to a dozen writers under contract, and several artists were already earmarked for the Apple Records label. Yet Apple concluded that if they were truly going to fulfill their promise to find and develop undiscovered talent, they needed to do more to encourage such talent to contact Apple. To get the word out about the Beatles' new company, Paul McCartney came up with an advertising concept that was sure to entice even the most reticent artist to submit samples of their work to Apple.

Under McCartney's direction, an advertisement was created featuring a photo of Apple Office Manager Alistair Taylor dressed up as a one-man band. The accompanying text read:

This man had talent... one day he sang his songs to a tape recorder (borrowed from the man next door). In his neatest handwriting he wrote an explanatory note (giving his name and address) and, remembering to enclose a picture of himself, sent the tape, letter and photograph to Apple Music 94 Baker Street, London W1. If you were thinking of doing the same thing yourself – do it now! This man now owns a Bentley!

The advertisement ran in several English music papers during April 1968 and was so successful that more than 200 tapes arrived at Apple within two weeks of the ad appearing. Even though Peter Asher admits that Apple really didn't need to run such a campaign, he still defends the project, explaining that, "We hated the way that record companies were. It's hard to remember now, but back then the artists had no power, the companies were run by serious suits, people who had never listened to a rock record. We really felt that it had to be changed, so we said, 'Listen, here's a new label run by people who actually like music, and therefore we will listen to your stuff. Bring us your ideas.' It was a worthy ambition and it didn't do any harm. It made us a little nuts for a while, all these mailbags of tapes and weirdos on the doorstep. But it was fun. Even the weirdos were great."

Some of the submitted tapes would be given cursory listens by Peter Asher's assistants in the A&R Department, but many of them were never even played. "Everything collected dust in the corner. We just couldn't cope," recalled Alistair Taylor. "The kids were sending all sorts of tapes and sheet music in, constantly. You'd come in the morning, switch on the answering machine and get some guy auditioning on the message tape. We used to send a lot of them around to the (Lew) Grade Organization."

"The A&R Department was really just me, and then I hired some people," explains Peter Asher. "There was no aspect of going out and looking for people because everyone was coming to us. We ran that campaign where we said send us your tapes and we will listen. So basically, I ended up with quite a number of people there just listening to tapes, and they would select the best moments and I would finally listen to the best of the best. None of it was much good, unfortunately. Out of the myriad of tapes we got in the mail, we didn't sign anyone. We tried to have A&R meetings once a week or so, whenever we could get a quorum of Beatles. But again, the Beatles tended to be more interested in their own favourite projects. We worked pretty hard, but most of our time was taken up with the process of listening to all those submissions. The actual A&R part didn't take much. Once you said, 'OK, Jackie Lomax, George is producing,' boom, that's done. Nowadays, A&R people do a lot more interfering with how records are made, but that didn't happen then. We did have some A&R meetings when all four Beatles would be there and I would play maybe six of the best submissions, so that they would know what was going on. They would discuss their pet projects, and I would bring them up to date with the ongoing projects. There would be occasional arguments and stuff because they had fairly abrasive relationships, but things got done."

The first recording artist to be discovered and signed to Apple by Peter Asher was James Taylor, a lanky American singer-songwriter from

North Carolina, who had most recently been in New York City playing with a group known as the Flying Machine.

Asher remembers that Taylor had been given his phone number by a mutual acquaintance, Danny "Kootch" Kortchmar. "Danny and James were old friends and Danny and I became close friends because Danny had been in a band, the Kingbees, that had backed Peter and Gordon on a US tour," recalls Asher. "Danny and James had been in a band together called the Flying Machine. I apparently met James at a Flying Machine rehearsal here in New York, which I don't remember. So Kootch gave James my phone number and said, 'If you get to London, here's my friend, you should give him a call.' James called me up, came over and played me a tape, and I loved it. It wasn't what was happening then, but the songs were brilliant. Coincidentally, I had just started this job with Apple, so I asked if he wanted to make an album. Within a week of arriving in London, he was hanging with the Beatles and signing with Apple. So at an A&R meeting I said basically, 'Here's this guy, an American, he's here, and we're going to sign him.' And Paul went, 'Oh yeah, he's great.' John, I think, didn't care one way or the other, and I think George kind of liked it."

Given the perceived limited commercial appeal of an introspective folk singer with a solitary acoustic guitar, Asher's vision was to form a group to back his new discovery. Auditions for a bass player were held in April and 22-year-old Louis Cennamo was selected to join Taylor's band. "I had just left the Herd and had answered an advert in the *Melody Maker*, just a little ad, a very small ad, saying, 'Apple looking for bass player,'" recounts Cennamo. "I went down to the Apple headquarters in Baker Street, and when I got there there was a queue of bass players coming out onto the street and going around the corner for about a hundred yards. I was just about to turn around and go home when someone called out to me, and it was a guy who was in a band who supported the Herd and he was working at the Apple offices. I went upstairs with him, past all of the other guys waiting, and I got ushered in to play with James. We started playing a blues together, and the next thing, I look around and John and Ringo were sort of cowering around the desk listening, giving him a few words of encouragement. James had been auditioning for some time and was quite tired, and I remember how John Lennon turned around to him and said, 'See, James? I told you it would be alright.' So James said, 'Well, that was great, can you come back tomorrow?' And that's how it started. We didn't do much rehearsing at all. It was only the two of us at first, and then we got Bishop O'Brien, the drummer, over from America."

James Taylor signed a record deal with Apple Records S.A. (an Apple subsidiary corporation set up in Switzerland for tax purposes) on 12 June

1968. The revelation that Apple now had a corporation registered in Switzerland was disconcerting to Paul McCartney. "It was the first time I'd seen 'S.A.' on companies," recalled McCartney. "I used to think it was South Africa. It implied Switzerland, it implied dodgy deals to me. Suddenly it was Apple S.A."

During the early months of 1968, almost everyone involved with Apple was looking out for talent. Mal Evans and Apple Publishing's Mike Berry had both been keeping an eye on a young, London-based group known as the Iveys. Consisting of three Welsh teenagers and another more recent recruit from Liverpool, the Iveys were an obviously talented, yet still developing pop group, who were one of literally a hundred bands that could be found performing around London in 1967 and 1968. Through a mixture of hard work and raw talent, the Iveys had managed to make a name for themselves on the London live circuit, playing solid versions of songs by the Beatles, the Animals, and other popular groups, as well as some of their own promising compositions.

Drummer Mike Gibbins believed that it was through the efforts of their manager, Bill Collins, that Mal Evans first became aware of the Iveys. Collins, a Liverpool native, claimed to have once played in a jazz band with Paul McCartney's father, James. Having also worked as a road manager for the Mojos, a group that featured his son, Lewis, Collins knew Mal Evans from the Liverpool club circuit. It was at Collins' suggestion that Mal Evans first came to see the Iveys. Gibbins explained, "Mal got really friendly with us. He really liked the band and he used to hang around our house with us. We used to do acid with him. Peter Asher came to the Marquee to see us with Mal, and he didn't like us. He thought we sucked, but then, so did Peter and Gordon, in my book."

Gibbins and his bandmates felt that Peter Asher never really supported the Iveys, noting that Asher tended to focus on James Taylor and other artists that he was considering for Apple. "Peter Asher was producing Yes for a while, too, then. We were in the next studio. This was before Yes was big, he was doing a demo with them. Peter wasn't really our A&R man at Apple, everybody was A&R at Apple. Everybody at Apple was stoned constantly, I mean everybody. We used to hang out there all the time. Mal was our main guy at Apple. Peter Asher took a few photographs. He did what he had to do. Everybody was a photographer at Apple, everybody was everybody."

"We owe it to Mal for getting us to Apple more than anybody," recalled Gibbins. "Mal and Bill, of course, because Bill put his foot in the door big time. Bill was turning down record deals and stuff. We were starving, but he was holding out for an Apple deal. He knew that Apple was going to be a happening thing. Mal used to come around to our house way before we signed. We would make him tape after tape on Revox recorders, cheap demos. The tapes that we gave Apple, if I gave that same tape to a record company today, they'd laugh at us. It was really chintzy, but they saw something in the sound."

The Iveys submitted three sets of demo tapes to Apple before Harrison, Lennon, and Derek Taylor agreed that Apple should sign the group. On 31 July, Apple Records signed the Iveys to a three-year contract with two one-year options. For reasons no longer remembered by any of the participants, it would not be until 31 October that the Iveys signed a five-year contract with Apple Music Publishing.

Mary Hopkin, a young folk-singer from Wales, was another one of Apple's early discoveries. Hopkin had come to Apple's attention after British fashion model Twiggy saw her perform on the television talent show *Opportunity Knocks* in early May. "Twiggy saw the show and, I think, the next day saw Paul McCartney," Hopkin recalled. "He was telling her all about the new Apple label, and she said she had seen this girl on *Opportunity Knocks* and he should check me out. So I received a telegram, two days after the show, which I ignored for a few days. It said, 'Ring Peter Brown at Apple Records,' and I'd never heard of either of them. I was a great Beatles fan, and I'd heard of the Apple Boutique, but nothing else. We didn't know that Apple Records was on the way. I left it on the shelf for three days, and then my mother said it would be polite to ring back." Hopkin dutifully dialed the number provided in the telegram and asked for Peter Brown. A man with a distinct Liverpool accent – who Hopkin assumed was Peter Brown – came on the line. For a few moments, Hopkin had no idea that she had been speaking to Paul McCartney.

It suddenly dawned on Hopkin that Apple Records probably had something to do with the Beatles, but when the man with the Liverpool accent asked if she'd be interested in coming to London for an audition, the young singer – who had only just turned eighteen – was understandably evasive. McCartney sensed her reluctance and asked Hopkin to put her mother on the phone. McCartney introduced himself to Mrs. Hopkin and explained his interest in having Mary audition for the Beatles' new record label. Several days later, Apple dispatched a car to the Hopkin's home in Pontardawe to take Mrs. Hopkin and her daughter to London, where Mary made some demo recordings and mother and daughter were treated to lunch with Paul McCartney. "I sang a few songs for him," Hopkin recounted, "and then I was called back about two or three weeks later, and he sang a little song for me, sort of hummed it, and said, 'I've had this song lying around for years. It's called "Those Were The Days." Let's go in and do it.'"

McCartney had apparently been looking for the right singer to record "Those Were The Days" ever since he had first heard the song performed at the Blue Angel nightclub in London by an American duo, Gene and Francesca, sometime in 1966. McCartney was convinced that, given the right vocalist and arrangement, "Those Were The Days" could be a massive hit.

Upon hearing Mary Hopkin sing in the demo studio of Dick James Music, McCartney instinctively knew that "Those Were The Days" would be the perfect song for Hopkin and decided that he would personally produce the record. Envisioning "Those Were The Days" with an "old-time" arrangement, McCartney tasked Peter Asher with securing an arranger for the recording session. Asher's choice was Richard Hewson, a London musician who had played drums in a jazz trio in which Peter Asher had once played stand-up bass. Arranging "Those Were The Days" was Hewson's first job out of music college.

"Apple was a funny old place," recounted Hewson. "It was very haphazard. Nobody really knew what anybody else was doing. Peter didn't know anything about arrangers. All he knew was he knew me, and that I'd been to the Guildhall and studied classical music and he thought, 'OK, Paul wants some orchestra on this, Richard probably knows how to write classical orchestra arrangements, let's try him.' That's how I got the job, because they didn't know anybody else. If they'd looked around, they could probably have found a real arranger."

Hewson proved to be an inspired choice, and McCartney was delighted with the results of Mary Hopkin's first recording session for Apple. Having proven himself to McCartney and Asher, Hewson was then hired to write arrangements for several of the songs that James Taylor had been recording over the summer. "We worked for about three months," explained Taylor in a 1971 interview with *Rolling Stone*. "We just got all the basic tracks down as good as we could to all these tunes. Then Peter would take the basic tracks to Richard Hewson. Richard would just write out an arrangement completely. There was no head session involved, except on "Carolina" and "Rainy Day Man." It always happened in two separate phases. "Sunshine Sunshine" – I recorded a demo of it. And he took it and wrote a very specific arrangement to it with 3 against 4. And I had to play guitar inside that, too. I remember it as being pretty confining. And Richard is a fine arranger, indeed." In addition to writing the arrangements, Hewson would also be given the responsibility of conducting the orchestral sessions.

Of the four Beatles, it was initially Paul McCartney who was most interested in using Apple as an outlet for his songwriting and record production skills. But George Harrison – the Beatle most skeptical about the Apple concept – also spent several months throughout 1968 producing material for Apple. Harrison's principal project was to record an album for Jackie Lomax. Lomax recalled: "I think it was before they went to India with the Maharishi trip that George came to me and said, 'I heard some of your songs from upstairs. I really like them and I'd like to produce something when we get back from India. Are you into that?' I said, 'Yeah yeah yeah, of course.'" Lomax was in for an even bigger surprise when Harrison returned to England. While in India, Harrison had written several new songs, and upon returning to London, offered one of them – "Sour Milk Sea" – to Lomax to record as his first Apple single. With Harrison producing, Lomax recorded "Sour Milk Sea" and his own composition, "The Eagle Laughs At You," early in the summer of 1968. Lomax signed a three-year recording contract with Apple – with options for two one-year extensions – on 28 June 1968.

By May, all of the disparate pieces of Apple were finally falling into place. On 12 May 1968, Paul McCartney, John Lennon, and the heads of several Apple divisions had flown to New York City, where the two Beatles were scheduled to discuss Apple on *The Johnny Carson Show*.

Facing off against Joe Garagiola, a middle-aged former baseball star who was filling in as a guest host for Johnny Carson, and the unsettling Tallulah Bankhead, an elderly actress who was also a guest on the show, a nervous looking Lennon and McCartney presented their unfocused concept of a company that they hoped would utilize the collective influence, talent, and money of the Beatles to help discover and nurture deserving artists and to serve as a model of "Western communism." It was not an auspicious start for the Apple organization.

During their stay in America, the Apple team held a press conference in New York City, where John Lennon, Paul McCartney, and Derek Taylor further enlightened the world about their new company. During the 14 May press conference, John Lennon took the lead, explaining to the assembled press: "It's a business concerning records, films, and electronics, and as a sideline, whatever it's called, manufacturing. We want to set up a system whereby people who just want to make a film about anything don't have to go down on their knees in somebody's office, probably yours." Apple's last order of business during the whirlwind trip would be to hold an Apple business meeting on a motor yacht that had been rented to sail around Manhattan.

Several weeks after the New York press junket, Paul McCartney, Derek Taylor, Ron Kass, Tony Bramwell, and Ivan Vaughan (a childhood friend of John Lennon and Paul McCartney who was now on the Apple payroll as a consultant working on the Beatles' idea of starting an Apple school) returned to America to attend a Capitol Records convention in Hollywood. They brought with them a copy of one of the few films ever made by Apple Films to show to the Capitol executives.

Featuring a searing, Eric Clapton-led instrumental track from George Harrison's still unreleased *Wonderwall Music* album entitled "Skiing" as its soundtrack, the five-minute promo film shown in Hollywood gave a brief summary of Apple and featured just-signed Apple Records artist Mary Hopkin performing a song in Paul McCartney's sun-dappled backyard, as well as a bizarre greeting from Magic Alex filmed in the Apple Electronics lab.

Images of the Apple Boutique could be seen in the film, but little was said about Apple's latest addition to their retail operation. To complement the Apple Boutique, Apple Retail had set up a second store – more high-end than the Apple Boutique – known as Apple Tailoring (civil and theatrical) in a shop at 161 King's Road. Established on 2 February 1968 and officially opened on 23 May, the shop was a partnership with John Crittle, a celebrated London designer whose previous boutique, Dandie Fashions, had been favoured by the Beatles. Crittle was named Director of the enterprise along with Apple's Neil Aspinall and Stephen Maltz. Apple also opened an ex-directory men's hairdressing salon in the basement of Apple Tailoring, run by Leslie Cavendish, a former assistant to Vidal Sassoon.

"I had started cutting Paul McCartney's hair in late 1966. In 1967, I was asked to go on the *Magical Mystery Tour,*" recalls Cavendish. "When we came back, the Beatles mentioned that they wanted to open a hair styling shop up and that's how it happened. There was a shop called Dandie Fashions that became Apple Tailoring. The owner, John Crittle, was a friend of George Harrison. The combination of opening a tailoring shop and a hairdressing shop downstairs appealed to them at the time, I suppose. The Beatles funded everything. They spent around £10,000 on the shop. There was no salary. I just paid some token rent to John (Crittle), who was then supposed to pay Apple. Whether or not that ever happened I don't know. I was paid by the clients. I was on call for all of the Beatles and would cut their hair at either the salon or Savile Row. I would go from James Taylor and Grapefruit to even Doris Troy. I would do all of their hair and other artists, too, like Keith Moon. I thought Apple Tailoring was a revolutionary shop. They started with all those crushed velvet jackets and pirate shirts. It wasn't cheap. And I charged two pound twenty for haircuts, which was a lot in those days."

Equal little attention was paid to Apple Films in the promo clip, even though they were reportedly developing two projects in the spring of 1968. Initially, Apple Films had announced plans to produce a film adaptation of John Lennon's *Spaniard In The Works* and *In His Own Write* books, as well as a Beatles version of *Lord Of The Rings*. But by May, Apple Films had shelved both proposed films and instead started work on two entirely new projects. The first film was to be an adaptation of a short story by Julio Cortazar, called *The Jam*, filming for which was scheduled to begin in England in July. Apple Films also announced that a film called *Walkabout*, written by Edward Bond, was scheduled to begin filming in Australia in November 1968.

There was, in fact, a new Beatles film in the works, but Apple Films was only tangentially involved with the upcoming *Yellow Submarine*. The animated film – which revolved around a story line loosely based on characters and subjects lifted from Beatles songs – had been in development since 1966. The Beatles were under contract to deliver a third film to United Artists. But by 1966 the Beatles had lost their enthusiasm for making feature films, and when film producer Al Brodax – who had previously produced a Beatles cartoon series shown on American TV – pitched the idea of creating an animated film featuring the Beatles, the group readily agreed to his proposal, reasoning that it would allow them to fulfill their contractual obligations to United Artists without having to go through the trouble of acting.

Production began in 1967 and the film quickly took on a very "trippy" psychedelic feel, complete with bright colours and "far-out" otherworldly visual images. Once Beatles songs such as "It's All Too Much" and "Lucy In The Sky With Diamonds" were inserted into the soundtrack, the film became something of a psychedelic touchstone and it remains a fascinating encapsulation of the era.

Yellow Submarine would be promoted as an "Apple Presentation," yet neither Apple Films nor the Beatles had much to do with the creation of the film. Even the Beatles' voices were supplied by actors. The band's sole contribution was limited to a few minutes at the end of the film, when the four Beatles appeared on-screen to warn of approaching "blue meanies" and to preside over a jolly sing-along sequence of Paul McCartney's "All Together Now."

Ironically, all four Beatles were quite taken with the charm and imagination of the finished work and they later were said to have regretted not being more actively involved. The Beatles may have had little to do with the actual development of *Yellow Submarine*, but they would take an active role in promoting the film. It was premiered at the London Pavilion Theatre on 17 July and all four Beatles as well as several of their guests attended the premiere. "I went to the premiere of *Yellow Submarine* with James Taylor, which was a little strange because we were worlds apart," recalled Mary Hopkin. "I was so shy that I barely uttered a word, and James was totally spaced out. A fine pair, turning up in a huge limousine!"

Unlike *Magical Mystery Tour*, which had been savaged by the British press, *Yellow Submarine* received generally positive reviews. For reasons that were (and are still) not clear, the film was given only limited distribution in the UK, and it was not a major financial success. *Yellow Submarine* fared far better in the United States, where the film received glowing reviews and was rewarded with a strong box office performance.

The *Yellow Submarine* premier was a major news event for the English press. For the first year of Apple's existence, Apple would be an almost bottomless well of newsworthy stories for a media with a still insatiable appetite for Beatles-related news items. To ensure that Apple would be able to fully publicize their music and film ventures, Derek Taylor hired 33-year-old Jeremy Banks in June 1968. Assisting Taylor with publicity matters and acting as Apple's Photographic Coordinator, Banks was responsible for placing, as well as selling, photos of the Beatles and other Apple-related projects to the press.

Banks would spend his first month at Apple working alongside Derek Taylor in the claustrophobic conditions of the tiny publicity office at Wigmore Street. This arrangement would thankfully be short-lived due to Apple resolving its shortage of office space by buying a property that would become Apple's new headquarters.

Situated in the heart of fashionable Mayfair, Apple's new building at 3 Savile Row was an elegant, five-storey Georgian townhouse for which the leasehold was purchased for approximately £500,000 on 22 June 1968. Prior to Apple purchasing the property, the building had housed a theatrical management firm owned by bandleader Jack Hylton.

The building was in need of substantial refurbishment, but members of Apple's staff started moving in as early as 15 July. For the next two months, workmen swarmed in and around 3 Savile Row, turning the somewhat run-down townhouse into a stately space suitable for a company that was positioning itself to revolutionize the entertainment industry. In addition to reconditioning the facade, the building's interior was painted a cream color and the floors were covered in thick apple-green carpet.

Though primarily intended to be Apple's corporate headquarters, the four Beatles also envisaged their new building as being something along the lines of their personal London clubhouse. To cater to their whims and the soon-to-be-frequent business lunches, Apple hired several young chefs to man the small kitchen on the third floor. In keeping with Apple's utopian spirit, the Beatles decreed that even Apple's junior staff would be allowed to order lunch from the kitchen.

The new Apple building would eventually also incorporate a recording studio, so that the Beatles would have ready access to first-rate recording facilities whenever inspiration struck. Apple Electronics was tasked with constructing a state-of-the-art studio in the basement. Even before the plans for the studio had been drafted, the Beatles had lured several Abbey Road Studios employees to come over to help establish Apple Studios. One of the first to join was Malcolm Davies, who was hired to set up and run the cutting room in the Apple basement for the

Beatles' exclusive use.

In the days when vinyl records were the primary medium of recorded sound, it was the responsibility of the cutting room engineer to transfer the music captured on the recording studio tapes to a metal "master" that would be used to manufacture a record. In addition to mastering records, the cutting room engineer also "cut" acetates, which were essentially short-lived records that were made in small numbers in order to check the sound of a performance or a mastered recording.

To assist Davies in the cutting room, George Peckham was hired to train as a cutting room engineer. Peckham was a veteran of the Liverpool music scene. "I started out playing bass in a band called the Fourmost, who were also managed by Eppy," he explains. "In early 1968 when I was twenty-three, the Beatles told me that they were thinking of getting a studio together. I went to speak to Peter Brown and told him I wanted to work in the studio, start at the ground level, no favours or anything, and work my way up. When the Beatles decided to put a studio together at Savile Row, I had these interviews with Peter Brown. Peter introduced me to Ron Kass and then said, 'OK, you can start in September, but there won't be any favours. (Peckham's first day of work was actually 9 November). You'll start like any other employee.' So I gave my notice to the band and started at Apple. I was already living in London while the rest of the band was still in Liverpool. With the Fourmost, I was always interested in what Geoff Emerick was doing in the control room. I used to drive Geoff mad with asking about what all the different meters did and all that. A few months later when Geoff came over from EMI to become the Apple Studio Manager, I had already been at Apple for a while. When I was introduced to him, and he saw me and it was like, 'Oh my god, what are you doing here?' The actual mastering room was up and running in Savile Row by the summer of 1968. They were still putting walls around it when I got there. "Hey Jude" was being cut when there were still three walls there, there wasn't a fourth wall yet. When I started, Malcolm Davies did the mastering and he let me do all the acetates. But that changed around because the better I got, the easier it became for Malcolm, so he could spend more time at the pub around the corner."

The studio was originally planned to be for the exclusive use of the Beatles, as well as musicians and songwriters affiliated with Apple, but many outside artists were soon clamouring for an opportunity to cut their records at Apple. Peckham remembers, "I used to go out clubbing every night after work, and I would bump into a lot of musicians that I knew from when I played music. When they found out I worked at Apple, they used to ask me to cut their records. Eventually, I had to sit down with George Harrison and the others and tell them that people want to come and cut at Apple, and I asked if we could open Apple up to outside clients. They agreed, and the next thing you know, Apple Studios was up and running. It was busy as hell after that. At other studios of the time, you would have these guys in white coats cutting your records, they wouldn't say anything, and they wouldn't let you give any input. But with me as an ex-musician, I'd say, 'Oh you need more bass on that,' and you work with the artist. Apple got a reputation for cutting records that had that magic, which was what the Beatles wanted, they wanted to make a better record. Soon I was cutting records for the Stones, Clapton, Led Zeppelin and those early Genesis albums. All of these artists were coming in. It was like working day and night."

Apple Electronics would not be able to complete a fully functioning recording studio until 1969 at the earliest. But since Apple Electronics was only involved with the creation of the recording studio, a makeshift cutting room was operational by the late summer of 1968 and the Beatles and Apple would soon begin cutting most of their acetates in the Apple basement instead of at EMI.

Given that the Apple Studio was only in the earliest planning stage, the Beatles had returned to EMI's studio at Abbey Road to work on what would become the "White Album." Such was the backlog of songs that had been written in India that it had been decided to record them all and release the recordings as a double album.

Throughout the summer of 1968, when not recording with the Beatles or engaged in Apple business meetings, Paul McCartney spent what little free time he had producing sessions for an eclectic collection of new and potential Apple artists. Even the break-up of McCartney's long-term relationship with his fiancé, Jane Asher, in early July, did not impact his output in the recording studio or his ability to work with Peter Asher. Several Apple employees recall some initially awkward vibes in the office between McCartney and Peter Asher after the split, but McCartney and Asher had been close friends for years and were able to maintain both their friendship and working relationship. "We were very English about it," explains Asher. "It was a separate issue, and we left it that way."

Soon after completing work on "Those Were The Days," McCartney's next production project for Apple was to record several tracks with a traditional English brass band, the John Foster and Sons Ltd. Black Dyke Mills Band. One of the songs was an instrumental entitled "Thingumybob" that McCartney had written a few months earlier to be used as the theme song for a London Weekend Television show of the same name starring Stanley Holloway. Unimpressed with an earlier attempt to record "Thingumybob" with London session musicians, McCartney hired the Black Dyke Mills Band to record a new version of the song. To capture an authentic brass band feel, McCartney opted to record the song live in the band's hometown of Shipley, in Yorkshire.

On Saturday, 27 July, Paul McCartney drove up to Shipley to "produce" an outdoor recording session by the Black Dyke Mills Band. The band were part of a long-standing English tradition of factories sponsoring employee brass bands and orchestras. Given that the members of the Black Dyke Mills Band spent most of their days toiling in a distinctly unglamorous area of the textiles industry, even the older members of the band were thrilled to be making a recording with one of the Beatles.

Joining McCartney on his trip to Shipley were Peter Asher, Tony Bramwell, Derek Taylor, and McCartney's sheepdog, Martha. On Sunday morning, Peter Asher set up the portable recording equipment they had brought from London for the recording session. Apple had booked the local Victoria Hall to use in the event of rain, but the morning turned out to be the start of a lovely English summer's day and over a hundred fans turned out to see McCartney and Martha grace the streets of their small, usually quiet town. The session was a success, and at the end of the day, Apple had a fine recording of "Thingumybob" as well as a rousing brass band version of the Beatles' "Yellow Submarine" to use as a B-side.

Less than two weeks after the "Thingumybob" session, McCartney was once more back in the studio on behalf of Apple. This time, he was working with Drew and Dy, a young duo who had signed a contract with Apple Records on 8 July.

In May, Drew (Keith Drewett) and Dy (Pete Dymond) had been passing Apple's Baker Street office in a taxi when they saw Paul McCartney on the street. They immediately stopped the taxi and ran up to McCartney to ask if they could get his opinion on their songs. McCartney agreed to give them a listen and took them into the Baker Street building where they recorded six songs on the Apple Publishing Revox. McCartney said he would listen to the tapes and get back to them, though Pete Dymond admits that they did not expect anything to come of the meeting. But their tape – particularly the song "Tales Of Frankie Rabbit" – quickly became a hit around the Apple office (the Beatles can actually be heard busking a version of the song during the Get Back sessions in early 1969), and Drew and Dy were signed as writers to Apple's new publishing company, Python Publishing.

Eventually, McCartney and the other Beatles decided that they also liked Drew and Dy as performers and signed them to a three-year (with two one-year options) recording contract with Apple Records. "We knew this singer, Billy Nicholls, quite well," explains Dymond. "Billy was involved with George Harrison for a short while, and he told me that he had gone to George's and George gave him a ride in his Mercedes. Billy said that George had a copy of the tape we made on the stairwell at Baker Street playing all the time in the car. George told Billy that he and Ringo Starr wanted to put out the tape exactly as it was, really rough, but that Paul wanted to do a proper record of it. On 12 August, we went into Trident Studios to do three tracks with Paul McCartney.

"We were only about seventeen and weren't that good at playing and singing, so Peter Brown was meant to book session musicians. But when we got there at two in the afternoon, they weren't there, because he had forgotten to book them. So, Peter got a drummer in who was drunk and who was very overwhelmed to be working with Paul McCartney. I remember Paul saying, 'Well, that isn't going to help.' Then there was a Hawaiian bass guitarist for some reason, and Paul McCartney worked out the bass parts and showed the bass player how to play the part. Goodness knows where they found those two, but we were really disappointed. The session cost Apple 1100 quid, and even at the end of the session, McCartney knew that we probably hadn't made a record and that we would have to do it again. What we did that day didn't come out like a record. It was ok, but it wasn't up to "record" status because it was us playing. Paul McCartney did a bit of bass and the piano. At the end of it, he sent us the acetate a week later with a letter that essentially said, 'It's not really there as a record, but it's our fault so we'll do it again.'

"What I remember most about the session was that he was incredibly down-to-earth and he had tireless energy. He kept running up and down the stairs between the control room and the studio, telling us what he wanted, and playing things to us on our guitars. The session lasted thirteen hours, and his energy never waned. But like many other celebrities, as long as you were saying everything was great, he was fine, but as soon as you made any criticism, he'd go very cold indeed. I made a bit of a mistake when he played us an acetate of "Those Were The Days," which hadn't been released yet. He asked me, 'So, what do you think?' and I told him, 'Brilliant for the continent, absolutely brilliant production, but I can't see it doing very well in England.' Well, that was the wrong thing to say to him, and he just said coldly, 'Well, we'll see, won't we?' It was a great song, and I could see it doing well in Germany and France, but not in England. But I guess I was wrong."

McCartney had been trying to find an outlet for Drew and Dy's "Tales Of Frankie Rabbit" ever since the duo had signed to Python Music. Earlier that summer, he had pitched the song to Timon (born Stephen Murray), a seventeen-year-old singer/songwriter from Liverpool who was being considered for a contract with Apple Records. "Paul McCartney had heard "Bitter Thoughts Of Little Jane" (Timon's January 1968 single for Pye Records) on the radio and wanted me to re-record that for Apple," explains Timon. "I went in to see Derek Taylor at Apple at Wigmore Street once, and he said, 'The Beatles want to meet you,' and I thought, 'Well yeah, why would the Beatles possibly want to meet me?' Obviously, they were investing some money in me, so I understand now, but at the time, I thought they must be bugged by everybody. I met Paul at Wigmore Street before we did any sessions. I left the big room and went across the hallway into an office where Chris O'Dell was. I had just gone in to check it out, and then Paul followed me into the room just on his own and we started talking.

"He had sent me a demo of a song called "Golly Miss Pringle" – he wasn't singing it – and he asked me if I liked the song, and I told him that I didn't want to do it. He asked me if I had some songs, but there was no guitar, so I couldn't play anything for him. Then he played me a tape of some writers that Apple was working with. Back then, Paul used to take an ordinary bus to the Apple office, and he said he met these guys one day when he got off the bus at Apple and they came up to him and said, 'Here's our tape, Paul. Nobody wants it. We've tried every record company and everybody's turned it down.' So Paul thought, well then it has to be good. He put it on for me and asked if I was interested in doing one of their songs. There was this song, "Tales Of Frankie Rabbit Bringing Me Down." Paul was interested to see if I wanted to do it, because he thought my stuff wasn't poppy enough or whatever. He really wanted me to re-record "Bitter Thoughts Of Little Jane," and I told him that I didn't want to do it again, because it was my last single and people would think I had dried up if I put it out again. I was really concerned with what my friends would think more than anything else."

Several weeks passed before Apple reached a tentative decision to offer Timon a record and publishing deal. "I still have the unsigned contract with a company called Python," says Timon. "I never signed the contract, for some reason. Basically, I did three tracks at Trident Studios for Apple and a few other bits with Peter Asher above the Apple shop at Baker Street. I did a few songs on those Revoxes at Baker Street, and Derek Taylor was there. I wanted to make an LP, and Apple sort of wanted me to make a commercial record, and I didn't think that was what Apple was about, personally. That summer I recorded three tracks with Peter Asher at Trident Studios, but they were more than just demos. If they were demos, they were expensive demos. They had Mike Vickers from Manfred Mann in to arrange the session. There was full orchestration. We did my session in the same studio where James Taylor was recording his Apple album. Paul McCartney came down and played piano on a track called "Something New Every Day." I was backed by James Taylor – who borrowed John Lennon's white Epiphone guitar for the session – and the band who had been working on James's album, Bishop O'Brien on drums and Louis Cennamo on bass. I had been sitting around playing guitar with James at Peter's house, and he liked my songs, so we got him for the session.

"In the middle of the session, Paul came down to the studio, probably to see how his money was being spent. Mike Vickers was playing piano on the session, and Paul asked if he could play on a track. It was a funny situation; I had met Paul once or twice before in the Apple office, but he started playing piano. This was before the "White Album" had come out, and he was sitting there between takes playing really amazing stuff like "Martha My Dear," which no one had heard yet. Really amazing. But for some reason, I was aware that we only had three hours for the session. In those days you would go in at 2pm and end at 6pm. So he was going up and down the piano, and I realized we were only on the second song. Everyone in the studio was silent as Paul doodled on the piano, though it sounded fantastic; it sounded like Beatles songs that you had never heard before. I knew it was great, but something came over me and I shouted to Louis Cennamo across the room, 'Hey, Louie, what time is it?' Louis pretended he never heard me, so I shouted again, and he replied it was, like, twenty past five. Suddenly, Paul stopped playing and saluted to me like a soldier and said, 'Aye aye, sir, let's get back to work,' and we started straight back into the song we were working on. I've always respected him for that."

There was an additional act that Apple had been considering for a possible deal that was also given a full session at Trident, though none of the Beatles nor Peter Asher were directly involved with the recordings. It was a group known as Contact, though "the group" was really just a vehicle for aspiring singer/songwriter Trevor Bannister.

"My contact with Apple came about through Mark Davis, who was working in some capacity with Apple Films. Mark was a close friend of John Lennon, and I was a good friend of Mark and his wife. I was nineteen at the time," recalls Bannister. "I was writing songs, and Mark heard one of my songs and introduced me to John Lennon. John heard a couple songs and really loved "Lovers From The Sky." He told me that he wanted to arrange to get it recorded. This was in the early days of Apple, before they started advertising for people to send in tapes. It was a different situation.

"John later invited me back to play my songs for him at a different building on Wigmore Street. After I played the songs, they asked if I could get a few musicians together. I later came back again and played the song to the rest of the Beatles, and they decided to get me into a studio to record. I then went to see Terry Doran to sign a publishing deal for the songs. The other song I had, "Midsummer Night's Dream," was a bit of a spoof. The band was me on guitar, Peter Cassidy playing bass, Tony Furguson on keyboards, and we were going to get someone else on drums. When we went into the studio, Jim Capaldi from Traffic was playing drums.

"I thought up the name Contact as in terms of contact with people from another planet, which was a big interest of mine at the time. There was actually someone I knew at the time – Johan Quanjer – whom I thought was from another planet. He was the first president of the UFO society. But the next time I saw him, he was working in the furniture department at Harrods, and I was so disappointed. I thought, 'He ain't no alien, with a posh English accent in a suit working in the furniture department.'

"The plan, from the best of my recollection, was to cut a single and maybe an album. Paul McCartney was interested in having me record at Trident, which was an eight-track studio, because at that time, the Beatles had only been using four tracks at EMI. They were interested in seeing how I would get on. Peter Asher wanted to produce the session, but I didn't like his style. I thought he was a little too "establishment," and I really wanted to get something a little more dynamic. So, Jim Capaldi ended up producing and playing drums on "Lovers From The Sky." I don't remember how I met him, but we became very good mates. Jim was very interested. He liked the song after I played it to him on acoustic. Yoko Ono, who I also knew through Mark Davis, wanted to be involved in the recording. I wanted to practice the song before going into the studio, and she said, 'You should go out into a field and practice,' and I told her, 'Yeah, good idea, but we're looking to add drums to it.' It was a bit crazy.

"After the tracks were recorded, I met John and Paul to have a talk about the record. Paul actually thought that it was a bit too heavy for the time in terms of musical style. John wanted it released, but they wanted me to get a group together to promote the record. But at that time, I was working with these two musicians – Tony Furguson and his brother – who were getting into those things that people got involved with in those days that tended to take people off course. One committed suicide, and a few weeks later, the other committed suicide."

With no group to promote the recordings, the proposed Contact single never came to pass, though Bannister would cut several demos in Apple's studio several years later. "Lovers From The Sky," however, was a fantastic recording. Propelled by the galloping drums of Jim Capaldi, Bannister's hypnotic psychedelia was oddly catchy, though, as McCartney noted, it was a heavy track, and it would have been at odds with the more pop oriented records that Apple was preparing for the launch of the label.

Notwithstanding the abortive attempts to record singles by Timon, Contact, and Drew and Dy, by early August, Apple had amassed a backlog of master recordings to release on the Apple label. Concluding several months of negotiations, Apple had signed a worldwide manufacturing and distribution deal with EMI in late June. The deal struck with EMI covered only Apple Records releases by non-Beatles artists and was totally independent of the Beatles' existing contract with EMI. With a deal in place, Ron Kass dedicated July and August to getting Apple integrated into the EMI distribution system. Under the agreement with EMI, Capitol Records would manufacture, distribute, and promote Apple in the United States, and EMI would handle the rest of the world. Once Apple Records was formally launched later that summer, all new Beatles records would be issued with an Apple label, even though the Beatles were not actually signed to Apple. The Beatles would remain under contract to EMI until 1976, and money earned from sales of Beatles records issued with an Apple label would continue to go to Capitol and EMI, and not Apple. Apple would not earn any money from the sale of Beatles records until the Beatles' contract with Capitol and EMI was renegotiated in 1969.

To represent Apple at Capitol's Hollywood office, Capitol's Director of Independent Labels, Ken Mansfield, was appointed North American Manager of Apple Records. Mansfield remembers, "Capitol President Stanley Gorticov called me one day and told me that the Beatles, mainly Paul McCartney and Ron Kass, has asked for me to head up Apple Records in America. 'You don't have to tell us where you are, or what you're doing, and you don't have to clear your expenditures. You only have one responsibility – to keep it together with the Beatles.'"

Mansfield first met the Beatles in 1965. "I was head of Capitol's Artist Relations and District Promotion Manager for the West Coast out of the Hollywood office. When the Beatles first came through, they were like any other band, and they were my responsibility. It was my responsibility on any major tours to set up all the press conferences – anything to do with artist relations – and if it was a major act, to just fall in with the band and spend the time with them. When they came to L.A. to do the 1965 Hollywood Bowl concert, that was my job. We did the press conference downstairs in the Studio A recording studio in the basement of the Capitol Building. The Beatles were really enamoured with L.A., with California, and Hollywood. George was asking me where all these things were, Paul asked me if I could get him any Gene Vincent records, and Ringo asked me if he could meet Buck Owens while he was at Capitol. They just really wanted to know more about California. Because we kept on getting interrupted, I said to them, we have a day off tomorrow and that we could take care of all their questions then. The next day we just spent the day by the pool at this house in Benedict Canyon, and I got to know them pretty well. When they decided to set up Apple, I was kind of the only young executive they knew. Everyone else was a lord at EMI or a chairman of the board. Everyone was old and grey, while I was twenty-four and starting to grow my hair long. When they set up Apple, America was unquestionably *the* market. So they flew me, Stanley Gorticov, and Larry Delaney over to London, and we put it together over there, then I came back and ran Apple for them in America. It wasn't like I changed offices or that they put up a special logo or sign, the only thing that happened was that my stationary changed to US Manager of Apple Records. But Capitol paid my salary. I became their personal liaison. Everything had to go through me; I was responsible for everything: promotion, release dates, American mastering, keeping track of the parts and artwork. Most of my day-to-day work and dialogue was with Jack Oliver in London.

"It was crazy, but it was more to do with the sheer volume of the work. The unfortunate, in a way, announcement that Apple was open to the people and that they wanted to do this different thing just made everyone in the world think that Apple was their home and that would drive you crazy. And Apple was not just a record company, there were five companies there. When I got to London, they had already made me a special packet of acetates of the first four records. We spent the days in London going over how we were going to present and position Apple in America. They were really gearing up for the American release, because America was the market. The office at Savile Row had just been painted white on the outside and white on the inside, and they had put in green carpeting, but there was no furniture. When they brought me over to London, we would have our meetings in a hotel in Hyde Park, and then we'd go to the Apple building and we'd sit on the floor. The only thing in the whole building was a big sound system that Paul had brought in so that we could decide what our first releases were going to be and a portable table where they put food on.

"It was always very clear what the first four records were going to be, except for "Hey Jude." Paul was really concerned about "Hey Jude" because it was seven minutes long and unlike any other single at that time. We spent a lot of time going back and forth whether we should do "Revolution" as our first record instead of "Hey Jude." Finally, because we kept playing it over and over every day and going back and forth, I said, 'Tell you what, Paul. I'll just go back to America, I'll work my way back to L.A. and I'll hit the major cities, and I'll run the two songs by the big stations.' Because I had been National Promotion Director for Capitol, I had good relationships with a lot of the major music directors and program directors across the country. I flew into WFIL in Philadelphia, Jim Hilliard was the hot ears in Philadelphia at the time, and then WQAM in Miami, a fellow named Jim Dunlap was there, and I went into St. Louis, and they all fell all over "Hey Jude," so I called

London and told them we had to go with "Hey Jude."

"When I came back to L.A., I set up a special promotion team to handle independent labels, but it was really because of Apple. I took my best men out of the fifty national promotion people I had at Capitol and created a six-man team to promote Apple. But I was the only person in America working specifically for Apple. Neil Aspinall once told me that the London office never had a clue what was going on with me in the States. I was their only contact in America. Paul Wasserman was their American PR man, but other than that, it was just me. I just got inundated all the time. It was madness, but it was fun."

Once Ken Mansfield was in place to manage Apple in the United States, Ron Kass had the opportunity to finalize the staffing of Apple Records' London office. Tony Bramwell was brought over from Apple Films to handle promotions for the record label. "Since nothing was happening with Apple Films when Apple Records was getting ready to release 'the first four,' they came to me and said they needed someone to do the promotion," recalls Bramwell.

Bramwell was joined by Jack Oliver, who was moved out of the press office and into the record department on the ground floor of the Savile Row office. Jack Oliver recalls: "I had moved from Apple Publishing to working with Derek Taylor. Ron Kass wanted me to work with him, and Derek wanted me to work with him, and I chose to go into records, because I thought I could go further, which I did. Ron Kass was very gentlemanly, a gentle person. He was a very smooth, Californian-type American. He was a very good businessman. He was very together and made some good decisions. When I first went into the label and worked with Ron in the record division, he gave me the foreign department, so I handled all of the foreign licensees. And then they gave me the advertising department, and then the production department, so I did all the workings of a label, and I knew exactly how it all worked and I would go meet with the people at EMI and took care of everything, basically. Tony Bramwell did the promotion, and I did everything else."

Looking back on those hectic days, Oliver recalls: "I thought Bramwell was pretty good. He knew a lot of people. To be honest, I don't see it as being too difficult to promote anything that came out of Apple Records. We were with the fab four, and everyone would listen to us, no matter what we said. At that time, we could do anything we wanted because we were so big. It wasn't a difficult job, but he played it very well."

With only weeks to go until the highly anticipated launch of the Apple Records label, the staff focused on completing last-minute preparations to support the inaugural batch of Apple releases and finalized the details of an international promotional campaign designed to introduce Apple to the world. The campaign would position Apple as a serious, professionally run music company, albeit one with a stated intent of discovering and supporting unheralded talent.

The image of business competence that Apple had hoped to portray would be somewhat undermined when Apple made headlines around the world in late July with the sudden and chaotic closing of the Apple Boutique. The real reason why the Beatles decided to close the boutique may never be known, but many of the people involved with Apple at the time – and the Beatles themselves – have claimed that the Beatles simply got tired of being involved in retail.

Long suffering boutique manager John Lyndon claimed that the catalyst for the closing of the boutique was an article in an English music paper by disc jockey John Peel that chastised the Beatles for their involvement in retail. Lyndon remembers being summoned to a meeting at the new Savile Row office with the four Beatles and Yoko Ono (now John Lennon's romantic partner after Lennon's split from his wife, Cynthia) to discuss ongoing operations of the Apple Boutique. He recalled that Harrison and Starr had little interest in the discussion and that Paul McCartney was the only Beatle who still wanted to make a go of the boutique. Peel's comments had apparently struck a nerve with Lennon. When Yoko Ono suggested that the Beatles simply give away the remaining stock and walk away from the boutique, John Lennon latched onto the idea, and from that point on, there was no hope of turning back. "Give it away, you are not a Jewish rag merchant," Lyndon remembered Yoko Ono saying to Lennon, which he thought was rather bold considering it was not her money that she was advocating giving away to the public.

Only the remarkably prescient Derek Taylor seemed to comprehend that closing the Apple Boutique signaled the first cracks in the façade that was the Apple dream. Despite Taylor writing an impassioned letter to the Beatles, imploring them to not give up on "promising openings for the hopeless, riches and Bentleys for clerks, shops for the young where even the counter was for sale, adventurous music, progressive films."

On the evening of 29 July 1968, the Beatles, Yoko Ono, and Neil Aspinall entered the boutique after it had closed for the night and gleefully set about taking whatever clothes they wanted. All of them left with some choice merchandise, except for Ringo Starr, who lamented to *Rolling Stone* that he had been unable to find anything in his size.

The next morning, Apple Boutique employees informed shocked customers – the first being American actor Michael J. Pollard – that there was no need to pay for their selections and then set about giving away the remaining £10,000 worth of stock. Once word spread that the Apple Boutique was giving away all of its merchandise, a frenzied mob gathered on the corner of Baker and Paddington, intent on taking away anything they could lay their hands on. Bolts of unused fabrics from the Fool's workshop, ashtrays, and even the carpeting that covered the floor of the shop were taken away by the ravenous horde.

Future Apple recording artist Joey Molland even managed to get a piece of the shop itself as a souvenir of the final hours of the Apple Boutique. "I got a hold of the Apple Boutique door handle," recalls Molland. "It used to be a hand sticking out that you could put your hand in. I was in London with Gary Walker and the Rain and our manager, Maurice King, his office was right off of Baker Street, about two blocks north of the Apple shop. I still have a jacket from the Apple shop. It was beautiful. It was a little far out with a lot of velvet."

It was over quickly, and on the evening of 30 July, after only eight months in operation, the Apple Boutique closed its doors forever. In a press statement, Paul McCartney explained: "Originally, the shops were intended to be something else, but they just became like all the other boutiques in London. They just weren't our thingy... All that's happened is that we've closed our shop in which we feel we shouldn't, in the first place, have been involved." McCartney whimsically concluded his prepared statement by proclaiming that "Apple is mainly concerned with fun, not frocks," and assured the public that the staff of the Apple Boutique would be given three weeks' pay and an opportunity to get a job with another division of Apple.

One Apple Boutique employee whom John Lennon, at least, was particularly keen to keep on Apple's payroll was the enigmatic Caleb (aka Caleb Ashburton-Dunning). "At the Wigmore Street office in the early days, it (the I-Ching) was thrown every morning," recalled Derek Taylor, adding that Caleb "wore all white and his white-blond hair parted in the middle. He got 50 quid a week."

Not wanting to lose the services of a good mystic, the Beatles brought Caleb over to Savile Row, where, with the aid of his I-Ching coins, he apparently was asked to weigh in on business decisions that were being made at Apple. But Caleb would not last long at Savile Row, his position being terminated after he was alleged to have incurred Lennon's wrath by predicting that Lennon's relationship with Yoko Ono would not last and that he should go back to his wife, Cynthia. Peter Brown later claimed that Caleb ended up in a mental institution, which was certainly feasible given the acid-induced mental health issues that several other associates recall Ashburton-Dunning struggling with at the time.

Within weeks of the Apple boutique being shuttered, the decision was made that Apple should extract itself from all retail operations. Though the King's Road shop would continue operating into the autumn of 1968, Apple signed the entire operation over to John Crittle and ended their brief and certainly bold experiment in the fashion business.

1968: The Revolution Begins

The sad, strange tale of the Apple Boutique had only just faded from the headlines when the first Apple singles were finally released in the United States on 26 August 1968. The Beatles' "Hey Jude," Mary Hopkin's "Those Were The Days," Jackie Lomax's "Sour Milk Sea," and the Black Dyke Mills Band's "Thingumybob" were the recordings that had been selected to inaugurate the Apple Records label. Due to scheduling problems with the record pressing plants that Apple used in England, the Beatles and Mary Hopkin singles came out in the UK on 30 August, while the Black Dyke Mills Band and Lomax singles came out the following week, on 6 September.

To promote the official launch of Apple Records, Apple had engaged the Wolfe Olins advertising agency to develop a campaign to introduce Apple to industry VIPs and the press. The agency came up with a sleek plastic presentation box on which a sticker reading "Our First Four, 3 Savile Row, W3" was affixed. Each box contained the four records along with a photo and short biography of each artist.

Seeking maximum press coverage of Apple's launch, Jeremy Banks devised a plan to have Richard DiLello deliver "Our First Four" presentation boxes to the residences of English Prime Minister Harold Wilson, the Queen Mother, and other members of the royal family. Driven to the residences by Apple's chauffeur, Joe Marchini, and accompanied by favoured Apple photographer John Kelly, a slightly inebriated DiLello delivered the packages with little incident. George Harrison was reportedly less than pleased that DiLello had delivered a set of records to Prime Minister Wilson (the Mr. Wilson featured in Harrison's "Taxman"), but the publicity stunt worked well and Apple would even receive a thank you note from the office of the Queen.

In a more offbeat attempt to publicize "Hey Jude," a few weeks earlier Paul McCartney and a new girlfriend, a young American named Francine Schwartz, found themselves spending a few hours of the evening of 7 August in the vacant Apple Boutique on Baker Street. Scraping away the whitewash that covered the abandoned shop's windows, the two proceeded to write "Hey Jude," "Revolution" and an Apple logo on the windows of the empty shop. Unfortunately, when local residents and merchants saw the handiwork of McCartney and Schwartz the next morning, some mistook "Hey Jude" to be an anti-Semitic slur, and the windows had to be hastily covered over.

Schwartz had come to Apple in April 1968 with the hope that Apple would finance a film of a script she had written. Though her script was probably never read by anyone at Apple, she did manage to have a brief fling with McCartney, who secured her a position in the Apple press office. At one point during the summer of 1968, Apple assigned Schwartz to start going through the reams of unsolicited poetry that were being sent to Apple on a weekly basis to see if there was anything that could be used for a possible book. Unbeknownst to the literary hopefuls who sent in their unpublished works, Apple had no real plans to start a book publishing division, and most of the poetry and book manuscripts would end up unread in a closet known as "the black room" next to the press office on the second floor of the Savile Row building.

Having Schwartz review the accumulated poetry manuscripts was probably the closest that Apple ever got to having a book publishing division. Apple did actually put out one book in early 1970, which was the book that accompanied the initial English pressings of the *Let It Be* album. Although the book was credited to Apple Publishing, all of the work on the project was done by freelance employees.

By the time Apple Records had launched in August 1968, it was obvious that Apple's main focus would be music, and by almost any standard, Apple Records had got off to a spectacular start. In England, the Beatles shot to number 1, only to be replaced in the number 1 spot by Mary Hopkin. Both singles were also massive hits in America. Apple was ecstatic with Mary Hopkin's success but were disappointed and perplexed as to why the Jackie Lomax single failed to get into the top 100 in either the United States or England.

No one could explain why "Sour Milk Sea," a catchy, high-energy rock song written and produced by George Harrison and featuring instrumental support from Harrison, Ringo Starr, Paul McCartney, Nicky Hopkins, and Eric Clapton, failed to become a hit. John Hewlett, who had been hired by Apple mid-summer as a promotions manager, admits that his effort to promote Lomax's single did little to help the commercial prospects of "Sour Milk Sea."

Hewlett, the former bass player of the notorious UK pop band John's Children (who also featured a young Marc Bolan), remembers that he joined Apple after the band split in the summer of 1968. "I came back to London and Simon (Napier-Bell, the manager of John's Children and several other groups) introduced me to a woman who worked at Apple. She was leaving and Simon happened to know her, and he asked if I wanted to step into her job. So I called Terry Doran and went to meet him at the Baker Street office, and Terry just hired me instantly, so I had a job. He was a really nice man. Initially, I was hired to do promotion. The first day I was asked to go to the BBC with a Jackie Lomax record. I had never been a promotion man, so I just went over with the record. And I recall clearly what I said to the BBC guy, which was, 'My job is to get it played. I think it's pretty crap, but would you play it?' When I left, the BBC producer called Apple and told them that I said that 'the record was crap, but would they play it?' So when I got back, they called me up to the office and fired me. But Terry was cool and gave me another job. They gave me the job of sifting through all the tapes that had been sent in after they did that promotion where they announced that anyone could send in a tape."

In a 1968 interview with *Melody Maker*, Lomax admitted that he never expected his association with the Beatles to make his career, although he probably also never thought that his record label promotions man would be as frank and as opinionated as John Hewlett. "When people heard that I was on Apple, they said, 'You got it made,' but I'm not really connected with the Beatles, just with George as an individual." In the same interview, Harrison added: "When we started Apple, we thought that, even if we don't have a hit, as long as the record is good, that's all that matters. We never think of anything as A or B sides. We just try to make them all very good with what's around us, with the musicians and the studios."

Given the exposure that came with the immense success of "Hey Jude" and "Those Were The Days" and the media interest generated by the Beatles' direct involvement with the company, it did not take long for Apple to become an almost mythical part of the youth culture of the day.

For a brief moment in time, Apple was idealized as a place where you could go and meet the Beatles, find a receptive outlet for almost any sort of creative idea, or to just go and "hang out." Speaking on behalf of Apple in a 1968 press interview, Derek Taylor summed up the goal of Apple: "What we are trying to create is a situation where an unknown can walk through our door, be welcomed and talk ideas, work projects over with, say, a Beatle. If they are good, he'll be backed and given artistic freedom for his work." With such warm, well-publicized invitations, it was little wonder that the Apple office was besieged by a steady flow of would-be artists, con-artists, well-wishers, and curious tourists.

To their credit, and occasional detriment, the Apple staff were exceptionally tolerant of the unusual individuals who turned up at the office. During the first year of operation, Apple would be visited by Hells Angels from San Francisco and even a family of American hippies, dubbed "Emily's Family," who apparently came to London to convince John Lennon and Yoko Ono to join them on a proposed trip to the Fijian Islands. Emily's Family were a particular nuisance given Emily's penchant for walking around naked and breast-feeding an infant while her older children ran unsupervised through the office. It would have been very easy for Apple to have barred these people from the building, but instead, they were given use of the third-floor guest lounge during the day and access to the Apple kitchen.

"One day I got a call from customs at Heathrow asking for George Harrison, to inform him that there were six Harley-Davidson motorbikes in customs that he needed to pay the duty on," recalled Apple receptionist Debbie Wellum, "And we paid it. And then the Hells Angels turned up at the office. The stink of patchouli was unbelievable, and they came with all these women and girlfriends. We put them in our green room, about 11 feet by 8 feet, and they all lived in there for weeks. They would constantly play chicken on their Harleys, from outside of Apple to about 250 yards down the street to West End Central Police Station and back, to see how fast they could go. It was terrifying."

The Hells Angels eventually grew tired of London and left on their own accord, but Emily's Family and the other hippies who had come to Apple with the Hells Angels would only leave after George Harrison – who had allegedly developed a strong aversion to hippies after an unpleasant visit to San Francisco in 1967 – finally took it upon himself to rid the building of the interlopers that had taken over the guest lounge. Richard DiLello recalled the day that Harrison sauntered into the lounge and asked, "Well, you moving all your stuff out of here tonight?" There was then a long silence in the room, which was only broken when one of the stunned hippies asked Harrison, "Do you dig us or don't you?" Harrison's simple reply was, "Yin and Yang, head and tails, yes and no." Apparently, Harrison's cosmic response managed to connect with their hippie logic, and the lounge was empty by the end of the day.

The popular public perception may have been that the Apple office was a haven for crazed hippies and wide-eyed, post-adolescent dreamers, yet once past the imposing front door at Savile Row – watched over by doorman Jimmy Clark – on most days Apple generally looked and operated like any other mid-sixties record company. For most of Apple's first year, Peter Asher, Derek Taylor, Tony Bramwell, and many of the other male staff would be attired in stylish jackets and ties, while senior executives such as Peter Brown and Ron Kass were renowned for their fine suits and keen sense of style. Drinks, and to a lesser extent, drugs, may have flowed freely at 3 Savile Row, but the Apple staff probably had more in common with the typical London office worker than with the disaffected students who were spreading civil unrest across Europe in 1968.

Still, Apple was a much more hospitable office than your typical mid-sixties English record company, and Apple seemed to attract a good number of the more extreme members of the counterculture movement. The focal point of this idealized counter-culture utopia was unquestionably Derek Taylor's chaotic press office on the second floor.

Fuelled by his experience in Los Angeles during the summer of love, Taylor was the perfect person to preside over the Beatles' daring attempt to bring youth, culture, and commerce together under one roof. More than anyone else at Apple, Derek Taylor actually believed in what the Beatles were trying to achieve with Apple.

In addition to his Press Officer duties, Taylor evolved into Apple's unofficial master of ceremonies. Sustained by a daily diet of alcohol, and on some occasions, mind expanding drugs, Taylor would prove to be as adept at dealing with the Hells Angels and hippie families who stopped in at Apple as he was setting up record receptions and fielding incessant press inquiries.

For most of 1968 through to mid-1969, there seemed to be a perpetual party in Taylor's spacious open plan office. Each morning Richard DiLello would stock the Apple-shaped ice buckets with ice, make sure the drinks cabinet was fully stocked, secure a fresh supply of Benson and Hedges cigarettes, and then wait for the daily parade of artists, staff, and visitors to pop into the press office for some entertainment, gossip, and refreshment. At the peak of Apple activity, the drinks bill often reached £600 a month.

Of all the Beatles, Paul McCartney was Taylor's harshest critic (he justifiably admonished Taylor for tripping on LSD during work hours) and, as illustrated in Taylor's *Fifty Years Adrift*, would send Taylor mean-spirited post cards and letters that questioned the relevance of his press office. One of McCartney's more pointed notes featured a cartoon drawn by McCartney showing two people drunk at a bar, over which he wrote, "We probably don't want a press department. Do we?" Later in life, Taylor would come to understand this friction between himself and McCartney, explaining that "It was all too much for him, I can see that now," adding that "He was a young man and I was ten years older than him and not as easily manipulated or controlled as I should have been since they were paying my salary. I was becoming autonomous."

Peter Brown explains that while Taylor often seemed quite caught up in the high spirit of the times, the press office "also served as PR for Apple, not just in the sense that they handled Apple's publicity, but rather that they conveyed Apple's style at the time. Derek and the press office certainly helped shape the public's perception of Apple. It was swinging London as everyone imagined it to be."

George Peckham readily agrees with Brown's assessment. "Derek Taylor's office was the nucleus of Apple. Everyone used to hang out there and there was always something happening with Derek. Many a time his missus would call and ask if we'd seen Derek, and we'd have to go up and get him. He'd be in his office on the floor of the bog, out cold, pissed or stoned. We'd have to get him in a cab and send him home."

Kosh (born John Kosh), a graphic artist who designed several Apple album covers and who spent many happy hours at 3 Savile Row, sums up the feelings of many of Apple's staff: "Derek enjoyed himself a lot and he liked his substances," adding that "He was older than everyone else, so it was a little more shocking."

Taylor would later admit that the Apple press office did not function as well as it should have. "The pity of it was that it would have run better if I'd been more sober. Less marijuana, less alcohol," reflected Taylor several decades on. "It would have been much less fun, but more coherent. The Apple press officer, in addition to everything else, was a practicing alcoholic."

Sheltered from the loud, chaotic environment of the press office by two sturdy floors and by their more traditional view of the record business, Ron Kass and Jack Oliver had little time to spend lazy afternoons in Taylor's press office. Though pleased with the international sales of "Hey Jude" and, in particular, "Those Were The Days," (the first true Apple hit) Kass knew that Apple Records could not afford to be lulled into complacency by their early success. Throughout the waning days of summer, he had continued efforts to build up Apple's artist roster. Being a jazz fan, Kass signed a deal with the venerable Modern Jazz Quartet, reasoning that an established jazz act like the MJQ would give Apple's roster some immediate prestige.

Getting Apple Publishing established in the United States was another priority project for Kass. In the summer of 1968, he had hired an American named Mike O'Connor to oversee Apple's American publishing operations. "I ended up at Apple because I knew Terry Doran and also knew Ron Kass," recalled O'Connor. "Ron Kass was from Los Angeles, and when he was made President of Apple Records, Ron talked to me and told me that Terry Doran was not going to be continuing with Apple Publishing. Terry was supposedly just a temporary head when the Beatles set up Apple Publishing, and Ron asked me if I would like to go to work for Apple and I said, 'Absolutely.' I had not worked in publishing, but I had been a musician and I was living in Surrey outside of London at the time. When I went to work for Apple, I was twenty-seven, and Ron was thirty-three. I had gotten out of the performance side of the music business by then and had become a personal manager for artists and a booking agent in Europe. I had not worked in publishing, but I knew how it worked having been a musician and manager of musicians. Basically, Ron Kass taught me the business.

"I joined Apple just as they opened the office at 3 Savile Row and closed the clothing store on Baker Street. I never worked out of the Baker Street office, though I went there several times. I always worked at 3 Savile Row in an office on the top floor. On one side of the floor was A&R, which was Peter Asher, and the other side was publishing. When I joined Apple, I had to go through all the writers that had been signed to Apple Publishing and see what we could do with them. One problem I found was that Terry Doran had signed a publishing deal with Terry Melcher that did not make any sense at all. It gave Terry Melcher the rights to the Apple Publishing catalog in America in exchange for the rights to Terry Melcher's publishing catalog in England. It made no sense, so Ron Kass, myself, and George Harrison spoke to Terry Melcher and, basically, Terry Melcher agreed to tear the deal up."

The deal that Doran had brokered would have given Terry Melcher the American publishing rights to the George Harrison and Ringo Starr compositions that would appear several months later on *The Beatles* double album (which sold many millions of copies) in exchange for little more than the English publishing for a poor selling Paul Revere and the Raiders album. Melcher stood to make hundreds of thousands of dollars from the deal, but he graciously allowed Apple to nullify the agreement that he had signed with Doran in December 1967. To thank Melcher, Apple let Melcher's Yolk Music retain the American copyright to Cream's "Outside Woman Blues" as well as the copyrights to a number of songs by George Alexander and Focal Point.

"Terry Doran was a really good guy, but he was not a businessman when it came to publishing," explains O'Connor. "As far as his musical ears were concerned, he had some acts that he was involved with which were pretty good and others which didn't work, but he didn't have a business background. He knew he was only temporarily heading up Apple Publishing. In fact, it was Terry Doran who told me at Baker Street, before I had even discussed working at Apple with Ron Kass, that he was going to be leaving Apple. Terry said that Ron Kass was going to become President of Apple Records and that I should talk with Ron, which I did. Ron and I met for breakfast at a hotel in London, and a week later Ron called and offered me a job as head of Apple Publishing. At the time I was hired, the Beatles were interested in expanding Apple in the United States. But I had already been living in England for three years. It was discussed that Apple would open up an office in Los Angeles or New York and that I would go there, but nothing definitive ever came of that. So, during the whole time I was at Apple, I worked out of the London office. By some weird set of circumstances, I was actually an employee of Apple's Swiss corporation, and I was paid by the Apple company in Switzerland."

In November, Doran would officially leave Apple Music Publishing to focus on managing Grapefruit, who also severed their links with Apple. Although Grapefruit would no longer be on an Apple retainer, George Alexander would remain signed to Apple Publishing until 1971.

Neither the members of Grapefruit nor Terry Doran could ever explain why the Beatles' patronage seemed to have blighted Grapefruit's career so decisively. Speaking to *Melody Maker* soon after leaving Apple, George Alexander explained: "What we want to do now is lose the Beatles' tag. Sure, it helped us in the beginning, and everybody knew us as the Beatles' group, but we want to make it on our own. If any mistakes were made in the past, it was getting four blokes off the streets and saying, 'You're Grapefruit,' and getting fantastic publicity."

Upon leaving Apple, Grapefruit attempted to update their sound by adding a new lead vocalist and a keyboard player to the original line-up after Pete Swettenham left the group in early 1969. In the process, they replaced their tuneful psychedelic pop style with earthy, riff-driven rock songs to fit the gruff voice of their new front man, Bob Wale. Their subsequent recordings were somewhat pedestrian efforts that lacked the charm and catchy pop melodies of their early singles, and the group failed to find an audience for their new sound (except in the Netherlands, where the Apple-published "Deep Water" was a top 20 hit in early 1969). Conceding that Grapefruit's days were numbered, Terry Doran relinquished management of the floundering group and returned to Apple in the summer of 1969 to work as George Harrison's personal assistant.

Like Grapefruit, the Iveys were another Apple act who were often accused of sounding too much like the Beatles, and both Apple and the band tried to downplay the Beatles connection. The Iveys' debut single, "Maybe Tomorrow," was released in November 1968, and it showed the group to be developing a distinctive style of their own. With a bold melody, sweeping strings, and an ultra-catchy chorus, "Maybe Tomorrow" perfectly captured the best elements of British pop circa 1968. The record's flip side, "And Her Daddy's A Millionaire," a bouncy pop-rock number powered by a driving, fuzz guitar riff, was equally impressive and both the band and Apple were certain that one of the songs had to be a hit.

"Maybe Tomorrow" was the first Apple single to be issued in England since the highly-publicized "First Four," and Apple desperately wanted to get a hit in order to prove that there was more to Apple than the Beatles and their assorted pet projects. The debut offering from the Iveys received a respectable amount of airplay on the BBC, but "Maybe Tomorrow" had only modest sales in the UK. The single would be issued in the United States in late January 1969, where it became a regional hit in some parts of the country and ultimately climbed to number 56 in the national charts.

Out of the first wave of Apple artists, the Iveys proved to be one of the most challenging to market. They had come to Apple at a time when the

British, and to a lesser extent the American, pop scene was moving away from the traditional show business approach that sustained such teen-oriented bands as the Herd, the Turtles, and Amen Corner into a more progressive rock scene heralded by bands such as Cream and the Jimi Hendrix Experience. With their tight harmony singing, two-and-a-half minute melodic pop songs, and matching outfits and haircuts, the Iveys were neither mired in the past, nor were they on the vanguard of the looming rock revolution. In the liner notes to their debut album, Derek Taylor would write: "They were not, nor are they now adventurous innovators, but they are ready, they are ready to be."

Given the rapidly changing tastes of the music buying public, Apple seemed somewhat unsure of how best to position the Iveys. Indeed, the promo film that Apple shot for "Maybe Tomorrow" featured the uncomfortable looking Iveys playing the song in Apple's unfinished basement studio. Under the advice of Mal Evans, the group were dressed in matching suits, although they had turned up the collars of their jackets in a vain attempt to appear hip. Still, "Maybe Tomorrow" was a significant step for Apple in that it was the first record released by the company that had no direct involvement from any of the Beatles.

"The biggest problem we had with the Iveys was with their manager, Bill Collins. He just had no idea about the music business," says Tony Bramwell. "Then later, when they were Badfinger, they had this American, Stan Polley. They had no idea of what they had. Collins always expected the impossible but not do the obvious. They would say, 'Oh, we don't want to do that.' And Tommy (Tom Evans) wanted to be Paul McCartney, but he didn't know how to behave like Paul McCartney. And that little drummer was a bit of a Welsh git. They were great performers, but they had this rock and roll lifestyle of living in the country before they'd earned it. Mal Evans was a bit overprotective of them. He thought they were the next Beatles, and he pushed them as the new Beatles before they were ready for it. But as songwriters, they were dreams, fantastic songwriters."

Ken Mansfield had high hopes for the Iveys in America. "I believed in the Iveys' "Maybe Tomorrow" record so much that I had 450,000 copies pressed up. We came out full blast, had radio play and acceptance from the stations, but we ended up probably selling 200,000 copies. From the business standpoint, we put all our resources behind Apple. What we spent on Apple was so out of proportion I don't know how Capitol could have made money on Apple. We did everything on those Apple records. Philosophically, we were supposed to treat the Apple records as a Capitol record. We were supposed to work Jackie Lomax equal to Glen Campbell or whatever. Apple was a plum for Capitol. It was the greatest thing we ever did."

Despite Capitol's enthusiasm for Apple Records, it would prove difficult to break the Iveys or James Taylor in America or England. Even being the pet project of Apple's A&R Director seemed to be of little help to James Taylor.

Working with Asher and Richard Hewson, Taylor had spent most of the summer of 1968 recording his debut album at Trident Studios. Taylor's album was Peter Asher's first album-length production project. Upon hearing the tapes of Taylor's songs for the album, Apple was particularly excited by a song called "Carolina In My Mind" and it was chosen to be Taylor's debut single. In a show of support, Paul McCartney had played bass on the track and James Taylor remembers that George Harrison also dropped by to add backing vocals to the song. Unlike the sparse, acoustic-based songs that Asher would produce for Taylor in the years to follow, Taylor's 1968 recordings featured some exquisitely produced arrangements.

Recording sessions for Taylor's album finally concluded in October 1968. It was a remarkable achievement, particularly considering that Taylor had only just turned twenty. His material drew on elements of folk, rock, and blues, but the end result – when combined with the distinctly English arrangements of Richard Hewson – was a wholly unique sound that was unlike anything else in pop music at the time. The twelve songs recorded for the album ranged from the stark acoustic guitar and voice performance of "Something In The Way She Moves," to "Circle Around The Sun," on which Taylor and Bishop O' Brien are slowly enveloped by a dense orchestral fog. Taylor played electric guitar on only two songs, with most of the tracks featuring Taylor on acoustic, backed by bass, keyboards and drums, which were augmented by Hewson's ornate string and woodwind embellishments and Peter Asher's backing vocals.

With recording complete, Peter Asher and Apple's record department began work on an album cover and finalized such details as sequencing and mastering the album in preparation for a late November release. Meanwhile, on the other side of London, James Taylor waited patiently and continued to write new material, including an early version of "Fire And Rain," which would ultimately become his signature composition.

Taylor had started composing "Fire And Rain" in his basement flat in Beaufort Gardens in Chelsea. The first verse was Taylor's reaction to hearing about the death of Suzanne Schnerr, a friend of Taylor's from New York. Taylor was clearly shaken by the news and within a week and a half of learning of Schnerr's suicide, he had written the first verse of "Fire And Rain" but was not able to complete the song. Jackie Lomax remembered Taylor playing him the unfinished song. "James came into Trident Studios where we were recording, and he comes into the control room and plays me the first verse and chorus of a song," recalled Lomax. "I said, 'Hey James, that's great. If you finish that up, we'll put it on the album. I'll do my own version,' and he thought that was great. Then he went away and disappeared shortly after. The song was "Fire And Rain," and I would have loved to have done it."

As James Taylor wrestled with his personal demons, the release date for his debut Apple album was drawing near. The 26 Oct 1968 issue of the US trade magazine *Billboard* reported that the album title was to be "James Taylor and Son" (indeed, photos were taken of Taylor frolicking in front of the James Taylor and Son bespoke shoe shop in London, presumably for use as an album cover), but when the album was issued in England on 6 December it was simply titled *James Taylor*.

The *James Taylor* album was packaged in a fold open sleeve that featured a front photo of Taylor reclining in a park, his tall frame stretched across both sides of the cover. Derek Taylor had hired 22-year-old Scottish photographer Richard Imrie to shoot the iconic cover photo. "I was called in one day in late September," remembers Imrie. "I met up with James at Apple and he was very mellow, let's put it that way. He asked 'Where should we go?,' and I told him Virginia Water would be the place to do it. He said, 'Alright, I got a car,' and, indeed, he had a car; he had a Cortina GT, which was quite a fast car for those times. He drove extremely fast, but he was safe. So, we went off to Virginia Water and found some places, and he was just drifting around amongst the ruins there and amongst the trees, and we snapped what we could. Then he sat down for ten minutes, and that's when we took that long one (that was used for the cover). We got back by six or seven in the evening, had a couple of drinks, and that was a day's work done."

Apple had also hoped to have Mary Hopkin's debut album ready in time for Christmas. Following the success of "Those Were The Days," McCartney had agreed to produce an album for Hopkin and had come up with a concept of having her record a combination of show business standards and new songs written by some of the top pop songwriters of the day. American singer-songwriter Harry Nilsson, whose work was greatly admired by Derek Taylor and all four Beatles, contributed "The Puppy Song," which was recorded for the album and almost released as a follow-up single to "Those Were The Days." McCartney had asked Derek Taylor to contact Randy Newman about contributing a song for Hopkin's album, and Taylor dutifully sent a telegram to Newman's home in November 1968. Newman eventually did compose a song for Hopkin called "I'll Be There," but Hopkin's album had already been completed by the time Newman's tape made it to London.

Recording sessions for Hopkin's album had wrapped up by November, but it was too late to get the album manufactured and into the shops in time for Christmas. Given the time constraints, the release date was reluctantly pushed back to February 1969.

Postcard was Paul McCartney's first album length production project, and the results were generally impressive. But on this occasion, McCartney's eclectic musical tastes seem to have trumped his fine-tuned commercial instincts. The final product sounded almost like a compilation album, with McCartney casting Hopkin as a folk singer, a French chanteuse, and on the old pop standards such as "There's No Business Like Show Business" (recorded after McCartney allegedly mistook a sarcastic suggestion from John Lennon as a genuine recommendation) as a cabaret performer. The best material on Hopkin's album were certainly the folk-pop compositions written by McCartney's friend Donovan, who contributed three songs to the project. Singing to the simple accompaniment of the acoustic guitars of McCartney and Donovan, Hopkin's exquisite performances of "Lord Of The Reedy River," "Voyage Of The Moon," and "Happiness Runs" showed her to be an accomplished folk vocalist.

During the course of sourcing material for Mary Hopkin, Apple had come across a group who would soon find themselves added to the carefully curated Apple artist roster. Mortimer, a trio of American teenagers who had released an excellent acoustic-pop album for Mercury-Phillips Records earlier in the year, were visiting London in October 1968. As Mortimer's drummer, Guy Masson, remembered: "We were managed by an Englishman named Danny Secunda, and we went to London for just a few weeks in the late fall of 1968, and we went over and knocked on Apple's door. We had heard over the radio in England that Apple was looking for songs for Mary Hopkin and for you to bring your tape to Apple Records, because they were looking to finish Mary Hopkin's album. So the three of us went down to Apple Records – we were still signed to Mercury-Phillips – and we walk in and we go, 'Hi, we're Mortimer, and we heard on the radio that you were looking for songs,' and we walk in with our acoustic guitars, and the receptionist said, 'You have to leave a tape.' So Tony Van Benschoten (Mortimer bassist) was pretty sharp and said, 'We can't make a tape. We don't have time; we're going back to the States tomorrow.' So she says, 'Alright, let me call up to the publishing office,' and she tells Mike O'Connor, 'Mortimer is here,' and he goes, 'Mortimer? John gave me their album. Send them all up!'"

Mortimer were dumbfounded to hear that O'Connor knew who they were, let alone that he was familiar with their debut album. Earlier that summer, Masson and a friend had delivered a copy of Mortimer's record to John Lennon and Paul McCartney when the two Beatles were staying in New York City at the apartment of Nat Weiss (the Beatles' American attorney). "We had heard on the radio that the Beatles were in town," recalled Masson, "and a friend of mine kept pushing me to take a copy of our record to Weissman's (sic) office/apartment, which was only around ten blocks from where we lived. So my friend and I went off down the street with our little album to give to the Beatles. I said to him, 'I don't know how we're going to get in there,' and when we got there, the whole block was surrounded. There were girls and cops everywhere. We're stuck in the middle of this crowd when suddenly one of the girls looks at us and screams, 'Oh, it's the Hollies!' So one of the cops thought we were the Hollies, and they grab us and pull us through the crowd. My friend Gary told them that we had to see John Lennon and Paul McCartney, so we went from being stuck in a crowd as Mortimer to being led into the apartment with a police escort as the Hollies. I could hear through the door that there was a party going on, so we knocked on the door, and Nat Weiss answered it. We told him we were Mortimer, and I said, 'I want to give this album to John and Paul.' He took the album and went back inside and came back a little later and said, 'I gave it to John, and he said he would seriously give it a listen.'" John Lennon was apparently a man of his word, and Mortimer's album not only made it back to London with Lennon but had also been passed on to Mike O'Connor in Apple Publishing.

Masson continues: "We went up to the office and sat around with our guitars and sang our songs. While we're going along singing a song called "Life's Sweet Music," there are two doors in this office, one opens up, and George Harrison walks in dressed in this Indian-styled, green, long jacket. He comes bopping in, and he's clapping and he's dancing all around, and the three of us are going, 'Holy Toledo, that's George Harrison,' and he says, 'Sign them up,' and he went out the other door. So we told our manager, and he followed up, and the next thing you know, they bought us off of Mercury, and we're signing contracts with Apple Publishing and Recording."

Mortimer signed to Apple on 30 November 1968. To extract Mortimer from their contract with Mercury-Phillips, Apple Records had to agree to give Mercury-Phillips 25% of any royalties generated from Mortimer's Apple recordings until the $17,065.54 which was still owed by Mortimer to Mercury-Phillips was recouped.

Apple Records now had more than half a dozen artists signed to the label, but as of November 1968, they had yet to release an album. The first Apple album, George Harrison's *Wonderwall Music,* was finally issued in late November. Recorded as the soundtrack to a quirky psychedelic film of the same name, Harrison's score (essentially the first solo album issued by a Beatle) was suitably colourful, featuring an eclectic set of instrumentals that ranged from Indian ragas to more rock-oriented recordings.

Since Harrison – like the other three Beatles – was unable to read or write music notation, he had to hire an outside music arranger to assist him with the *Wonderwall Music* recording sessions. His arranger of choice was London native John Barham, who would be Harrison's favoured arranger until the mid-seventies.

"I was twenty-five when I started to work with Apple in 1968," recalled Barham. "I had gone to the Royal College of Music in London and then the Trinity College of Music. In my third year there, I met Ravi Shankar and started working with him on the *Alice In Wonderland* film in late 1966. I met Ravi because I had been writing some music that used Indian scales, and that's why Ravi took an interest in me. George came down to some of our sessions at the BBC, and Ravi introduced me to him. From my work with Ravi, George knew that I could compose and arrange music, so he asked me to do *Wonderwall*. We started recording in early 1968 after George had returned from India where he had recorded the Indian music. I also played trumpet on the *Wonderwall* sessions. I hadn't played the trumpet for around six years. It was Paul McCartney's trumpet, it was a flugelhorn just lying in the studio, so I asked George if I could use this. So after I warmed up, George asked me to play this melody he had. He played it for me on piano, and I made up a melody to go above it, which was based on a tune that Ravi had given him to practice on the sitar."

Barham remembers: "For *Wonderwall*, I would go up to George's house in Esher, and he would play things on guitar and sing them to me, and I would write down the music. Most of the *Wonderwall* music wasn't composed when we went into the studio. It was usually improvised. We recorded it at EMI with Tony Ashton and the Remo Four. We also did overdubs on some of the Indian tracks. It was very much a collaboration with all of the musicians. Obviously, George knew what he wanted, and he was guiding it the whole time. He played on almost all of the sessions... guitar, bass, and piano. Ringo Starr and Eric Clapton were at the sessions. After the first day of playing the flugelhorn, George went out and bought me one. I ended up playing it on Jackie Lomax's "The Eagle Laughs At You." So I got a trumpet and a very generous fee for my work on *Wonderwall*." Impressed with Barham's work, Harrison hired Barham to play piano and score the string arrangements for some of the songs that Harrison was producing for Jackie Lomax.

Given that it was a soundtrack album with no vocal performances, *Wonderwall Music* sold reasonably well and was a respectable start for the Apple Records album catalogue. *The Beatles* – better known as the "White Album" – and *Two Virgins* by John Lennon and Yoko Ono would follow *Wonderwall Music* into the shops.

The Beatles was yet another critical and commercial triumph, but it was *Two Virgins* that arguably received the most attention. Housed in a sleeve that displayed a fully naked John Lennon and Yoko Ono on its cover, the album sent shock waves throughout the world.

Featuring "music" that consisted of little more than Lennon's tape recorder experiments and Ono's voice manipulations, the record itself was of little consequence. But the risqué cover of *Two Virgins* was another story altogether, and it caused the album to be banned from sale in many American cities. The very conservative EMI refused to have anything to do with *Two Virgins*, so Apple had to contract two independent record companies to distribute the album.

In Europe, *Two Virgins* would be distributed by Track Records, an independent label founded by the managers of the Who. In America, it was distributed by a small label called Tetragrammaton. "What happened was that EMI wouldn't touch it," recalls Jack Oliver. "They wouldn't even sleeve the record, so I had a bunch of the Apple Scruffs sleeve the record in the basement of the old Apple shop, and then Track picked them up to distribute to the shops."

Apple Records would close out the year by releasing James Taylor's self-titled debut and *Under The Jasmin Tree* by the Modern Jazz Quartet in England.

The Modern Jazz Quartet were unlike any of the other acts on the Apple label. They were a known entity and, since the mid-fifties, had been one of the most respected jazz outfits in the world. There was little that Apple could offer that they could not find at any other label. The MJQ's leader, John Lewis, explained: "When we signed with Apple, it was an interim time between our obligations to Atlantic Records, where we had been for many years. The Beatles had just started their record company, and the President of the company, Ron Kass, was an old friend of our manager, Monte Kay. We had known Ron Kass for many years. We were visiting Ron in Switzerland and we were having dinner, and the whole thing came up and Monte Kay made the deal. We never thought anything about it. We were busy making music. At the time, the deal was open, we could have done other albums, but we did two albums. We recorded 'Jasmin Tree' in New York City and sent it to Apple." Packaged in a colorful post-psychedelic cover designed by Alan Aldridge, *Under The Jasmin Tree* was a superb, if perhaps incongruous, addition to the Apple catalogue.

James Taylor was the first "rock" album by a new artist to be released by Apple. Swept along by Peter Asher's boundless enthusiasm for James Taylor, everyone at Apple expected Taylor's album to be a big seller. Packaged in a lavish gatefold sleeve featuring musician credits and lyrics, Apple had not spared any expense on the album. It was an excellent record, featuring the definitive versions of such well-loved Taylor songs as "Carolina In My Mind," "Rainy Day Man," and "Something In The Way She Moves" (a line that George Harrison would later "borrow" for his own composition "Something"). Taylor – backed by a trio comprised of Louis Cennamo, Don Schinn, and Joel "Bishop" O' Brien – turned in twelve exceptional performances that still sound fresh and vital, especially when compared to his subsequent work.

Under The Jasmin Tree sold as well as could be expected for a jazz record, but *James Taylor* underperformed commercially, despite several songs from the album receiving a good amount of play on the BBC. Apple's efforts to promote *James Taylor* had certainly not been helped by the artist suddenly being unavailable for interviews and promotional appearances. Taylor, whose heroin addiction finally caught up with him in the final months of the year, had suffered an emotional breakdown in late November and ended up in a hospital in New York City before transferring to the Austin Riggs psychiatric hospital in Massachusetts where he would spend several months getting his addiction under control.

Looking back on James Taylor's initial difficulty in finding an audience, Peter Asher stresses that Taylor's album "got a lot of attention because the songs were so good. In retrospect, both James and I feel that I kind of overproduced it in an effort to get people to pay attention, because at that time, the feeling was that if he was just some sort of folkie guy with a guitar, no one was going to pay any attention. That's why I added all that different instrumentation and links. In the end, I think the album still stands up due to the songs."

By the end of the year, it was clear that Apple would need to exert some significant effort in 1969 if they were going to make stars out of Jackie Lomax, James Taylor, and the Iveys. With 1968 coming to an end, Apple's senior management took time to re-evaluate some of the departments and personnel that were not living up to Apple's ambitions. Only months after having opened for business, Apple had already come under attack in the English music press for not having discovered any new stars other than Mary Hopkin and for the unkept promises and general chaotic atmosphere at Apple.

It had already become all too much for Stephen Maltz, who had resigned his position with Apple on 30 September and left the company a few days later on 4 October. On his way out, Maltz presented the Beatles with a long, detailed letter that outlined his reasons for leaving. Maltz believed in Apple and sincerely wanted the company to work, but he also had the fiduciary duty to ensure that the Beatles' personal finances were sound. In his letter, Maltz admitted that his role as an Apple Director had essentially been rendered impotent by the Beatles habit of regularly overriding board decisions, specifically in regards to the Apple Boutique, which the board had wanted to wind down in an organized and more traditional fashion in December 1968. He also admonished the Beatles for spending more than they were earning, particularly given their significant tax liabilities.

Maltz closed his letter on a grave and very direct note, "Apple is in a mess and I believe that the only way you can get out of it is by trusting Neil and talking to him not as a road manager but as a Managing Director," before wishing his former employers only the best and exiting the lives of the Beatles forever.

In a November 1968 article entitled "Has Apple Gone Rotten?" *Melody Maker* painted a bleak picture of an Apple that had failed to live up to the grand ideas that had been announced earlier in the year. Speaking on behalf of Apple, Derek Taylor was forced to admit, "We are now more or less a record company," though he added in typically Tayloresque fashion, "We started off with grandiose ideas, but it's difficult to be grandiose in a glum society like the one which we have here."

Melody Maker journalist Alan Walsh clearly put Taylor in a defensive mode. When Walsh brought up the subject of Apple appearing not to respond to most of the letters and tapes that were sent to Savile Row, the usually enthusiastic Taylor bitterly answered, "Why should we reply? We didn't ask for the letter in the first place, and we don't owe them a letter back at all." Trying to sum up Apple's first year, an exasperated Taylor concluded: "We certainly haven't brought about a revolution in the music business... we've failed in that. But all the other revolutions this year have failed, too!"

Paul McCartney was especially stung by this criticism and became briefly obsessed with making Apple a more efficient company. Upon reading that Apple was full of freeloaders and unnecessary staff, he asked Neil Aspinall, Peter Brown, and Derek Taylor to come up with lists of non-essential personnel, but none of the three Apple managers had the heart to draw up what would amount to an Apple hit list. McCartney even tried to take matters into his own hands by asking Derek Taylor to cut the head count of the press office and fire one of the department's several secretaries. In *Many Years From Now*, McCartney remembers how his attempt to cut costs in the press office was ultimately foiled by George Harrison, who bluntly informed McCartney that if he were to fire the secretary in question, he and the other two Beatles would "reinstate her immediately."

Ultimately, Jeremy Banks – whom Richard Dilello recounted as having a habit of starting many of his workdays at Apple by consuming a potent mixture of champagne and diet pills – was the only employee to be declared redundant. Banks left Apple in November 1968. To help out in the press office after Banks' departure, Derek Taylor hired Mavis

Smith to be his assistant. She started at Apple on 16 December.

The decision was also made to scale back Apple Films. Denis O'Dell explained that this was a matter of practicality more than anything else. Given Apple's expenditures on the record label and publishing operations, Apple Films simply did not have the capital needed to fund a major film project. According to O'Dell, Apple Films only had about "£40,000 at its disposal at any one time." Peter Brown – who had considerable experience in film production later in his career – felt that Apple could have maintained the film division had they approached things differently. "With Apple films, there wasn't enough time," he explains. "Film projects take a while to develop. Several things could have happened, it wouldn't have taken a lot of Apple money. It wasn't meant to be a full-blown film studio; it was more a film development or production company. One project I do remember is that we started a documentary on the Royal Ballet. There was footage of Margot Fonteyn. I don't know what happened with all that. It was a project that I brought in. There was some historic footage there. I guess Neil still has it somewhere."

Going forward, Apple Films would only be activated for projects that directly involved the Beatles. Denis O'Dell would remain with Apple for the time being, producing a proposed television special about the recording of a new Beatles album that was scheduled to begin filming in January 1969. O'Dell was also hoping to produce *The Magic Christian,* a new Peter Sellers film in which O'Dell had secured Ringo Starr a starring role, through Apple Films, but the project was ultimately funneled through Sellers' own production company.

Looking back on what they had accomplished in 1968, there was no denying that the Beatles had pulled off something quite special, even with Apple having abandoned their retail and film ambitions. It had been a highly successful inaugural year, which would be celebrated with a Christmas party held at the Apple office on 23 December 1968. Surprisingly, Ringo Starr and John Lennon were the only two Beatles to attend, as Paul McCartney had already gone up to Liverpool for the holidays, and George Harrison claimed to have overslept (Harrison would not admit that he skipped the party because he feared possible violence – on the part of the Hells Angels who were attending the party – until he was interviewed for *Anthology* in 1995).

Having entertained a steady flow of holiday visitors since midday with a generous supply of alcohol, by the time the party officially commenced at six o' clock in Neil Aspinall's office, the party guests were already in high spirits. The idyllic mood was unexpectedly shattered when Frisco Pete – one of the more menacing members of the California Hells Angels biker gang that took up George Harrison's innocent offer to "drop by and see us when you're in London" – decided that he was unwilling to wait any longer for Apple's cooks to serve the holiday turkey.

Within moments, Frisco Pete had felled Mavis Smith's husband, journalist Alan Smith, with a single punch after Smith tried to reason with the belligerent biker. Richard DiLello later recounted how Frisco Pete was moving towards John Lennon and Yoko Ono when Peter Brown intervened to head off any physical harm coming to Lennon. With his calm, collected manner and gift for being able to find the right words for any situation, Brown was able to get Frisco Pete to quiet down, and the party was soon able to get back under way.

Despite the unfortunate incident with Frisco Pete and the presence of only two of the Beatles, the party was, by all accounts, a wonderful affair. In addition to the magician who was hired to entertain the children in attendance, Apple's guests were treated to a costumed John and Yoko playing Mother and Father Christmas. As the evening wound down, John Lennon, Yoko Ono, and Mary Hopkin would lead Apple's guests on a rousing round of Christmas carols before bidding everyone a good night, ending 1968 in fine style.

1969: THE PRE-KLEIN ERA

The Beatles had done it. Apple had weathered a tumultuous first year in business and had even notched up an international hit record with a previously unknown singer, Mary Hopkin. It was now critical that Apple consolidate the momentum that they had achieved with the successful launch of the record label.

The last quarter of 1968 had been dedicated to getting the first batch of Apple Records to market, with only minimal thought and effort being dedicated to the mundane but just as essential task of developing an efficient back office to handle business affairs. Early in the new year, Apple took the first step towards better integrating their business and creative operations by moving the accounting department into an unoccupied third floor office in the Savile Row building. With Apple's one-year lease at Wigmore Street due to expire at the end of January, all of the departments that had remained at Wigmore Street were brought over to Savile Row. Yet even the seemingly straightforward task of consolidating Apple's personnel into a single building was a daunting project for Apple's inexperienced staff. Most of the furniture and files from Wigmore Street would eventually arrive intact at Savile Row, but important paperwork, photos, and other items went missing during the process. Apple had apparently learned little from the mistakes made when Apple Publishing moved out of Baker Street. During the course of that move, Terry Doran and the other Apple Publishing employees simply dumped all of their paperwork into several black cabs to have it driven over to Savile Row, only to later find out that some of their files – including several boxes of acetates and tapes – never arrived at Apple.

To support the additional personnel and the corresponding workload that came over from Wigmore Street, Apple added another office boy to the staff of their third-floor mail room, eighteen-year-old Nigel Oliver.

Like so many English teenagers who grew up during the peak years of Beatlemania, Oliver was captivated by the music and allure of the Beatles. He never thought that he would meet a Beatle, let alone work for the band. "I used to stand outside of the Baker Street shop just looking in, but I was scared to go in," he remembered. "I had left school and was working in a clothes shop at the time. One day, this Irishman I knew from my job asked me what I wanted to do, and I told him I wanted to work for the Beatles, so he wrote a couple of letters to Apple for me. They didn't have any jobs, but I kept writing to Apple each month until Alistair Taylor hired me in January 1969. The office boy who trained me was the one who nicked the lead off the roof but never got caught."

The incident to which Oliver refers – when Apple realized that someone was actually stripping the lead off of the office roof, dragging mailbags full of lead through the office, and then selling the metal to a scrap dealer – did little to dispel the popular perception of the Apple office being a soft touch for thieves and grifters.

Theft was certainly a problem at Apple. Richard DiLello later detailed a partial list of items that walked out of Apple's front door, which ranged from employee paychecks and electric typewriters to record player needles and cases of alcohol. One of the more enterprising thieves went as far as to remove the expensive speaker cones from some of the speaker cabinets in the basement studio. The admittedly clever thief simply unscrewed the back panel of the speaker cabinet, removed the speaker cones, and then re-sealed the cabinet, leaving the studio staff none the wiser until they attempted to use the now-worthless speaker. "Whenever you walked into Apple, it was party time," explained Klaus Voormann. "What they did in the Rutles film (a 1978 television show that parodied the history of the Beatles) was exactly how it was. People would walk in and walk out with equipment. I had this big Marshall amplifier that just disappeared from Apple. I had it in the studio, and I wanted to play it the next day, but it was gone. And nobody knew who took it. This definitely changed once Allen Klein came in, but it took time to change."

Tales of missing typewriters, cameras, and roof lead are now a fundamental part of Apple lore, yet the items most likely to be removed from the premises were copies of singles and LPs that were stored in the building. The Apple staff were also apparently overly generous when it came to giving records away. Upon realizing just how many records were being given to employees, friends of employees, and even people who simply came in off the street, Ron Kass was forced to implement a policy under which each employee would be given a single copy of each Apple release and the option to purchase up to three additional copies at wholesale cost.

Nigel Oliver admits that the Apple office boys were not always able to resist the temptation of the record riches that could be found around the office. "We used to take sacks of albums out of Apple. All of the albums that were supposed to be posted to America we never sent. I was the best office boy though; people thought I was the one who could be trusted. I wore a suit, and I was making seven pound fifty. The fiddles were amazing, but if you had to go somewhere late at night, Paul's house, or over to the studio, Derek would give you a couple of albums or a bottle of scotch. I took the job very seriously."

Having the core Apple departments (except for Apple Electronics, which remained in Boston Place) situated in a single building presented an opportunity to evaluate the performance of the company from the top down. There had already been several half-hearted attempts to identify inefficient or impractical divisions of Apple, but for the most part, efforts to downsize the under-performing departments and employees would prove difficult. Apple had managed to shelve the Apple Foundation for the Arts, Apple Films, and Apple Retail, but little progress was made when it came to evaluating the overall performance of Apple's music operations.

Come 1969, Apple's only fully functional business units were Apple Records and Apple Music Publishing, which was fine as far as Ron Kass was concerned. Kass was apparently relieved to not have to devote resources to non-music projects, and he was particularly eager to give Apple a proper launch in the United States. In mid-January, Kass announced an ambitious plan to establish an Apple office in Los Angeles, noting that Apple had already been searching for a building to house a proposed six-person staff. Since Apple's American distributor, Capitol Records, was responsible for most of the record production issues, Kass envisioned Apple's California office as focusing primarily on Apple Publishing, which he promised would soon grow larger than the English publishing operation.

Kass took an active interest in music publishing and he put his full support behind establishing an American presence for Apple Publishing. To represent the company's music publishing interests in America, Apple Music Publishing was split into two companies – one to correspond to each of the two major American performing rights organizations, BMI and ASCAP. Apple Music Publishing Co. Inc. was aligned with ASCAP, while Apple established a new company, Python Music, to focus expressly on American writers and to be affiliated with BMI.

But few copyrights would ever be assigned to Python Music in America. In England, Python Music – which had been incorporated on 16 May 1968 – had been quite active, though no one associated with Apple at the time seems to remember why Apple set up Python Publishing in the United Kingdom. Throughout 1968, Python Music and Apple Publishing appeared to be fairly interchangeable, with some new writers signed to Apple and others to Python.

As part of Kass's plan to expand Apple operations in America, on Saturday, 4 January 1969, Peter Asher was dispatched from London for a two-month stay in Hollywood, California. Kass knew that the United States was Apple's key market, and he sent Asher to California so that Asher could get a better feel for the American record business, look for American talent, and assist Ken Mansfield in establishing a presence for Apple in the United States.

In the London office, the Apple staff were gearing up for a new

Beatles project, which was to be a television program that featured the Beatles developing new songs that they would perform in front of a live audience at the conclusion of the program. The concept was that the group would create back-to-basics material that the four Beatles could play live, as opposed to building songs up using overdubs and advanced studio techniques as they had done on their most recent albums.

Filming began on 2 January 1969 on a desolate soundstage at Twickenham Film Studios. It was not a location that inspired creativity and the sessions were mostly unfocused and rough sounding. With Yoko Ono now permanently affixed to John Lennon's side, the atmosphere was fraught and grew more tense with each passing day. Matters came to a head on Friday, 10 January, when George Harrison quit the Beatles after a row with Paul McCartney. The argument – which was captured on film – was touched off when McCartney attempted to give Harrison a suggestion on how to play a guitar part. The situation quickly escalated and ended abruptly when Harrison left the soundstage and drove home.

Harrison would return on 15 January for a meeting with the other three Beatles to outline the conditions for his return to the group. Harrison was adamant that the Beatles abandon all plans to give a live performance in front of an audience and that the sessions be moved from Twickenham to Apple, where any recordings that were made could be used as a foundation for a new album. The performances filmed at Twickenham had been recorded by the film cameras only and the fidelity was not sufficient for use as an album. The meeting lasted close to five hours, but after heated discussion, the other three Beatles acquiesced to Harrison's conditions and it was agreed that recording would resume at Apple Studios the following week.

The Beatles had been anxiously awaiting the completion of Apple Studios. Tired of the corporate bureaucracy and outdated 4-track recording equipment at EMI, they had spent a good amount of time in 1968 recording at several of London's new independent 8-track studios. Between not having 8-track facilities at EMI, and sometimes not being able to record at EMI or Trident due to the studios being booked by other artists, the Beatles were looking forward to having a recording studio available for their exclusive use.

Having confidently assigned the task of creating the studio to Apple Electronics, the Beatles had assumed that the studio would have been mostly complete by January 1969. Instead, they were dismayed when they went down to the basement and found out that not only had Magic Alex been unable to create such promised technical innovations as a 72-track recording console, but that the recording studio he did assemble was barely even functional. George Harrison recalled: "Alex's recording studio at Apple was the biggest disaster of all time. He was walking around with a white coat like some sort of chemist, but he didn't have a clue of what he was doing. It was a 16-track system, and he had sixteen tiny little speakers all around the walls. The whole thing was a disaster."

From his vantage point in the Apple cutting room, George Peckham spent many hours watching Magic Alex working on the studio, and he remembers his creation quite vividly. "Magic Alex had some good ideas in principle, but it didn't work. All down one side he had these big stainless steel panels that inside were like sponge, so you had this reflection and absorption, which is how modern studios are today. But what let it down was that he didn't float the floor, so it was solid and you got reverberation everywhere. He also kept the old fireplace that was down in the basement, so the sound would reverberate up the chimney and then back down again.

"There was also this big set of lovely oak doors, and he kept them in and neglected to soundproof the other side of them, so the sound would hit the doors and the passageway behind the doors would become this kind of sound box, and you'd get all these rumbling sounds that you would pick up on the mics. He also made what we called 'the white elephant desk.' It was a big old white leather thing with bloody big knobs on it. We called it 'the white elephant' because if somebody switched it on, it wouldn't function. It would just make some nasty sounds and switch itself off. I think the only thing we ever recorded on it were some demos for John, his Saturday morning demos we used to call them. Alex had some great ideas. They had a window that shined light into the studio, and Alex was putting in these lights that would change with the different sound frequencies, but we eventually realized that it wasn't going to float. We ended up buying a desk from a guy called Dick Swettenham, which cost about 15 grand. They had to gut out all of Magic Alex's work when they rebuilt the studio." According to studio manager Geoff Emerick, the recording console that had been built by Magic Alex was eventually sold to a scrap metal dealer for five pounds.

Of all the Apple department heads and close associates of the Beatles, Magic Alex was perhaps the only person whose activities were never really questioned. "They should have called him Crazy Alex," offered Jackie Lomax. "That guy, Alex, kept promising that he could make a fantastic studio out of cheap bits, but he never could. I never heard it play more than two tracks at a time. That's Magic Alex for you. Every time something went wrong, he had a heart attack and went into the hospital. It was a nice studio, well done, except for the machines."

Jack Oliver agrees: "The studio was a waste of money. It never came together. When I was there it was nothing, it was a hole in the ground. We had a room down there, but there was never any electronics in it, all that would happen was that bands would rehearse down there. Most of the bands would have rehearsal studios elsewhere, but people would come and play now and again. Billy Preston would jam down there a lot, and Doris Troy would come in and sing and people would sit in. It was great fun. They were always in there at night, we would all descend down there at night after work, and they would play until two in the morning."

Magic Alex's efforts may have left the Apple Studio as little more than an astronomically expensive rehearsal room, but the Beatles decided that they still wanted to move their new project to the more hospitable environment at Apple. Given that Magic Alex's creation was non-functional, Apple had to borrow and install recording equipment from EMI so that the project could continue on schedule.

It was not only the locale that had changed when the Beatles abandoned Twickenham for Apple. When filming and recording resumed at Savile Row, the Beatles were now accompanied by a guest musician, American organist Billy Preston. Preston was in England performing with Ray Charles when George Harrison had spotted him on stage with the Ray Charles Band at the Festival Hall. The Beatles had first crossed paths with Preston while in Hamburg in 1962, and they had been very impressed by his dynamic playing and ebullient personality. In the ensuing years, Preston had become an even more accomplished musician, and Harrison extended an invitation to drop by Apple and sit in on a Beatles recording session.

Within an hour of arriving at Apple, the good-natured Preston had hit it off with the entire band, and he would stay with the Beatles until the end of the recording sessions. All four Beatles acknowledged that Preston's presence greatly improved the heavy atmosphere that had characterized their time at Twickenham. As a result, the Apple sessions would be much more upbeat, productive, and musical than what had been captured on film several weeks earlier.

To thank Preston for his contributions, the Beatles would bill the forthcoming "Get Back" single as being by "The Beatles with Billy Preston," an honour that was never bestowed on any other session musician who graced a Beatles' recording. George Harrison was so impressed with Preston – who at the time was signed as a solo artist to Capitol Records – that he requested Capitol re-assign Preston's contract to Apple. Capitol duly passed Preston off to Apple, and Preston was signed to Apple Records and given a contract with Apple Music Publishing in February 1969.

Even though the January 1969 recording sessions are typically regarded as the nadir of the Beatles' recording career, a good deal of exceptional music was recorded. Perhaps the finest moment of the Apple era took place at 3 Savile Row on 30 January 1969, when the Beatles made their last public performance on the roof of the Apple building.

During the initial filming of the proposed television show, the Beatles had been arguing amongst themselves about where they should give a live performance as the finale of the program, which included such ambitious ideas as filming a performance in a Roman amphitheatre in Tunisia or perhaps on an ocean liner at sea. But these grandiose proposals were shelved as a condition for George Harrison returning to the group. But as the sessions drew to a close towards the end of the month, the Beatles – including Harrison – agreed to give an unannounced live concert on the roof of the Apple building.

This final chapter of the Beatles' career – which was captured for posterity by the film crew – began on an overcast Thursday morning when road managers Mal Evans and Kevin Harrington loaded the band's equipment into the elevator at the back of the Apple building. Once on the roof, Evans and Harrington set up the drums, amplifiers, and Billy Preston's electric organ in stage formation and then watched and waited as the film crew made their preparations. A few hours later, around lunchtime on that cold winter's afternoon, the Beatles – augmented by Billy Preston – made their final public performance as a group on the bleak rooftop of the Apple office.

With film cameras rolling, the Beatles played for forty-two minutes, running through several versions of songs that they had been rehearsing in the Apple basement and at Twickenham. Performing five storeys above Savile Row, few people could actually see the band, but the raw, amplified sound that they created reverberated throughout the surrounding neighbourhood. As the Beatles played, the film crew captured perplexed people scampering onto the rooftops and fire escapes of neighbouring buildings to get a better look at the group that had not performed in public since 1966. The unannounced performance brought traffic in the street below to a stand-still. The Beatles managed to perform only seven songs before the police arrived at Apple's door and requested that they cease performing.

It has been suggested that someone at Apple or with the film crew called the police to add some drama to the proceedings, but those who were at 3 Savile Row that day are adamant that the police raid was genuine. "The police raided the building during the rooftop concert, and there was a whole chorus of toilets being flushed when the fuzz arrived," recalls resident Apple designer Kosh. "Ten minutes before the raid, someone called from Savile Row police station to say, 'You've got ten minutes.' We knew they were coming, and everyone was ready for it; the toilets had been securely flushed by then. There was all sorts of stuff around!"

By the end of the day, neither the Beatles nor any of the Apple staff had been arrested for disturbing the peace nor for possessing any illicit substances. The Beatles would return to Apple's basement studio the next day to finish filming what certainly ranked among the most dispirited recording sessions of their career, but there was no denying that for one brief moment on that windswept rooftop, the Beatles had managed to come together as a band one last time, each member seemingly charged to be playing to an audience and remembering what it felt like to play in a real working rock band.

Apple Publishing's John Hewlett, who was on the roof along with Ken Mansfield, Peter Brown, Ron Kass, and other Apple staff, artists, and guests, remembers: "The Beatles were fantastic. It was amazing, I had never seen them close-up like that. I had seen them in the studio every now and then, but I never heard them playing a whole song. It was great; it really was. I was blown away. It was so much fun seeing them playing, and they were really, really good. They were all enjoying it; Lennon, in particular. I was most impressed with Lennon and with Ringo Starr. His (Ringo's) drumming was knocked a lot, but he was great and really unique. I came in from lunch and heard all this noise, and we went up on the roof and just sat and watched them play."

The Beatles' rooftop performance was certainly one of the most exciting moments to ever occur on Savile Row, but by the next day, both the group and the Apple staff had put the excitement behind them and had returned to their usual work schedule. While the Beatles struggled to wrap up recording in the makeshift studio in Apple's basement, in the record office directly above the studio, the small staff of Apple Records was working round the clock to establish Apple as a hit-making record label in its own right. Apple's first new record in England for 1969 would be the debut single of White Trash, a five-man band from Glasgow, Scotland, who had come to Apple in late 1968 while they were still performing as the Pathfinders.

The Pathfinders may have had a beat group inspired name, but the music they made was a progressive, hard rock style that was very much in vogue in late sixties London. Since 1967, they had built a huge following in Scotland and had come down to London to further their career. In London, they hooked up with independent producer Tony Meehan (former drummer of the Shadows), who became their manager. Meehan took the group into a studio to record a song called "Road To Nowhere." It was Meehan who had brought the finished tape to Apple. Fraser Watson remembered: "One night we were sitting in the Cromwellian Club, totally depressed after a rotten gig, when Tony came in and said, 'Apple – the Beatles' company – want to release "Road To Nowhere!"' It was like a dream."

Meehan had paid a visit to Savile Row in late 1968 and played the Pathfinders' tape to George Harrison and Paul McCartney. Both Beatles were impressed by what Meehan had captured on tape, and the Pathfinders were given a contract to release a single for Apple Records. When the newly signed group voiced concern that their name might not be suitable for the progressive music scene of 1969, they asked Apple to come up with a new name. It was Richard DiLello who came up with White Trash.

Road To Nowhere was a brooding, dynamic version of a seemingly obscure Carole King song." It would be backed by "Illusions," a driving piece of poppy psychedelia written by Hugh Nicholson (a member of the legendary Scottish freakbeat band the Poets) that was subsequently assigned to Apple Publishing. "Illusions" was arguably even better than the A-side, and either one of the songs had the potential to become a hit for White Trash.

But only weeks after the band was signed, Apple learned that English singer Lesley Duncan had recorded her own rendition of the song for release as a single. Apple suddenly found itself with only a few weeks to get the record into the shops. Copies of "Road To Nowhere" were quickly pressed up and released in late January. As soon as finished demo copies of the record arrived at Apple, Tony Bramwell rushed the White Trash single over to the BBC to try to get "Road To Nowhere" added to the Radio One play list. Confident that Apple had discovered a new hit act, Ron Kass and Jack Oliver were extremely disappointed when an exasperated Bramwell returned from the BBC and informed them that the BBC considered the name "White Trash" to be offensive and that they would not be airing the song unless the group came up with a more suitable name.

Or so the story goes. In the 8 February 1969 issue of *Disc And Music Echo*, a BBC spokesperson denied that the record had actually been banned and added that "Road To Nowhere" had been played three times the previous week by the BBC. The most likely scenario was that Apple received some pushback from the BBC on the name, but there was never a formal ban initiated.

Regardless of whether there was a formal ban on the record or not, Apple felt that a name change was in order. Ron Kass pointed out that the name would certainly face even more resistance in the more conservative American market. As a compromise, Apple simply had the group shorten their name to Trash and then re-pressed the record with the group's revised name on the label. Unfortunately, by the time the re-pressed "Road To Nowhere" was in the shops, the single's initial commercial impact had been lost.

Despite the quality of both sides of the record and the group's well-received live shows, the single failed to chart. Iveys drummer Mike

Gibbins was quite fond of White Trash and was surprised that they were unable to get a hit. "White Trash went over really well in London," he recalled. "We used to hang out with White Trash and get stoned. They used to come to our house, we used to go to theirs. I loved them, they were a powerful band. They were heavy, but they weren't very successful with Apple. Their drummer is a taxi driver in London now."

Trash's failure to get a hit with "Road To Nowhere" is but one of several unsolved mysteries of the Apple story. Unlike the Iveys, whose upbeat Kinks/Hollies/Beatles-influenced style was arguably several years out of date with what London's taste-makers considered to be cutting edge, Trash's hard rock guitar and neo-gothic organ sound placed them at – or at least near – the forefront of the heavy rock style that was quickly becoming all the rage in England. Trash's only real liability was that none of the group members were accomplished songwriters. Tony Bramwell adds that the other problem that hampered the success of "Road To Nowhere" was that, "White Trash were too heavy. There was no heavy radio station at the time to play it. Also, there was a bit of a rejection of the name, although they were never actually banned."

Only weeks after the Trash debacle, Apple would have yet another record run into censorship problems, although this time it was Apple's distributor, EMI, who would be the censor. The controversy was over "King Of Fuh," a single by an American songwriter known as Brute Force that Apple had planned to issue in February 1969. A pretty, melodic song that combined subtle flower-power sentiments with a humorous and admittedly risqué lyrical hook, "King Of Fuh" was a perfect record for Apple circa 1969, and it could have realistically been a novelty hit of sorts had it received a proper release, even without airplay from the BBC.

Brute Force was the stage name of Stephen Friedland, a singer/songwriter from New York City specializing in satirical music and surreal performance art. Prior to his association with Apple, Friedland had been a staff songwriter for Bright Tunes Music Publishing (where he wrote songs covered by the Chiffons, UK pop-art sensations the Creation, and several other groups) and a member of the vocal group the Tokens. Friedland had also previously recorded a solo album for Columbia Records in 1966, featuring such quirky songs as "To Sit On A Sandwich" and "Tape Worm Of Love" – which earned him a good deal of notoriety but little in the way of record sales.

Friedland came to Apple's attention through the Beatles' American attorney, Nat Weiss. "I had a girlfriend who eventually became the girlfriend of Tom Dawes from the Cyrkle and they were managed by Nat Weiss," explained Friedland, "I got Tom Dawes to speak to Nat Weiss about a song I had recorded with the Tokens. This was early 1968.

It took me a long time to convince the Tokens to do "King Of Fuh." I had produced the song with the Tokens at Ohmstead Sound Studios which was on 40th and 6th Avenue in New York. They had a mellotron and we used that for violins, so we made the track. We did the B-side, "Nobody Knows," at a different session around the same time."

"We brought the song to Nat Weiss with the idea that it would go on Apple," recalls Friedland. "I wanted them (the Beatles) to hear it, and it came back to me one day that they wanted to do it, that's what I heard from Nat Weiss. Weiss sent the master tape to Apple in London and George Harrison took the track that I did with the Tokens and put on strings with the London Philharmonic. I believe he also re-did the bass and he might have done something with the drums, too. He changed the melodic line of the strings and made it prettier. I wasn't there when he did that. So they pressed it, put it on a 45 as Apple 08, and then they didn't do it. EMI banned "King Of Fuh." They found it offensive."

George Harrison, who had taken it upon himself to prepare "King Of Fuh" for release on Apple, commissioned John Barham to compose a string arrangement. The session to record Barham's string parts was held on Friday 10 January, the very same day that Harrison had only hours before briefly quit the Beatles. Despite the gravity of what had transpired earlier in the day at Twickenham Studios, Harrison was in good spirits for the session. "There was a lot of laughing when they played the tape in the studio," remembers Barham. "I did the strings when George produced the overdub session at Trident." The assembled session musicians may have been charmed by the subtle wit and good-natured fun of "King Of Fuh," but the powers that be at EMI would be less amused.

In fact, when EMI representatives heard "King Of Fuh," they flatly refused to press or distribute the record. Unwilling to be undermined by corporate censorship, Apple elected to press the single independently, and they gave a small run of records a very limited distribution in mid-May. Friedland recalls that, "They distributed it as much as they could. They must have pressed around 1,000 copies. They just sent it to friends and disc jockeys. I had two boxes of them, around a hundred copies."

Harrison had also wanted to have "King Of Fuh" issued as an Apple single in the United States, but Capitol decided that the record would be too controversial. In a lengthy 10 February letter to George Harrison, Capitol President Stan Gorticov conveyed that he, personally, liked the record, but that he was not the average American record buyer and that Capitol would in fact pass on their right to issue the record. Gorticov encouraged Apple to seek out another American record label to press and distribute "King Of Fuh," though he cautioned that the Beatles being associated with a record like "King Of Fuh" could jeopardize the goodwill that they enjoyed with the "squares" who owned American radio stations.

Friedland claims to have never signed a contract with either Apple Records or Publishing (although he has a letter from Mal Evans that mentions that Peter Asher had received his signed contract), nor did he ever receive any money from Apple. "I had no management at the time. I was a young artist, twenty-eight or twenty-nine, on Apple Records! I should have sat down with a manager, but it didn't happen. So in the spring of 1969, me and my wife, Cynthia, went to Savile Row. I essentially went to pick up the tapes, because it wasn't happening. I couldn't understand. I never did meet George. I remember when I was at Apple that I was hoping to meet George Harrison, and Derek Taylor said to me, 'Well, he's rather provincial,' meaning that George wouldn't come into the city to meet with me. I did get to meet with the other guy, Neil Aspinall, and Richard DiLello. It was a pretty sedate office."

Far away from London, Peter Asher – ensconced in his office in the Capitol Records tower in Los Angeles – had immersed himself in learning the intricacies of the American record business. Asher also used his California sojourn as an opportunity to reunite with James Taylor and to start preliminary work on Taylor's second album for Apple. During his stay, Asher recorded several songs with Taylor, including fully-produced early versions of "Sunny Skies," "Let It Ride," and "Fire And Rain" (which in this early incarnation featured countrified electric guitar licks and female gospel-style backing vocals).

Utilizing a full band that featured his old Flying Machine band mate, Danny Kortchmar, Taylor's lively new recordings sounded neither like the ornately arranged songs featured on his 1968 Apple album, nor the introspective acoustic musings that would characterize his later work. The three songs recorded during the session were a promising start to a new album and suggested that Taylor had managed to put his personal problems behind him and was once again ready to get back to making music.

The first non–Beatles Apple albums to be issued in the United States in 1969 were *James Taylor* and *Under The Jasmin Tree*, which were released simultaneously on 17 February. Both albums were heavily promoted, getting press advertisements as well as a special "More Apples Radio Co-Op Ads" dealer-only promo 45 that featured one-minute recorded ads for each album. But as had been the case in England, both albums – particularly *James Taylor* – earned excellent reviews but sold only a modest number of copies.

The Taylor and MJQ albums were followed into American record shops by several new Apple singles. Paul McCartney had once commented that he thought Trash had a sound that would be well-suited to the

American market, but that theory would be tested and found lacking when "Road To Nowhere" was issued in the United States in March 1969. Similar to the commercial reception given to the Iveys, the record sold well in several regional markets but never managed to break on a national level. James Taylor's debut single, "Carolina In My Mind," was also released in March and it, too, met with mixed results. "With James Taylor's "Carolina In My Mind" we had more airplay than any other artist that I have ever worked with and still nothing sold," recalled Ken Mansfield. "It was a total non-sale record. Nothing was wrong – they just didn't sell."

James Taylor was bitterly disappointed by the lack of chart action for "Carolina In My Mind," and he felt that the trouble was that Capitol was not fully behind Apple. "There were days when I'd go up to Capitol, and no one would even know that Apple was up there, in the Capitol Tower in Hollywood, much less James Taylor."

Taylor's single received steady radio play and positive press coverage, but it ultimately didn't shift many copies, nor did it do much to stimulate sales of the *James Taylor* album. It did attract the attention of Tony Orlando, an executive at April Music (the music publishing arm of Columbia Records). Orlando realized that James Taylor was still under a global publishing contract with April Music Publishing (Taylor had signed a deal with April in 1967 before leaving New York City for London), and he wasted little time in bringing this minor detail to the attention of Apple Publishing. Apple was subsequently required to relinquish all claims to Taylor's publishing copyrights and handed over all of the publishing royalties accrued from the sales of Taylor's debut album to April Music.

Following the release of the initial batch of Apple albums, Apple next turned its attention towards the launch of a subsidiary "art" label called Zapple. Since Apple's inception, Paul McCartney and John Lennon had been keen to develop a budget-line label to issue what would essentially be known decades later as "audio books." In October 1968, Apple hired Barry Miles, who co-owned the Indica bookshop with John Dunbar and Peter Asher, to manage the proposed spoken word label.

The Zapple concept was that the label would release avant-garde and spoken word records at a reduced price that would be comparable to that of a paperback book. The idea looked promising on paper, but the reality was that when the few records actually put out by Zapple finally made it into the shops, they were priced like any other full-priced music album. Zapple's first (and only) two releases were George Harrison's *Electronic Sound* and John Lennon and Yoko Ono's *Life With The Lions*. Both records were supposed to be issued in February but it would not be until 9 May 1969 that the records would be released in England, followed by the United States release on 26 May.

Apple had originally contemplated putting out every Zapple release in a generic Zapple sleeve, but of the two Zapple Records to be issued, both had traditional album cover art and the regular Apple label with a silver "Zapple" superimposed across the top of the Apple. Neither Harrison's nor Lennon's record really seemed to fit the original Zapple concept. *Electronic Sound* was an undistinguished recording of Harrison experimenting with his recently purchased Moog synthesizer, while *Life With The Lions* was essentially *Two Virgins* part 2, being little more than recent field recordings made by Lennon and Ono.

There was a third Zapple project planned that would have been more in keeping with the original idea for Zapple, which was an album of American author Richard Brautigan reading some of his poetry. The album, *Listening To Richard Brautigan*, was recorded, had a cover created, and was scheduled to be issued on 23 June. But the record was never released on Zapple (it would finally be issued by Capitol Records' Harvest imprint in 1970).

Despite the difficulties that Apple was having getting recordings out on the Zapple imprint, plans for Zapple continued to flourish throughout 1969. At various times, Zapple announced plans to release spoken word recordings by such acclaimed underground writers as Allen Ginsberg, Charles Bukowski, Kenneth Patchen, Ken Weaver, and Lawrence Ferlinghetti, and Barry Miles did, in fact, record several of these writers for proposed Zapple projects. Zapple even contemplated issuing a 24-album set of Lenny Bruce recordings. John Kosh remembers that, "There was a lot of Lenny Bruce being played at Apple. Derek Taylor decided to convert everyone to Lenny Bruce, which he did successfully."

American author Ken Kesey – of *One Flew Over The Cuckoo's Nest* fame – went as far as to venture to Apple's London office to begin work on his own Apple-sponsored project. Apple supplied him with a tape recorder, a typewriter, and the use of a small back office in the Apple building and requested that he record his impressions of late-sixties London. Though Kesey allegedly submitted a finished tape to Peter Asher, Asher never got around to doing any further work on the project, and it remains unreleased to this day. "Ken Kesey came over with the Hells Angels, and that was really bizarre," remembers Mike O'Connor. "We gave Ken a tape recorder to record stuff, and Ken was on a lot of acid and we had this problem where the tape recorder disappeared. Peter felt that Ken had probably stolen it, but I thought he wouldn't have done that. I was also involved with the Richard Brautigan album."

Perhaps the most anticipated non-Beatles Apple project to reach the market in early 1969 was Mary Hopkin's *Postcard* album, which was issued in England in late February. Paul McCartney had been involved with almost every aspect of the creation of *Postcard*. McCartney had even come up with the concept for the album cover and had his American girlfriend, Linda Eastman, take the pictures that graced the record sleeve. Speaking to the *Daily Sketch*, McCartney explained that his concept for the album had been to have Hopkin record songs by current leading songwriters as well as "songs that have been my favorites – carrying on the theme of "Those Were The Days." Songs that my dad used to play me."

Postcard is a charming, somewhat eclectic album. Nestled alongside the new songs and the old pop standards were two tracks that particularly stuck out from the rest of the album as they were both sung in a language other than English. One was in Hopkin's native Welsh, while the other was in French. Apple appeared to be working towards establishing Hopkin as an international recording property by having her record non-English language songs aimed at specific foreign markets. "Those Were The Days" was an obvious candidate for this international treatment, and English, Spanish, German, and French language versions of Hopkin's signature song were recorded and released in their respective local markets.

To capitalize on the international success of "Those Were The Days," Hopkin had recorded a new Paul McCartney-produced single, "Lontano Dagli Occhi," for release in Brazil, Italy, and a few select European markets in early 1969. Apple also tried to score a hit single in France with "Prince En Avignon," the French language song from *Postcard*. Both singles were backed with "The Game," a pleasant pop song written by Beatles producer George Martin and published by Apple Music Publishing.

Apple and EMI had been unable to get *Postcard* into the shops by the Paul McCartney-imposed target of Valentine's Day, but the album was still a massive success in England where it reached number three in the charts. In America, where Apple had added "Those Were The Days" to the album to help boost sales, the album sold well, and it became Apple's first non-Beatles album to break into the American top thirty, reaching number twenty-eight in March 1969.

Jackie Lomax may have not gotten the international push that Apple gave Mary Hopkin (a German language version of his 1970 Apple single, "How The Web Was Woven," was recorded but never issued), but Apple did put substantial promotional resources behind his *Is This What You Want?* album, which was given a worldwide release in March. Featuring Lomax's overlooked debut single, "Sour Milk Sea," plus well-crafted, self-penned ballads like "I Fall Inside Your Eyes" and sturdy pop-rock numbers like "Speak To Me," the George Harrison produced *Is This What You Want?* was expected to be a big seller. Instead, it garnered only average sales in the United States, sold relatively few copies in the UK, and fared little better in other territories. In an effort to stimulate sales, Apple even added an apple-shaped sticker on the cover of US pressings alerting potential purchasers that such famous guests as Paul McCartney, George Harrison, Ringo Starr, and Eric Clapton appeared on the album, but it was to little avail.

Ken Mansfield maintains that Apple put a great deal of effort and care into launching Jackie Lomax's career in America. "I took Jackie Lomax and Mal Evans on a radio promotion tour around the country, hitting up all the DJs and music directors in all the major markets. We really worked it. With Apple, though, we didn't have to do too much. It was the Beatles. It was Apple, so we were sort of above having to do too much. Anything on Apple had immediate acceptance, and it was considered to be very hip, very cool. Jackie got a really good listen because of it. Unfortunately, Jackie seemed to believe his publicity a little too much. I thought he was making great records and George was into it, but it didn't sell."

Mansfield and Apple may have been stumped as to why the Lomax album didn't make a bigger commercial splash, but both Lomax and Apple would be consoled by the fact that the album sold slowly but steadily for several years after its release as record buyers discovered the exceptional quality of the music on *Is This What You Want?*.

By the spring of 1969, Ron Kass and others at Apple were growing concerned with the lacklustre commercial response to James Taylor, the Iveys, Trash, and Jackie Lomax. Few would admit it publicly, but a good number of the staff at Apple had assumed that the quality of the music and the fact that it was associated with Apple and the Beatles would make success all but inevitable for any recording artists signed to Apple. It came as quite a surprise to many at Apple when Mary Hopkin seemed to be the only Apple artist to benefit from that theory.

Apple was taking no chances with Mary Hopkin. To help ensure that Hopkin would maintain her initial success, Apple took great care in developing Hopkin's recording career. Certain that there was no way that Hopkin could ever repeat the success of "Those Were The Days," Paul McCartney instinctively knew that there was no need to rush out a second single by his young protégée. When McCartney felt that the time was right for a new Mary Hopkin record, he presented her with a freshly written Lennon and McCartney song called "Goodbye." Boasting a breezy McCartney melody, a winsome arrangement by Richard Hewson, and McCartney's highly commercial production, "Goodbye" reached number two on the English charts following its release in March. Issued a month later in America, the song returned Hopkin and Apple to the American top ten, where "Goodbye" went all the way to number eight.

The B-side to "Goodbye" was a dark, folk-jazz song composed by Gallagher and Lyle entitled "Sparrow." Apple Publishing's John Hewlett recalls that "McCartney really loved their stuff, and he was responsible for the Mary Hopkin cover. McCartney was the only one taking any interest in publishing. He was actually genuinely interested, and he was thrilled when Gallagher and Lyle came through because the man's got a good ear. McCartney would actually come into the office on a regular basis and sit on the floor and listen to the songs with me, listen to these people singing in the bath in Wales sending a tape in. We'd laugh about a lot of it, but he'd also listen to the stuff that was half-way any good, and Gallagher and Lyle were really one of the better writers, or writing partnerships, that we signed during that period. The majority of the tapes were awful. I don't recall coming across anything else that was particularly good. The only guy I signed was a guy called Peter Cooper, who we got a record deal with Giorgio Gomelsky's label. But Peter was a little shaky. He had ability, but his marriage broke up and he had problems. It was an interesting sort of psychedelic guitar-based band. Giorgio produced some songs for him, but it never got released."

Graham Lyle recalls how Paul McCartney had asked all of the Apple Publishing writers to submit a song for consideration as a B-side for Hopkin's second single: "It was Paul McCartney who showed the most enthusiasm for what we were doing. I remember he was very involved with our song "Sparrow." What happened was that there were a few teams of songwriters who were signed to Apple: ourselves, the guys from the Iveys, and Grapefruit. McCartney said, 'Mary Hopkin's making this record, and we need you to write something for it, and whoever writes the winning song I'll present with a cake. We weren't too concerned about that, but we wanted desperately to get a cut on a Mary Hopkin record. Well, we won the cake with the song "Sparrow." The word came back that Paul liked what we had written, but could we change a little bit at the end and things like that. So we finished the song, and she recorded it in the studio. Paul even asked us to be on the session."

Mortimer's Tom Smith also remembered the competition, recalling that, "We got a memo from McCartney saying that he wanted material for Mary Hopkin's new single, and he had everybody in the company trying to write her something. We wrote a song and put it down, but nothing happened. I remember I was down in the main studio. I was at Apple by myself, and I went down to the studio and heard a guitar strumming. It was just George Martin and Paul McCartney in the studio, and the lights were out. I sat in the corner and listened to Paul put down a version of "Goodbye," and George was putting it down on tape. The studio was in shambles, but they recorded that demo there."

Despite the relative lack of success experienced by any (outside of Mary Hopkin) of the artists that had been signed to the label, Apple continued to sign new acts throughout the first half of 1969. During the sessions for Billy Preston's debut Apple single, George Harrison became re-acquainted with Doris Troy, an American R&B vocalist from New York City. Troy, who had been living in London for several years, remembers that she had been asked by her friend Madeline Bell to help out on Preston's session and that she had no idea that the session was being produced by George Harrison.

Harrison, a great admirer of Troy's mid-60s hits like "Just One Look," was knocked out by Troy and her dynamic voice. Harrison decided that Troy would make an excellent addition to the Apple roster, and she ultimately would sign record, publishing, and production deals with Apple. Troy was given an office next to Peter Asher's on the fourth floor of the Apple building, and she set to work writing material for herself and with other artists. Her first Apple project was on behalf of Apple Publishing, co-writing several songs with Billy Preston.

From his small office next door to Doris Troy's, Peter Asher was still responsible for Apple's entire artist roster, although he was clearly dedicating most of his time to developing the career of James Taylor. Having been exposed to the American market while he was in Hollywood, Asher was more confident than ever that Taylor would be Apple's next star. As he waited for Taylor to write enough material for a second album, Asher agreed to produce an album by the new Apple group, Mortimer. In an unusual move, Asher assumed control of the whole project, which included taking promo pictures and even penning a biography for the group.

Mortimer's Tom Smith recalls that Asher had high hopes for Mortimer and that Apple spared little expense when it came to recording the album. "We recorded mostly at Trident Studios. We did lots of sessions over a span of four months. Peter brought in some outside musicians to help us. We had an upright bass player named Spike Heatley playing on our song "People Who Are Different." On our song "Dolly," Richard Hewson brought in a choir of twelve people to sing the parts he had written. Richard Hewson also played piano on a song we hoped to make a single, "Pick Up Your Heart." Peter Asher sang on "You Don't Say You Love Me," and he also played bass on a track."

The twelve-song Mortimer album was completed and mastered on 17 April. Peter Asher was making final preparations for the release of the album when Paul McCartney paid an unexpected visit to Asher's office. Smith remembers: "McCartney popped in on us – he used to drop in and see how things were going with all the artists that were signed to Apple – and we had just recorded a song, "You Don't Say You Love Me," and Peter thought that it might be the single, so he played it to Paul. Paul said that he liked it but said, 'I don't know if it's a single.' Paul noticed that we played a lot of acoustics, and he said, 'I've got a song I think you guys would be perfect for,' and he played us "Two Of Us," which was then still called "On Our Way Home." He played us an acetate of him and John playing it on acoustic guitars. They were joking together like the Everly Brothers, saying, 'Take it, Phil,' and things like that. It was nice, but honestly, I don't think any of us thought that it was a single. But the fact that Paul gave it to us, and that Peter said, 'Let's go and try it,' we went and recorded it."

Asher dutifully took Mortimer back into the studio to record "On Our Way Home," and the song was completed and mixed on 1 May. Given the acoustic foundation of Mortimer's sound, it's obvious why McCartney thought that the song would be ideal for the group, but it didn't work. Mortimer's arrangement smoothed out the song's rough edges, and their performance failed to capture the charm and warmth of the Beatles' demo. It didn't sound like a hit, but several songs were dropped from the original track list and "On Our Way Home" was added as the first song on Mortimer's Apple album. Mortimer were unsure about how the song had turned out but felt that they were in no position to turn down a Beatles song. "When we finished the album. Peter invited us out to his place in the country to take pictures for the album cover," remembered Tom Smith. "It was a frantic time. Apple showed interest in our finished album, but no one was raving about it. I wouldn't say we took the place by storm."

Their album complete, Mortimer played a few shows around London and waited for Apple to release the record. "We rehearsed at Apple in the Beatles' storage room, which was upstairs on the top floor of the Apple building where they had all their equipment," recalled Guy Masson. "There was still plenty of room and it was quiet, they had all of their original Beatle drums, George's painted guitar that he played in *Magical Mystery Tour*. It was something, a great place to rehearse."

The Mortimer record was but one of many projects that Apple was working on that spring. With nine recording artists under contract and the Beatles as busy as they had ever been, Apple was operating at full capacity. Indeed, Neil Aspinall and Peter Brown found themselves increasingly overwhelmed by all of the Apple activity and the busy personal lives of the individual Beatles. To help out with the administrative duties at Beatles and Co., Brown had been given permission to secure an assistant, and in April 1969, he hired 20-year-old Londoner Bill Oakes.

Oakes – who had previously worked as an entertainment reporter for the news wire service UNS – first met Brown while covering a press reception for Mary Hopkin. "I had already met Paul McCartney and

Peter Brown at St. Paul's Cathedral of all places," remembers Oakes. "It was in the summer of 1968 at a press reception for Mary Hopkin, who was performing in the cathedral. I caught the tail end of it and then coming out of it were Peter Brown and Paul McCartney. I ended up writing an article on Apple. The next time I ran into Peter and Paul was in April 1969. I had just come back from hitchhiking around Europe.

"I happened to be cutting down Savile Row as a shortcut to Oxford Street, when I saw Peter Brown and Paul McCartney coming out of Nutter's, the tailor. Tommy Nutter was Peter Brown's friend and tailor to the Beatles. I said hello and was amazed that Peter Brown recognized me. Peter Brown said, 'Hello, come into Apple,' so I went past the Scruffs and went in with them, and the next thing I know, they were offering me a job. Although I had a couple of O-levels, no one was interested in my qualifications. It was more of, 'Oh, he seems like a good geezer, when can you start?' Paul had just got married, and I think he was already moving away from Apple mentally. Klein hadn't been hired yet, but he was in the wings. I was to work for Peter Brown, but there was no question that my first and foremost priority was meant to be McCartney. That was quite clear, although the others, of course, regarded me as being their slave, too, so you had to juggle it."

Unbeknownst to Oakes, he was joining Apple just as the Beatles and Apple itself were both starting to fracture. Having now had most of their earnings funnelled into Apple for more than a year, by early 1969, all four Beatles were becoming increasingly alarmed as they realized just how much money was being consumed by the company. Of course, it never occurred to any of the Beatles that much of the money that Apple had paid out during 1968 was directly attributable to their personal spending.

Slowly coming out of his drug lethargy, John Lennon was especially concerned by the developments at Apple. Speaking to Ray Coleman in an interview for *Disc And Music Echo,* the brutally frank Lennon exclaimed that Apple "needs a new broom and a lot of people will have to go. It needs streamlining. It doesn't need to make vast profits, but if it carries on like this, all of us will be broke in six months." Clearly on a roll, Lennon continued to bare his soul to Coleman, adding: "We have enough to live on, but we can't let Apple go on like this. We started off with loads of ideas of what we wanted to do... but like one or two Beatles things, it didn't work out because we aren't practical, and we weren't quick enough to realize we needed a businessman's brain to run the whole thing."

Due to the lavish spending habits of the Beatles and to the rapid expansion and carefree business practices at Apple, the company was simply spending more money than it was taking in. Derek Taylor later noted that the problem at Apple was that, "The weirdness was not controlled at the start. You can't control weirdness anyway... weirdness is weirdness."

"The Beatles weren't together; they didn't know what they wanted out of Apple," explained Taylor in 1988. "George and Paul wanted different things, while John and Ringo didn't know what they wanted at first. What Paul wanted was a publishing company, a record company, the Apple shops. I'm not sure that he wanted Apple Electronics and Magic Alex; John was the big sponsor there, but George liked Alex and Paul didn't dislike him. I don't know what Ringo's idea of Apple was."

Eventually, it became apparent that Apple had to find a suitable person to oversee business operations. Peter Brown recalls: "There was a point when Paul, with the support of the others, went looking for a major figure to run Apple, on the basis of they were so big and powerful that Neil and I were not qualified to do it. Paul felt that the Beatles needed the biggest and the best to run their corporation. They interviewed English tycoons like Cecil King and Dr. Beeching, but these people were not interested. Not only that, they knew nothing about the music business."

Having rapidly exhausted the list of potential saviours for Apple, it suddenly dawned on Paul McCartney that Lee Eastman, the father of his new wife, Linda, would be the perfect person to run Apple. Eastman, a successful New York City attorney who had extensive experience with music copyrights, was certainly a viable candidate for the job. The other Beatles were not particularly comfortable with the idea of Paul McCartney's father-in-law running Apple, but they agreed to discuss the issue with Eastman and, for a short while, even let Eastman and his son, John, act as business advisors to Apple.

It was Derek Taylor who convinced Peter Brown to put Allen Klein in touch with the Beatles.

By 1969, Klein, a New York City-based artist manager who had been involved in the music industry since the early sixties, had already developed a formidable – if somewhat unsavoury – reputation on both sides of the Atlantic. Klein, an accountant by trade, had started in the music business by auditing the books of agents, managers, record companies, and music publishers that he believed were shortchanging artists on their royalties. Since undertaking his first audit on behalf of singer Bobby Darin, Klein roared through the New York City music industry, becoming the manager of Sam Cooke and later acting as the American manager of such top English acts as the Rolling Stones, Donovan, and Herman's Hermits, amongst others. Only thirty-seven when he began courting the Beatles, Klein had already managed to acquire the American music publishing interests of the Rolling Stones, Ray Davies, and Pete Townshend, leaving some of the most important

English songwriters of the era bitter and resentful of their association with the self-styled "Robin Hood of Pop."

Klein's business dealings were common knowledge to most people in the music industry, yet he was also celebrated for being a ruthless negotiator who had a remarkable ability to secure fantastic deals for the artists he represented. The Beatles – Paul McCartney in particular – were far from happy about the fact that the Rolling Stones, thanks to Klein, had a much more lucrative record deal than the Beatles.

Klein's interest in securing a meeting with the Beatles had been conveyed to Derek Taylor by Tony Calder of Immediate Records. Taylor, who commuted daily to London from his home in Surrey, was driving to the train station with Calder when Calder mentioned that Klein had been trying to get in touch with the Beatles. Klein had apparently read the John Lennon interview with Ray Coleman where Lennon had proclaimed that if Apple continued on its present course that the company would be broke in six months. Klein wanted to share with John Lennon how he could solve all of Apple's problems and Calder intimated to Taylor that Klein was under the (false) impression that the reason he was not getting through to John Lennon was due to interference from Taylor. Taylor explained that he had no idea that Klein was trying to secure a call with John Lennon and agreed to bring Klein's request to the attention of Peter Brown.

Unbeknownst to Taylor, Allen Klein had been actively pursuing the Beatles ever since he had heard the news report of Brian Epstein's death in August 1967. Peter Brown and Clive Epstein had even met with Klein, but as Brown recounted, "He was so foul-mouthed and abusive that I ended the meeting in a few moments and had him shown the door." Yet despite Brown's less than favourable first impression of Klein, Brown arranged a phone call between Klein and John Lennon as a personal favour to Taylor.

The call was made, and by the end of the conversation, an intrigued John Lennon had agreed to meet with Klein in a London hotel, out of sight from the prying eyes of Apple's staff and his fellow Beatles. The beleaguered Beatle was particularly interested in getting Klein to sort out his and Yoko Ono's personal business matters. Speaking to *Playboy Magazine* in 1971, Klein explained that, "He [Lennon] made it clear that he was there for himself and Yoko, period. He told me that the Eastmans were handling the Beatles' financial affairs."

During the course of the meeting, both John Lennon and Yoko Ono were highly impressed by Klein's down-to-earth manner, knowledge of the Beatles music, and obvious business savvy. Lennon would later characterize Klein as a real person, as opposed to the Eastmans, whom he thought were pretentious. Lennon also liked the fact that Klein didn't look like a businessman. Unlike the reserved Eastmans, who were typically attired in immaculate suits, former Apple staff recall that Klein dressed casually, even for important business meetings.

Lennon found Klein's attitude refreshing, and at the end of the meeting, Ono typed out a letter authorizing Klein to look into Lennon's business matters and Klein agreed to see what he could do on behalf of John and Yoko. It was during a lunch meeting at Apple the next day that the other Beatles first found out that Klein was looking after Lennon's financial affairs. Klein later admitted to *Playboy* that during the meeting, "Paul was pretty cool. I don't think he made up his mind about me."

Reflecting on how Allen Klein came to power at Apple, Peter Brown feels that the other three Beatles were ultimately motivated to choose Klein over Eastman due in part to a feeling that Apple was becoming too dominated by McCartney. John Lennon was especially disturbed by what he perceived as McCartney's dominance at Apple. Brown concedes, "The day-to-day driving force at Apple was Paul, and therefore, it was Paul that Neil and I dealt with. I would be there all day. Neil would come in the late morning and Paul would come in most days. So naturally, Paul was the person we spoke to. Paul was the most reliable about making decisions. He was the most conventional about structuring a business. He liked the idea, so Apple was built in Paul's image. What happened was that when John woke up, partly as a result of Yoko's prodding, he found the structure in place. Then when he said he'd like to do this or like to do that, we had to say, 'Well, you can't do that because we've already got a structure, it's already done.' And that was the start of many of the problems, because John came along and said, 'I want something different,' and we would say, 'It's already done, this is how it's done.' So, he would say, 'Well, I don't like it,' and we would say, 'Well, it's too late, you should have been here before.'"

Peter Brown still considers Lennon's enthusiasm for Klein perplexing, given that Klein's style of doing business was no secret to the London music community. "Part of John's perverseness was shown by that awful situation when Mick Jagger wanted to come around and tell the Beatles what Klein was really like. He went to John and told him: 'Before you make a commitment to Klein, let me tell you my experience.' And I told John that Mick was gonna come around and do this, which was a very sensible thing to do. Mick was a very bright man, and he was far more business orientated than either John or Paul. Mick was going to say, as a friend, 'Listen, before you make any decision, I should tell you what happened to me.' So John tells Klein that Mick was coming, and when Mick arrived he was presented with not only the four Beatles but also with Klein. There wasn't much that Mick could say. It was a very, very bizarre thing for John to have done."

Lee and John Eastman, who a few weeks earlier had assumed that they would soon be representing the Beatles, were naturally upset by Klein's arrival in London. They knew Klein from New York City and they did not relish the thought of having to battle Klein for control of Apple.

For the next few weeks, both parties worked hard to curry the favour of all four Beatles, yet the balance of power soon tipped towards Klein as John Lennon grew disenchanted with the upper-class Eastmans and threw his full support behind the scrappy, unpretentious accountant.

The fierce competition between Allen Klein and Lee and John Eastman to be appointed business manager for Apple and the Beatles could not have come at a worse time, given that the group needed to address a pressing, high stakes business issue that unexpectedly materialized in the spring of 1969. Due to the protracted power struggle between Klein and the Eastman family, the Beatles would be forced to rely on the often contradictory advice of Lee and John Eastman and Allen Klein.

Ever since Brian Epstein's death, NEMS – now known as Nemperor Holdings and run by Brian's brother, Clive – had continued to receive 25% of the Beatles' recording income (per the terms of the EMI contract negotiated by Brian Epstein in 1967), despite the Beatles not having signed a new contract with NEMS when their original management agreement expired in the autumn of 1967. The company had languished under Clive Epstein's leadership, and it was thought that Nemperor would not have the cash on hand required to pay the death taxes on Epstein's estate, which were due to be paid on 31 March 1969. John Eastman realized that this presented an excellent opportunity for the Beatles to purchase Nemperor outright, which would bring the 25% of the Beatles income that was being paid to Nemperor back to the group. Eastman even arranged for EMI to loan the Beatles – as an advance against future royalties – £1 million to purchase Nemperor.

Clive Epstein appeared to be initially receptive to Eastman's proposal and it seemed – to Eastman at least - like a done deal, until Allen Klein arrived on the scene and explained to the Beatles that they would have to earn twice as much in pre-tax royalties to pay back the EMI loan. A stalemate ensued and little action was taken until McCartney and John Eastman abruptly left a critical meeting after coming to a major disagreement with Klein. With McCartney and Eastman out of the room, Klein was able to convince Harrison and Starr to side with Lennon and support Klein's alternative plan for securing Nemperor.

Klein's acquisition tactic was to threaten a rigorous audit of Nemperor's books, suspecting that the company owed the Beatles a substantial sum of money from tours and merchandising. John Eastman recalled Klein telling the Beatles that they would essentially "get NEMS for free" when the money owed the group by NEMS was factored into any prospective deal. Klein then sent an ominous letter of intent to Nemperor – via Eastman – warning Clive Epstein of an imminent audit and suggesting that NEMS' retaining its 25% share of the Beatles deal with EMI through 1976 would also need to be addressed.

Clive Epstein – who had by now grown wary of the deal proposed by John Eastman given that Eastman had "loaded the offer with so many conditions and warranties" - reacted to Klein's threat by promptly selling a majority stake of Nemperor to a London-based consortium of investors, the Triumph Trust, on 17 February 1969.

Shaken but unbowed by this setback, Klein quickly pivoted and turned his sights on Triumph. Klein met with Triumph head Leonard Richenberg, making the same claims that he had presented to Clive Epstein. But Richenberg was a far more formidable adversary than Klein had anticipated, and he was not overly concerned by Klein's threats. Unable to get Richenberg to capitulate to his demands, Klein decided to up the ante. His next move was to instruct EMI to pay approximately £1.3 million in royalties that they were due to pay to Nemperor (who would have deducted their 25% share and then paid out the remainder of the royalties to the Beatles) directly to Apple.

The matter ended up in court, with Klein insisting that Nemperor no longer represented the Beatles in any way, and Nemperor insisting that they were entitled to 25% of the Beatles record royalties though 1976, even if the Beatles were no longer under contract to NEMS. EMI found itself in a no-win situation and opted to not pay out royalties to any party until the conflict was resolved.

Triumph then went on the offensive, engaging a detective agency to investigate Klein's prior business dealings in the United States. The resulting report was then leaked to London's *Sunday Times*, who used the findings for the basis of a highly critical article on Klein. Klein realized, now that his past dealings were public knowledge, that it now might be difficult for him to prevail in court and that it was in his and Apple's best interest to settle with Triumph as soon as possible. Klein eventually negotiated a settlement that stipulated that Apple would pay Triumph £750,000 in cash, plus 5% of the Beatles gross royalties earned between 1972 and 1976. Triumph would also get a 25% share of the royalties that were still being held by EMI. As part of the deal, Triumph would receive £50,000 from Apple for the outstanding shares of Subafilms that were owned by Nemperor, which would then bring Subafilms completely under the ownership of Apple.

John Eastman would later point out in a memo to the Beatles that the figure that Klein paid to free the Beatles from Nemperor far exceeded the original £1,000,000 deal that Eastman had proposed to Clive Epstein several months earlier. But there was an immediate financial upside to Klein's deal, in that the Beatles briefly became Triumph shareholders when they traded the Nemperor shares held by the group – which represented 10% of the company – for Triumph stock that was worth approximately £420,000 (and which the Beatles promptly sold). Emancipating the Beatles from Nemperor had been a costly and questionable victory for Klein, but Lennon, Harrison, and Starr did not hold Klein accountable for the inflated price that they were forced to pay to end their association with NEMS.

Klein may have taken the lead in the clash with Triumph Investments, but it was still not certain if it would be Klein or the Eastmans who would ultimately assume management responsibility for Apple and the Beatles. John Lennon finally broke the stalemate when he decreed that he wanted to be represented by Allen Klein. Peter Brown remembers: "John wanted to bring in Allen Klein and John managed to persuade George and Ringo to support him, so it was a case of they were the majority shareholders and they wanted Klein to come in and take charge. And the way that Klein wanted to take charge was to eliminate costs, because that could be seen to be doing something, and to remove anyone who could stand up to him that he could get rid of. So he got rid of everyone, effectively, except for Neil and myself, and he would have liked to get rid of us. But there was a line drawn where they wouldn't let him go. I stayed long enough to prove he couldn't get rid of me, and once I made my point, I didn't want to stay any longer. He would have liked to have had a clean sweep of everyone so he could run Apple as he wanted, but as it was, we were left with so little authority anyway that it was very difficult for us to be a problem for him."

With the backing of John Lennon, George Harrison, and Ringo Starr, the Beatles and Apple signed a three-year management contract with Allen Klein in March 1969. To mark the occasion, press pictures of a staged signing ceremony, with McCartney, Lennon (with Yoko Ono by his side), and Starr gathered around a desk with Klein were taken. Contrary to the collective image presented by these photos, Paul McCartney's signature was still missing from the contract. In fact, McCartney would never sign the document.

Several of the photos from this session show McCartney playing around with a magnifying glass, as if he were scrutinizing every detail of the contract. Given the lucrative deal that Klein had negotiated for himself, one wonders if the Beatles had ever even looked at the contract before it was signed. Peter Brown admits he had no idea of why the Beatles would offer Klein such generous compensation. "They had no idea of what the going rate was," he concludes. "They had no idea how to negotiate. I don't know where their heads were."

In exchange for Allen Klein and his company, Abkco, assuming management of the Beatles and Apple, Apple would pay for a London apartment for Klein and for "reasonable expenses" incurred by Klein and other Abkco employees in the line of Beatles and Apple business. Klein would also receive 20% of the gross income earned by the Beatles and Apple during the period in which Klein was acting as manager. In addition to his base commission, if Klein were to renegotiate any previously existing deals on behalf of the Beatles, he would earn 20% of the gross income generated from the difference between the original royalty rate and the new royalty rate that he had negotiated.

McCartney appeared to be the only Beatle to have raised an objection to Klein's handsome commission. Given that the Beatles operated under the concept of majority rule, McCartney knew that it was inevitable that Klein would assume control of Apple, but he didn't think the Beatles needed to pay Klein 20% of their gross income. In *Many Years From Now*, McCartney relates how on Friday, 9 May, the other three Beatles arrived at a mixing session for the proposed *Get Back* album at Olympic Studios, with the express purpose of having McCartney sign the management contract. Klein claimed he needed to have McCartney sign the document so that he could return to New York to present the contract to the Abkco board (which did not exist). But McCartney reasoned that the Beatles were "the biggest act in the world" and that Klein would take 15% instead of 20%, so he attempted to convince the other Beatles to get Klein to accept 15%. To McCartney's dismay, the others were insistent that Klein should get 20%, and they angrily accused McCartney of "stalling." McCartney wanted to have his lawyer review the contract the following Monday and he refused to sign the document. On realizing that McCartney was not going to sign the agreement, the other three Beatles abruptly left, leaving McCartney alone in Olympic Studios.

Running into Steve Miller, an American singer & guitarist (coincidentally signed to Apple Publishing in England) who was recording at Olympic that night, McCartney consoled himself by playing drums and bass on one of Miller's new songs, appropriately entitled "My Dark Hour."

1969: LIFE AFTER KLEIN

Conceding that he would not be getting McCartney to sign the management contract, Klein returned to New York where he informed the Abkco staff that the company would now be representing the Beatles and Apple. Klein had been very secretive about his courtship of the Beatles, and even his closest business associates were surprised when it was announced that Klein had been appointed to manage Apple. Al Steckler, a New Yorker who had been looking after the record production side of Abkco's business since 1966, recalls that, "In early 1969, Klein suddenly became less available to us in New York. He spent a lot of time in England, and nobody really knew why. We heard rumours that he was doing something with Apple, but we didn't know. He was there for almost a year straight at one point. Then, all of a sudden he just told us that we were involved with Apple. So I flew over, met all the people, and started getting involved. Peter Asher was already gone, but Tony Bramwell and Jack Oliver were still there."

With the ink still wet on his partially signed management agreement, Klein turned his full attention to assessing the current status of Apple. Undertaking an exhaustive review of Apple's finances, Klein began looking for ways to reduce the mounting expenses and to bring some stability to the company's balance sheet. But less than a month into his job as head of Apple, Klein found himself having to contend with yet another crisis when the Beatles' long-time music publisher, Dick James, announced his intention to sell his shares of Northern Songs to ATV Music publishing.

Upon learning of James's intention to sell his Northern Songs shares, the Beatles were rightfully infuriated. It was the songs of Lennon and McCartney that had built Northern Songs into such a valuable company, and then suddenly, without even offering the Beatles a chance to buy his shares, Dick James sold the fruit of their labours to a third party. With Lennon, McCartney, and Klein out of the country when the news broke, Apple sent George Harrison, Derek Taylor, and Neil Aspinall to meet with James to try to persuade him to postpone the sale. As Peter Brown later noted, the meeting was contentious and emotions quickly got out of hand. The anger that the Apple contingent directed towards James – however justified it may have been – only fortified James's resolve to sell.

Harrison, Taylor, and Aspinall had been unable to convince James to not sell his shares to ATV, but there remained a chance that the Beatles would still be able to gain control of Northern Songs, regardless of James selling his stock to ATV. James did own a significant portion of the company, but as Northern Songs was a publicly traded company with a large number of shareholders, James no longer maintained an outright majority share. After purchasing the shares held by James and his business partner, Charles Silver, ATV held roughly 35% of Northern Songs.

Given that the four Beatles and Apple collectively controlled approximately 29% of Northern Songs, either the Beatles or ATV could conceivably end up with the majority share of the company. An all-out battle to secure the outstanding shares of Northern Songs stock still held by private investors was soon underway. It would be a long, difficult and, for the Beatles and Apple, expensive undertaking. Complicating the battle for control of Northern Songs was that a consortium of London stockbrokers had noticed that Northern Songs was "in play" and quickly amassed their own block of Northern Songs stock that represented approximately 14% of the company.

ATV and the Beatles became locked in an intense contest to come up with the winning bid for the outstanding shares of Northern Songs. The key to gaining control was to win over the consortium, and by mid-May, it appeared that the consortium was prepared to sell its shares to the Beatles and ATV had all but conceded defeat.

It only took a few choice words from John Lennon to totally change the dynamics of the negotiation. The proposed deal with the consortium stipulated that after the Beatles took control of Northern Songs the company would be overseen by an independent board of directors and that neither Allen Klein nor anyone else from Apple would sit on the board. John Lennon, who had been very engaged in monitoring the progress of the Beatles' quest to secure Northern Songs, was infuriated by this requirement. As Peter Brown noted in *The Love You Make,* during a meeting to finalize the details of the deal, Lennon lost his temper and exclaimed to a key member of the consortium: "I don't see why I should work for a company in which I have no say. I'm not going to be fucked around by men in suits sitting on their fat arses in the city." While it is highly unlikely that Lennon's outburst alone cost the Beatles the deal, it was certainly a contributing factor in the consortium's prompt decision to sell its shares to ATV.

Negotiations would drag on for several months, with Klein coming close to securing a very good deal for the Beatles with ATV. The deal that Klein brokered would have had Paul McCartney and John Lennon extend their contracts with Northern Songs for an additional three years until 1976 and George Harrison and Ringo Starr re-sign to Northern Songs through 1976. In exchange, Apple Publishing would get the sub-publishing rights for the United States and Canada. ATV would have also purchased the Beatles' Northern Songs shares for a combination of cash and ATV stock, making the Beatles shareholders of ATV. The

APPLE

94 BAKER STREET
LONDON W1

TELEPHONE
Shop: 01-935 2887
Office: 01-486 1922

PADDINGTON
STREET, W.1

The big break

BELIEVE IT or not—but I'm assured that it's true—the group above, known as Focal Point, actually met Paul McCartney while he was exercising his dog in the park. They persuaded him to listen to them—and the result was a contract with Apple and a new disc, titled "Love You Forever". Quite a break for the four Liverpudlians and one Reading man who make up the group.

WHAT BRINGS THE BEATLES, DONOVAN, BRIAN JONES & CILLA BLACK TOGETHER FOR A SUMMIT MEETING?

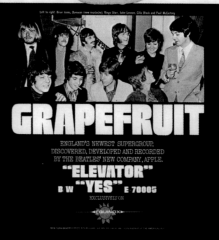

Left to right: Brian Jones, Donovan (rear moustache), Ringo Starr, John Lennon, Cilla Black and Paul McCartney

 3 Savile Row London W.1.

Ò JAMES TAYLOR

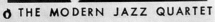
THE MODERN JAZZ QUARTET

Apple Records Ltd 3 Savile Row London W1

deal would have been a win–win for both parties (except, perhaps, for George Harrison, who would have been handing over the copyrights to some of his greatest and most lucrative songs to Northern Songs), but under the advice of John and Lee Eastman, Paul McCartney refused to participate, and the deal fell through.

With no deal on the table, the Beatles wanted nothing more to do with Northern Songs, and they sold their shares to ATV, which ATV was legally compelled to purchase at the premium price that they had offered during their takeover bid. From a short-term financial perspective, the Beatles had profited from ATV's takeover of Northern Songs, but they also lost any chance they would have of ever getting ownership of their songs. To add insult to injury, Lennon and McCartney would both be required to have their songs published by ATV until 1973.

If there was any bright side to the Northern Songs fiasco, it was that both George Harrison and Ringo Starr had not renewed their songwriting contracts with Northern Songs when their original contracts had expired in March 1968. Instead, they had both signed to Apple Publishing, which meant that the Beatles would at least own the publishing rights for songs written by Harrison and Starr.

Klein's first few months working for the Beatles had not been particularly distinguished. After leading the costly separation from Nemperor and then losing the battle for Northern Songs, Klein needed a successful deal to prove his worth to the Beatles. Klein's first real coup would be his re-negotiation of the Beatles' contract with EMI. By early 1969, the Beatles had already produced the minimum number of records required under their 1967 agreement with EMI, and Klein realized that this gave him the leverage needed to renegotiate the EMI contract.

Klein went on the offensive against EMI, suggesting that the Beatles would not make another album until their demands were met. Klein's aggressive tactics during meetings with EMI head Sir Joseph Lockwood nearly cost him another deal, but an agreement was finally reached where, in exchange for the Beatles supplying two albums a year until 1976 (either collectively or as solo artists), the group would receive an unprecedented royalty rate of 58 cents per album in the United States until 1972, at which time the royalty rate for any album that sold more than 500,000 copies would escalate to 72 cents per album. It was an excellent deal – even Paul McCartney was impressed.

In addition to negotiating a significantly increased royalty rate for the Beatles, Klein also secured a piece of the action for Apple Records as part of the deal. The new agreement was quite clever as it stipulated that EMI – who retained ownership of the Beatles' master recordings – would grant Apple the right to manufacture and sell Beatles albums in the United States. Apple in turn would pay Capitol to manufacture the actual records at various Capitol pressing plants. The finished records would then be purchased from Apple by Capitol, who would then sell the finished goods to record stores. The difference between what Apple paid Capitol to manufacture the records and the amount that Capitol would pay to purchase the finished albums from Apple was Apple's profit. Prior to this deal, Apple made no money from the sales of Beatles albums, so it represented a significant flow of income to the company.

Klein's masterful negotiation with EMI was a turning point in his relationship with the Beatles, and John and Lee Eastman were soon eased out of any Apple business, other than to the extent that they would still represent McCartney on the Apple board. Bill Oakes recalls that the new record deal sealed Harrison and Starr's support of Klein, noting that, "Klein's mandate, from George and Ringo anyway, was go and get us a better deal. They were tired of hearing of all these rock groups coming along with these huge percentages. They wanted a better deal, and they were right; they really had a stupid deal, Paul couldn't argue with that. His point was that Eastman could have got them the same deal or more, and they didn't have to go with someone with as unsavoury a reputation as Klein.

"Paul was always conscious and protective of the group's image, even when he didn't want to be known as a Beatle. He felt that Allen Klein was a poor representative for the Beatles. Linda was providing him with the dirt on Klein as she came from New York and knew of his reputation. But John didn't give a shit about that. No one was going to argue with John except Paul, and Paul did it his way, which was he didn't talk to him. I think he knew he was going to be outvoted three to one. Klein's mandate was get the money, and he fulfilled it. It was when he started doing things like the *Hey Jude* repackage (an album of miscellaneous Beatles tracks that Klein released in the United States in February 1970) that Paul's teeth really got on edge. The interesting thing was that almost within weeks of them signing with Klein, there was Mick Jagger appearing. My first encounter with Mick was when he came breathlessly into the Beatles' room to talk to John, to tell him, 'Don't sign, man, cause we're suing him,' but it was too late. They had already signed."

Renegotiating contracts to bring in more money was one part of Klein's strategy to stabilize the finances of the Beatles. The other part would be to sort out Apple. Predictably, he determined that Apple's inflated head count and lax business practices were to blame for the company's financial problems. Though it has long been assumed that it was the excessive Apple-related spending that led John Lennon and the other Beatles to start worrying about their financial well-being, Bill Oakes, the employee who had to sign off and log all of the Beatles' personal expenditures, takes a very different view of the Beatles' financial predicament at that time. In fact, Oakes is adamant that Apple played only a small part of the band's financial woes.

"Trash was really Apple's only flop up until that point," says Oakes. "People think that there was a lot of money spent, but the money at Apple wasn't being spent on things like records. I remember that EMI were horrified at the cost of *All Things Must Pass*, which they said was the most expensive album ever made in EMI history, but the total was just around £70,000. But the money hemorrhaging out of Apple was never really a creative thing. It was not the fact that the Beatles were investing large sums in creative endeavours; it was the rampant kind of waste of things, the houses and things they were treating themselves to. I don't think that Apple could ever be accused of pumping money into creative projects. Klein was able to save the Beatles a little money by having stricter things put on, but the Beatles continued to live exactly as they had before – he couldn't control that. Effectively, I was working for a company called Beatles and Co. which was their own partnership. Apple was a separate entity, and I assume that Apple Records was subject to the usual Capitol and EMI structure when it came to spending. Beatles and Co., which I was paid by, was the Beatles' own holding company from which they paid themselves and all their own expenses, their helicopters, planes, all of that. Beatles and Co. was where there was a large expenditure."

"I think that Apple must have given out a considerable amount of money," recalled Derek Taylor, "but it wouldn't get to six figures in all. What John was initiating with Yoko would add up. John should have recognized that when he was getting panicky and saying, 'We've been bled dry,' and all that. A lot of the bleeding was done by Bag Productions."

Realizing that it would be both difficult and politically unwise to attempt to curtail the Beatles' lavish spending habits, Klein instead attempted to control costs by cutting back the expenditures directly associated with Apple. Having been assessing Apple's situation for several months, Klein's first public course of action was to introduce more traditional business practices to the loosely structured Apple organization.

Where it had once been possible for an Apple employee to go to a shop and charge an item to Apple or to simply get reimbursed from petty cash, Klein instituted a strict purchase order system so that every Apple expenditure had to be cleared through his office. Klein was so determined to cut costs that he even instituted a policy where staff members could order a sandwich from Apple's kitchen only if they were actually working through their lunch hour. But that was just the beginning. Apple's staff knew that it was only a matter of time before

Klein would start cutting jobs.

They didn't have to wait long. The first wave of dismissals came on a sunny spring day in the first week of May. After several months under close scrutiny by Klein, Apple Records President Ron Kass was one of the first people to be fired. "Ron Kass told me that Klein was coming in and that we were all going to be out," remembers Mike O'Connor. "I never met with Klein. Ron told me that he was going to be leaving and that he was going to become president of a record company in the US and that he would be in touch with me and offer me a job. He said the same thing to Peter Asher. And that's how Peter Asher and I went to MGM, Peter going into A&R and me going to be Professional Manager at Robbins Music. We were all fired from Apple. We all knew that there was already a separation between Paul and the other Beatles, so it was no surprise."

Apple office manager and long-time Beatles aide Alistair Taylor was also let go. Taylor, a hard-working, modestly paid employee, was devastated to find out that his position had been eliminated. Taylor repeatedly tried to get a phone call through to John Lennon or Paul McCartney to find out why he was being fired, but neither Beatle would take his calls. The British music press – which had been looking for cracks in the Apple facade since late 1968 – gleefully ran stories of Taylor's dismissal and the other Klein-mandated firings. When finally asked about the way that Apple was handling the termination of employees, Paul McCartney curtly replied, "It isn't easy to be nice when you're sacking someone."

It was Klein's intention to make Apple more efficient and cut down on overhead by getting rid of those he deemed to be non-essential personnel, though many at Apple believed that Klein was also trying to consolidate his power by firing anyone he felt was too close to – or too influential with – the Beatles. The problem was that Klein was not exactly sure which employees were truly close to the group, so he fired or pushed for the resignations of almost all of Apple's senior management just to be on the safe side.

Given his reputation for being a ruthless businessman, Klein uncharacteristically put Peter Brown in charge of carrying out the actual firing. Wanting to avoid any direct confrontation, or perhaps in an effort to not look like the bad guy to the Beatles as he fired loyal, long-time employees, Klein had Brown serve notice to the targeted Apple employees while he was either back in America or out to extended lunches. Barbara Bennett, who was now supporting Peter Brown as well as Neil Aspinall, remembers that Brown was extremely displeased to be given this task. "Poor old Peter Brown had to sack a load of people," she recalls. "Peter used to say, 'Oh god, where's my jacket?' and I would say to him, 'Oh no, not another one you have to sack.' It was awful."

Both Jack Oliver and Tony Bramwell had proclaimed to their fellow Apple employees that they would resign if Ron Kass was ever fired, but both stayed on after Kass was dismissed by Klein. Jack Oliver's decision to stay at Apple was rewarded when, shortly after Kass was fired, Oliver was appointed the new President of Apple Records. "Klein pushed Kass out because Ron Kass knew what Klein was up to. Ron tried to bring it up to the Beatles, but they didn't want to listen," explains Oliver. "What happened was that John brought in Klein, and Paul hated him. Paul wouldn't even want to talk to the guy. In fact, one of the only meetings Paul had with Klein was with me, and that's when he told Klein that he wanted me to be head of the label. I was twenty-three. Looking back on it, I thought I was equipped to run the label, but I wasn't."

Klein also made drastic changes to Apple Music Publishing. The same week that he fired Ron Kass, Klein fired Apple Publishing's Director, Mike O'Connor, song plugger Wayne Bardell, and most of the department's support staff. The only people that Klein retained were Copyright Manager Jean Griffiths and John Hewlett. Hewlett left Apple on his own accord later that summer. "I quit Apple when I got the opportunity to go to the States to work for Tetragrammaton Records, which was Bill Cosby's label," says Hewlett," I didn't get fired."

Out of all the departments that were cut or restructured by Klein, his decision to effectively close down Apple Publishing made the least sense from a business perspective. Located on the top floor of the Apple building and operating in a quiet, reasonably efficient manner, Apple Publishing had signed some excellent songwriters, including George Alexander of Grapefruit, Tony Hill of High Tide, the Iveys, Jackie Lomax, Dave Lambert, Billy Preston, and Gallagher and Lyle. Apple also held the European publishing rights for several high-profile American acts, including the Steve Miller Band, Dr. John, and singer-songwriter Kenny Rankin, who had his song *Peaceful* turned into a top 20 hit by Georgie Fame in early 1969.

Even though Apple Publishing had a staff of five at the time it was reorganized, the overhead for the department was modest and they consistently delivered a return on Apple's investment. According to Mike O'Connor, Apple was ready to sign English publishing agreements with both Randy Newman and Harry Nilsson when Klein shut the department down. O'Connor remembers being very surprised that Paul McCartney allowed Klein to shut down the publishing department, explaining how "Paul was the Beatle who was most interested in Apple Publishing, which was funny because we didn't publish Paul's stuff. We only published George and Ringo. Paul would come up to publishing and listen to songs and writers. One of Paul's big initiatives was changing how we stored songs. We used to cut acetates in Apple's basement studio from reel to reel tapes, so we had these reel to reel tapes with all these songs on them. One of the things that Paul wanted to do was to get very small reels and small boxes and have all the songs in individual boxes. This required a lot of manual labor, and I remember coming in on Saturdays with John Hewlett and doing that stuff. If someone came looking for a song, we had a supply of acetates on hand. And both Wayne and John were running around town with briefcases seeing producers, and they would take acetates with them. Whenever we gave out anything it was on an acetate, but the master was always on a reel to reel tape."

Once most of the Apple Publishing staff had been let go, Essex Music – a large publishing company headed by David Platz – was assigned to temporarily oversee the catalogue of Apple Music Publishing. From this point on, no new songwriters would be signed to long-term deals with Apple, although several artists who signed to Apple Records would be given contracts with Apple Music Publishing. Later in the summer of 1969, Klein would hire Bernard Brown – previously the Copyright Manager at Campbell Connelly Music Publishing – to handle the day to day operations of Apple Publishing.

Having seen firsthand the troubles that Lennon and McCartney experienced as a result of having an outside party control their publishing, George Harrison and Ringo Starr both left Apple Music Publishing around this time and established their own individual publishing companies. Harrison was the first to launch his own company, setting up Sing Song Music in June. The first and only song to be copyrighted by Sing Song Music – which Harrison would soon replace with a new company, Harrisongs – was "Old Brown Shoe." Both Harrisongs and Ringo Starr's Startling Music would operate out of Apple's Savile Row office, and the copyrights to all Starr and Harrison compositions that had been originally published by Apple were transferred to their respective new companies.

Apple Publishing would be paid a fee to administer Harrisongs and Startling Music, but Apple lost a substantial source of revenue when the two Beatles struck out on their own. In addition to losing out on the income derived from the copyrights of five George Harrison compositions (Harrison's four songs on *The Beatles* plus "Sour Milk Sea") and Ringo Starr's "Don't Pass Me By," Apple Publishing also lost its lucrative 50% share of the Cream hit "Badge," which Harrison had co-written with Eric Clapton in 1968.

Once Klein had completed his clear out of Savile Row, Magic Alex and his cozy electronics den in Boston Place was the next Apple department to be identified as a drain on Beatles' money. Klein moved in and suspended all of Apple Electronics' research, and as of Friday,

29 August, Apple Electronics ceased operations. To get some return on Apple's investment in the Boston Place building that had housed Apple Electronics, Klein discarded most of Magic Alex's equipment and prototypes and moved Apple Studios' disc cutting operations into the building.

George Peckham explains: "When they got into rebuilding the studio, they turned the Apple Electronics space into Apple Studios. They moved the desk there and any other equipment that we could move. You'd walk into the reception area of Boston Place and that was where we put John Smith and the tape copying area. You'd walk into the main area – that was the Apple Electronics area – and that was where we had the lathe and did the cutting. We were there for a couple of years. All we had there was copying and cutting, Magic Alex was long gone. He must have gone in the Klein purge, but he still got away with an armful of goodies."

In the wake of the mass firings and other changes at Apple, many of the remaining English staff came to resent Klein and his heavy-handed way of doing business. Peter Asher was one of several Apple employees who grew disenchanted with Apple once Klein took control of the company. At first, Asher tried to work with Klein, but within months of Klein taking over, Asher resigned as head of Apple's A&R on 14 June. Soon after announcing his departure, Asher explained to *Billboard*: "Apple has been changing a great deal recently, and it made it more and more difficult for me to do my work with the same enthusiasm and effectiveness as before," although he diplomatically added, "I shall also be happy to produce for Apple on a freelance basis." In Asher's absence, the responsibility for booking and coordinating recording sessions for all of the Apple artists was assigned to his American secretary, Chris O'Dell.

In a subsequent interview with *Disc*, Asher explained: "When I joined Apple, the idea was that it would be different than other companies in the record business. Its policy was to help people and be generous. It didn't mean actually that I had a tremendous amount of freedom; I was always in danger of one Beatle saying, 'Yes, that's a great idea, go ahead,' and another coming in and saying he didn't know anything about it. But it did mean that it was a nice company to work for. Now that's all changed... it's lost a great deal of its original feeling."

At the time Asher made those statements, both he and James Taylor assumed that they would soon be recording a second album for Apple Records. "There were some discussions about an album," remembers Asher. "We did some recording in L.A., which we had no trouble doing. If we had wanted to do an album, I don't think anyone would have stopped us. Capitol would have paid the bill." After the initial recording session in Los Angeles, James Taylor did, in fact, return to England in June 1969 to start work on a new album for Apple, but as he lamented to *Rolling Stone* later that year, when he finally returned to Savile Row, "nothing was happening. I wanted to record, we were ready to record. They knew I was coming to record, but we couldn't get moving. So I did two television shows, a radio show, two guest club appearances, and came home again."

Taylor was perplexed as to why he was not able to record upon his return to England, but it was most likely nothing more than a simple case of bad timing. Taylor arrived back in London just as Allen Klein was in the middle of his reorganization of Apple. Ron Kass was gone and Jack Oliver had yet to start running the day to day operations of the label, so there was essentially no one in charge of Apple Records who was able – or willing – to authorize a new recording project when Taylor returned to London.

Taylor and Asher returned to the United States to undertake a series of live performances that would ultimately transform Taylor into an underground rock sensation by the end of the summer. Starting with a week at the Bottom Line club in New York City, Taylor went on to a highly successful week-long residency at the Troubadour in L.A. before making a triumphant appearance on 20 July at the Newport Folk Festival. Taylor and Asher made tentative plans to record a new Apple album in New York City sometime in August, but this idea was scuttled after Taylor broke both of his hands in a mini-bike accident on Martha's Vineyard.

While Taylor was recuperating, Asher made the fateful decision to leave Apple and secure a new record deal for Taylor, largely based on the discomfort that he and Taylor had with the prospect of working with Allen Klein. Miles Lourie, an attorney working with Nat Weiss, who was representing James Taylor and Peter Asher, sent a letter to Apple Records S.A. (in care of Apple's London office) on 17 September 1969 informing them that James Taylor was terminating his record deal with Apple. Lourie based the termination on Taylor having been under twenty-one years of age when he signed the contract, and he also claimed that Apple had breached the terms of the contract when they did not provide accounting and royalties as stipulated in July 1969.

Reflecting on Taylor's exit from Apple, Peter Asher is still amazed at how easy it was for James Taylor to leave the label. Indeed, Taylor was under contract to Apple until 1973. "He just kinda left," says Asher. "I knew about Allen Klein before, well, I knew people who had dealt with him. There were certain admirable things about him, but I knew I didn't like his style. It was clear that it was going to be a very divisive issue between the Beatles with John being for him and Paul so against him. All that stuff was going on, and James met with him in London. Allen was convinced he impressed the hell out of James. But James came out of the meeting going, 'I never want to come near that guy again,' so I told him I thought we should get off of Apple. So we just sort of left."

Asher initially attempted to sign Taylor to MGM Records before ultimately signing a deal with Warner Brothers Records on 15 October 1969. "Eventually I met with Joe Smith of Warner Brothers and made a deal for James Taylor, which included them indemnifying us completely from any lawsuits," remembers Asher. "I told him that James and I couldn't afford to get sued, and they gave us complete indemnification, which nowadays a company wouldn't do. Allen Klein served me some sort of legal paper – a notice to appear – but I didn't have to do anything. He did this interview with *Playboy* where he said he sued us for some massive amount. I got one bit of paper, which was like some notification of a suit being filed. I consequently heard that Allen really was going to sue us and that the Beatles talked him out of it. I don't know that for a fact, but I think George told me, 'Oh no, Allen was going to do something,' but then he and Paul had said, 'No, this is not how we wish to be perceived. If an artist is unhappy and wants to go, let them go.' So, in that sense, I may indeed owe George and Paul a debt."

To help pay the bills while he waited for James Taylor to strike it big, Asher had taken an A&R job with MGM Records, where he would report to his former Apple boss, Ron Kass. Upon leaving Apple, Kass was hired to be the new President of MGM, and he quickly brought on several ex-Apple employees to help him revive the faltering MGM label. In addition to bringing Asher and Mike O'Connor to MGM, Kass hired Ken Mansfield away from Capitol to be MGM's Director of Exploitation and Artist Relations. Ken Mansfield remembers: "I ended up leaving Apple at the end of 1969. Peter Asher, myself, Mike O'Connor, and Ron Kass all went together to MGM Records. MGM had been through five presidents at that time and they thought that their salvation, by taking advantage of what was going down at Apple, was to slice off the top of Apple and plug it in on top of MGM. Then three months after we started at MGM, the company was sold and the new owner got rid of Kass and brought in Mike Curb as President of MGM!"

The arrival of Allen Klein at Apple and his subsequent reorganization of the company had totally transformed the working environment at 3 Savile Row. By mid-summer, a once inflated staff of fifty had been slimmed down to approximately thirty employees. The remaining staff were generally able to cover the increased workload, though a few promising projects did seem to fall through the cracks due to the sudden departure of key staff members. With Peter Asher gone, Mortimer had lost their representative at Apple and their proposed single and album were put on temporary hold as Klein determined how best to proceed with the non–Beatles Apple artists.

Another project seemingly lost in the shuffle was an album by the American rock-soul act Delaney and Bonnie. Apple had planned to release their album entitled *Accept No Substitute* on 30 May. Given the catalogue number Sapcor 7, copies of the album had been pressed and were waiting for covers when Apple cancelled the whole project due to contractual disagreements with the duo. Mike O'Connor remembers that the project fell apart due to a money dispute, though he suggests that the project might have been saved had Ron Kass still been running Apple and been available to finalize a deal. "Due to the Beatles popularity, there was such an opportunity to sign talent and sign talent for not a lot of money, because the policy at Apple was that we don't pay any advances," explains O'Connor. "Ron Kass put in the policy that Apple wouldn't pay advances on anything, which cost us a few projects. One was an LP by Delaney and Bonnie, which George really wanted on Apple. George was really pissed off about that."

The plan to issue the Delaney and Bonnie album in the UK may have been scuttled in part by Apple's reluctance to pay advances, but the inconvenient fact that Delaney and Bonnie were under contract to Elektra Records in the United States is likely to have played a more significant role in the non-appearance of a Delaney and Bonnie album on Apple. For the next year or so, lucky visitors to the Apple office would be given copies of the sleeveless Apple pressing of the album. Copies would also be given to any interested Apple staff and artists. A copy of the Delaney and Bonnie album certainly ended up in the Iveys' communal home in Golders Green, where the group added the Delaney and Bonnie song "Someday" to their live set and even recorded the track for a BBC broadcast.

The departure of Ron Kass and Peter Asher had left a gigantic void in the record department. Apple Records' newly appointed President, Jack Oliver, clearly remembers having to work at a frantic pace to compensate for the absence of Kass and Asher. "I had two secretaries, and then there was Bramwell. I did everything. I worked all the time; it was my entire life. I worked from maybe nine, nine-thirty in the morning, to maybe four in the morning, because we would go out to dinner and maybe clubs and socialize. Bramwell and I would hang out all the time, we would go out every night together to the Revolution or one of those clubs. They had a table there for us. Klein cut us down a bit, but not a lot. But we never spent outrageous amounts of money. I was always one of the first ones in. The record department was pretty sane, and the press office sometimes would look down on us with disdain because we did so much work. We'd go up and hang out with them, because it was so much fun up there. Anyone that ever came to London from the States would come to our building and would end up in Derek's office. I never had any problem with Klein. I kept out of his way, and I did my job. He knew that. We worked most weekends, not in the office but outside. We would take off on Sundays and go to the pub."

Of all the remaining Apple staff, Apple Director Neil Aspinall was perhaps the most impacted by the arrival of Allen Klein. Previously consumed with the responsibility of setting up the company, and then with keeping Apple running as smoothly as possible, Aspinall found his duties at Apple greatly diminished once Klein took over operations. Jack Oliver points out that, "When Klein came in, Neil became, I suppose, a lame duck president. He came in every day and worked on his Beatles film and basically acted as a referee between the Beatles and Klein and everybody else."

Klein may not have been given the authority to fire senior employees like Aspinall and Peter Brown, yet he was able to put limits on their power and influence, and the Beatles did little to intervene on their behalf. Reflecting on this period during an interview in the late nineties, Peter Brown explained: "With all of us who came up from Liverpool with them, it was a case of, 'How could they be good since they came from Liverpool with us?' With Neil, for instance, Neil is a very good businessman who is savvy with artists and patient, but he's never been rated like he should have been by the Beatles, because they still think, 'He's our roadie.' The only reason he's survived is the fact that he's the only one that everyone can tolerate. Basically, he's been underestimated in terms of all he's achieved over the years. He's made the Beatles millions of dollars. Not even the generous-minded Ringo valued Neil as much as he should be."

Once Klein had taken control of Apple, Aspinall shifted gears and devoted most of his time to working on a new Beatles film. Steve Brendell – who had joined Apple in 1969 after Rupert's People (a pop group in which he played drums) failed to make it big – worked closely with Aspinall on this film project. "It was through Kevin Harrington (hired to replace Neil Aspinall as Beatles road manager) that I got my job at Apple," remembers Brendell. "Kevin and I had become good friends when we both worked at NEMS, and I had kept in contact with Kevin. Kevin told me to come to Apple to see about a job. So I went to Apple and was interviewed by a woman called Terry, who was the personnel lady at 3 Savile Row. She was in the accounts department, but she also handled people. She interviewed me for a job, and the job I was given was "film librarian." They had collected all of these films over the years, but nobody had done very much with them. I started off in a room in the back of Apple on the ground floor, just below George Harrison's office. It was a room that you wouldn't know was there, and it didn't have any windows. All of the film cans had been just dumped in there, so I went into the room and started sorting films out. Eventually I got to know Neil, because he would call down and ask me to bring a film up to his office. He had a projector in his office, and it became a case of me sitting there every day – with Neil – and we'd run through every piece of film. For a guy my age, who was a big Beatles fan, it was like cloud nine. Neil then started getting very serious, and he had a film cutting room made on the top floor of Apple where Apple Publishing used to be. They spent a fortune on having the floor strengthened so that they could bring all the film up from the room where I had been in, and they had a cutting room made for these two guys to do their cutting work, and I had a small room at the back of the fourth floor, which became my office."

"We would get started around noon. The first thing Neil would have was a bacon sandwich and a cup of tea. He would basically come in and phone the kitchen, Joy Perkins and this girl, Primrose, they were the two cooks. They would cater the lunches that Peter Brown had in his office. He had this big round table set up for lunch when he had visitors. And they would also cook steak dinners for Jack Oliver, who would eat at his desk, and Tony Bramwell. People would drop in while we viewed the films. Ringo would come in, George maybe. Harry Nilsson was quite often there, as was John Gilbert, who was one of Neil's very good friends. Quite often by five o' clock there was always a bit of a party going on, all of these people watching Beatles films and having scotch and cokes or whatever they want. Every week Neil's drinks would come, a box of bottles of scotch and bottles of this and that. A bit like Derek Taylor's office. I was like a fly on the wall. I sat through it every day, and that was generally how it went. By about five or six o' clock I would pack up and go home, and Neil would probably stay there."

In 1996, Aspinall would explain to *Mojo* magazine: "In '69, in all that chaos, the traumas – things were falling apart but they were still making *Abbey Road* – Paul called me saying, 'You should collect as much of the material that's out there, get it together before it disappears.' So I started to do that, got in touch with all the TV stations around the world, checked what we had in our own library, like *Let It Be, Magical Mystery Tour*, the promo clips, what have you. Got newsreel footage in, lots and lots of stuff. We edited something together that was about an hour and three quarters long."

While Aspinall toiled on his Beatles film, Allen Klein was cooking up a Beatles movie project of his own. Realizing that Apple had hundreds of hours of film footage from the January *Get Back* sessions at their disposal, Klein decreed that *Get Back* should be a feature film rather than a television documentary as originally intended. During the course of reviewing Apple's books and contracts, Klein had learned that the Beatles still owed one final film to United Artists and making a feature film out of the *Get Back* footage would enable the group to discharge that contractual obligation.

Once that decision had been made, the *Get Back* project seemed to take on a life of its own. Somewhere along the line it was decided that the project should also include a book. Much of the responsibility of putting together the *Get Back* album cover and book was assigned to 23-year-old John Kosh. Kosh – who as "Kosh" was to become one of the best-known album cover designers of the seventies – remembers that it was John Lennon who brought him to Apple. "I was working in the design department of the Royal Opera. The Royal Opera House housed the Royal Ballet and the Royal Opera and it was real fashionable for pop stars like Mick Jagger and John and Yoko to sort of show up in the royal enclosure, as it were. I was also working as a creative director for a magazine called *Art And Artist* who did a piece on Yoko. All of these things sort of converged at the same time and the next thing I knew I had to go and see John. I got this phone call from John, 'This is John Lennon. Will you come and see me?' I was like, 'Yeah, right.' I was convinced it was someone playing a joke on me, but I showed up at Apple anyway, and it wasn't. We hit it off immediately and we had a lot of fun, and I suddenly found myself working at Apple. I wasn't exactly staff, but I had an office. I started out on the ground floor in Ron Kass's old office until Lennon kicked us out because he wanted the office, then I ended up on the second floor with Derek Taylor. They didn't have an art studio; we just had an office. I used to do the design work at night, come in at lunch and get stoned and then go home again. I was just hanging out, I actually did the work at home."

Kosh considers the *Get Back* project to be one of his greatest professional memories. "Looking back on it, Apple's fees were ridiculously low, but you didn't need much money in those days. We would sometimes get paid in substances, though I don't know how it was channelled. None of the suits and ties ever got an idea of what was going on. But wherever we went, we went first class. Apple sent me to New York for six months, and I lived off the fat of the land, all paid by Apple. We were trying to get the *Let It Be* book published. I had an office on the 45th floor. I got on very well with Allen Klein, he was very good to me. He was very appreciative of what I was doing and very flattering. United Artists had no intention of ever letting that book come out (in America)."

As Kosh recounted, Ron Kass had barely departed Savile Row when John and Yoko commandeered Kass's spacious ground floor office in the front of the Apple building. Having become increasingly involved with activist capers such as their infamous 28 March bed-in for peace at the Amsterdam Hilton, the couple needed a base from where they could coordinate their activities, grant interviews to the world's press, and work on their avant-garde films. To handle their personal projects, the Lennons hired several assistants and established a company called Bag Productions.

Despite the disruption caused by the personnel changes and new business procedures that had been instituted by Klein, Apple was still able to maintain a healthy release schedule. In May, Apple issued a new Jackie Lomax single called "New Day." Produced by Lomax and Mal Evans, "New Day" was a highly commercial pop/soul song that inexplicably failed to garner much radio play or interest from record buyers. The B-side to "New Day" was an old Coasters song, "Thumbing A Ride," that featured Paul McCartney acting as both producer and drummer. During the "Thumbing A Ride" session, Lomax recorded an original composition entitled "Going Back To Liverpool." The McCartney produced track featured the talents of McCartney, Harrison, and Billy Preston, but Apple didn't think that the song made the grade as a single, so it was not released at the time.

In June, Apple scored their biggest hit since Mary Hopkin's "Goodbye" when Billy Preston's "That's The Way God Planned It" reached number 11 on the English singles chart. Unlike the records of the Iveys, James Taylor, Jackie Lomax, and Trash, Preston's dazzling fusion of gospel-influenced R&B and rock proved very popular with the record buying public. "Billy Preston was a dream to work with," remembers Tony Bramwell. "George gave me a finished acetate of "That's The Way God Planned It" on a Friday, I went to Kenny Everett's on a Friday night, and on the following morning he played one minute sections of the song twenty-seven times, and we had a hit."

Preston's record had been released in July in the United States, but despite receiving rave reviews, "That's The Way God Planned It" reached only number 62 during its sixteen week chart run.

Apple would have better luck in the United States with "Give Peace A Chance," John Lennon's debut solo single issued under the moniker, the Plastic Ono Band, in July. Recorded live on 1 June in a Quebec hotel room during John and Yoko's honeymoon "bed-in," the record made number 14 on the American charts. The record did even better in England, where it stopped just short of hitting number one. On the B-side was Yoko Ono's "Remember Love," a song featuring just Ono's voice and Lennon's acoustic guitar that was published by Apple Publishing.

"That's The Way God Planned It" had made getting an English hit look deceptively easy, but the fact remained that the majority of the artists on the label had not yet experienced any significant success. In July, Apple made an odd attempt to reach a wider – and presumably younger – audience by releasing a promotional four-song EP in conjunction with Wall's Ice Cream. Featuring Mary Hopkin's "Happiness Runs," the EP also included album tracks by James Taylor and Jackie Lomax, plus a new song by the Iveys called "Storm In A Tea Cup." Apple hoped that the EP would stimulate some interest in Taylor, Lomax, and the Iveys, but the project did not work out as successfully as anticipated, and it is doubtful that the record helped create any appreciable interest in the featured artists.

Encouraged by the success of the "That's The Way God Planned It" single, Apple issued Preston's *That's The Way God Planned It* album in late August and a few weeks later in early September in the United States. The album was a combination of new tracks produced by George Harrison in London and songs that Preston had already recorded for Capitol Records while he was in America in 1968. Derek Taylor captured Apple's enthusiasm for the record in his somewhat over-the-top liner notes, where he proclaimed that Preston "was the best thing to happen to Apple this year. He's young and beautiful and kind and sings and plays like the son of God."

Given all of the press interest that Preston had generated through his recording activities with the Beatles, Apple was disappointed when Preston's album did not replicate the success of his single. Featuring an extended version of the hit single and catchy pop-soul numbers such as "This Is It," *That's The Way God Planned It* was a fine album that deserved to do much better than it did in England or the United States.

Apple released yet another George Harrison production in August, which was a single by the Radha Krishna Temple called "Hare Krishna Mantra." It was a surprise hit for Apple, who were amazed to see the single reach number 12 in the English charts. Even by 1969 standards, "Hare Krishna Mantra" was a record that could have only come from Apple. In the months since several temple devotees had arrived in England in the autumn of 1968, they had quickly become – with their shaved heads, loud street celebrations, and colourful clothes – a common sight in London. It was inevitable that the Radha Krishna Temple would end up at 3 Savile Row.

One of the temple members, Mukunda Goswami, recalled that the Krishna devotees first came to Apple after Allen Ginsberg arranged for them to meet Peter Asher in late 1968. Asher introduced them to George Harrison, who was aware of the Krishnas and even owned one of the records that the temple members had recorded in New York City the previous year. Harrison was particularly interested in the hypnotic chants performed by the temple and he thought that one or two of them might make a good single for Apple. A session at Trident Studios was booked, and with Harrison playing guitar, bass, and harmonium, the temple members added their vocals and percussion to "Hare Krishna Mantra" and created one of the most distinctive hit singles of 1969. The single did so well that the group was even invited to perform the song on *Top Of The Pops*, which Mukunda Goswami claims to have delighted George Harrison.

The Iveys debut album, *Maybe Tomorrow*, was another record on Apple's summer release schedule. But the album would never be issued in England. Presumably due to the lackluster commercial performance of the "Maybe Tomorrow" single in the UK, Apple elected to only issue the album in Europe, Japan, and America. The Iveys were gutted by Apple's decision not to release their album in England, but they were somewhat consoled by the fact that the album would at least be released in America. Or so they thought. A week before the album's 14 July release date, Apple cancelled the American release of the album. The last-minute decision to scrap the album was most unexpected, especially since Apple had gone through the trouble of assigning the album a catalogue number and had even designed a unique cover for the American market.

The Iveys album did come out in Germany, Italy, and Japan, where it was issued in its original cover featuring a colour photograph of the group, credited to Peter Asher. Asher has no recollection of ever taking photos of the Iveys, and he freely admits, "I didn't have much to do with the Iveys, they were Mal's project." Asher was even unaware that he had ever been credited with taking photos of the band. "I am very much into holiday snaps, but I don't think that was me. It's odd because there were so many cool photographers hanging around."

Contrary to Asher's modest claim of not being a photographer, it appears that he was, in fact, taking an interest in photography during this period. The Apple photo archive still contains three complete Mortimer photo sessions for which Asher was the photographer.

To stimulate interest in the *Maybe Tomorrow* album in several of the foreign territories where it was issued, Apple released the album track "Dear Angie" as a single. Apple apparently neglected to inform the Iveys of the record's existence as "Dear Angie" songwriter Ron Griffiths claims that the band were unaware that the song had been issued as a single until many years later.

Featuring the A-sides to the "Maybe Tomorrow" and "Dear Angie" singles, along with ten other tracks that had been recorded at various sessions in 1968 and 1969, the Iveys album was a solid collection of late sixties English pop. *Maybe Tomorrow* had been assembled from tracks produced by Tony Visconti as well as others produced by Mal Evans that were credited as being arranged by Mal Evans and John Barham. "That was a bit naughty of Mal," chuckles John Barham, who was involved with many of the Iveys sessions. "He was a lovely guy, but he had nothing to do with the arrangements. The Iveys were Mal's first production. Mal was always around when I was working with George. He was spending a lot of time with George at that time, so I knew Mal very well. So when he came to do the Iveys, he brought me in. It was a bit strange, because he didn't have a background in music.

"I had a free hand to do whatever I wanted, so the Iveys didn't have much input on the arrangements. I remember them being very busy at the time. They were always on the road, so they didn't have a lot of spare time anyway. We did most of the recording at Trident and that studio in Barnes, Olympic. I also did some recording with the Iveys in this small studio that I haven't been to since. I remember Nicky Hopkins being at a session as well. Mal had strong ideas and opinions. It was not a question of him sitting around and being passive, he was actively involved with the recording. He would sort of suggest what he wanted by singing something or comparing it to another song. But he certainly wasn't an engineer."

Mal Evans was a tireless champion of the Iveys at Apple, yet despite Evans's obvious passion for the group, Apple seemed hesitant to get fully behind them. In retrospect, members of the Iveys claimed to understand why they had such problems establishing themselves at Apple. Iveys guitarist Tom Evans recalled: "It was very difficult, because you had to be accepted by their [the Beatles'] standards, and we weren't that good. We weren't in the bag of four different people, as everyone now knows they are. Like, McCartney would like one thing and Lennon wouldn't. It was like that. It must have been a weird time for them. They'd got all these groups to promote, and one would be interested and one wouldn't. But all that really doesn't matter. The main thing was that we had to please them to get a record released. That was a good thing, because they wanted a record company that would be fairly well respected."

But in the summer of 1969, and with only one single to their credit in England, the Iveys' confidence had been severely shaken by the way that Apple was handling their career. In the 5 July issue of *Disc*, Iveys bassist Ron Griffiths explained, "We do feel a bit neglected... we keep writing songs for a new single and submitting them to Apple, but the Beatles keep sending them back saying that they're not good enough. We've now come up with a song that Mal Evans says he likes, so perhaps we stand a chance at last." As luck would have it, Paul McCartney read the article and was very concerned to learn that the band felt abandoned by Apple. McCartney decided to become personally involved with re-launching the Iveys, and he soon hit upon the ideal project for the group.

Earlier in the year, McCartney had been commissioned to write the theme song for *The Magic Christian*, a film featuring Ringo Starr. Not having the time or inclination to record the song himself, McCartney convinced the producers of the film to hire the Iveys to perform his composition, "Come And Get It." The Iveys found out about McCartney's gesture on 23 July when they returned home from a gig to find a letter from Paul McCartney requesting a meeting with the group. The next afternoon, they met McCartney at EMI's Abbey Road Studios, where the Beatle informed the star-struck Iveys that he had read the *Disc* article and that he wanted to help. McCartney told the group about the *Magic Christian* project, and the Iveys were given an acetate of McCartney's solo recording of "Come And Get It" so that they could learn how to play the song. The group was given a week to work up a suitable version and on 2 August, McCartney took the Iveys into Abbey Road to record "Come And Get It."

It would be a memorable day for the Iveys. In addition to being given the opportunity to record with Paul McCartney, John Lennon made an unexpected appearance while McCartney was working on the arrangement for "Come And Get It" with the Iveys. Ivey Tom Evans recalled seeing John Lennon and Yoko Ono walking into the studio, noting that, "Lennon stopped and looked over at Paul, bowed his head, and said, 'Oh wise one, oh sage, show us the light.'"

In a 1970 interview with *Disc*, Tom Evans elaborated on the uncertain environment that the Iveys found themselves in at the time McCartney offered to let them record "Come And Get It." "We were just making album tracks and weren't doing anything as far as a single was concerned, so we began to feel depressed. We kept submitting tapes to Paul and George, but they were always returned as 'unsuitable for release.' The Beatles were worried when we weren't doing well, but Paul has always taken the most interest. When he wrote "Come And Get It," he offered it to us because he knew we had nothing to do... he told us, 'I'm going to do this, but don't expect any more.' When we did the single, we thought it was too simple because only piano, bass and drums are used... but now we realize what a genius Paul is... he knew what he was doing. Our music is simple – it has teeny-bopper appeal – and is aimed at middle-of-the-road people who like neither reggae nor progressive music. But, like the Beatles, we're gradually going to progress... we don't intend to be a real way-out group; just a simple, hard rock group."

Despite their initial lack of success, the Iveys remained confident that Apple was the best possible label for the group. Iveys drummer Mike Gibbins recalled: "Apple regarded us like we were kids. We were young lads. Little did they know we'd sell a lot of records. We'd always go to Apple for a reason, and then we'd end up staying all day because Apple was like one big happy family. George worked with us, Paul worked with us, Ringo used to hang out at our sessions. John was a bit aloof – he never bothered with us much. I saw James Taylor around, but I never got a chance to talk to him. We used to rehearse down in Apple Studios before they gutted it out. It looked great, but nothing worked. Mad Alex (sic) was there all the time, trying to fix things. The guy was a maniac. We used to hang out with the Apple staff a lot, go out to pubs. Especially Debbie at the front desk. She used to eat daffodils all day. They used to bring in a bunch of flowers, put them on her desk, and she'd eat them. We used to be a bunch of stoners. It was later on that we got introduced to all the good stuff. Mal used to come over with the Beatles' stash and get us stoned. Mal used to come over to our house and stay all night, and we'd just be tripping all night. They were good times."

Being young musicians who were suddenly given the opportunity to work with the Beatles, it's not surprising that the Iveys look back at their time at Apple with fondness. For Paul McCartney, however, Apple was rapidly becoming a source of great displeasure. While McCartney would continue to release his records with an Apple label until 1974, the Iveys recordings for *The Magic Christian* soundtrack would be the last production work that McCartney would undertake on behalf of Apple. McCartney had been the Beatle who had been the driving force behind its creation, but he seemed to lose interest in Apple once Klein assumed control of the company. By Christmas 1969, McCartney had for the most part stopped visiting the Apple offices, and the few times that he did come in, it was only to attend critical business meetings.

It was painfully clear that no real working relationship would ever develop between Allen Klein and Paul McCartney. To his credit, Klein tried hard to gain McCartney's confidence. McCartney was certainly pleased with the increased royalty rates that Klein had negotiated with Capitol and EMI on behalf of the Beatles, but he remained unwilling to simply go along with the other three Beatles and accept Klein as his manager.

Peter Brown believes that the problems at Apple were not only due to Klein but also to differences in opinion between McCartney and Lennon. "I think one of the problems that surfaced was because, in the early days, Paul had always been the most conventional and most business minded of the Beatles, and when Apple was set up, he took the most interest in it. He was the driving force behind the record company and virtually everything else we did. John at that time was pretty out of it, and the other two liked the idea, so they just went along with it. After Klein came in, Paul saw Apple as a place that had been taken over by someone he saw as an enemy, and he wasn't going to contribute to it. He saw Apple as an obnoxious place to come to, and he wouldn't come to Apple. Paul tried to avoid coming to Savile Row, so he would send John Eastman to the Apple meetings."

Reflecting on the strained relationship between McCartney and Klein, Bill Oakes suggests that, "Klein became absolutely obsessed with McCartney, in my opinion, by virtue of not being able to see him. He never had an artist who wouldn't see him, and it drove him nuts. Everyone thinks that Paul went off his rocker and was quite mad and rude about Klein, but the fact is that Paul had a nice, wicked sense of humour about him. There was a time when McCartney made an appointment to meet with Allen Klein at Marble Arch one afternoon. Klein kept on badgering me, asking, 'Where's Paul, where's Paul?' and he wanted to know if he was in town. I told him that Paul was in town, and I called Paul and told him that Klein wanted to meet with him. Paul said, 'Oh yeah, I'll meet him.' At first, he told me to send him around to his house on Cavendish Avenue, which obviously Paul then thought better of, because how then would he get rid of Klein? So Paul said, 'Tell you what, tell him to meet me at 2 o'clock at Speakers Corner at Marble Arch.' So I called Peter Howard and this secretary, Jane, who actually worked for Klein and told them what Paul had said, and Klein was flabbergasted that Paul actually agreed to meet him. Then I told them, 'Well, there's a catch. He doesn't want to meet here at Apple or at Cavendish Avenue, so how about Speaker's Corner at 2 o'clock?' Then a bit later Paul called back and had me ask, 'Paul wants to know, how will he recognize you?' He wanted to rub it in, and he knew that this would be an insult.

"It turned out that the clouds flew over and it got dark around lunchtime, and it really got raining by 2 o'clock; it was a downpour. Even if it hadn't rained, Paul had no intention of going, of course. He loved the idea of Klein standing in the rain until nightfall. For him, it wasn't enough that it happened. He had to tell people, which was his downfall, and that's when he sounded a bit cruel. Klein was a charming villain. He knew all the words to the Beatles' records, which made him even more villainous to Paul. They weren't happy campers from day one with Klein. John and Paul wouldn't want to be caught hanging out together after that."

Given the tensions that existed between McCartney and the other three Beatles at the time, it was most surprising that the group were able to put aside their differences long enough to venture into Abbey Road Studios in the summer of 1969 to record what would turn out to be their final album.

During the sessions for the album that would become *Abbey Road*, McCartney squeezed in time to produce two final songs for Mary Hopkin, "Que Sera, Sera," and a song written by Apple Publishing's

Gallagher and Lyle, "The Fields Of St. Etienne." Hopkin recalled the session for "Que Sera, Sera" as: "Just one of Paul's fun ideas. It was one sunny afternoon, we were sitting in Paul's garden, and he said, 'Do you like this song?' I said, 'Well, I used to sing it when I was three,' and he said, 'My dad likes it, let's go and do it.' And so Ringo came along, it was all done in one afternoon. I was sort of swept along with Paul's enthusiasm, really. By the time I was halfway through the backing vocals, I said, 'This is awful.' I really thought it was dreadful and I didn't want it released."

Hopkin may have been unimpressed with McCartney's efforts, but McCartney's final burst of Apple production activity during the summer of 1969 would provide a massive lift to the professional fortunes of the Iveys. Drew and Dy, the Apple group for whom McCartney had produced a session for the previous summer, had been hoping to receive a similar boost to their now dormant career, but neither McCartney nor anyone else at Apple had ever reached out to schedule a new recording session for the duo.

"Because we had been signed to the Beatles, we had a few record companies like Phillips and Fontana who wanted to sign us up," explains Pete Dymond. "So we did a really silly thing. We had McCartney's number at his house at St. John's Wood, and I phoned him up and asked him to let us know what was happening. He said, 'Don't you trust me?" and I told him, 'Yes, of course we trust you, but it's been a year and we haven't had a record out.' So, he asked, 'Do you want to be let out of your contract then?' and I said, 'Yes.' It was a silly thing to do because he said he would get around to recording us again, but he said if you don't trust me, I'll let you out of the contract. He had us call someone at Apple who cancelled our contract with Apple Records and gave us the rights to the songs (which had been assigned to Python Publishing) back. It was the stupidest thing I ever did in my life. And then, like that, we couldn't contact him anymore. He used to change his number a lot, but we always knew what it was being changed to, but suddenly we no longer knew his number. We had a big change of heart about six months later. We wrote to him two or three times, but he wouldn't answer."

Given the changes that had taken place at Apple over the preceding months, the summer of 1969 had been a time of uncertainty for both the Apple staff and the artists who were under contract to the company. But there was a palpable air of excitement around the Apple office that summer as the Beatles put the finishing touches on their new album. There was a fresh, upbeat quality to the music found on *Abbey Road*, yet the recording sessions did little to reduce the tensions within the group. With each passing month, John Lennon was growing increasingly tired of being a Beatle, and by September 1969, Lennon seemed to have also grown tired of Apple.

Speaking to Zapple Records head and journalist Barry Miles, Lennon seemed to be particularly upset about the state of the company. "Apple was a manifestation of Beatle naivety, collective naivety, and we said we're going to do this and help everybody and all that. And we got conned just on the subtlest and grossest level. We didn't get approached by the best artists, we got all the bums from everywhere... they'd been thrown out from everywhere else. And the people who were really groovy wouldn't approach us because they were too proud... that's why it didn't work. And then we quickly have to build up another wall around us to protect us from all the beggars and lepers in Britain and America that came to us. And the vibes are getting insane. And I tried, when we were at Wigmore Street, to see everybody, like we said, 'You don't have to get on your knees.' I saw everybody, day in, day out, and there wasn't anybody with anything to offer society or me or anything. There was just, 'I want, I want,' and 'Why not?' – terrible scenes going on in the office with hippies and all different people getting very wild with me."

It was certainly true that Apple – with the notable exceptions of Magic Alex and the Fool – had found no non-musical artists to back, but Apple Records had accomplished far more than Lennon seemed willing to admit. In fact, earlier in the same interview, he had been enthusiastically praising Hot Chocolate's version of Lennon's "Give Peace A Chance."

Contrary to what Lennon may have thought, many top artists had indeed tried to align themselves with Apple. Mick Fleetwood (who was married at the time to Jenny Boyd, sister of George Harrison's wife, Patti) tried to get his group, Fleetwood Mac, signed to Apple. Although there were some preliminary discussions, Apple seemed to be unable to follow through with a deal and Fleetwood Mac eventually signed to another label. Tony Bramwell remembers that several of the biggest rock acts of the seventies came to Apple early in their career. "We almost signed Queen, Gilbert O'Sullivan, but no one was really interested," he recalls. "I remember going to see Yes at the Marquee with John Lennon, and he really liked them. We put them into the studio to do some demos, but nothing came of it. By the time we got to the signing stages, John would say, 'Aah, I don't really like it, let's just forget it.' So we did."

Peter Asher also remembers pursuing Yes for Apple. "I don't remember why we didn't sign them. I heard them in a club, maybe the Scotch, and I loved them. They did a Beatles song, too, "Every Little Thing," it was a very cool version, very original. I did some demos with them with Andy Johns engineering at Morgan Studios. It sounded great. I don't know what happened with Yes." The members of Yes were enthused by the prospect of signing to Apple, and they had hoped to get Paul

McCartney to produce them. But during the audition session for Apple, guitarist Peter Banks's recollection was that Peter Asher spent most of the session reading a newspaper before finally just walking out of the studio. No offer was ever tendered from Apple, and Yes would ultimately sign to Atlantic Records, for whom they would sell millions of albums in the years that followed.

Crosby, Stills & Nash had also approached Apple to see if Apple was interested in their debut album. The group was guaranteed to be a highly commercial act, but Apple allegedly passed on Crosby, Stills & Nash due to the band wanting too much money and their stipulation that Paul McCartney produce the album. Stephen Stills recalled: "We invited George Harrison over to listen, to see if Apple might be interested in us. After we finished, he went, 'Wow.' Then he turned us down. The English attitude towards American musicians was a lot more competitive than I expected."

Mike O'Connor remembers being told that Harrison cooled on the idea of signing CSN to Apple after his initial meeting with the group. "George wanted to sign them, and then there was a meeting – where I wasn't present – but I was told by Peter that what broke the deal was that one of them made the remark that, 'Well, do you think that Apple is good enough for us?' and George replied, 'Well, is CSN good enough for Apple?' and then George turned off on them."

Graham Nash recalled speaking to George Harrison about Apple in the early eighties: "George told me he heard us on tape, but I don't remember making any tapes in England then. We *could* have. But, anyway, George tells me, 'It's damn lucky CSN didn't end up on Apple, because things were so totally chaotic you would have been swallowed up in the bullshit.' So I guess the luckiest thing that ever happened to CSN is that we didn't end up on Apple."

The list of artists who would go on to great success but who had first approached Apple for a record deal is extensive. And for every group – such as Yes, CSN, Fleetwood Mac, or 10cc – who were granted auditions or were in preliminary discussions with Apple, there were others who had sent in tapes, only to receive a form rejection letter back from Apple. Future member of the Eagles and popular 1970s American solo artist Joe Walsh submitted a tape to Apple in the summer of 1968 and still has a rejection letter signed by Derek Taylor thanking Walsh for submitting a tape of his soon-to-be-successful group, the James Gang, informing Walsh that Apple was not interested in the James Gang at the present time. So, while Lennon may have thought that all of the truly creative artists were not coming to Apple, the reality was that a good number of them were and that Apple simply didn't have the infrastructure and processes in place to properly evaluate the submissions that were coming in, and as a result, the company missed out on several artists who would go on to great success in the seventies.

Justified or not, Lennon's frustration with Apple was yet another source of friction between him and McCartney. "We could hear them arguing sometimes through the wall," remembers Graham Lyle. "We left in late 1969. We were forming McGuiness Flint when we were still with Apple during the summer of 1969, but there was never any discussion of McGuiness Flint being on Apple. In fact, I remember going to see Neil Aspinall and saying, 'We've got this offer from an American record company, and they want the publishing as part of the deal,' and Neil said, 'Just do what you need to do and don't worry about it.' He was very generous from that respect, and that was the end of our relationship with Apple. My experience at Apple was very positive. I know the Beatles were going through a tough time, and we were aware of that. Apple was a bit chaotic. Each day you would go in there and there would be something totally different happening. It was a very exciting time to be around, but it was chaotic."

Gallagher and Lyle went on to enjoy considerable success after leaving Apple. Their new group, McGuiness Flint, scored an English hit single with "When I'm Dead And Gone" in early 1970. Former Apple Publishing staff member John Hewlett managed the group.

The period immediately after Klein's reorganization of Apple was a confused, sometimes dispirited time for those who remained with the company. But the staff did their best to carry on business as usual. It was not always an easy task given that most of the employees that Klein had fired or drove out of Apple were those who had the most music industry experience. Once Apple had released all of the records that had been in the pipeline before Klein's arrival, Apple seemed uncertain of how it should best proceed.

The seemingly straightforward task of deciding what song to issue as Mary Hopkin's next single exemplified the lack of direction at Apple in the aftermath of Klein's staff purge. Apple was looking to release "Que Sera, Sera" or perhaps a dramatic new version of "The Fields Of St. Etienne" (produced by Apple Studio head Geoff Emerick) as an English single in September. The catalogue number Apple 16 was reserved for the record. But at the last hour, Apple cancelled Hopkin's single, and for a moment, it looked as if Apple 16 would be Mortimer's long-delayed recording of "On Our Way Home." But Mortimer's single never materialized, and Apple 16 would never grace the shelves of English record shops. Apple 16 would ultimately be utilized as the catalog number for "Que Sera, Sera" in several European markets when it was issued as a single several months later.

Mortimer's Tom Smith recalled that the group were never given an explanation as to why "On Our Way Home" was not released. Once Mortimer had finished recording their album, they could do little else but hang around the Apple offices and wait for Apple to release their album or even a single. "We used to hang around with Pete Ham and Tom from the Iveys," he remembered. "We used to hang around downstairs and rehearse and go out to pubs. We didn't go to each others homes – we didn't have a home actually – but we used to hang around Apple together and have a few drinks after that."

In retrospect, it was probably just as well that neither Mortimer nor Mary Hopkin put out records in September, given that most of Apple's resources would be consumed by the release of the Beatles' *Abbey Road* album. Apple wouldn't release any new non-Beatles records until October, when they released three new singles in both England in America. The first was Trash's version of the Beatles' "Golden Slumbers."

Trash had experienced a great deal of difficulty coming up with a suitable follow-up to "Road To Nowhere." At one point, it was not even clear if Trash would get the chance to record another record for Apple. Earlier that summer, Richard DiLello had secured a meeting with Paul McCartney and Jack Oliver to plead his case for Trash, only to have Neil Aspinall walk in on the meeting to proclaim that he heard Trash rehearsing in Apple's basement and that "they were no fucking good." DiLello argued that Aspinall had heard the band under less than ideal conditions, and the house hippie was ultimately able to get McCartney to agree that Trash should record some demos so that Apple could determine if the group had enough material for an album.

But before demos could be cut, Trash needed material to record, and they solicited suggestions from several members of the Apple staff. Richard DiLello gave them a few ideas, before Derek Taylor came up with an inspired solution. Knowing that Trash needed a really strong second single to get their career off the ground, Taylor suggested that Trash listen to a copy of the still-unreleased *Abbey Road* album and select a song that they could cover. This opportunity could not have come at a better time for Trash. "We had been hanging around Apple and doing a lot of gigs but not making much money, and things were getting a bit desperate with the band," remembers Fraser Watson. "There was no money, and we were starving. We didn't get any money from Apple. Just money we got from gigs. We hadn't had any money for seven weeks, we lived on a bag of crisps for two or three days. Tony Meehan was that tight; he didn't want to spend any money.

"Derek Taylor realized we were struggling, and he did an incredible thing. The Beatles had just got back together to do *Abbey Road,* and there were five demo acetates that had been made, one for each of the Beatles and one for Neil Aspinall. Derek went into Neil's office when he went out for lunch and stole the acetate, gave it to us, we went home to the house on Ladbroke Grove, recorded it on our reel-to-reel tape recorder, and took it back to Apple. Derek said, 'Pick the most commercial song off that, and I'll stick you into Trident Studios where George Harrison has time booked that he's not been using, and we'll record it.' So we picked "Golden Slumbers" and did our own version of it. It was George Harrison's studio time, and we even got to meet George Martin when we went to get the orchestra score for the strings. We just used, like, ten strings. By that time Colin Morrison, the bass player, had left the band. He had decided that music was not for him, and he was getting a bit tired of traveling, so I played the six-string bass and guitar. We also recorded the B-side, "Trash Can," at that session. It was just thrown together quickly for the B-side."

Trash recorded an absolutely superb version of McCartney's "Golden Slumbers." Fresh from playing countless shows in clubs across England and Scotland, Trash gave McCartney's gentle ballad a much-needed rough edge and turned the neglected album track into a highly commercial rock single. Fraser Watson recalled that: "Derek was happy, but the Beatles had to be consulted and at least two of them had to agree on any project. George Harrison was away somewhere, Ringo agreed, but McCartney didn't. So we were sitting in the office with our (press) reception all set up, waiting from a reply from Lennon. Yoko took the thing to him, then came back and said, 'OK. It's going to be released.' That kept us going for a wee while, but there was a kind of Apple backlash going on in the media and we didn't get to do *Top Of The Pops*."

McCartney's refusal to authorize the release of "Golden Slumbers" took Trash and their champions in the Apple Press Office by surprise. McCartney had been under the impression that Trash were simply going to record a few demos for further consideration. Instead, the band went off and recorded a full-blown single of one of his songs, complete with orchestral overdubs and a B-side. McCartney was so incensed by what he considered to be an unauthorized recording session that he refused to sanction the release of the single. Richard DiLello remembered that it was an exasperated Taylor – who, along with DiLello, had become quite fond of Trash – who took the acetate to play to John Lennon in the hope that Lennon would overrule McCartney. As Taylor had expected, Lennon listened to the acetate and proclaimed, "That's a good imitation of us... it's going out."

Whether or not Lennon actually liked the single or if he was just trying to upset McCartney will probably never be known, but "Golden Slumbers" was issued in October. It was extremely well done and received the full support of the Apple Press Office, but Trash's version of "Golden

Slumbers" only reached number 35 in the English charts. The chart performance of the Trash record was not helped by an EMI Records group, the Orange Bicycles, rush releasing a cover version of "Golden Slumbers" to compete with the Trash record. This gesture underscored the less than perfect nature of the relationship between Apple and its distributor.

Billy Preston's "Everything's Alright," a remixed version of the *That's The Way God Planned It* album track that Preston had written with Doris Troy, did not even chart when issued as Apple's next single. Given that Preston's previous single had only just missed the English top ten, Apple was surprised by the profound lack of interest in "Everything's Alright." Jack Oliver believes that the problem was that, "Things like Doris Troy and Billy Preston were difficult to break in England. It was a very American style of music and, at that time, that type of music wasn't selling that well."

Oliver maintains: "We had to put a lot of effort into non-Beatle acts, because the Beatles themselves would sit on us. In the case of Trash, I think that the Beatles weren't that fond of the group. I don't think that they thought Trash were that good. The trouble was that if they didn't like it, and they didn't bring pressure to bear on everybody, then people would push their efforts in other directions. Trash never even got the chance to record an album."

Trash did cut additional material for a possible album in early 1970, but only two tracks – including their final Apple recording called "Would You Believe" (cut on 4 March 1970) – remain in the Apple tape vault. "We started working on an album for Apple," explained Fraser Watson. "We were a great live band. Unfortunately, we weren't songwriters. We demoed another Hugh Nicholson song, who was still with the Poets at the time, called "Bad Weather" (recorded 2 Feb 1970), which was a good song. We did a couple of our own songs; I think we put four tracks down, but when Allen Klein came in, that was it, no more money. Tony started hawking the band around again to different record companies, trying to get something happening. By that time, the band was changing. We had got another guitar player in, and I started to draw back from the band, and I eventually left."

The final single that Apple issued in October 1969 was a fascinating cover version of John Lennon's "Give Peace A Chance" done in a reggae arrangement by an unnamed group that had literally walked into Apple from off the street. The group came to the Apple office with a finished master tape and asked if Apple would release the record. Derek Taylor recalled that, unlike most of the visitors to Apple at that time, "They were not awfully friendly. They didn't want a drink, they didn't want a cup of tea, they wanted to play this fucking song to John Lennon.

So we went down to the record department's office with Jack Oliver, heard this fabulous little record, and John liked it. And again, they went somewhere else to succeed."

Lennon, like most of the Apple staff, absolutely loved what this mysterious group had done with "Give Peace A Chance," and they were offered the opportunity to release it as an Apple single, despite only three months having elapsed since the Plastic Ono Band had issued the original version of the song. Since the group didn't have a name, they asked Apple to provide them with one. It was Mavis Smith from the press office who came up with the Hot Chocolate Band. Their Apple single received enthusiastic reviews from the music press but didn't chart, and no one at Apple gave any thought to seeing what else the Hot Chocolate Band may have had to offer. The following year, the Hot Chocolate Band would modify their name to the simpler Hot Chocolate and sign with producer Mickie Most's RAK Records. Under Most's tutelage, they would hone their pop skills and go on to become one of the best-selling English pop bands of the seventies.

Apple also issued an album that October, which was the Modern Jazz Quartet's second and final Apple album. Entitled *Space*, the album had been recorded in England in March. But now that their principal contact at Apple, Ron Kass, was no longer with the label, Apple took minimal interest in the MJQ, and no one was surprised when the group returned to Atlantic Records soon after the release of *Space*. The MJQ's John Lewis remembered: "We were on tour in Europe, and at the end of our tour we took a few days in London to record *Space*. We recorded it at Trident and Peter Asher supervised the session. I was the music director. I like the Apple albums very, very much. They're some of the best things I think we ever did. The Beatles were having difficulties getting the company started, and when Ron left, that was the end of that deal. We met George Harrison once because Connie Kay played on an album with him, so George came by the studio one day. We didn't meet the other Beatles, so after Ron left, we went back to Atlantic."

The official wind-down of the Zapple label also came to pass in October, the victim of Allen Klein's ongoing efforts to nurse Apple back to financial health. The dysfunctional subsidiary label was one of the last active components of Apple's original goal of being an altruistic, arts-based organization, but from a business perspective, actions like this were long overdue. As Klein dug deeper into Apple's books, he was shocked by the irregularities that he uncovered. Preparing the financial accounts of Apple up until only the end of 1967, Klein learned that during this period, Apple's accountants had written off three cars that could simply not be accounted for and had authorized Apple Electronics to issue non-business related cash advances to art gallery owner John

Dunbar in the amount of $4,800 and to Magic Alex for $2,400.

Out of necessity, Klein had transformed Apple into a new, more American-styled type of company. "At the time when he came over, he had this American attitude, which was 'better in my bank account than theirs,'" explains Barbara Bennett. "He changed the system and wouldn't let us pay vendors at the end of the month, which is the way the English always did it. I went to him one day and told him this not paying at the end of the month is wrecking so many of our contacts because they are small companies. If you don't pay this guy who delivers George's milk, he's gonna stop delivering George's milk, and you're going to have to explain to George Harrison why he has to go out to the shop to buy it. I was always having to find new contacts and laundry people, because he wouldn't pay them until sixty days later."

Apple's English staff had to adapt to the curious cultural differences that existed between them and the sundry Abkco employees who would turn up with Klein at Savile Row. To this day, many of Apple's former artists and staff still vividly remember Apple's American Promotion Manager, Pete Bennett.

Bill Oakes stresses that, "With Klein, when he came to England, at that time he was about as curious a figure as the Maharishi. Suddenly there was this scruffy little guy from Brooklyn at Savile Row with a five o'clock shadow with these guys in spats. They acted like American gangsters from the movies. Pete Bennett was a boy playing at it, but Phil Spector was the real deal, going around with loaded guns. Pete Bennett was the first physical evidence that Klein had arrived. Suddenly there was this ridiculous person in a loud double-breasted suit at the top of the stairs checking people's credentials in an office where they had lived and worked for two years."

Pete Bennett concedes that he and most of the Abkco employees were quite unlike the people working at Apple in London at the time. "I didn't look like them, I didn't have the long hair, I was a different character, everyone was asking, 'What the hell is Peter Bennett doing with these guys?' The continuity wasn't there. They were saying, what is he, a Mafia guy, a tough guy? The thing with the Beatles and Apple was that I produced. I got them hits. When I told them I was gonna break a record, I did it. The Beatles required a lot of attention. When they came to America, I would pick them up at the airport, set up media interviews at the airport. I was acting as almost a personal manager. I was an advisor, I took them to dinner, I did everything besides the records. We had a lot of fun. We had a close relationship."

Tony Bramwell acknowledges that however unlikely an Apple employee Pete Bennett appeared to be, "John adored Pete Bennett. He might have been an effective promotions man, but he wasn't in the

Beatles' or Apple's image."

Fortunately for Apple's English staff, Klein still needed to devote significant effort to running Abkco, and he and Bennett were generally unable to remain in England for extended periods of time. Klein had an office in the Savile Row building, but the office was seldom used. To ensure that Apple continued operating in an orderly fashion in his absence, Klein had appointed a trusted Abkco employee, Englishman Peter Howard, to oversee operations at Savile Row. Howard was given the empty room in front of the press office on the second floor. "Klein wasn't too involved with the day-to-day running of Apple," remembers Pete Bennett. "Peter Howard worked for Klein in London and Terry Mellis helped him out, but they were mostly into the accounting end of it."

Klein also established an American office for Apple in late 1969. Apple had originally intended to base their American operations in Los Angeles, but Klein decided to locate the office in New York City. The Apple office was set up in space leased from Abkco on the 41st floor of a new skyscraper at 1700 Broadway, on the corner of Broadway and 53rd Street. The North American Beatles Fan Club would soon follow Apple to 1700 Broadway, moving into an office on the 40th floor.

Apple's English staff were disappointed that Apple would not have an office in California, but the shared office space arrangement with Abkco was the best possible way for Apple to establish itself in the American market. Unlike in Apple's London office, all of the employees working on behalf of Apple in the New York office were actually Abkco employees. In addition to keeping costs down by using Abkco support staff, Apple now had the services of Pete Bennett, a highly regarded independent radio promotions man.

Bennett recalls: "I ended up with Apple because the Beatles wanted the same promotion guy as the Stones. In 1969, I was an independent promoter and was working with Klein on the Stones. They actually came to me first; they wanted me, not Klein. The only reason Klein got them was because of me. He told them that he was working with Pete Bennett, and that was how he got three of the Beatles to agree to let him manage them. They wanted me for promotion. Then they found out Allen Klein knew nothing about the recording business, he was just an accountant, and not even a certified accountant. I first got involved with Klein when Allen got Sam Cooke, and Sam told Klein that the only way I'll go with you is if you get Pete Bennett to promote me. Cooke was a big fan of Nat Cole, whom I was promoting, and he wanted the same promotion man as Cole. So Allen says, 'I know Pete very well,' although we had never actually worked together. Allen was doing work for Scepter Records, a company which I was promoting. So Klein made a deal with me and with Sam. Then in 1964 Mickie Most came in and was involved with Klein, so I ended up working with Most, too — Herman's Hermits and the Animals. But Klein didn't know anything about promotion. I was not an Abkco employee, I was independent. I was collecting a check from Abkco and Apple Records. It was a real busy time working for Apple and the Stones. I was still doing the Stones up until 1976, even after the Stones left Klein in 1970."

Having secured an American office and the services of a seasoned radio promotions man, all that Apple needed now was some product to release. That new Apple product turned out to be the second single from the Plastic Ono Band. Inspired by the withdrawal symptoms that John Lennon and Yoko Ono had experienced during their recent flirtation with heroin, "Cold Turkey" was a raw expression of personal pain. Lennon had originally hoped to record "Cold Turkey" with the Beatles, but after McCartney and Harrison balked at the idea, Lennon decided that "Cold Turkey" would be issued by the Plastic Ono Band. With the Beatles unwilling to put the group name on his latest creation, Lennon recruited Ringo Starr, Eric Clapton, and Klaus Voormann to back him on the recording.

To drive home the extremely personal nature of the song, the record came packaged in a sleeve that displayed x-rays of John and Yoko's heads. Kosh, the designer of the record sleeve, remembers: "The "Cold Turkey" sleeve was kind of scary, putting John Lennon's head under an x-ray machine. I didn't know if he was going to go blind or something. John and I thought it up on a drunken afternoon. That's really his head and his glasses, it wasn't retouched or anything, and Yoko was on the other side." Given the song's unpleasant subject matter and the raw, visceral nature of the recording, "Cold Turkey" was only a minor hit on both sides of the Atlantic.

In England, Apple's final release for 1969 was scheduled to be the Iveys recording of "Come And Get It." For several months, the music weeklies had noted the imminent release of "Come And Get It" by the Iveys, but when copies of the record finally materialized in the shops in early December, the group's name had been changed to Badfinger.

The Iveys had apparently been unhappy with their name for quite some time. As the sixties progressed, the group felt that their name was sounding increasingly dated, and they also found themselves being confused with the mid-sixties harmony-pop hit makers the Ivy League. When Iveys bassist Ron Griffiths was asked to leave the band in November 1969 (he was replaced by guitarist Joey Molland, with Iveys rhythm guitarist Tom Evans switching to bass), the remaining Iveys decided that the time had come to finally change the name of the group. After rejecting Paul McCartney's suggestions of "Home" or

"Mama's Boys" and John Lennon's "Prix," the group finally agreed on "Badfinger," which had been put forward by Neil Aspinall. Badfinger had been derived from "Badfinger Boogie," which had been the working title of "With A Little Help From My Friends."

By the final days of 1969, most of the remaining Apple staff had begrudgingly resigned themselves to being part of "an Abkco managed company" (a phrase that Klein would add beneath the Apple logo on the record sleeves of almost all of the albums released by Apple in the United States in 1970) and had adapted to the new business parameters put in place by Klein. Klein's arrival at Savile Row had brought to an end the freewheeling guest admission policy that had characterized the Apple of 1968 and early 1969. With Klein in command, colourful characters like the Hells Angels, Emily's Family, and Stocky – the drug frazzled American teen who spent two months perched on top of a filing cabinet in Derek Taylor's office drawing pictures of genitalia – were no longer welcome. The Apple building had become more subdued, and sights such as Jeremy Banks leading a donkey that he wished to present as a gift to Derek Taylor through the Apple office would not be seen again at Savile Row.

Still, Apple would remain open to guests who managed to get an audience with one of the Beatles or a senior Apple executive. Even after Klein had assumed control of the company, Derek Taylor remained exceptionally dedicated to keeping at least some spark of Apple's original idealistic fire alive. It was this sense of duty to Apple's original goals that had briefly pitted Taylor against the future Virgin Group founder, Richard Branson.

Taylor met Branson in December 1968 when, at the age of eighteen, Branson came to Apple to see if he could get one of the Beatles to contribute music for a flexi disc that was to be distributed with a magazine he was running called *Student*. Taken by the young Branson's impassioned pleas, Taylor innocently promised a tape of words and/ or music by John and Yoko. In *Fifty Years Adrift*, Taylor recalled how, "Branson kept coming in to see if there was any progress, and one afternoon he helped me address Christmas cards as one of a team of visitors I had seconded to essential office tasks. He looked so pessimistic and young, seated on the floor, that I wrote on a card I was signing, 'Trust me, Richard... [signed] Derek.'"

It was in early 1969 that Taylor finally got John and Yoko to submit a tape, which turned out to be a recording of the fading heartbeat of the couple's miscarried baby. After what Taylor described as a "retrospectively hilarious listening session at Apple Studios," Branson and his recently acquired lawyers found the recording to be quite unacceptable.

Soon after that meeting and using the Christmas card that Taylor had signed as evidence, Branson served Taylor with court papers and attempted to sue the hapless publicist for breach of contract claiming £10,000 in damages. Taylor was very upset by the incident and even circulated a memo to Apple management stating that they could take the damages out of his wages should Branson prevail. Fortunately for Taylor, Branson decided against taking him to court.

As for Derek Taylor, perhaps he learned – as the Beatles had done before him – that the best intentions are often abused by the very people that they are intended to benefit.

1970: AND THEN THERE WERE THREE

The grey winter skies of January 1970 were typically English and a harbinger of the new decade that had been ushered in with great fanfare on New Year's Eve 1969. The sixties had ended, and there already was a discernable feeling in the air that the days of London being the fashion and music capital of the world may be nearing a close. Before the end of the year both Janis Joplin and one-time Apple guest Jimi Hendrix would be dead, and the Woodstock and Isle of Wight music festivals would prove to be high water marks of the dynamic sixties youth culture that was starting to recede. The curtain had come down on the sixties, and music, politics, and even society itself would enter a sustained period of marked change. Come December 1970, John Lennon would sum up the feelings of the generation who grew up listening to the Beatles when he sang in a harsh, world-weary voice that "the dream is over." While the dream may not yet have been completely over, the sixties dream that the Beatles had come to represent for so many people was certainly entering its final hour.

Inside the Apple office, the arrival of Allen Klein, and his subsequent remaking of the company, certainly contributed to a general feeling that the passing of the sixties had indeed been the end of an era. Yet in many ways, Apple had not changed all that much from what it had been a mere eighteen months earlier. Despite the numerous staff dismissals that had taken place throughout 1969 and the looming presence of Klein and Abkco, many of the original faces could still be found at 3 Savile Row. In the second-floor press office in the rear of the building, Derek Taylor, Richard DiLello, and Mavis Smith still held court, constituting perhaps the last remaining bastion of Apple's original idealism. In the record department on the ground floor, Tony Bramwell, Jack Oliver, and Oliver's two secretaries were busier than ever with a myriad of Apple Records projects, and from his well-appointed first floor office, Peter Brown still attended to the increasingly divergent needs of the four Beatles.

By the start of 1970, the staff at 3 Savile Row had more or less come to terms with Apple's traumatic transformation into what was now little more than a fairly orthodox independent record label. The staff kept calm and carried on, largely unaware of the growing tensions between the four Beatles and having no idea that the entire Apple organization was being drawn into the drama of the impending split of the band.

The new decade had started on an auspicious note for Apple when Badfinger's "Come And Get It" crashed into the English top ten in January, validating Mal Evans's intense belief in the humble, hard-

163

working rock band from Wales. To Joey Molland – who had been an unemployed Liverpool musician only a few months earlier – Badfinger's sudden fame was a particularly surreal experience. One of Molland's most vivid memories from that era was the first time he met one of the Beatles: "A couple of months after "Come And Get It" hit, we went into Apple, and George Harrison was coming down the stairs. He congratulated us and said, 'Well, you know that from now on, you'll have to play that song every day for the rest of your lives!'" Full of youth and optimism, it would be many years before Molland and the rest of Badfinger would appreciate the prophetic nature of Harrison's remark.

"Come And Get It" was swiftly followed into the English top ten by Mary Hopkin's new single, the calypso influenced "Temma Harbour." The bright and breezy "Temma Harbour" was a particular milestone for Hopkin in that it was her first Apple single to not be produced by Paul McCartney. McCartney has since said that the primary reason he stopped producing Hopkin was that he was not particularly interested in the folk-oriented direction that Hopkin wanted to pursue at the time. But "Temma Harbour" was not remotely folk. If anything, McCartney appeared to have lost interest in making any further creative contributions to Apple. The Apple staff remember McCartney as having stopped coming into the Apple office soon after the September release of *Abbey Road*. Having begrudgingly come to accept that the other three Beatles had given Klein their full support, McCartney seemed to have lost interest in Apple, and perhaps even the Beatles.

There had been a Beatles recording session on 3 January, when McCartney, George Harrison, and Ringo Starr got together at EMI to record "I Me Mine." But after the session, McCartney went into virtual seclusion, leaving London and decamping to his remote Scottish farm.

With McCartney out of the picture, Apple had needed to find a new producer for Mary Hopkin. Mickie Most – a proven pop hit maker – was eventually given the job. Since 1965, Most had produced a formidable string of hits for the Animals, Donovan, the Yardbirds, Herman's Hermits, Jeff Beck, and others. Most was one of the top English record producers of the sixties and a logical and quite sensible choice to produce Apple's most successful pop artist. Most also had strong ties to Allen Klein (who had represented Most, Donovan, and Herman's Hermits in the United States), so it was not surprising that he was selected to be Hopkin's new producer.

Mary Hopkin did not initially object to Most being hired to produce her new recordings. Hopkin explained: "The reason I worked with Mickie was that, obviously, Paul and I agreed that it wasn't going to work out, because he hadn't the time, and I had to get more material out. We came up with Mickie Most, and I thought, 'Oh, that might be good,' because he'd produced Donovan, who was very sensitive and does beautiful music. Unfortunately, Mickie took a different approach with me, and that's when the rot set in. The crunch came when Mickie visited me at my final summer season. We'd been going over some songs to record, and he said, 'Choose the keys, and I'll go away and record them. When you got a chance, you can come down and do the vocal.' I said, 'No way, I have to be there, I want to discuss the arrangements. I don't want to be a session singer.'"

Despite Hopkin's misgivings about the material she was being asked to record and Most's polished, highly efficient production style, she eventually acquiesced to the wishes of both Apple and her management and recorded several singles with Most.

To this day, Hopkin seems to have little affection for the majority of the material that she recorded with Most, but it should be noted that all of the records did make the English top 40. Other Apple artists were far less fortunate than Hopkin when it came to getting their music into the pop charts. Billy Preston was finding that even if you could get one of the Beatles to produce and perform on your records, there was no guarantee that the record would be a hit. In January 1970, Apple released "All That I've Got," a soulful new song by Preston, produced by George Harrison, and which was Preston's first new recording since the release of his *That's The Way God Planned It* album. Co-written by Preston and Doris Troy, "All That I've Got" was a fine, earthy R&B number, but lacking the pop appeal of Preston's earlier singles, it failed to make the charts in either England or America. Doris Troy also recorded a spirited version of the song, but it would not be heard until more than two decades later.

Like Preston, Jackie Lomax was also finding it difficult to establish himself as a pop star. In February 1970, Apple gave Lomax one last crack at stardom when they released the gospel-influenced "How The Web Was Woven," a song that George Harrison had produced for Lomax in November 1969. Lomax remembers: "Apple seemed to have a hard time picking singles. "How The Web Was Woven" was supposed to be my commercial song that they found for me. We recorded it at Trident and Leon Russell played everything – the drums, the bass, the slide guitar, the organ – he was like a mad genius."

"How The Web Was Woven" certainly sounded like a commercial pop record and it was given reasonable airplay by the BBC, yet it failed to chart and Apple declined to pick up their option on Lomax. "How The Web Was Woven" likewise saw little action in the way of radio play or sales when it was released in America in March.

Lomax felt that the failure of "How The Web Was Woven" was due in no small part to the way that Allen Klein was running Apple. "Allen

Klein was not going to spend any more money, period. No one could figure out what was happening. I tried to get to see him at Apple, and he wouldn't see me. I was just going to say, 'Look, am I ever going to record again, or what?' and I never did get an answer, I never did get an interview with him."

Since recording "How The Web Was Woven" in November 1969, Lomax had spent several months kicking around London as he waited for Apple to release his new single. Considering that *Is This What You Want?* had sold around 50,000 copies and had – to his knowledge – not lost money for the label, Lomax assumed that Apple would be willing to continue to back his career. In a 1970 interview with *Rolling Stone*, Lomax confided that, "He [Klein] came in and put a stop to everything going out of the company, to get a chance to re-evaluate things. There I was, with a band, set to go out on the road. He didn't know me at all. It was, 'Hey kid, where do you think you're going?' I think I wound up going out with 50-watt amps... Apple was always saying, 'We're your record company, not your booking agent,' so Klein never spoke to me to find out what I was into. They stopped answering my phone calls. I owed them a certain number of sides a year, but all I cut was a single that George produced. Finally, I had a solicitor's letter sent to them asking what was going on. They said the man in charge of the matter would get back to me in three weeks. Well, I got some pride, so I had another letter sent saying, 'I consider our association terminated.' They haven't yet answered that one."

With his recording career at Apple in limbo, Lomax had returned to playing live music, touring around England in early 1970 and recording an album with a blues-rock band called Heavy Jelly. Pete Ham and Tom Evans of Badfinger were featured on the album, contributing backing vocals to a song called "Take Me Down To The Water." The Heavy Jelly album was a good record but was never released due to business problems experienced by Head Records, the label that paid for the recordings. Finally giving up on both Apple and England, Lomax left for America just before Christmas 1970, where he later recorded several unsuccessful albums for Warner Brothers Records.

Contrary to Lomax's belief that it was Allen Klein's indifference to his music that was at the root of his inability to crack the charts, Derek Taylor explained that Klein had little to do with Lomax's failure to get a hit. "Jackie was given all the shots that a young rock and roll hopeful could have had in the sixties, both at Apple and later at Warners, but he never came through as a star. Perhaps the problem was that stars at that time had a lightness of spirit, while Jackie was a little melancholy. Anyway, his time was not to be. I agonized a lot about him, because I knew it wasn't happening for him the way that it should. I had a big joint one day on Virginia Water Station; when I got to Waterloo I went to the bar, had a couple of large gin and tonics, and I thought I had it cracked. I went into the office and said, 'Jackie Lomax should go MOR.' He should become The Gaucho, dressed in incredible boots, baggy pants, a moustache, and a huge shirt with large sleeves and knock 'em dead in the clubs. My assistant, Richard DiLello, said, 'I think you need to calm down, Boss. This is an appalling idea, and Jackie Lomax will never forgive you for it.' So I never put it to Jackie myself..."

Jackie Lomax was one of several Apple artists to be cut from the label's roster in the early part of 1970. During the same period, Apple decided to cease working with Trash and Mortimer. They were not formally dropped, rather, Apple simply stopped answering their calls and let their respective contracts expire. Guy Masson of Mortimer clearly remembers trying to get a meeting with Allen Klein so that he could find out where Mortimer stood in relation to Apple. "In early 1970, I ran into George Harrison and said, 'Hi George, do you know when our record's coming out?' and he said it would be out in two weeks. I told him I think that the group is breaking up, and he didn't know what to say, so he told me, 'Oh well, you'll make more money that way.' Our album had already been done for months and was sitting there. I had seen everything there was to see in London, and the group was dissipating in front of me."

Masson finally lost his patience and decided that his only option was to confront Klein directly. "At the time I might have had a warm beer from one of the pubs across the street or something," he remembers, "so I went in and said, 'Where is Allen Klein?' They said he's on such and such floor in such and such office, and I just charged in there and saw this man behind a desk with a light, with these two huge business guys, all in suits. I don't remember what I was doing, but I was ranting and raving about our album and what was going on, can we get this finished, and Allen Klein just kinda looked at me and said to these guys, 'Could you escort this man out, please?' so they took me out, they escorted me right out of his office, down the stairs and to the lobby and said, 'Please leave Mr. Klein alone.'"

According to Masson, Peter Asher had expressed interest in taking Mortimer with him to Warner Brothers. "Peter knew about Mortimer breaking up before it was happening, and Peter, I know, approached our manager and said, 'Let's go back to the United States, let's take the group with us, and we'll go with James Taylor and Mortimer to Warner Brothers.'" In the end, Mortimer's management chose not to go with Asher. Masson believes that Iveys manager Bill Collins was also interested in managing Mortimer, but with the group collapsing, nothing ever developed from that interest. As Masson feared, Apple never did release any of Mortimer's recordings, and the group broke up.

Mortimer's Tom Smith confirms that Peter Asher was indeed interested in Mortimer and says that Asher actually invited him to join James Taylor's band. Smith explains: "After our Apple album was shelved, Peter played me a tape of James Taylor's "Fire And Rain." By that time, I had had enough of Mortimer and that acoustic business. I wanted to go back to playing electric, so I had decided to leave Mortimer. Peter was putting a band together to go to America with James Taylor, and he asked me if I was interested in playing lead guitar for James Taylor. Arrangements were being made for all of this when I got a letter from my draft board in the United States. I remember both Apple and Peter sent the draft board letters saying that I was under contract for another year, but they took my passport and put out a warrant for my arrest, so I couldn't join Taylor's band. It was a big disappointment."

Listening to the excellent record that Mortimer made for Apple, it's not immediately clear why Apple chose not to release the album. Recorded in one of London's top studios and having been given expensive orchestral overdubs and a final mix, Apple certainly spent a good deal of money on the recordings. "The group visited arranger Richard Hewson's apartment several times, where we worked out beautiful orchestrations," explained Guy Masson. "We had a full tilt, ten-person chorus sing on some of the songs. I remember that for "On Our Way Home" he worked out this little trumpet sound, a popular sound back then (arranger Mike Vickers was hired to play this "trumpet sound" on George Harrison's new Moog synthesizer). As far as I know, Apple never did any test pressings, only acetates, and they never did a cover."

The Mortimer album was by no means a ground-breaking work, but it is an excellent collection of acoustic-based rock. Several tracks, including the poppy "You Don't Say You Love Me" and "Pick Up Your Heart" – a soulful rock ballad on which Mortimer's acoustic guitars and conga drums are blended with a swirling Richard Hewson string arrangement – could have both realistically done well as singles in America, where Mortimer was already a known entity through the positive press and radio exposure they received with their 1968 debut album for Phillips Records.

Mortimer had delivered a very good record with definite commercial potential, but what most likely scuttled the release of the album was that Allen Klein reviewed their contract and realized that Apple was obligated to give Mercury-Phillips 25% of any royalties generated from Mortimer's Apple recordings until the $17,065.54 that was owed by Mortimer to Mercury-Phillips was recouped. In 1970, you had to sell a lot of records to earn $17,000, and Klein rightly determined that Apple stood to make very little money by releasing the Mortimer record. So they never did.

With Jackie Lomax, Trash, and Mortimer out of the picture, a good deal of Apple's attention shifted to Doris Troy. Since the spring of 1969, Troy had been working on material in Apple's basement rehearsal room, but nothing had yet been issued. In addition to her own material, Troy had been spending time writing and recording music with keyboardist Chris Hadfield for an Apple Films project. Ringo Starr – then father of two young boys – had decided to engage Denis O'Dell and Apple Films to produce *Timothy Travel*, a new children's show that was developed in conjunction with puppeteer Gerry Anderson of *Thunderbirds* fame. Working with Hadfield, who had come to Apple's attention through his session work for Jackie Lomax, Troy recorded close to a dozen songs and pieces of incidental music for the show. A pilot episode of *Timothy Travel* was completed (and still exists), but the proposed series never materialized. None of the music developed and recorded by Troy and Hadfield for the show would ever be released either.

Apple decided, finally, to issue a Doris Troy single in February 1970. "Ain't That Cute" – a powerful hybrid of R&B and rock that was co-written and produced by George Harrison – should have been a big hit for Troy and Apple. It received favourable press and respectable airplay, but the record failed to sell. Troy had no idea why it took Apple so long to release her debut single, although she suggested that, "While we were doing the sessions at Trident Studios, George's mother died and that kind of stopped the sessions for a little while, and I had to finish it up on my own."

Even after Troy had been signed to Apple, she continued to work as a session singer and remembers that she didn't feel any real pressure from Apple to release records. Perhaps because of her previous success in the mid-sixties, Troy seems to have received a much better deal from Apple than the other Apple artists. In sharp contrast to Jackie Lomax or the pre-Badfinger Iveys, who subsisted on meagre publishing advances and the receipts from live performances, Troy recalls: "I was on a nice salary. I never had any problems with money; the money was always there. I never wanted for anything. Apple rented me a gorgeous flat. It was fun being there and we got a lot of things done. They even gave me my own office next to Peter Asher. The next thing I know Peter Asher had left with James Taylor. We had fun, it was a wonderful time."

The commercial indifference to Doris Troy's single had been genuinely unexpected, and it was a big disappointment to Apple. Fortunately, the label would have better luck in March with a new Mary Hopkin record. The single – a frothy, Mickie Most produced pop number called "Knock Knock, Who's There?" – was given the dubious honour of representing the United Kingdom in the 1970 Eurovision Song contest. Though "Knock Knock, Who's There?" did not secure top Eurovision honours, the resulting publicity made the song Hopkin's biggest hit since "Those Were The Days." Packaged in a special "Song for Europe" picture sleeve, the single climbed to number two in the English charts. For reasons unknown, Apple elected not to release the single in America.

Hopkin, who by this time was more interested in pursuing her folk muse than being a showbiz personality, was particularly aggrieved at being – as she saw it – coerced into representing England in the Eurovision contest. But as Derek Taylor would later note, "The middle of the road did not seem to us to be the wrong direction for someone who had come from *Opportunity Knocks*."

Apple's next single would be "Govinda," the second George Harrison produced offering by the Radha Krishna Temple that was literally a world away from the saccharine pop of "Knock Knock, Who's There?." Featuring a haunting string arrangement composed by John Barham, the record had much more of a contemporary rock feel than "Hare Krishna Mantra," and it managed to climb to number 26 in the English charts.

Apple held an outdoor press reception on 5 March to promote the single in the U.K. "I remember hiring a marquee in a big garden in Sydenham... a lunchtime reception," recalled Derek Taylor, "and watching with apprehension as the devotees casually wet-shaved each other's heads in the conservatory of the big house in order to look their best for the press, who turned up in great numbers hunting in vain for the bar. The journalists were thoroughly puzzled, thirsty and quite annoyed by the direction in which things had taken their mop tops and their press officer."

The Radha Krishna Temple record was released in multiple international markets at different times throughout March. "Govinda" did not emulate its UK success in America, but Apple's US operation finally saw some respectable chart action that month with several singles that had been released earlier in the year. Mary Hopkin scored with "Temma Harbour," which climbed to number 39 in the charts. More impressively, Badfinger's "Come And Get It" made the American top ten. Badfinger's *Magic Christian Music* album was released the same month, and by April it had reached a very respectable number 55 on the American album charts.

In the UK, Apple had released the *Magic Christian Music* album in January, where it sold a decent number of copies but not enough to make the charts. Perhaps due to the simple nature of "Come And Get It" and the fact that the song was written by Paul McCartney, Badfinger were perceived to be something along the lines of a teeny-bopper pop act in England. As far as the English market was concerned, this unfounded perception of Badfinger being a pop band would stick with the group for the remainder of their career.

Apple promotions manager Pete Bennett remembers that breaking Badfinger in America was not a simple task. "Come And Get It" may have been written by Paul McCartney, but Bennett claims that American radio was initially reluctant to get behind the single. "We spent thirty to forty thousand dollars breaking that first Badfinger record. George Harrison was pleading with me to do something for Badfinger, so I broke "Come And Get It" on WLS in Chicago by buying air-time, one minute commercial spots, and playing "Come And Get It." It was like a paid advertisement, but the radio station didn't make us say it was. After we started playing the spots, people started calling in and the program director started playing it, so that's how we broke Badfinger in America."

Despite the substantial effort and resources that were being spent on Badfinger's behalf, Apple seemed to have been caught off guard by Badfinger's sudden success. Once "Come And Get It" was scheduled for release in England, the *Magic Christian Music* album had been hastily thrown together by Apple in order to get an album into the shops to capitalize on the almost certain success of the single.

Magic Christian Music was the debut album of Badfinger, but the record was to all intents and purposes an Iveys album, given that new guitarist Joey Molland did not perform on any of the songs. Faced with the prospect of having no album to cash in on the success of a hit single, Apple compiled *Magic Christian Music* from tracks taken from the Iveys' *Maybe Tomorrow* album, the three songs that the Iveys had recorded for the soundtrack to the *Magic Christian* film, and several other songs that the band had recorded in the summer and autumn of 1969.

Apple was in such a rush to release *Magic Christian Music* that they could not even arrange to have a picture taken of Joey Molland in time for inclusion on the album cover. The liner notes, written by "Mal," state that "Badfinger are four" and lists Molland as a band member, yet only the three remaining Iveys are pictured on the back cover. "It didn't bother me, these kind of things seem to happen," offers Molland. "I just got to work learning their songs and trying to put my two cents into things, and that's just how I worked it. I thought it was kind of weird that they put my name on it, and it was a bit of a joke within the band that I was the shadow coming around the corner on the cover!"

The cover and record label also neglected to give Paul McCartney credit for the three songs he had produced, simply stating that the songs were from the soundtrack of the *Magic Christian* film. A fourth McCartney production, "Crimson Ship," was incorrectly attributed to Tony Visconti.

Released at a time when some English albums still featured 14 songs (as opposed to the 11 or 12 tracks found on typical American albums), the UK edition of *Magic Christian Music* included two songs that were not on the American album – "Angelique," a remix of a pleasant ballad from the *Maybe Tomorrow* album, and "Give It A Try," a group composition that the Iveys had submitted to Apple as a possible follow-up to the "Maybe Tomorrow" single but which had been rejected by Apple. *Magic Christian Music* was essentially a patchwork compilation of tracks that had been recorded over a two-year period, but the end result was an impressive album that showed great promise, despite being stylistically rooted in the decade in which it was recorded.

Successful records by Badfinger and Mary Hopkin did much to dispel the perception that Apple was merely an outlet for Beatles projects, yet there was certainly a great deal of Beatles-related activity at Apple in the early months of 1970. Making up for the lacklustre public response to "Cold Turkey," John Lennon – this time credited as John Ono Lennon (with the Plastic Ono Band) - reached the top ten in February with his third solo single, "Instant Karma." Produced by legendary American producer Phil Spector, "Instant Karma" served as an informal production audition for Spector. Both Lennon and George Harrison – who had assisted Lennon on the "Instant Karma" session – were impressed with Spector's work, and they engaged Spector to assemble an album out of the *Get Back* tapes, hoping that Spector would be able to make the rough performances suitable for release.

Much of the first quarter of 1970 would be devoted to preparing for the release of what would ultimately be known as the *Let It Be* film and album. Work on the *Let It Be* project was almost complete by early spring, and on 1 April, Richard Hewson joined Phil Spector at Abbey Road Studios to record the string arrangements that Hewson had written for "The Long And Winding Road" and "I Me Mine." Hewson was well respected at Apple, but he was not Spector's first choice to arrange the songs. On George Harrison's recommendation, Spector had originally tapped John Barham to write and conduct the string parts. Unfortunately for the recently married Barham, the session was scheduled to take place while he was to be away on his honeymoon, so Spector assigned the project to Hewson instead.

With Apple Records having scored several non-Beatles hits and a new Beatles album scheduled for an April release, on the surface it appeared that all was well within the Beatles organization in the early months of 1970. The reality of the situation, however, was that there was serious in-fighting going on between the four owners of the company, or rather between Paul McCartney and the other three Beatles.

Still reeling from Allen Klein gaining control of Apple, McCartney's next battle with the other Beatles came over their decision to have Spector produce the *Let It Be* album. Enraged by the orchestra and choir that Spector had overdubbed onto his poignant ballad "The Long And Winding Road," McCartney was adamant that Spector's version of the album not be released. "Paul McCartney hated the strings on *Let It Be*," remembers Pete Bennett. "He didn't want Phil Spector producing the album. Paul complained to us, but we put it out anyhow. It wasn't even Klein's doing; we put it out because John Lennon wanted it out. You have to understand that Lennon was the Director of Apple Records. Lennon had the last say. The four of them owned the label, and for whatever reason, they made Lennon the president when they set up Apple."

McCartney's anger over *Let It Be* was compounded by the fact that he had been informed by Apple that the release date of his solo album, *McCartney*, would have to be postponed so as not to draw sales away from the *Let It Be* album and *Sentimental Journey*, the Ringo Starr solo album that had already been scheduled for release in April or May.

Tensions were running high between the four Beatles, yet almost everyone working at Apple was as surprised as the rest of the world when the 10 April issue of *The Daily Mirror* broke the story that Paul McCartney was leaving the Beatles. "There was never any watershed day when they broke up," maintains Bill Oakes. "The depth of the ignorance about the Beatles actual personal situation was amazing to me. The fact that the Apple Records staff, the accountants and the promotions people, they had no idea that the Beatles weren't still living and sleeping in one bed. I remember after I had been there about a year, I brought up some small domestic thing and people were shocked. They still viewed the Beatles in some sort of time warp. I don't think that the people outside of myself and Peter Brown, the people working for Beatles and Co., had any idea that this time bomb was ticking. They were all very affected when the Don Short story was published. They all thought they were going to be pink slipped the next day, which I thought was a bit naive. Peter Brown had to remind me that not everyone was privy to the inside world of the Beatles."

The *Daily Mirror* story was based on information that came directly from Derek Taylor. The actual interview from which McCartney's quotes were taken was conducted by Oakes: "I remember the interview that Paul had me do which was then quoted around the world as 'Paul quits the Beatles.' Although Derek has been taking credit for it, I did that interview. Paul didn't want to talk to anybody, but he wanted to get it out in the air and he wanted the information available to everyone. So he asked me to write down twelve questions that I would consider key if I was a journalist. Then he gave me the answers and wanted them printed up and included with every promotional copy of the *McCartney* album. So I told Derek that we would have to handle it quite carefully as the answers were quite incendiary, so Derek said, 'Let me handle it,' but I told him, 'No, you don't get it. He wants this printed up and sent out to every journalist who is reviewing the album.'"

Quoting the "interview" that McCartney had done with Oakes, Taylor proceeded to "leak" the information to Don Short of the *Daily Mirror*. "All of a sudden it was 'Paul quits Beatles,' when it really was not about him quitting the Beatles, it was about promoting his album," says Oakes. "Actually, each of them was saying they'd quit. It was sort of a self-fulfilling prophecy. By saying he was quitting the Beatles, he ended the group because none of them liked the idea that it was him who was quitting."

John Lennon, in fact, was furious that McCartney had trumped him by announcing that he was leaving the Beatles. As early as the fall of 1969, Lennon had been telling the other Beatles that he "wanted a divorce" and it was only at the urging of Allen Klein – who was still finalizing a new contract for the Beatles with Capitol Records – that Lennon had agreed to keep his intention to leave the group to himself until the new contract had been executed. Regardless of the circumstances, it was clear that the Beatles would not be working together again anytime in the near future.

Fittingly, it was Derek Taylor who was called on to offer Apple's official statement to the world. A brief press release issued on 10 April reflected the complicated nature of the split as well as Taylor's eternal optimism and reticence to believe that the Beatles had ended. Taylor wrote:

> "Spring is here and Leeds play Chelsea tomorrow and Ringo and John and George and Paul are alive and well and full of hope.
>
> The World is still spinning and so are we and so are you.
> When the spinning stops – That'll be the time to worry, not before.
>
> Until then, The Beatles are alive and well and the beat goes on, the beat goes on."

Today, the break-up of the Beatles is often seen as nothing less than an end of an era, and as perhaps a fitting and convenient end to the sixties. The Beatles were certainly mourned in many circles when the group split in April 1970, but it was hardly looked upon at the time as an epoch defining event. To pop fans of the day, the Beatles' split was seen as little more than a very popular rock group deciding to go their separate ways. Once *Let It Be* had been released and the immediate repercussions of McCartney's split with the Beatles had subsided, new idols were soon found and the pop music machine marched on to a new tune.

Mere weeks after McCartney announced that he was leaving the Beatles, fans were given the opportunity to see the group disintegrating before their very eyes when the *Let It Be* film was released in May. *Let It Be* captured the Beatles in the final stage of their musical partnership, still making music together, but seemingly without any genuine enthusiasm and often with a significant amount of tension clearly evident between the members of the group. The London premier of the film drove home the intensity of the split. Where once all four Beatles could be counted on to attend the premier of a new Beatles film, not a single Beatle attended the 20 May premier of *Let It Be*.

The Beatles had ceased working together, and many in the music industry and press naturally assumed that Apple would soon implode as well. But Bill Oakes stresses that McCartney's announcement had little direct impact on Apple. "It really made no difference to me on a day-to-day basis. They were all still there, they still had records coming out. It really got sticky later in the year. I left at the start of 1971, by which time it was real cloak and dagger stuff. Initially, it was quite funny. Paul used to write to me as 'Bill Oakes – An Abkco managed company,' and he would use me to find out what Klein was doing at Apple. But it was not too attractive when all the lawyers started coming in."

Once *Let It Be*, Ringo Starr's *Sentimental Journey* and Paul McCartney's solo album had been issued, Apple entered a relatively quiet period, and there was limited activity in Apple's London office during the summer of 1970. In March, Derek Taylor had started a six-month sabbatical to work on a book project. He would come into London each Thursday to check on any new developments and to get his mail, but with each visit to Apple he became aware that there was precious little to do. In Taylor's absence, Apple press matters would be handled by his assistants, Mavis Smith and Richard DiLello.

The summer lull at Apple was not due to any lack of effort on the part of the Apple recording artists. With Mal Evans producing, Badfinger had recorded three new songs in April, including a catchy, Beatlesesque rock song written by group leader Pete Ham called "No Matter What." Mal and Badfinger thought that the powerful "No Matter What" would make an excellent follow up to "Come And Get It." An excited Evans proudly brought a tape back to Apple and played it to everyone in the office, but after the tape had been listened to, word came back from the record department that the song wasn't commercial enough and that Apple was not going to issue "No Matter What" as a single. According to members of Badfinger, Apple even suggested that Badfinger record a version of Ringo Starr's recently completed composition, "It Don't Come Easy," as the follow-up to "Come And Get It."

"What probably happened with "No Matter What" was that the tape was brought in and listened to by Paul or John and that they didn't like it," suggests Jack Oliver. "That would happen sometimes. It was their label, and if they didn't like something, no matter how good we thought it was, if they didn't approve it, we couldn't put it out. I do remember trying to get Badfinger to record "It Don't Come Easy," but I don't remember why."

With no new records being issued and the ex-Beatles lying low after McCartney's announcement that he had left the band, there was little excitement to be found in Apple's once bustling headquarters. In the eerily quiet press office, Richard DiLello and Carol Paddon were perfectly content to while away the hours reading magazines, gazing out the window and generally enjoying the calm that had engulfed Apple. But the lack of activity became unbearable for acting Press Officer Mavis Smith, who resigned from Apple in June 1970.

With Smith's departure, the press office was left in the hands of Richard DiLello. Speaking to *Rolling Stone*, DiLello admitted: "The day after Paul's statement was released it was bedlam. But for just that one day. Then it got quieter than it had been before... I guess it's just the summer doldrums. I got worried one day and called Jo Bergman at the Stones' office, but she said everything was quieter than usual in her office, too – that it's always like this at this time of year. Anthony Fawcett has left John and Yoko, but there haven't been any sackings. We'll all have jobs as long as we want them. The accountants will always be busy. They're not going to assassinate the building... I think it [the Beatles' split] will go on for about a year, then there will be a reconciliation. It won't jump like it used to jump. We're not going to sign any new artists for a while, we want to hand pick them. But it's still a gig for the Beatles, you just get what they want."

Peter Brown elaborated on DiLello's statements: "We still have four employers... they still demand the same amount of attention. They're all releasing albums, after all. Allen Klein's arrival caused much more of a bomb than Paul's announcement... people did leave then. It's a bit quieter. We don't have Mary Hopkin or Jackie Lomax now. But Doris Troy, Billy Preston, the Radha Krishna Temple will be recording... George is working on a solo album. And there will be another Beatles film. They are to be seen together again for the first time in a documentary being put together from the vast collection of film bits and pieces collected over the years and from around the world. It is being produced by former Beatles road manager Neil Aspinall, now head of Apple films. The tentative title is *The Long And Winding Road*, with release set for Christmas."

Given that Doris Troy, Billy Preston, the Radha Krishna Temple, and

Badfinger were still in the studio working on new material, Apple found itself with little product to issue or promote in the summer of 1970. In America, Apple released Mary Hopkin's almost year-old recording of "Que Sera, Sera" in June. Despite it being Apple's only project, the single made little impact and struggled to reach number 77 in the American charts. Other than Hopkin's single, Apple would release no new records until the autumn of 1970. Work on the new albums by Billy Preston and Badfinger was further delayed when George Harrison enlisted both Apple artists to assist him on the recording sessions for his debut solo album throughout the summer of 1970.

Ironically, several months after Richard DiLello's optimistic proclamation to *Rolling Stone* that the Apple staff would have jobs for as long as they wanted, Allen Klein closed down the Apple Press Office in July and fired DiLello and secretary Carol Paddon after they both commented on the depressed state of Apple's affairs in an interview with an English magazine. The article generated a good deal of negative publicity for Apple, so Klein used the opportunity to purge the press office and gain even more control of Apple's image in the press. After closing the in-house press office, Klein hired the more traditional Les Perrin Agency to handle Apple's publicity.

Several weeks after the dismissal of DiLello and Paddon, Derek Taylor returned to Apple full-time, but with most of the press inquiries now being fielded by the Les Perrin Agency, Taylor would have little to do with Apple's day-to-day publicity. As Taylor poignantly recalled in his 1973 book, *As Time Goes By*: "When my office closed and I gave up writing this – I returned to a different Apple. My artifacts and posters and friends had gone, and the room was as smooth as silk and dead. Really dead. I would sit with Neil in his room, and we would both get drowsy by the fire and then go out for lunch."

Sitting alone in the now empty press office, Taylor probably took little notice when Apple finally started to show some signs of life in August 1970, when "Jacob's Ladder" – a new George Harrison-produced single by Doris Troy – was released. Troy's single was followed in September by three new albums – Doris Troy's debut album, John Tavener's *The Whale* and Billy Preston's second album for Apple, *Encouraging Words*.

Of the three albums released by Apple that autumn, it was the John Tavener record that would receive the most acclaim, but – being an album comprised of challenging, religious themed classical music – achieved the least in terms of the number of copies sold. Tavener had been an unusual and brave signing for Apple. Apple – who had both Yoko Ono and the Radha Krishna Temple under contract – had never shied away from signing non-traditional artists, but Tavener was the first artist signed to the label whose music had nothing to do with pop whatsoever. That said, Tavener was already something of a "pop star" within certain circles, and in 1968, at the age of twenty-four, he was considered to be one of England's most promising young composers of contemporary classical music. Tavener was by no means a typically tweedy classical music academic. With his long hair and contemporary clothes, he had become something of a media darling. Yet despite having had several of his compositions performed on critically acclaimed BBC broadcasts, none of Tavener's work had been captured on record by the time he met John Lennon in the spring of 1969.

Tavener met Lennon and Yoko Ono at a dinner party in Kensington that was hosted by a wealthy American. Tavener recalled that despite the host's cook having prepared an elaborate meal, John and Yoko arrived in their white Rolls Royce carrying their own specially prepared macrobiotic food. Dining on the floor of the American's luxurious home, Tavener played John and Yoko a tape of an opera he had recently composed, while Tavener was treated to tapes of John and Yoko's "experimental" recordings. Tavener remembered John and Yoko having little interest in the opera's religious message, but both seemed captivated by the actual sounds and effects on the recordings.

Lennon was impressed and the very next day called Tavener to tell the young composer that Apple would be interested in recording his work. Within days of that conversation, Tavener was summoned to Savile Row to meet with Lennon, Ringo Starr, and Ron Kass. It was by all accounts a productive meeting, and John Tavener was soon signed to Apple Records.

By strange coincidence, Ringo Starr was already somewhat familiar with Tavener's work. For close to a year, John Tavener's brother, Roger, had been pitching the idea of having Tavener record for Apple to Ringo Starr. Roger Tavener – known in the mid-sixties as "the swinging builder" – managed an up-market construction company that had been doing work for England's brightest young pop stars. The Beatles were among his many clients, and he had done work for both NEMS and Apple. Roger Tavener had been hired to renovate Ringo Starr's Highgate home, and he spent almost two years working on the property during 1968 and 1969. Each day, Tavener would join Ringo and his wife, Maureen, for breakfast to discuss what he would be working on next. During the course of these breakfast discussions, Roger brought up the possibility of his brother, John, recording for Apple, and he brought Ringo a tape of an early BBC performance of *The Whale* for his consideration.

Once signed to Apple, John Tavener had the full backing of two of the Beatles, yet little progress was made on recording his Apple debut until early 1970. Tavener felt that Apple's difficulty with getting the album recorded was largely due to no one at Apple having any idea of how to set up a classical music recording session. Sensing this problem, Tavener brought his friend Nicholas Snowman to Apple, hoping that Apple would agree to let Snowman coordinate the recording of Tavener's album. Tavener remembered that when he took Snowman to Savile Row to meet Ringo Starr, Ringo did not seem up to getting involved in a long conversation about classical music. Instead, he expressed his admiration for Tavener's work, reiterated Apple's commitment to John Tavener, and then sent out for an order of chips and tomato sauce, sending Tavener and Snowman downstairs to meet Apple's record department.

In the record department office on the ground floor, Tavener and Snowman discussed their plans with Jack Oliver. Though impressed by the well-stocked drinks cabinet and the ice-buckets that were shaped and coloured to resemble giant apples, it did not take long for Tavener and Snowman to realize that no one at Apple had the slightest grasp or interest in classical music.

With little coaxing, the record department was more than happy to hand over all responsibility for producing an album of Tavener's music to Snowman. In what he today considers "one of the great deals of all time," Snowman negotiated a "colossal" management fee for the London Sinfonietta Orchestra, then he selected a church in Islington in which to record the album, hired a technical crew, and negotiated all of the necessary royalty deals.

Sessions for Tavener's album finally took place on 22, 23 and 24 July 1970. By the time Tavener had actually started recording for Apple, Lennon had taken to spending long stretches of time abroad, and he had little day-to-day involvement with the label. In Lennon's absence, Ringo Starr assumed responsibility for Tavener at Apple, attending several of Tavener's performances as well as the recording sessions for the album. Starr even provided a brief vocal contribution to *The Whale*. The album earned bountiful critical acclaim when released in September 1970, yet it was not a big seller, mainly because, as Derek Taylor would later admit, "We didn't promote it; we really couldn't." Fortunately for Apple, the English media was already very interested in the dashing young composer. In addition to being featured in articles in *Vogue* and *The Daily Mirror*, Tavener had even been the subject of a BBC Television special.

The Whale was unlike any record that Apple – or almost any other English record label for that matter – had ever released. The first movement opens with BBC news announcer Alvar Lidell reading a scientific analysis of whales as the foreboding music slowly builds behind him. Inspired by the biblical allegory "Jonah and the Whale," Tavener deftly wove symphonic passages, opera and spoken word into a strikingly original work that was arguably several years ahead of its time.

Tavener had delivered a challenging piece of music in a genre in which Apple had no experience, and there was no expectation on the part of Apple that *The Whale* would appeal to any audience other than a small cadre of modern classical music enthusiasts. But the new albums by Doris Troy and Billy Preston – which deftly spanned the increasingly divergent worlds of rock and R&B – were both thought to have significant commercial appeal, yet Apple was not able to shift many copies of either record. Apple purchased the obligatory print advertisements for both albums in the English and American music papers, but neither album received much in the way of press or radio exposure, which was surprising given the quality of the albums as well as the high calibre of musicians who were involved with the projects.

The superb *Encouraging Words* had been produced over several sessions held in 1969 and 1970 by George Harrison. In addition to co-writing "Sing One For The Lord" and performing on Preston's funky remake of the Beatles' "I've Got A Feeling," Harrison let Preston record several of his finest new compositions – "My Sweet Lord" and "All Things Must Pass" – several months before Harrison was due to release his own versions on his solo album, *All Things Must Pass*.

Apple had even scheduled Preston's rendition of "My Sweet Lord" to be an English single, and it was given the catalogue number Apple 29 and coupled with the non-album B-side "As Long As I Got My Baby." Only after someone at Apple realized that Preston's record might diminish the impact of Harrison's forthcoming "My Sweet Lord" single did Apple cancel the release at the last moment.

Preston's "My Sweet Lord" – now backed by the album track "Little Girl" in place of "As Long As I Got My Baby" – was issued on 5 December in the United States, several weeks after Harrison's hit version of the song had been released. It would not be until February 1971, once George Harrison's rendition had started slipping from the charts, that Preston's stirring version of "My Sweet Lord" reached its peak chart position of number 90. In the end, Apple did not even release a single from Preston's album in England, which certainly limited the commercial prospects of *Encouraging Words*.

The commercial failure of Doris Troy's album was equally surprising to Apple. Before signing to the label, Troy had established herself as an in-demand session vocalist and songwriter, and she had scored several English and American hit singles in the mid-sixties. She was hardly an unknown artist. Troy's album featured an impressive list of players, including George Harrison, Ringo Starr, Eric Clapton, Billy Preston, Peter Frampton, and Stephen Stills, yet the cover made no mention of these musicians. At a time when "super-groups" were all the rage and an album could sell many copies just on the names of the famous musicians who played on a record, Apple's decision to put little more than a dark photo of Troy taken by Mal Evans and a list of song titles on the cover of the album was a questionable marketing move.

Jack Oliver claims that this was intentional and that Apple did not list the names of the performers on the album in order to avoid any contractual entanglements with the record labels of the musicians involved, as well as the Beatles long-standing efforts to try to let Apple artists succeed on their own merits rather than on the strength of their Beatles connections.

Both Billy Preston and Doris Troy were keenly aware that a listing of credits for session musicians would have helped sales of their albums. "That was another mistake," said Preston in a 1971 interview with *Rolling Stone*. "No credits or liners. Like on ...*God Planned It*, there was Doris Troy, Madeline Bell, Richie Havens, Eric Clapton, Ginger Baker, and Keith Richards and on "My Sweet Lord" on *Encouraging Words* the Edwin Hawkins Singers sang, the Temptations' rhythm section played on a couple of tracks, Delaney and Bonnie's band played, Ringo and Klaus Voormann were on it. George got them all in."

Doris Troy offered that, "The way they explained it to me was that because we had so many guest artists on the record that by the time we got around to calling everybody in the States to get permission to have all these people on the album, we would have never got the album out and everybody would want points and all that. It was basically done to keep us from having to deal with all those different record companies, because at that time, it just wasn't done. Also, Apple didn't give it mass promotion because at the time there was some chaos at the label, but we got some action on it, but not as much as it could have been or should have been."

Complementing the illustrious cast of session musicians appearing on Troy's record, the album featured songwriting collaborations with Harrison, Stephen Stills, and Ringo Starr. George Harrison would later admit that this had not been his original intention, explaining that, "I was producing her album, and we got to the session and she didn't have any tunes, so we had to make them up on the spot!"

Troy also appeared to have written several songs with her Apple label mates Jackie Lomax and Billy Preston, including a soulful R&B number credited to Troy and Lomax called "I've Got To Be Strong."

Having had little to do with Apple since leaving England in late 1970, Lomax was, until 1992, unaware that Troy had received a writing credit for "I've Got To Be Strong." Lomax recalled: "After Doris first came to Apple in the summer of 1969, I knew that she was having a bad time. I don't like to speak ill of people, but messing around with dope is really bad. She had a problem with that, and that's why I wrote "You've Got To Be Strong," and she was being strong, and she was really getting it together; she had a great voice. So I ran into Doris in the studio one day and told her I had a song that she might be interested in doing, so I went round to her place and just played it to her on guitar and she liked it, so she did it; she didn't write any part of the song (outside of changing "You've" to "I've). I had the complete song before she went into the studio; she did a nice job with it, though."

Klaus Voormann had a similar experience with his composition, "So Far," the magnificent ballad that is one of the finest moments on the *Doris Troy* album. "I wrote that song myself. Doris just changed a few words, and now she has part of the song," he explains. "But I don't mind. I don't write many songs, and I have no idea of who owns my songs. I never got any royalties for the song."

The publishing rights to "So Far," as well as Voormann's composition "Lu La Le Lu," which was a European hit for the group Wishful Thinking in 1972, are, in fact, held by Apple Publishing. But even the curious lack of royalty payments have not diminished his enthusiasm for the song. "We recorded "So Far" at Trident Studios, and we were about to start recording when suddenly the door opens and Eric (Clapton) walked in with all of the Derek And The Dominoes people. They were all tired from the plane but they were all wired up with the help of some "medication," and I said, 'C'mon, let's play on this song.' So Eric played the guitar, Bobby Whitlock played the organ, and Jim Gordon didn't want to play because we already had Alan White there to play the drums. We had Delaney and Bonnie on backing vocals and Rita Coolidge singing on it, too."

Ultimately, neither *Encouraging Words* nor *Doris Troy* did much to contribute to Apple's bottom line. Apple's most financially rewarding project in the autumn of 1970 was their effort to cash in on the *James Taylor* album that Apple had first issued in 1968. After Taylor scored an international hit with "Fire And Rain" in September 1970, Apple realized that Taylor's debut album was now the most valuable asset in the Apple catalogue. To promote sales of the Apple album in America, Apple re-released Taylor's "Carolina In My Mind" single. With "Something's Wrong" replacing the single's original B-side, the record reached number 65 in the American charts. To coincide with the reissue of the single, Apple also put a new promotional push behind Taylor's album. Their efforts were rewarded when the album settled into the American hot 100 album charts from October 1970 to April 1971. Hoping to repeat that success in England, Apple finally released "Carolina In My Mind" as a UK single in November, but the record failed to chart.

Taylor's single was followed in November by "Think About Your

Children" – a new Mary Hopkin recording that Apple issued in both America and England in the hope of scoring a lucrative Christmas hit. The song was easily one of Hopkin's best and most commercial numbers in quite some time, but it failed to match the success of her previous efforts. Despite having been given significant promotion, the Mickie Most produced "Think About Your Children," an uplifting pop-soul song written by former Apple artists Hot Chocolate, reached only number 19 in England and number 87 in America.

"Think About Your Children" is alleged to have been taken from a series of recording sessions held over the summer that were intended to form the basis of Hopkin's second Apple album. "I'm about halfway through my second album," Hopkin explained to NME in November 1970, "but it's difficult getting the time to finish. I'm not even sure how it's going to work out. It's supposed to be on one theme – children – and I want it to be good. But it's such a shame having to cram everything in and then not being happy about it or doing it as well as I should."

It would be Badfinger who would finally return Apple to the charts. Not willing to give up on "No Matter What," Badfinger had enlisted Mal Evans to lobby Apple management to release the song as a single. But Evans made little headway with his campaign to get "No Matter What" released until Badfinger's Tom Evans played a tape of the song to Al Steckler, who immediately recognized that the song was a sure-fire hit and scheduled it for release as Badfinger's next record.

The consensus at Apple was that Badfinger had the potential to become a hit-making group, yet the company had been strangely reluctant to release "No Matter What" as the follow-up single to "Come And Get It." They may well have been concerned that "No Matter What" sounded as if it were performed by a totally different band than the one that had recorded "Come And Get It" only a year earlier. Technically, they were, as "Come And Get It" had been recorded when Badfinger were still the Iveys. On "No Matter What," Pete Ham's rich tenor vocal replaced the lead vocal of Tom Evans, who had sung "Come And Get It." In place of the simple piano, bass, and drums arrangement of "Come And Get It," "No Matter What" featured bold electric guitars, soaring three-part harmonies and exceptionally powerful drumming from Mike Gibbins. The addition of Joey Molland to the Badfinger line-up had totally transformed the band, giving them an edge that they had not had – at least on record – as the Iveys. By late 1970, Badfinger sounded very little like the band that had recorded "Come And Get It," a point that was certainly not lost on Apple Records.

Badfinger were confident that "No Matter What" would make a great single, but even they were genuinely surprised by just how well it sold. In a 1971 interview with NME, Pete Ham admitted: "There wasn't much promotion done on it I don't think, because there suddenly wasn't anyone at Apple to work on it, so it plodded on. Then out of the blue, it appeared in the charts."

Reflecting on how Apple operated in the early 1970s, Joey Molland confirms Ham's observations. "We'd go down to Apple once a week at least. We'd see Derek and stuff and maybe have a glass of scotch and sit around for half an hour. There was a lot of coming and going at Apple. When I first joined in 1969, we used to go down there quite a lot and see everybody at Christmas parties and all that stuff. But as the group got successful, we'd be away on tour, so things like Derek leaving and all that stuff happened when we were away. We'd get back from tour, and all of the people had changed. It was hard to believe when Richard DiLello was leaving. That was a bit of a weird thing."

"No Matter What" was followed by the release of Badfinger's *No Dice* album in November, which failed to chart in England but made the American top thirty. Produced by Geoff Emerick (with two tracks produced by Mal Evans), the album had been recorded at several London studios during July and August 1970. Apple Studios was still more than a full year away from being operational, but Apple had started to assemble a team of engineers and producers to work for their new studio. Emerick had been lured away from EMI in June 1969 to be the studio manager and a staff producer for Apple.

Members of Badfinger remember that Mal Evans had hoped to produce the album that became *No Dice*. Despite Evans's lack of formal production experience, Badfinger had been pleased with his production work on "No Matter What," and they were more than willing to record their album with Evans at the controls. Joey Molland recalls: "Mal seemed to be able to do whatever he wanted. He was always at the George Harrison sessions taking care of things. He was very positive and encouraging. He knew how to make a good record from being around the Beatles." Evans was all set to produce Badfinger's album until, during a June 1970 meeting at Apple, Badfinger manager Bill Collins told a bewildered audience of Derek Taylor, Mal Evans, Allen Klein, Badfinger's Tom Evans, Geoff Emerick, and a few other Apple personnel that Mal Evans was not welcome to produce Badfinger and that Emerick would be producing the album instead.

Joey Molland explains: "It turns out that Collins was very jealous of Mal Evans, and Collins manipulated the situation so that Mal wasn't involved. To this day, Collins is obsessed with the idea that Mal wanted to manage the band. I talked a lot with Mal, and he never, ever mentioned anything about managing Badfinger."

Two songs that Mal Evans had produced for Badfinger in the spring of 1970 — "No Matter What" (which would be remixed by Geoff

Emerick) and Tom Evans's "Believe Me" – were ultimately included on *No Dice*, with the remaining songs on the album being produced by Geoff Emerick. The twelve songs that comprise the album – which include the sublime power pop of "No Matter What," heartfelt ballads like "Midnight Caller" and "Without You," all-out rockers like "I Can't Take It" and even the countryesque "Blodwyn" – showed that Badfinger had developed into a first-rate hard pop band that was able to effortlessly perform many different styles of music.

The provocative *No Dice* album cover, featuring a scantily clad model pointing suggestively at the camera, was designed by Richard DiLello and Gene Mahon, the graphic artist who had developed the Apple logo. DiLello, a friend of Badfinger, had little difficulty convincing Apple that he and Mahon were the right team to design the cover of *No Dice*. When DiLello was fired by Allen Klein, Derek Taylor had promised to hire DiLello to work on Apple projects on a freelance basis, and the Badfinger album cover seemed to be a perfect assignment for Apple's former "house hippie." DiLello and Mahon would also design the cover for John Tavener's *The Whale* and Taylor would hire DiLello to design the 1970 Apple Christmas card.

To promote *No Dice*, Badfinger departed for America for what would turn out to be a tour lasting nearly three months. Kicking off the tour in Grand Forks, North Dakota on 25 September, the group would remain in America until December. Met by audiences who were under the impression that Badfinger were the Beatles in disguise, that Joey Molland was Paul McCartney's brother, or that one of the Beatles would be appearing on stage with the group, the tour was well received, especially after "No Matter What" was released on 12 October.

Towards the end of the tour, George and Patti Harrison flew to the United States from England to introduce the group on the first night of Badfinger's three-night booking at Ungano's in New York City. *Circus* magazine reviewed the show, noting how the arrival of George and Patti electrified the usually blasé New York City audience and press. *Circus* writer Janis Schacht reported that just before Badfinger began their set, Harrison stepped to the stage microphone and announced, "Hello everybody, thank you for coming tonight. We'd like to have you welcome one of Apple's bands: Badfinger!" Harrison then returned to his front row table, opened a briefcase containing a tape recorder and proceeded to tape Badfinger's entire performance, which did little to soothe the nerves of the band.

In the final months of 1970, Apple shifted its attention from its non-Beatles acts to focusing on the solo careers of George Harrison and John Lennon. Despite having been integral members of the most popular rock band ever, the two ex-Beatles were genuinely concerned that they would not be accepted as solo acts. Having seen the *McCartney* album go into the top ten earlier in the year, both Lennon and Harrison wanted their solo debuts to do as well or even better than McCartney's, and they instructed Pete Bennett to devote as much time as possible to making their respective solo albums successful. Pete Bennett recalled that there was a keen sense of competition between the ex-Beatles: "The Beatles didn't give a shit about the other Apple artists. The only one that George and Paul cared about was Badfinger. We couldn't promote all of the non-Beatle Apple albums, it took too much time to promote the Beatles themselves. They were concerned about themselves first. It was a lot of work promoting the records by the individual Beatles, and I was still doing the Stones. Not only that, but if one of Paul's records hit the top ten, John would call me and say, 'How come Paul's record is at number 10 and mine's at number 15?' and I would tell him, 'Alright John, we'll make your record number 5,' and then Paul would say how come his record is at number 5, and George Harrison would say my record isn't even on the chart. Every week was another problem at Apple. There was a lot of competition between them."

In the end, neither Harrison nor Lennon had much reason for concern, as both of their solo albums made the top ten in both the United States and England. Harrison's *All Things Must Pass* triple album box set and the "My Sweet Lord" single were particularly well received, and for the next several years, Harrison was the most commercially and artistically successful ex-Beatle.

The release of John Lennon's *Plastic Ono Band* coincided with the start of Yoko Ono's career as a full-fledged Apple Records recording artist. Ono's album - confusingly, also entitled *Plastic Ono Band* – featured the same group that backed Lennon on his album. But Ono's music, which ranged from a spooky improvisation with the Ornette Coleman quartet to Klaus Voormann, Ringo Starr, and John Lennon backing Ono on wild, proto-punk rock like "Why," was unlike any other album issued in 1970. John Lennon's raw, uninhibited guitar work was a revelation, sparring forcefully with Ono's shrieks and wordless vocals. On tracks like "Greenfield Morning I Pushed An Empty Baby Carriage All Over The City," Ono created rhythmic soundscapes that were shockingly similar to what German "Krautrock" groups were creating at the time. Yoko Ono's *Plastic Ono Band* was a record that came totally out of left field, and while her music was certainly ahead of its time and could have possibly even been considered remotely commercial towards the end of the seventies, in 1970, Ono's music was as far removed from the popular music scene as you could possibly get.

Inaugurating a tradition that would extend for the next three years, Yoko Ono would release an album of her own music roughly every time John Lennon put out an album. Over the course of her four-year recording career with Apple, Ono would be a considerable drain on Apple's finances. The four albums – two of them double record sets – she would release on Apple between 1970 and 1973 were recorded at Abbey Road and in New York City's premier recording studios utilizing some of the best and most expensive session musicians available. Given Ono was John Lennon's wife, Apple also spent far more money promoting her records than was warranted by her commercial potential. "The reason why we put out Yoko singles," confessed Pete Bennett, "was just to keep her happy. I promoted her to pacify her. But Klein never pacified her. He told her she couldn't sing. He told her to her face that she didn't have 'the sound.'"

Al Steckler agrees with Bennett's assessment that Klein had absolutely no idea of what to do with Ono. "I don't profess to really like Yoko's music, that kind of music," explained Steckler, "but I understand what she was trying to do. One of the biggest problems that Klein had – on a personal level – was that when John and Yoko were living in New York, they were doing many projects and were going through a huge amount of money. Klein and John really liked each other; they were very close. On one very rare occasion that he opened up to me, Klein came into my office late one night and asked, 'How do I tell a man that his wife is fucking away millions of his dollars? I'm his manager, and I have to do this. I don't know what to do,' he said, but he never said anything to John. The general public and mainstream press treated her albums as a joke. It is what it is. They didn't sell all that well."

Each of Ono's Apple albums would chart in the lower reaches of the American top 200, although this was mostly due to aggressive marketing by Apple and interest from curious Beatles fans rather than any realistic commercial viability. Perhaps the greatest financial strain that Ono brought upon Apple was her and Lennon's insistence that Apple release singles from Ono's albums. Ono's small following of artists, feminists, and adventurous Beatles fans may have been willing to purchase her albums, but there was little prospect of Ono's offbeat attempts at straightforward rock songwriting such as "Mrs. Lennon" and "Death of Samantha" becoming successful pop singles. Due to Ono's position as wife of one of the co-owners of Apple, however, Apple Records was obliged to buy advertisements, send out promo copies, and promote records that would never recoup Apple's investment of time and money.

Jack Oliver can still remember the discomfort he felt when John Lennon would come into his office with an acetate or tape of one of Yoko's latest creations. "John would sit me down and make me listen to all of Yoko's records. It wasn't salable. I would sit there for an hour listening to it, and John would say, 'What do you think?' Being politically correct, I would tell him that it was very nice but not particularly commercial, to which he would always say, 'What the fuck do you know?' I told him that I didn't think that it would sell a lot of copies, and he would tell me 'Well, it's your job to make sure it does, isn't it?'"

Tony Bramwell – who by this time had known Lennon for close to a decade – had the distinct impression that Lennon was fully aware of where Yoko Ono's records stood in relation to the music of the time. "John used to snigger about Yoko's music behind her back," he recalls. "He knew it was impossible to sell, but I was always polite. I remember when he came to me with *Two Virgins*. He was laughing, saying, "You've got to listen to this!" I think it appealed to him as a practical joke."

Despite having a difficult-to-sell Yoko Ono album to push as one of their Christmas priorities, 1970 had been a good year for Apple. The company had managed to maintain its momentum with hits by Mary Hopkin and Badfinger, defying the widely-held perception in the music industry that Apple would not survive the break-up of the Beatles. That is not to say that the Beatles' split had no effect on Apple. Tellingly, there had been little new growth in 1970. All of the records that had been released throughout the year had been from artists who had been signed in 1968 or 1969 when Ron Kass was still running the record division.

By the end of 1970, it was clear that Apple had changed and that it would never again be the kind of company it once was, nor what it had once hoped to be. Few, if any, at Apple felt the changes at the company as keenly as Derek Taylor. Sensing that Apple would never regain its initial energy and promise, and with little to actually do in the way of publicity, Taylor resigned from his position as publicist for Apple Records on 31 December 1970.

Peter Brown handed in his resignation the same week as Taylor, leaving Apple to join his former NEMS associate Robert Stigwood at his burgeoning RSO organization. Bill Oakes recalls Peter Brown taking him to a very elaborate lunch at Indigo Jones and not telling him why. "He told me, 'Robert Stigwood has invited you and me to start up his new American company (which was working on *Jesus Christ Superstar*). You met Tim and Andrew (Rice and Lloyd-Webber) when they came pitching "Superstar" to Apple.' Apple was the first place they came to, and Apple turned them down. I thought it would be great to go to New York, and I also realized that by saying no that I would be staying at Apple at a time that I could easily fall between the cracks. By then I was really not sure about staying at Apple. Without McCartney being there, it was really not clear what I would do there. I had to write out my resignation to John and George, because they were the Directors of Apple. George was the one who didn't want to accept it, because he knew where I was going. George felt a bit betrayed because he didn't think I'd go off with Stigwood, whom he hated because Stigwood kept sending Apple bills for Eric Clapton's services on George's records. Eric didn't know that Stigwood was billing George. George kept sending them back unpaid because he said that Eric was doing him a favour. The irony was that I did split after a few months in New York. I just got fed up with the daily grind, I just didn't like being there."

Oakes worked only a few months at RSO before being asked by Paul McCartney to come to London to be the head of McCartney's new MPL organization. Oakes accepted the position, but after several months at MPL, he once again returned to New York to become President of RSO Records.

Peter Brown remembers that McCartney begged him not to resign because Brown and Oakes were McCartney's last sympathetic contacts at Apple. Indeed, with the unanticipated resignations of Derek Taylor, Peter Brown, Bill Oakes, and Jack Oliver – who would leave Apple during the last week of February 1971 – Apple suddenly bore little resemblance to the company that McCartney had helped launch only three years earlier.

The sudden exodus of a good portion of Apple's senior staff only helped fuel media speculation that all was not well at Apple and that the Beatles split was becoming an ugly, acrimonious affair. But while the legal aspects of the dissolution of the Beatles and certain isolated incidents between one or more of the ex-Beatles did get rather nasty, there were also times when the four ex-Beatles carried on as if nothing had happened between them. George Peckham, a fellow Liverpudlian who was familiar with the camaraderie that existed between the four Beatles, is adamant that the split was not as bad as it was portrayed in the papers.

"I remember being in New York with George Harrison mastering *All Things Must Pass*," he recalls. "It was all in the papers about the troubles between John and Paul and the rest of the stuff, but I remember we went out to dinner and John was there and Paul was there and some other people, and George turned to me and said, 'You know nothing, do ya?' and I told him, 'As you say, I know nothing.' It was all friendly talk going on, but in the press the total reverse was going on, it was all about how much they hated each other's guts. All I could read between the lines was that they were going through a divorce, but it wasn't all that bad. But we were told to keep our gobs shut, basically. Klein did instruct the entire Apple staff that we were to say nothing to the press. He would close the doors and let us have it. He'd really try to make us all feel really small. All we were doing was trying to give the best we could to the company. We'd work extra hours, and we'd often be there until eight or nine at night, not putting down overtime, just getting the job completed, and Klein would come to us the next day and ask what we were doing because we hadn't signed out until nine.

"One night it was around eight, and John called and asked if I was busy at the moment. I told him no, I was just finishing up. He asked if I wanted to come over to Abbey Road because he was making a record, and he wanted me to play a bit of guitar. I got there and it turned out to be "Instant Karma," and I got to sing on it and play tambourine. The next day, one of Klein's guys comes down and says, 'You were over at EMI last night, what were you doing?' and I told him I was working with John, and it had nothing to do with him. He said, 'Well, were you being paid for those hours?' and I told him no, I hadn't asked for a penny. Klein always had people nosing around trying to find out what you were doing. He had this guy at Apple, Terry Mellis, he was English, and he had worked for Abkco in England when Klein managed the Stones. When I went with George over to the United States, I saw how he (Klein) ran the Abkco office. He treated them with an iron rod, and there was fear in the corridors. The only nice person over there was Apple's London receptionist, Laurie McCaffrey, who went over to New York to work at Abkco."

For Taylor, Brown, and others at Apple, the final symbol of the complete dissolution of the Apple dream came when Paul McCartney served John Lennon, George Harrison, and Ringo Starr with court papers. Having made several attempts during 1970 to get out of the Beatles partnership, McCartney and the Eastmans (who were McCartney's legal advisors) realized that the only way to get out of the Beatles and Co. partnership agreement was to sue the other partners of Beatles and Co. – John Lennon, George Harrison and Ringo Starr.

McCartney was reluctant to initiate court proceedings against his three estranged friends, though he was eventually convinced that he had no other option. In *Many Years From Now*, McCartney recalled discussing his desire to get out of the Beatles partnership and off of Apple Records with George Harrison, only to have Harrison reply, "You'll stay on the fucking label. Hare Krishna."

Claiming that it was ridiculous to be legally bound to a group that no longer existed, McCartney's main objection to the Beatles and Co. partnership agreement was that all of the money that was earned from the solo projects of the ex-Beatles – with the exception of publishing royalties – was being put into Apple to be theoretically shared equally by all four Beatles. It's not unreasonable to conclude that McCartney found it unacceptable that Ringo Starr would earn as much money from McCartney's solo records as he himself would. McCartney's biggest point of contention, however, was that he was adamant that Allen Klein should not be involved with his career in any way. To that end,

McCartney took Apple and the other three Beatles to court in order to have a receiver appointed to oversee the assets of Apple until all four ex-Beatles could come to an agreement on how to end their partnership. The court case would begin on 20 January 1971.

McCartney's overriding goal was to disassociate himself from Allen Klein. Pete Bennett explained: "Paul never really knew Klein, he never really started with Klein. Paul had heard about Klein and knew he was a crook. Paul had to put out his records through Apple, but he never had any interactions with Klein after 1969, just with me. I used to deal with John and Lee Eastman. I was their contact at Apple. They wanted nothing to do with Klein. I remember being in the Stage Deli in New York with Allen in 1972, and Lee Eastman, who had offices on 54th Street, walked in to pick up sandwiches, and when he turned his head around to walk out, he saw us and he came up to us and said, 'Pete, how are you?' and then he turned to Klein and said, 'You, you're no good, you're shit,' and he walked out."

1971: IT DON'T COME EASY

Having put out an impressive number of records during the last quarter of 1970, Apple assumed a low profile during the first few months of 1971. Temporarily free from having to work new releases, Jack Oliver and Tony Bramwell instead turned their attention to a new group, the Apple Band. "The band was started by George Peckham and I," explained Steve Brendell. "We brought in my friend Rod Lynton (former lead singer and songwriter for Brendell's previous band, Rupert's People) and Mike O'Donnell, who didn't work at Apple, but who did later get a job in Apple Studios and who went on to marry Barbara Bennett. The band was started as a joke. For the 1970 Christmas party at Savile Row, the idea was that we would play at the party. So we started rehearsing at Boston Place, which was where Magic Alex has been, maybe once or twice a week. For the party, the film guys had linked together all these films which were projected on the wall. We set up everything in Peter Brown's office, and we played a set and everybody liked it. Then Ringo came up and started playing guitar, and it went on into the night as a jam session. It was a good party.

"It went so well that we decided to continue, and we got the idea of having a record out. So we thought, "We're the Apple Band, let's get Apple to release a record." I think Jack Oliver was assigned to the task of asking the Beatles if they'd sign us, and they would have, but I think it was John who basically didn't think it was a good idea for staff to have a record out on Apple Records, and that was the bottom line. But we didn't want to give up on it, so Jack Oliver went and got us a deal with Mickie Most's RAK Records (Oliver also secured a US deal with Andy Williams' Barnaby Records label, which was now managed by Ken Mansfield) and we released the single "Don't Shut Me Out." Because of our connections with Apple, it got really good airplay. By this time, Tony Bramwell was also involved, and he was getting us airplay on national radio. Because the record came out on RAK, we didn't put it out as the Apple Band. I don't know why we called ourselves Matchbox, but we did. Tony Bramwell even got us on *Top Of The Pops*, but the record never took off. It sold ok, but it didn't happen for us, so that was that. At that point I was working down at Tittenhurst Park, and I watched the show there the next night. The day after, I was walking through the house and John came down and said, "I saw you on *Top Of The Pops* last night!" Ringo Starr even joined in on the fun, naming Matchbox as one of his favourite new groups in interviews that he gave at the time.

There may have been few new Apple Records releases to work during the early months of 1971, but despite Derek Taylor's conclusion that the Apple era had ended when Paul McCartney sued his fellow Beatles at the end of 1970, plans were already well underway to re-launch and re-configure Apple in the coming year.

Lennon, Harrison, and Starr were united in their desire to give Apple a fresh start and agreed to do whatever they could to revitalize the label. Al Steckler remembers, "The first thing that I was asked to do was by George. He asked me to find out what artists wanted to stay with the label and who didn't. Basically, he said, 'Look, there were artists that we signed up, with all good intentions, but we really don't know if we have the time to nurture them as we should. It's been a year and a half – two years – and we really haven't done anything for them. It's not fair to them. Try to call each one and find out if they want to stay or if they want to leave, and if they want to leave, let them leave.' What I did, I went to Billy Preston in California, and he said he wanted to stay for a while. I spoke to Mary, who was in the studio working on the *Earth Song* album. They played the album for me, and I fell in love with it. I told them I really believe in the album and I'll do whatever I can, so she stayed."

Allen Klein was also committed to rebuilding Apple, and as part of the plan he developed to give Apple increased presence and effectiveness in the American market, he opened up an Apple office in California in February 1971. Curiously, Jack Oliver claims the he and the other members of Apple's English staff had no idea that Apple was opening an office in California. "I don't remember anything about setting up an Apple office in California, so it must have been one of Klein's projects," says Oliver.

Located close to the Capitol Records tower, the new Apple office was to serve as a liaison point with Capitol for distribution, promotion, and sales. To run Apple in California, Klein hired former Capitol Vice President of Independent Labels Charlie Nuccio to be General Manager, and former Capitol National Promotion Manager Tom Takayoshi to be Apple's National Promotion man. Having succeeded Ken Mansfield at Capitol when Mansfield went to MGM, Nuccio had already developed a good working relationship with Klein and Apple.

Opening the California office had relatively little direct impact on the other Apple offices, as all of the creative and accounting work would still be handled out of New York and London. "The Apple office in California was set up to make Apple look good by having someone work there, to give them a bit of presence, nothing else," recalls Pete Bennett. "We had Capitol and the Capitol sales force, we didn't need anyone else. Apple had good distribution with Capitol. Tom and Charlie were basically there to work on distribution, they didn't do any work with radio."

Charlie Nuccio admits: "The California office was Klein's idea. He wanted to establish an image for Apple outside of Capitol, and he felt that it would be good for Apple if I just concentrated on the Apple line, so they offered me a position as General Manager for Apple US. We moved to an office on Sunset Boulevard, which we shared with Phil Spector. We just had four people there... me, Tom Takayoshi, and two girls. It was a very small office – two rooms in a three-and-a-half, or four-room suite that we shared with Phil Spector. He had his own entrance. We didn't really need a force, because that was handled by Capitol. We just gave them our input and helped with what we could do on the side, and Pete Bennett did some more out of New York."

Unlike the London or New York offices, Apple's Sunset Strip office would rarely be graced with a visit by a Beatle. "Occasionally the Beatles would come in," recalls Nuccio. "Harrison would come in, Ringo occasionally. Mostly George Harrison. Harrison was more concerned about Apple than any of them. He brought more artists to Apple than the other three, so he was concerned with promoting the other artists on Apple, not just himself. We tried very hard to push all of the Apple acts. There was a lot of effort put behind Badfinger and also the Radha Krishna Temple album. The only time I did business with John Lennon was when I was in the New York office. I used to go out to New York, once or twice a month. I never even met Paul McCartney when I was at Apple. I think Paul's problem was with Allen Klein. I got along very well with Allen Klein. I never had any problems with Allen. As a promoter and a manager, I'd rate Allen Klein number one, he was fantastic. He was a hard deal maker, he made the Beatles a lot of money. He wasn't a record head, the everyday stuff didn't interest him at all; he was on the next project already."

Establishing an American distribution and retail promotions office was a long-overdue effort on the part of Apple. Since 1968, getting adequate distribution and promotion for non-Beatles albums had been one of Apple's biggest challenges. Although EMI and Capitol were always eager to work on Beatles albums, both companies seemed to have less enthusiasm for working with acts like Doris Troy or Billy Preston.

Being familiar with Capitol's set-up at the time, Charlie Nuccio explains: "Capitol was a giant label, they had the Beatles, the Beach Boys, Anne Murray, you can go on and on. At the time, the Capitol salespeople were selling one on one to accounts. A salesman would go to a store with twenty new releases, one of which was the Radha Krishna Temple and the other was a Glen Campbell or a Beach Boys album and so on, so the Krishnas would get the least attention. Normally a dealer wouldn't say, give me that, I want that in my store. What I'm saying is that when an album like the Radha Krishna's came out, there was no reason for Capitol to push it. Capitol at that time had a very strong pop roster with a lot of chart items. I was Apple's liaison with Capitol really, trying to get the best image we could for Apple Records through that giant distribution system. There was no problem with a Beatles record or a John Lennon record, but when Apple started to build a catalogue, Capitol didn't understand the importance of that to Apple. So when Harrison wanted to do a Radha Krishna album, they were sort of second-class citizens when they went through the distribution centre at Capitol. But we would treat them as a prime album, a number one promotion, so we had to instill that throughout the Capitol system. Sometimes we did, sometimes we didn't. All the production was done in New York, and we did the promotion and marketing."

Geographically insulated from Abkco, the California office lacked much of the efficiency and discipline of Apple's New York and London operations. Billy Preston's manager, Robert Ellis, recalled going into the Apple office in Los Angeles and asking one of the women in the office for two of Billy Preston's albums to which she responded, "Billy who? Oh yes, I remember him." In general, Apple's L.A. operation was a relatively low-key affair. Charlie Nuccio remembers: "We had a few people coming into the office and dropping off tapes. We tried to discourage them, but we'd send them on. It wasn't like it was in London. In London, everyone knew where Savile Row was, it was a landmark. It was a mecca for young kids who thought they had some talent. I can understand that. We didn't have that problem. We did have some with the local Krishnas, when forty of them would come in and sit on the floor and want to know how their album was doing. It wasn't well known that we were an Apple Records office, we didn't have a sign out."

Not long after Klein opened the Apple office in California, Jack Oliver resigned from Apple Records. "I left Apple in the last week of February 1971 and came to L.A. on 1 March 1971," recalls Oliver. "I saw what was going on, I knew the Beatles were breaking up, and I just couldn't see where it was going to go. Peter Asher, in L.A., had been calling me for three years since he left Apple, so finally, I relented and went to work with him at Peter Asher Management. Klein was always on my case, but I wasn't worried because I had Paul's backing and that of the others as well. There was a list that Klein got when he came in of people that he wasn't allowed to fire, and I was on that."

With Oliver's departure, the responsibility of running the Apple label fell largely on Al Steckler. Even before Oliver's resignation, more and more Apple business was being conducted from the Abkco office in New York City. Steckler remembers that, "At one point, Abkco had a floor and a half. The Beatles' fan club was there downstairs. I had an assistant and this other young man – Jeffrey Michelson – he came in off the street one day. He was dressed very outlandishly and said he wanted to work for Apple. I didn't hire him then, but he did eventually work with us on a job to job basis. But basically, I ran the Apple label by myself. I didn't have anyone to help. I ran around like crazy. Anything that had to be done, I did. I coordinated all the releases and got designers to do the art. George and Ringo came in fairly often. Once George came into the office and said, 'I don't like how your office looks, let's get you some nice stuff,' so we went out and got this big Indian chair and a couch. Ringo got me one of those big egg chairs with speakers in it. When the guys would come up into the office, they would go in to see Klein first, and then they'd come in to see me in my office and that's where they hung out. I would get tapes to listen to that I would listen to and audition. You can't believe how many we got, and I tried to listen to as many as I could. We used to get 15 to 20 tapes a day."

Steckler continues: "I was in a very difficult position at Apple. I was the only American to ever have an Apple business card. George wanted it that way. I got on very well with the artists, but I worked for Klein, I was an Abkco employee. Klein knew that my allegiance was to him, but when it came to artistic issues, I would always side with the artists if I could, and the artists knew that as well. They also knew that I tried very hard to stay out of the negotiations. It worked pretty well. There were times when I had problems with Allen, especially when Phil Spector was involved, but the artists respected me, they knew they could come to me and they did."

To give Steckler some support from the London office, Klein directed Bernard Brown – the genial Englishman who ran Apple Music Publishing – to assume management responsibilities for Apple Records in England. Brown had joined Apple Publishing in 1969, when he was hired to replace Jean Griffiths as Copyright Manager. Having worked in the English music industry for several decades, Brown was well-suited to be General Manager of Apple. But Brown's appointment was also a symbol of how far Apple had drifted from its original intentions. Well into his fifties when he joined Apple, Brown was typical of the old-school music industry professional from which Apple had originally set itself apart. Klein was attracted to Brown due to his extensive experience with contracts and royalties. As for the Beatles, they had all had enough of the crazy atmosphere and drama that had characterized Apple in 1968 and 1969, and George Harrison, Ringo Starr, and John Lennon simply hoped that Brown would help turn Apple into a more efficient record company.

One of Brown's first projects would be seeing to the completion and release of Badfinger's follow-up to the *No Dice* album. On the eve of their second American tour in March 1971, Badfinger delivered the tapes of their proposed new album to Apple's Savile Row office. Given Badfinger's success in 1970, Apple was looking forward to releasing a follow-up to *No Dice*, and they had already tentatively scheduled a Badfinger single and album for release in May.

But after listening to the album that Badfinger had recorded with Geoff Emerick, Apple management felt that the tapes were not commercial enough and they declined to release them, just as they had previously done with "No Matter What." Al Steckler believes that the primary problem was that Geoff Emerick – who co-produced the recordings with the band – was simply not up to the task of producing a commercial pop album. "Geoff had a very good ear as an engineer," he explains, "but I didn't think much about his abilities as a producer." Steckler points out that Badfinger had experienced the same problem with *No Dice*, which was also produced by Emerick. "After I became involved with Apple and Badfinger, I heard the tapes of the album that would become *No Dice* and I thought it was good, but that it wasn't commercial. There wasn't a single on it. So I didn't know what to do with the group. I think it was Tom Evans who told me, 'We have some other stuff that we recorded, would you like to hear it?' and I said sure, and we went back into the studio and he played me this stuff that Mal did, and I heard all this great pop stuff. I told him that I heard two singles, maybe three."

Even though Apple had determined the album that Badfinger delivered to the label was not strong enough to release, they were impressed with a stately Pete Ham ballad called "Name Of The Game." Tentative plans were made to issue "Name Of The Game" as Badfinger's next single, and arrangements were made for the group to finish the track at Bell Sound Studios in New York while they were on tour. Noted session player Al Kooper was hired to overdub additional keyboards onto Badfinger's original recording, and a new mix was completed. But even after all this effort, Apple was unsure if "Name Of The Game" made the grade as a single. George Harrison – who rated the song highly – attempted a new mix with Phil Spector, but the results presumably failed to meet expectations and "Name Of The Game" was shelved as a potential single.

Listening to the album that Badfinger recorded as the follow-up to *No Dice*, it's clear that it contains no songs that were as effortlessly commercial as "No Matter What." Instead, Badfinger had recorded an album that reflected their live sound at the time, ranging from the all-out rock of "No Good At All" and "Baby Please," to the poignant acoustic pop of "Perfection." It may have lacked an obvious single, but it is a very strong "rock" album and was certainly as good as almost any other record issued in 1971.

Perhaps Badfinger had simply submitted the tape to Apple at the wrong time. On Friday 12 March, Paul McCartney won the first round in the legal battle to dissolve the Beatles' partnership. It is quite possible that the decision makers at Apple were simply unable to give Badfinger's new album a fair listen. In the 12 March decision, England's High Court ruled in McCartney's favour and appointed accountant James Spooner as the temporary receiver for the Beatles' business affairs. The appointment of a receiver had immediate implications to Apple's business, as it meant that all Apple expenses would now need to be cleared through the receiver.

Lennon, Harrison, Starr, and Apple considered appealing the High Court decision, but on Monday 27 April, they abandoned any such attempt. In addition to now having their finances overseen by an independent third party, Apple had also incurred legal costs estimated to be in excess of $200,000.

With the Beatles now officially estranged, and Klein firmly ensconced at the helm of Apple, Neil Aspinall found himself with even less to do at 3 Savile Row. Pete Bennett remembers: "Neil seemed to just be around. He was just there. No matter what Neil said, it didn't mean anything anyhow." In a 1996 interview, Aspinall himself admitted: "It was traumatic for everybody, including me. I didn't have a clue what I was going to do. And in all that there was Allen Klein and lawsuits starting. I really started making movies and music for movies. I put together the music for (the David Essex film) *That'll Be The Day* then I was making a little movie out at George's place, but I never finished it."

Yet even as Paul McCartney was dragging Apple through the English court system in an attempt to free himself from what Apple had become, Apple was working to transform itself into a viable business. In May 1971 Apple Electronics "officially" ceased operations when Alex Mardas formally resigned from the company. Since Mardas had not been seen at Apple since 1969, this gesture was more symbolic than practical. But it did signal that Apple was continuing to make meaningful efforts to streamline its operations. Since its inception in 1968, Apple Electronics had not produced a single invention or product for commercial use. After clearing out the electronics equipment and moving the cutting room and tape copying back to Savile Row later in the year, Apple would use the Boston Place building that had once housed Apple Electronics to store its film and audio tape library. And although they would not fully appreciate it until many years later, Apple wisely kept Apple Electronics registered as a company.

One of the most interesting developments at Apple in 1971 was the emergence of Ringo Starr as a successful solo artist. Written off by everyone as a musical has-been after the breakup of the Beatles, Ringo Starr found himself with a worldwide hit when his single, "It Don't Come Easy," was released in May. Written by Starr (with some uncredited help from George Harrison), the single was produced by Harrison and featured the talents of Harrison, Stephen Stills, Badfinger's Tom Evans and Pete Ham, and several other musicians.

Apple's first new, non-Beatles project of 1971 was the Ronnie Spector single "Try Some, Buy Some," which came out in April. Between 1963 and 1966, Ronnie had been the lead singer of the Ronettes, a vocal group that scored half a dozen major hits on Phil Spector's Phillies label, so her return to making records was greeted with great anticipation by the music industry. "Try Some, Buy Some" was written by George Harrison, who had produced the single with Ronnie's husband, Phil Spector. Ronnie Spector – who later professed to have had serious doubts about the commercial appeal of Harrison's grandiose and lyrically awkward ballad – claimed that Phil Spector had been hired as Apple's "unofficial" A&R manager under the condition that he secure Ronnie as an Apple artist. But Al Steckler disagrees with Ronnie Spector's recollection and emphatically states that Phil Spector "never had a position at Apple," although he admits that Spector did serve as an A&R consultant by default, given that he was working so closely with both Lennon and Harrison throughout 1970 and 1971.

"Try Some, Buy Some" was gloriously produced, featuring trilling mandolins, an epic rhythm section, and an impassioned vocal performance by Ronnie Spector. But even Phil Spector's "wall of sound" production could not compensate for Harrison's dark, dreary melody and obtuse lyrics that made references to meeting a mysterious "big fry." The single was heavily promoted in the US and reached number 77 on the American charts, which was good enough for Apple to be interested in a second single and possible album.

Nearly an album's worth of material was recorded, ranging from the bouncy, Motown-inspired Harrison composition, "You," to several songs – "I Love You Like I Love My Very Life" and "Lovely La-De-Day" – that were brought in by Phil Spector. A cover of the Beatles' "Two Of Us" was also cut, but the sessions were never completed and no further Ronnie Spector records appeared on Apple.

Klaus Voormann, who played bass on the sessions, remembers tension developing between Ronnie and Phil Spector as the sessions progressed. "We were recording at Studio Three at EMI," he recalls, "and Ronnie was supposed to sing the song, and then Allen Klein came in. Allen Klein and Phil Spector, those two together were very, very funny, making jokes all the time. Phil and Allen were actually having a conversation for close to one and a half hours, and the whole time Ronnie was sitting on a stool in front of the microphone. Then suddenly you heard this big sigh coming out of the studio, which was Ronnie. Phil just bollocked her and told her to keep quiet after she had been sitting there for one and half hours! But I love Phil Spector. He had a very fine feeling for a situation, he's not just some crazy guy. He can be very delicate. When we were working with John and Yoko, he was very sweet to Yoko."

Apple's next project was to release the long-delayed album by the Radha Krishna Temple, which was issued in May. The album – packaged in a lavish gatefold sleeve that provided listeners with Krishna prayers and a list of the locations of temples around the world – also came with a mail-order insert offering Krishna merchandise. Both "Hare Krishna Mantra" and "Govinda" were featured on the album, as well as six additional recordings that Harrison had produced at various sessions throughout 1970.

Considering that the Radha Krishna Temple had scored several successful singles in England, the album did not sell particularly well in either England or America. Pete Bennett remembers that he didn't really have any idea how to promote the album. "I told George, 'We'll put it out, a lot of Krishnas might buy it, all these guys on the street corners.' I sent the record out to radio, but I really couldn't promote it. But it wasn't bad like Lennon's "Woman Is The Nigger Of The World," but there still wasn't much we could do."

Al Steckler agrees that Apple had problems promoting the Radha Krishna Temple album. "I met the Krishnas in London," he remembers. "George was very into it, and I told him that I would help him. But it was very hard to tell people like Charlie Nuccio and Pete Bennett that this was a record we felt really strongly about, so it was not an easy album to sell. I did my college radio mailings and hoped for the best. I think we sold 20,000 copies, and the single "Govinda" got a fair amount of radio play." It was hardly a mainstream record, but the *Radha Krishna Temple London* is a very good album. Perhaps if Apple had released the Radha Krishna Temple album a year earlier, when "Govinda" was still in the charts, the album might have enjoyed greater commercial success.

Since new albums by Badfinger and Mary Hopkin were not scheduled until later in the year, Apple had little choice but to look to its back catalog to drive sales. In June 1971, Apple once again re-promoted James Taylor's 1968 debut album. Having been forced against his will to release Taylor from his multi-year contract with Apple, Allen Klein was determined to make as much money as possible from the James Taylor album that Apple owned.

June also saw the release of a second album by John Tavener, *Celtic Requiem*. Given Tavener's non-existent media profile in America and the fact that – unlike the BBC in England – American classical music radio stations did not typically broadcast avant-garde recordings such as Tavener's, *Celtic Requiem* was not released in the United States. A dark, haunting work that was in some ways more accessible than *The Whale*, *Celtic Requiem* was warmly received by the classical music fraternity and sold respectably for a classical music release. *Celtic Requiem* would be the last record that Tavener would record for Apple, but he would return to work on another Apple project later in the year.

To maintain the label's profile on the pop scene, Mary Hopkin's "Let My Name Be Sorrow" was issued as her new single in mid-June. It was Hopkin's first record to be produced by Tony Visconti, who had previously worked for Apple as the producer of several Iveys sessions in 1968 and 1969. Hoping to stem Hopkin's declining commercial fortunes, Visconti's vision was to resurrect the formula that had brought Hopkin so much success by hiring Richard Hewson to provide the musical arrangement for the single.

Hewson's diary notes that he met Visconti at Apple's office at eleven thirty on 19 May 1971, where Visconti expressed Hopkin's interest in having Hewson work on her new single and her admiration for the work that Hewson had done on her previous hits. Hewson welcomed the opportunity to collaborate with Hopkin again. Although he had recently accepted an offer from Paul McCartney to write and conduct an orchestral version of McCartney's *Ram* album, Hewson found the time to write a tasteful arrangement for "Let My Name Be Sorrow." He also conducted the orchestra on the session, which was held in George Martin's newly opened AIR Studios in London and which featured future Yes keyboardist Rick Wakeman as a session musician.

Unfortunately, Mary Hopkin's reunion with Richard Hewson proved to be less successful than Visconti had hoped, and the single only reached number 46 on the English charts. Both Hewson and Visconti had done admirable work on the recording, but the overly dramatic, almost dirge-like "Let My Name Be Sorrow" was not half as good a song as either "Those Were The Days" or "Goodbye," so it was not particularly surprising that the song did not capture the fancy of English record buyers.

In the wake of the failure of "Let My Name Be Sorrow" to crack the top 40, Apple management should have stepped in and provided some career direction to their best-known artist. But when it came to Mary Hopkin, Apple had developed a curious hands-off approach ever since she had stopped working with Mickie Most the previous year. If Hopkin wanted more artistic control over her recordings and the freedom to pursue her interest in contemporary folk, Apple was willing to give her that freedom, even if that decision resulted in diminished record sales. Many at Apple — some slightly embarrassed by Mary Hopkin's "pop" image – were not in the least bit troubled by Hopkin no longer having hit records.

Billy Preston's decision to leave Apple in the summer of 1971, however, was a cause for much greater concern at the company. Despite his lack of recent hits, Preston's close ties to the Beatles would have ensured that he would always have a place on the Apple roster. Surprisingly, in mid-summer 1971, Billy Preston requested to be let out of his Apple contract. George Harrison was reluctant to see Preston leave, yet he nevertheless made arrangements for Preston to be released from his Apple Records and Apple Music Publishing contracts. Apple Publishing would retain the global rights to Preston's Apple-era songs, though the American publishing rights for several songs reverted to Preston.

Preston's release from his Apple commitments may seem to have been a magnanimous gesture on the part of Harrison and Apple, but Pete Bennett suggests otherwise, noting that, "The Beatles thought that Billy was a great musician, but they never thought that he would ever be a star."

In a 1971 interview with *Rolling Stone*, Preston explained, "They had to get their thing together... how could they do anything for me if the Beatles' affairs were messed up? The same people who were supposed to be doing my things were theirs, and they had to look after them first. I just bowed out rather than try to be there and hassle them. It's better for them, too, 'cause George did everything he could, but the people in the office just sat around... It was comfortable at Apple at first until they started changing all the key people... like the President... and people left right in the middle of getting my product out, and people came in to start from scratch and it just never got out."

Once free from Apple, Preston signed to A&M Records in July 1971. Within a year, his first A&M album was in the top ten and spawned several hit singles. Preston believed that it was A&M's superior organization and infrastructure that finally helped him break through as a recording artist. "When I was at Apple, you know, you could only record one day out of a week because Trident and all the other studios were always booked up." Despite Preston leaving Apple, Harrison would continue to work with him, inviting Preston to perform at the Concert for Bangladesh as well as making a guest appearance on Preston's first album for A&M.

Preston's decision to leave Apple was a significant loss for the company, as he was one of the few high-profile artists still on the Apple roster, yet even this setback did not deter Apple's ongoing reorganization efforts. As Ringo Starr related in a July 1971 interview with *Melody Maker*: "The only thing they [Apple] are doing now is getting it all together. It's like pruning the tree, then you get the great flowers. If you have a big tree with a thousand million rose bushes, you get little roses. Prune it down and you get maybe ten fantastic roses, that's what's happening... The problem with Apple is that we're so involved, we can't sign anyone unless one of us is personally involved. Like George was involved with Jackie, Doris, Billy and who else, and he had to produce them. I've got involved... the only one I've got involved with is John Tavener, and I had to go round with him and get it together with him. You see, we haven't got anyone at the moment who can do it. Tony King will soon be able to. He'll have the right to get people who he thinks are good for the company. We've gotta start giving responsibility. Right now Apple isn't like that, which is why we're pruning it down so you can say, 'Right, that's your job, you like them, it's up to you.'"

Tony King had been the last employee to be hired by Peter Brown before he left Apple. Brown remembers that, "Tony King was hired in December 1970, just before I left. I gave Tony King the job. When I gave him the job, I felt guilty getting him to come to work knowing that I was leaving, but I couldn't tell him I was leaving, I couldn't tell anyone. He came in to take care of publishing, mainly. We brought Tony in to be the professional manager of Apple Publishing."

Tony King recalls: "I started at Apple in late 1970. I had been asked before, when they first started and Terry Doran was in charge. At the time I was working for George Martin, and George Martin's offices were right across from the original Apple office in Baker Street. I was asked to go work for them then, but I refused. Well, I politely turned it down, because I sort of felt at the time that Apple seemed a little chaotic and my job with George seemed more secure. George Martin had an independent production company called AIR, and I was doing record promotion for him and three other record producers he had the company with. George had just lured me away from Andrew Oldham and the Rolling Stones. There was Ron Richards who produced the Hollies, John Burgess who did Manfred Mann and Peter Sullivan who did Engelbert Humperdinck and Tom Jones, and they did other artists, too. I used to promote any records that they made, so I had a nice job over there working with George and Co.

"I knew the Beatles when they first came to London," continues King. "I used to work for the Stones in '65, so I used to hang out with the Beatles when they went to nightclubs like the Ad Lib and the Scotch, so I was very friendly with them and Terry Doran and Neil and all those people around them. It became more business-like when Allen Klein came in. I was offered the job again in late 1970, and I took it more seriously because they had more serious people in there. I went to see Ringo, who I was very friendly with, and he said to me, 'Oh come on, take a chance, we got Bernard Brown here, we got Allen, it's much more business-like now, so take a shot,' and I did. Initially, I was employed in the publishing end working for Bernard Brown. He was an older man, a sweet man, and I think Bernard provided a lot of stability at Apple. Anyway, I gradually moved into the record company. I started to do record promotion and A&R work. Peter Brown and Jack Oliver both left right after I arrived, but I didn't mind because Apple had changed – they were a much more professionally run outfit."

Apple had been in dire need of an A&R Manager ever since Peter Asher left in June of 1969. Before the arrival of Tony King, Apple had not signed a single new act since Asher had left the company.

Badfinger's Joey Molland recalls: "We never got any A&R direction from Apple, until we got into a recording situation. Then, they were very supportive usually. For instance, George was very supportive of everyone's tunes. Mal was the same way. There were a lot of positive, gentle people around. We never gave Apple demos. We would do our sessions and leave, and a few weeks down the line some mixes would be made for Apple."

Throughout the music industry there remained a widely-held perception that Apple was ready to cease operations at any time, but both Harrison and Starr – and to a lesser extent Lennon – were committed to making Apple a successful venture. Tony King confirms that Harrison and Starr were very interested in re-launching Apple. "In early 1971, there was a drive to encourage Apple to take on some more artists and to concentrate on the career of Badfinger," he recalls. "I think there was a concerted effort to make Badfinger bigger and also to encourage new artists. Ringo and George were the two behind that, because by this time John had gone to America. George and Ringo were very optimistic about Apple. They were very hands-on and I think they wanted it to continue."

In his 1972 book, *The Longest Cocktail Party*, Richard DiLello recalls speaking to Harrison in the summer of 1971 about the future of Apple. DiLello remembers that after he had mentioned to Harrison that he had recently completed a history book on Apple, Harrison replied: "Well, it's only just beginning."

Despite George Harrison's optimistic declaration, there were Apple employees who were finding it hard to fill their days. "When Tony King came in, I had been promoted to chief office boy, which meant that they sat me in the accounts office with two or three telephones and I ordered stationery once a week, that was it," remembered Nigel Oliver.

There may have been a handful of idle employees at Apple, but the majority of the staff were expending a great deal of time and effort trying to make Apple a commercially viable record label. At the same time, the company was also attempting to re-establish its somewhat faded reputation as a record label with a conscience and a sense of altruism. During the summer of 1971, Apple released no less than three benefit singles, including George Harrison's "Bangla-Desh," and several other singles from which any proceeds would go to help specific causes championed by ex-Beatles.

The first single, released in July, was "God Save Us" by Bill Elliot and The Elastic Oz Band. Still at the height of his involvement with the counterculture movement in both England and the United States, John Lennon had been enlisted to record a song to raise money for the legal defence fund for the English "underground" magazine *Oz*, which was involved in a high-profile obscenity trial. "God Save Us" was written by John Lennon, who produced a version of the song at his home studio in Ascot with assistance from Phil Spector and Mal Evans. Given that Lennon was under contract to EMI and EMI would thus be entitled to most of the money generated by sales of "God Save Us," Lennon decided to get around his contractual obligations to EMI by having another vocalist sing lead on "God Save Us." Lennon reasoned that if he did not sing on the record, EMI could not claim any rights to the recording, which meant that more money would go directly to *Oz*. For some reason, there was apparently no problem with having Lennon sing on the bizarre B-side, "Do The Oz." Based on a mutated blues guitar riff, the song featured Lennon extolling listeners to "do the Oz," as Yoko Ono shrieked in the background.

Lennon's vision was to have members of the *Oz* staff perform on the record. To augment the *Oz* contingent – including the well-known music journalist Charles Shaar Murray on rhythm guitar and Felix Dennis (who would go on to create the men's magazine *Maxim*) on percussion – Lennon brought in Ringo Starr and Klaus Voormann to serve as rhythm section. Lennon sent a van to pick up the *Oz* staff from the then-scruffy neighbourhood of Notting Hill Gate to take them to his Ascot estate.

To provide the lead vocal, the *Oz* staff brought along Magic Michael, a performer who was well-known on the benefit concert circuit (and who would later go on to record for Stiff Records). Recorded in a single day, both Lennon and the *Oz* delegation were quite pleased with "God Save Us." But when copies of the finished product arrived at the Oz office a few weeks later, the assembled staff were shocked to hear that Magic Michael's voice had been replaced by that of 20-year-old English singer, Bill Elliot.

Elliot had come to Apple's attention after his manager sent a tape of his group, Halfbreed, to Apple. "Rob Hill, our manager, always aspired to go for the best, and his opinion was that Apple was for us," explains Bill Elliot. "So he sent our demo to Apple where it found the ears of Mal Evans. Mal picked up on us. In particular, he picked up on my vocals and Bob Purvis's songwriting. We, unfortunately, didn't get a deal with Apple." Halfbreed recorded several demos for Apple – including a session with George Martin – but were ultimately not awarded an Apple contract. Despite this setback, Mal Evans continued to work with Elliot and Purvis. "John Lennon needed someone to sing "God Save Us," and Mal put my name forward," remembers Elliot. "I got the job, but I never met John. John actually sent me an acetate of "God Save Us" with his vocals on it, and I learned the song. I put on my vocals at EMI, where they took John's voice off and overdubbed it with mine." Although Elliot's involvement allowed Lennon to get around EMI owning "God Save Us," Lennon hadn't considered that the voice of the little-known Bill Elliot might not have the same commercial appeal as the voice of former Beatle John Lennon. Despite Apple's reasonable promotional efforts in both England and the United States, the single sold few copies, and Apple did no further recordings with Elliot.

George Harrison, however, took note of Bill Elliot's vocal on "God Save Us." When Harrison started his Dark Horse label in 1974, the second act signed to the label was Splinter, a duo comprised of Bill Elliot and Robert Purvis. Speaking to *NME*, Elliot noted that he had first met Harrison in a recording studio: "George was there doing a couple of mixes, I think he was in the studio with Badfinger at the time, and he just came through to see what was going on."

The other two benefit singles to be released in the summer of 1971 were both George Harrison projects. In August, Apple released a three-track single of Indian music by Ravi Shankar, the lead track being "Joi Bangla." This record, along with George Harrison's "Bangla-Desh" single which Apple had released the same month, was intended to raise money for the refugees of Bangladesh. Unfortunately for the refugees of Bangladesh and the beleaguered litigants at *Oz* magazine, few people purchased either the "Joi Bangla" or "God Save Us" records.

Though not as successful as his previous singles, Harrison's impassioned, if somewhat clumsily worded "Bangla-Desh" sold well enough to earn some much-needed money to aid the refugees of Bangladesh and to publicize their plight to Western nations. But the single was only part of a much larger gesture of support that Harrison was planning. On 1 August, Harrison performed two critically acclaimed benefit concerts at Madison Square Garden in New York City. Apple Films filmed both concerts, and within days of the event work was started on a concert film and an accompanying soundtrack album.

The members of Badfinger were among the many artists who joined Harrison on stage at Madison Square Garden. Prior to organizing the concert, George Harrison had spent several weeks in June producing tracks for Badfinger at Studio 2 of Abbey Road. Harrison had agreed to produce Badfinger at the urging of Al Steckler, who explains, "When I first became involved with Apple, none of them (the Beatles) were very involved with the label. I did get George involved with Badfinger. I went to George and said, 'Look we have a group, they're signed to us, they've had some pretty good success, you like them, they have some new songs and they need a producer. Do you have some time to take them into the studio?' He didn't have as much time as he wanted, so I got Todd Rundgren to finish the album. But I don't think that George produced Badfinger because they were on Apple, but because he liked the group."

Harrison assumed the role of producer and helped Badfinger arrange several new songs. He also played on the sessions, contributing his distinctive slide guitar playing to "Day After Day," a potential new single written by Pete Ham, and also played electric guitar on Joey Molland's "I'd Die Babe." Harrison was able to complete only four tracks before he had to suspend the sessions with Badfinger in order to devote all his time to preparations for the Bangladesh benefit concert.

Badfinger were disappointed when Harrison had to stop work on their album, but they understood the importance of the Bangladesh project to Harrison. Their disappointment was further tempered after Harrison invited the group to perform as part of the backing band at the concert. Harrison asked Badfinger to reprise their roles from the *All Things Must Pass* sessions, providing percussion and acoustic guitar backing for performances by Harrison, Ringo Starr, Leon Russell, and Billy Preston. The members of Badfinger considered it an honour to have been asked to appear, and Harrison even brought Badfinger's Pete Ham into the spotlight to accompany him on a moving acoustic version of "Here Comes The Sun."

The concerts – which featured the then-reclusive Bob Dylan's return to the concert stage – were a triumph and they cemented Harrison's reputation as the most relevant of the ex-Beatles.

Badfinger returned to England a few days after the concert to resume recording their album, but no further sessions would take place until late September. With Harrison preoccupied with mixing the tapes of the Bangladesh concert with Phil Spector, Badfinger needed to find a new producer. Apple ultimately selected twenty-three-year-old American musician Todd Rundgren to finish Badfinger's album. "I guess, at first, my involvement with Badfinger just started as a series of rumours," Rundgren recalled in an interview with *Melody Maker*. "Finally, one day somebody from Apple called me up and said they thought it might be a good idea if I went to England and did some work with them. I went to England and worked with them a couple of days, and then we decided that we'd finish the album together. I met George about a couple of days after I started recording with them, and he said that he had these four tracks. He gave me the tapes and said do whatever I want with them. So I took the tapes and recorded things on them and re-mixed them myself. One of them ("Day After Day") turned out to be a single. Somebody just didn't pay attention and said that George Harrison produced it, when he had actually given up the production of the act. He had turned the tapes over to me and said, 'I'm not doing this project anymore – you finish it.' So actually, the entire album is my production even though George Harrison is credited in four places. I'm sure he's aware of this as much as anybody. It was more of an administrative mistake than anything."

Rundgren and Badfinger would complete work on the album over the course of two weeks at several different London studios. The Badfinger sessions ended just a week after Apple finally opened their new 16-track studio in the basement of the Apple office. A party to celebrate the opening of the studio was held on the evening of Thursday, 30 September 1971 with guests including recent Apple signings Lon and Derrek Van Eaton, several members of Badfinger, and George Harrison. To Harrison, the opening of the studio was a bittersweet experience. In an interview he gave to journalists at the event, Harrison noted that: "It's a bit sad now that Apple is in the position all four of us planned three years ago. I just wish Paul would use the studio if he wants to. It's silly not to. I can't see the four of us working together again, but I'd like us to be friends. We all own the business, and it's doing well. I'd like the four of us to enjoy it now."

McCartney would eventually record in the Apple studio, but only on a handful of occasions. In forgoing the option to record at Apple, he was not only denying himself the opportunity to use the studio that he had helped pay for, but also missing out on utilizing a recording facility that would soon be regarded as one of the finest in Europe. By the end of 1971, both the Van Eaton brothers and an American, all-woman group known as Fanny had recorded albums at Apple Studios. Cilla Black would also be among the first artists to record at Apple. John Barham remembers that, "Around the same time as the Lon and Derrek Van Eaton album, George wrote a song for Cilla Black called "I'll Still Love You." It's a nice song, but it never came out. It was a complete track with Cilla's vocals. I put strings on it, and we recorded it at Apple."

The studio had been under planning and construction since the *Get Back* fiasco in January 1969, and by the time it was completed, Apple had spent an estimated $1,500,000 on the project. Extensive work was required to build the studio in the basement, and the exterior of Apple's Savile Row headquarters had been obscured by scaffolding since the autumn of 1970.

Building the studio had been a monumental undertaking. Since being appointed studio manager, Geoff Emerick had spent most of his time designing and developing the studio. George Peckham still maintains, "Sound-wise, it was a very good studio indeed. You had good engineers, good equipment, you couldn't have asked for more. It was small, but you could fit an orchestra in there. The studio was constantly booked." Unlike many of the independent recording studios that had sprung up around London in the late sixties, Apple's studio measured a relatively snug 30ft x 45ft with an 11½ft ceiling and a 12ft x 22ft control room. Now relocated back at Savile Row, Apple's cutting room was even busier than the studio. Since 1969, Apple's cutting room had been cutting masters for albums by the Stones, the Who, the Zombies, Cat Stevens and many other artists.

The first act to record in the Apple Studio would be Lon and Derrek Van Eaton. Derrek Van Eaton remembers that he and his brother were surprised to get a deal with Apple. "After our first group, Jacobs Creek, split up, Lon and I got together and made demo tapes in our house in Trenton and sent them to every record label we could think of. A couple of weeks after we sent out the tapes, we got a call from George Harrison. We had already had a couple of bites from small labels in New York and Philadelphia when George called us up and asked if we wanted to do an album on Apple. We got on Apple just by sending them a demo tape. We didn't even send them a picture. Klaus Voormann, who was with George Harrison when George first listened to the tape, thought we were black."

Lon and Derrek's manager, Robin Garb, had sent a tape to the Apple office in London, where it was heard by Tony King. "I really liked "Warm Woman." I loved the sound of it, it sounded like a fifties record," says King. "I played the tape to Ringo first, because he was in the office next door to me at the time. Ringo really liked it, and then George came in later that week and I played it to George, and he loved it too. So I got in touch with them."

"I got a letter dated 11 June telling me that Apple had received the tape and that George Harrison would be bringing it to New York with him the following week for an A&R meeting with other members of the Apple organization," remembers Garb. "Then I got a call from Tony King telling me that George Harrison wanted to call me at some ridiculous hour in the morning the next day, and sure enough, I get the call and he tells me how much he loved the music, how he would like to produce it and that I should please contact Apple in New York to start negotiating a contract. Lon and Derrek were elated."

Harrison took the Van Eaton's tape with him to New York where he played it for Allen Klein, Al Steckler, and Pete Bennett, who agreed with Harrison's assessment that the demo tape showed great potential.

"I fell in love with the tape," remembers Steckler. "John happened to be in the office the same day, and George grabbed him and said, 'Listen to this.' John loved it too and they said, 'Sign them up.'"

The Van Eaton brothers – who lived less than two hours from New York City in Trenton, New Jersey – met George Harrison for the first time in late July. "We met George when he came to New York to do Bangladesh," recalls Derrek Van Eaton. The brothers were invited to attend the concert, and the following week Robin Garb and Nat Weiss – who coincidentally was a mentor and business associate of Garb – started negotiating a contract with Apple.

Robin Garb is adamant that Nat Weiss – who had been a business partner of Brian Epstein and had been close to the Beatles before Allen Klein started managing the group – played no role in getting Lon and Derrek Van Eaton signed to Apple. "I had met Nat Weiss when I had the idea of renting the *Magical Mystery Tour* film to use in place of an opening act for concerts that I promoted on the east coast. It had never been released in the United States, and he had the rights to it and physically had the film with him and he allowed me to use it for several concerts. It was received very well. I became friendly with him, and one day he calls me up and asked if I wanted to manage Jacobs Creek. Nat told me he didn't want to manage them on a day-to-day basis, but he would continue to be the business manager and that we could partner on managing Jacobs Creek."

Jacobs Creek broke up in 1971, but Garb and Weiss continued their partnership. Initially, Garb tried to shop the Van Eatons as a duo with the assistance of Nat Weiss. But Garb maintains that whenever labels saw that Nat Weiss was involved, they would pass on the project, assuming it would be too expensive to pursue given that Nat Weiss was typically associated with only major acts. "I called Nat and told him, 'Vanguard's passed, Mercury's passed, everybody has passed. I want to send one to Apple, but I don't want to make them aware of my association with you.' Because I didn't want them to go through the motions of doing something nice for Nat Weiss. I wanted to get a reaction from the merits of the music only. So I sent a tape to Apple with just my name on it, no mention of Nat or Nemperor."

It was not until after Apple expressed their interest in signing Lon and Derrek Van Eaton that Garb made his affiliation with Nat Weiss known to Apple, and he brought in Weiss to help negotiate the contract. On Wednesday, 15 September, Lon and Derrek signed a five-year deal with Apple Records and Publishing at Apple's New York office. Four days later, the Van Eaton brothers – accompanied by Garb – were on a plane bound for London. "We were in England for around three months, and we would stay at George's place at Friar Park just about every weekend while we were there," remembers Derrek Van Eaton. "Our first night in England, Apple put us up in this place that was pretty dumpy, right by Heathrow Airport. We asked them if it was possible to put us in a different place, so they put us up in one of Ringo's places up in Mayfair, which was really nice and we stayed there until we left England."

Despite his schedule being totally consumed with work on the Bangladesh album and film, George Harrison was able to find a few days to produce a proposed single for Lon and Derrek Van Eaton. Two weeks after they had signed to Apple, Harrison took the duo into Abbey Road where they were joined by Ringo Starr and several other musicians to record a song called "Sweet Music." Derrek Van Eaton believes that, "The reason that George ended up producing "Sweet Music" was that it was the song on the demo that he had first heard, and he liked it a lot. Also, it was the same approach he was using in those days, four acoustic guitars, the harmonium, two drummers – the same sound he was using on his own albums."

With Harrison unable to devote any further time to working with Lon and Derrek Van Eaton, Klaus Voormann was given the job of producing the album. Derrek Van Eaton feels that, "Klaus came in as a producer because Klaus was with George when George first heard the demo. Klaus was really into it, so George told him that he could produce it. I don't think Klaus had any previous production experience. It was more of a joint production effort with us, outside of when George was producing. When George was there it was his stuff – he did it. He was a lot stronger personality. George dropped in a lot during the sessions that Klaus produced. We even ended up using the demo of "Warm Woman" on the record, because we couldn't recreate it in the studio the way we wanted to do it. We had everybody try to do it – Ringo played drums on one version – but it didn't come across with the same feel, so we just tried to doctor up the demo to make it sound good enough. While we were working on our album, we also met Richard Perry when he came to Apple Studios to work on sessions for (former Righteous Brother) Bobby Hatfield and Harry Nilsson. We didn't finish the album until we got back to New York. We got back from England a few days before Christmas 1971. After Christmas we did some more recording in New York, another six or eight cuts, then we mixed it all in New York and decided what to put on the album."

"I was in Los Angeles, staying with George at his house in Nichols Canyon while he was preparing stuff for the Bangladesh concert, and he played me Lon and Derrek Van Eaton and asked me if I would produce them," remembers Klaus Voormann. "I had not done any production, but he knew I had taste, and he didn't know and I didn't know at the time if I could be a good producer, so I did it. George thought it turned out ok. At least we didn't have an argument about it! I loved the song "Sweet Music," and I liked the songs they were writing. They got some sounds on their demos that were just fantastic. They got some very interesting results just by recording at home, and it's difficult and frustrating when you know how to do something, and then lots of those sounds that were done with very simple means you can't do in a studio, because the good equipment just doesn't sound the same. I was the guinea pig for Apple Studio. When I first saw it, it was like a building site, everything was hanging from the walls. It wasn't really ready when we recorded. You need some months to find out that things aren't working. We spent a lot of time working on the album. It was Apple's studio and everything was very loose, and we just took our time. No one was pressuring us, though we had a certain deadline when Lon and Derek had to return to New Jersey. But it was difficult recording at Apple because it was so new. Most of the time, you know a studio and are used to a sound, but in this case, it was all new. Geoff Emerick used to come in from time to time to take care of technical stuff."

The Apple staff in London were somewhat surprised by how much studio time George Harrison was giving Lon and Derek Van Eaton. To give an unknown act close to three months in a top line studio was an almost unheard of occurrence in the early seventies. Curiously, the most vivid memory that many former Apple staff have of the Van Eaton recording sessions is the artistic temperament displayed by the confident young Americans. Brought in by George Harrison to work on arrangements, John Barham recalls: "I remember working on the Lon and Derek Van Eaton album. I did a couple of sessions for them. One of the guys, the slightly younger one, the prettier looking one, was a bit abrasive. I got the feeling that he resented me as an arranger. I think he wanted to do it."

George Peckham adds that, "We spent a few bob on Lon and Derek Van Eaton. They were in the studio for ages. Everyone was saying that they made great album tracks, but they had a problem coming up with a single, but it was nice, gentle music. I think George got a bit fed up with them, everybody at Apple did. They were going on and on, and they were acting like superstars, looking down on all of us." Regardless of the friction that the group generated with Apple's staff, Harrison remained firmly committed to seeing that the album was done right and that no expense was spared.

By the time Lon and Derek Van Eaton left London a few days before Christmas 1971, they had completed an album, along with several recordings that were destined to remain outtakes. One of the most interesting songs they recorded during the sessions held at Apple Studios was a track called "The Sea," which was a collaboration between the Van Eaton brothers and fellow Apple artist John Tavener. In a 1972 interview with *The Daily Express*, Tavener recalled how Ringo Starr had asked him to take time off from the opera he was working on so that he could contribute "a bit for some pop record they're producing – just something for the middle, different from the rest. Ringo just said, 'You write whatever you want to write.'" Tavener's contribution was ultimately added as a coda to "The Sea," a heartfelt piano soundscape that would subsequently sit unissued on a shelf in the Apple tape vault for decades.

In addition to his production work, Klaus Voormann spent a considerable amount of time working with George Harrison on several Apple projects throughout 1971. Prior to the Bangladesh concert and the Van Eaton sessions, Harrison and Voormann had worked as session musicians on John Lennon's most recent album, which had been recorded over the summer at Ascot Studios, a recording studio that Lennon had built on the grounds of his Tittenhurst Park mansion. Entitled *Imagine*, the album was issued in the United States on 7 September and in the United Kingdom on 8 October. Unlike the emotionally raw *Plastic Ono Band* album, *Imagine* featured some of Lennon's most melodic work, particularly the stately title track, which became a major hit when issued as an American single on 11 October. But there were also several jagged edges on *Imagine*. At the time of the album's release, the most talked about song on the album was "How Do You Sleep," a scathing attack on Paul McCartney that was presumably motivated by McCartney's court victory over the other three Beatles earlier in the year and the hurt feelings that remained from the group's still recent split. George Harrison – who played guitar on most of the *Imagine* sessions – contributed a particularly stinging slide guitar solo to the song, and his presence on the track left no doubt as to Harrison's feelings on the subject.

Unlike Harrison and Lennon, outside of his "It Don't Come Easy" single, Ringo Starr released little music in 1971. He appeared to be focusing on films, accepting roles in the Abkco produced *Blindman* (which also featured Allen Klein and Mal Evans making cameos as bandits) and the Frank Zappa film, *200 Motels*. Starr also developed an interest in producing movies, and he took the lead in resurrecting Apple Films, although Tony Bramwell is quick to note that "Apple Films was just Ringo's hobby, there was nobody actually working there." Nevertheless, under the guidance of Ringo Starr, Apple Films would soon start preliminary work on a film about Marc Bolan called *Born To Boogie* and a feature-length documentary on Ravi Shankar called *Raga* in mid-1971.

Neil Aspinall's Beatles documentary was another project that was being considered for Apple Films in 1971. By mid-1971, Aspinall had finished work on what was now known at Apple as *The Long And Winding Road*. Unfortunately, as Aspinall recalled in an interview with *Mojo*, "The Beatles had split up by then, so there was really no chance of anything happening with it. I sent them a copy of it each, which they all quite liked, then I put it on the shelf. And it stayed on the shelf from 1971 till '89, about twenty years!"

Considering that Apple's four owners were now tied up in highly visible public squabbles, the company itself was actually doing surprisingly well. Only a year earlier, many people in the music industry had thought that Apple was doomed. But after a temporary lull, Apple was once again buzzing with activity. With Apple's finally completed studio the talk of the London music scene, and with several new artists having been signed to the label, it looked as if Apple may have found a new lease of life.

Allen Klein had also started to utilize Apple as a vehicle for his personal business ventures. Since Klein would not launch his own label, Abkco Records, until early 1972, he released the soundtrack albums to several unsuccessful films that were produced by his new film company, Abkco Films, through the American record division of Apple. The first Abkco Films soundtrack to be released on Apple was *Come Together,* which was issued in September 1971.

Released in America the same month as *Come Together* was Yoko Ono's new double album, *Fly*, which was accompanied by her first solo single, "Mrs. Lennon." The haunting piano–based ballad didn't trouble the charts, but it registered with the few people who actually heard it. One of those individuals was Alex Chilton, the lead singer of Big Star, who subconsciously lifted the melody of "Mrs. Lennon" for his celebrated 1974 song "Holocaust."

Yoko Ono's debut as a singles artist may have left music industry insiders wondering what the hell Apple was thinking, but Ono's single was almost a mainstream release when compared to an album that New York City beat poet Allen Ginsberg recorded for Apple in November. After being given what he considered to be a verbal contract from an enthusiastic John Lennon, Ginsberg went into New York's Record Plant Studios to record an album for Apple that was to have been called *Holy Soul And Jelly Roll*. Backed by a band that included Bob Dylan, Ginsberg recorded a full album of poetry and songs. But Apple declined to release the album, leaving Ginsberg with a hefty studio bill that he had paid for out of his own pocket. The recordings would not be released until 1994, when they were included on the Ginsberg box set, *Holy Soul Jelly Roll: Poems And Songs 1949-1993*.

The final months of 1971 also saw the return of Mary Hopkin. Having released only singles since her debut album was issued in February 1969, Hopkin's second album, *Earth Song/Ocean Song*, finally found its way into the shops in October. Produced by Tony Visconti – with whom Hopkin had become romantically involved – the album abandoned the upbeat pop feel of her debut album and subsequent singles, replacing the carefree pop stylings of her early work with a highly contemporary acoustic folk sound. *Earth Song* featured musical contributions from some of England's finest folk musicians, including Ralph McTell, Danny Thompson of Pentangle, and Strawbs guitarist Dave Cousins. The ten-song album was comprised of songs written by well-known folk artists of the day, including material by McTell, Cat Stevens, Tom Paxton, and Harvey Andrews, as well as several songs written by previously unknown songwriters. Apple Music Publishing also got a song on the album in the form of Gallagher & Lyle's "International," an exquisite song the pair had written in 1969 while still signed to Apple.

Earth Song was not a commercial hit, but it received excellent reviews and earned Hopkin some well-deserved critical respect. Al Steckler remembers Hopkin's *Earth Song* as being "probably one of the most difficult Apple albums to promote, because her image was so pop. There was a huge distinction between pop AM stations and FM stations in those days. The FM stations wouldn't touch her because she was an AM artist, and the AM stations wouldn't play her because there was no pop single there. Being aware of the importance of college radio, I did some mailing to college radio, but Pete Bennett didn't understand that market at all. Pete was a real, old time record promo man. He didn't understand the changes that were going on, he didn't understand the importance of the college market, he didn't even really understand the importance of the FM stations. So I just went to Klein and told him, 'I want to do mailings to college stations, and I want 500 copies of each album to do mailings,' and Klein said, 'Fine, just do it.' Whatever success the album had was due to that.

"I don't think that Capitol really believed in *Earth Song*. It wasn't a distribution problem as much as a problem that Capitol had with Apple. We were really one of the first independent labels; Capitol resented us. They resented the fact that we started doing our own advertising. We started doing our own advertising because we didn't like the ads they were doing for us. We were just another cog in their wheel, which is understandable. When a Beatles record came out, of course it was important, but anything else... Capitol had nothing to do with Apple other than to press and distribute the records. Tom and Charlie were hired away from Capitol by Klein to make sure that Capitol was doing the job they were supposed to do. We did the advertising ourselves, all the records were cut in New York, we told them when we wanted to release the records, we did the artwork in New York. There were always people at a lower level at Capitol who were trying to cut costs and be heroes. Like on the Bangladesh album, we wanted to print it on a certain high-quality orange paper, but Capitol wanted to print it on cheap orange stock, those kind of things. But we didn't want it, it was our label."

In December, Apple marked the end of 1971 by issuing several soundtrack albums. The first, *Raga*, was an Apple Films project. *Raga* was the soundtrack to a 96-minute documentary about Ravi Shankar that had premiered on Monday, 22 November at the Carnegie Hall Cinema in New York City. Both George and Patti Harrison and John Lennon and Yoko Ono attended the premiere. George Harrison, who appeared in a brief sequence of the film, was also credited with producing the accomplished Indian music that comprised the soundtrack album. For reasons unknown, the *Raga* album was only released in America.

The second soundtrack album Apple released that month was that of another Abkco film, *El Topo*. Like the poor selling *Come Together, El Topo* was only released in the United States. Fortunately for Apple, it was also the last Abkco soundtrack to be released on the label.

But unlike *Come Together* – a strange tale of a movie stuntman's road trip in Italy with two uninhibited American women - that faded into oblivion shortly after its release – *El Topo* was a controversial, critically respected film that received a fair amount of attention from the underground media. A surreal, twisted movie, both the film and the soundtrack album have since acquired a sizeable cult following. John Barham was hired by Apple to work on the soundtrack. Barham remembers: "I got the *El Topo* work through John Lennon, who I knew through George. I first met John at the *Sgt. Pepper* sessions at Abbey Road. George had asked me to come down to hear his recording of "Within You Without You." When I got there, John was coming down from an LSD trip, and I remember when I was introduced to him he almost jumped out of his chair. He recovered very quickly, though, and he was very charming. So when Allen Klein wanted to record the soundtrack to *El Topo*, Al Steckler mentioned to John Lennon that he wanted to record it in London, which I guess was cheaper, and so John recommended me to do it. I got a phone call from Al Steckler in New York saying, 'You don't know me, but John mentioned you,' and he flew me over to New York, which in a way was unnecessary, to see a private screening of the film and to sign a contract. I went over on a Thursday, and on the Saturday ten days following we had to record it at Island Studios. I wrote two or three additional pieces to fill it out. We did the album in two sessions over the weekend. It was a very interesting album. It had a Latin style, and it was hard to get the English musicians to play like that. Al Steckler produced the recordings and he was a really nice guy."

Al Steckler recalls that John Lennon was extremely enthusiastic about *El Topo*. "It was an independent film that was shown at this theatre in the Village every Friday and Saturday night at midnight," explains Steckler. "John saw it, flipped out, and went to Klein and said, 'I want it, I want you to buy the film,' and Klein did. He bought the movie to launch on a national basis and we released the soundtrack on Apple, but it was too far out."

The soundtrack albums to *Raga* and *El Topo* sold modestly as expected, but it was Badfinger's new album, *Straight Up*, that was the highlight of Apple's December release schedule. In America, the album had been preceded by the single "Day After Day," which had quickly risen to the top ten. *Straight Up* would not follow "Day After Day" into the top ten, but it sold extremely well in America where it reached number 31 in the *Billboard* album charts. Once again, Apple hired Richard DiLello to take photos for the publicity stills and the album cover, which, like *No Dice*, had been designed by DiLello and Gene Mahon.

In December, Apple also made one last vain attempt to resuscitate Mary Hopkin's rapidly fading pop career. Several months since its release, *Earth Song/Ocean Song* had barely dented the charts in either England or the United States. Surprised by the universal indifference to Hopkin's superb new album, Apple tried to generate some renewed interest in the record by releasing the stirring (and oddly Pagan) track "Water, Paper and Clay" as an international single in December. The single was certainly one of the most commercial songs that Hopkin had recorded for some time, yet it failed to meaningfully chart in any country. It appeared that Apple was not going to be able to re-establish Mary Hopkin as a commercially successful recording artist.

But with Badfinger riding high in the charts and with the recently opened Apple Studio booked for months to come, there was a new sense of optimism at Apple as 1971 drew to a close. But that optimism was apparently not sufficient enough to keep Tony Bramwell – Apple's Promotion Manager since 1968 and one of the few remaining senior staff members to have been with Apple since the launch of the company – from resigning from Apple to join his former Apple boss, Ron Kass, at Hillary Music Publishing. "I left on New Year's Eve, 1971," recalls Bramwell. "I was bored. There was nothing going on, so I left. It wasn't because of Klein. When Allen Klein came to Apple I wasn't affected at all. I always got along very well with Klein, I still do. He couldn't get rid of me. He got rid of everyone else, but John said he couldn't get rid of me, so he had to live with me."

Of all the Apple staff, it was Bramwell who was best known to London's pop music community, as his position required him to interact frequently with BBC radio personalities and the music journalists who played a critical role in promoting any record.

Upon Bramwell's resignation, Apple A&R man Tony King was assigned the task of handling promotion duties for Apple Records and Publishing. King remembers: "For most of 1971 I was working in publishing, except that I seemed to be doing more and more work for the record company. Then I sort of split from Bernard, and I was the boss of my own department, where I was reporting directly to George and Ringo. I was made General Manager of Promotions/A&R. Chris Stone was my assistant, and he did the promotions after Bramwell left. Chris was an English promotions man who worked for another English company, and I poached him. He stayed at Apple until the end."

1972: THEY SEEM TO BE GETTING IT TOGETHER REALLY WELL

It was now 1972. The sixties had been consigned to history, and pop music was becoming increasingly corporate and calculated. Apple, too, had changed. It was no longer regarded as the anarchic hippie haven that it had been perceived as being several years earlier. The company had evolved into what was, by standards of the day, a fairly orthodox record label. Busloads of tourists still regularly stopped in front of the Savile Row office to snap pictures and try to catch a fleeting glimpse of an ex-Beatle or two, but most left with little more than a photo of the building. For those who still showed up at Apple's door to see if Apple was really as wild as depicted in magazine articles from 1969, the reality of Apple circa 1972 – the once familiar building now almost totally obscured by scaffolding – was disappointing to say the least. No longer could Apple office boys be witnessed dragging bags of stolen roof lead into the street, nor did visitors generally have to contend with the territorial "Apple Scuffs," who were now seen only fleetingly outside 3 Savile Row. By this time, one former Scruff, Margo Stevens, had even been given a job inside Apple by Tony King.

Apple Records was the most visible division of the company in 1972, enjoying international hit records by Badfinger and releasing recordings by several promising new artists. With the departure of Tony Bramwell, the responsibility for running Apple Records in England had transitioned to Tony King and Bernard Brown. "It was a true joint effort," recalls King fondly. Bernard Brown – having proved himself to Klein through his successful management of Apple Music Publishing – was given the title of General Manager of Records and Publishing. Under Brown's direction, Apple became more active than it had been since 1969. The year opened on a high note in America when Badfinger's "Day After Day" sold so well that it became Apple's second non-Beatles gold record. In England, Apple ushered in the new year with the January release of "Day After Day," which was followed by the *Straight Up* album in February. "Day After Day" climbed to number 10 in the English charts, but the album sold only modestly, despite featuring a hit single and having been given a reasonable promotional push by Apple.

Apple's most fantastic success of 1972 would be Apple Music Publishing. Thanks to Pete Ham and Tom Evans, Apple Publishing would experience a remarkable year, though not just from the sales of current Badfinger records for which Apple owned the publishing, but rather from a song that Ham and Evans had composed in 1969 while

Badfinger were still known as the Iveys.

American singer Harry Nilsson had first heard "Without You" – the brooding ballad that closed the first side of Badfinger's *No Dice* album – at a party in 1971. The next day, he called his hosts from the previous evening to find out the name of the record that had been played with "you" in the title. Nilsson initially thought it was a John Lennon song, but after being unable to find it on any Beatles album, he (incorrectly) concluded the song was by Grapefruit.

When a listen to Grapefruit's *Around Grapefruit* album did not offer up the song he was seeking, it was eventually determined that the song was "Without You" by Badfinger. Nilsson secured a copy of *No Dice* and was finally able to reevaluate the song that he had been unable to get out of his head since the party. Upon further reflection, he felt that Badfinger's rendition was somewhat lacklustre but that the song itself had tremendous potential. Nilsson took the song to his producer, Richard Perry, who agreed with Nilsson's assessment and who proceeded to rework Badfinger's subdued arrangement into a dramatic, impassioned love song that became a massive global hit. Thanks to Nilsson's version of "Without You" – and the countless cover versions and muzak renditions that followed in the wake of the Nilsson record – the song became a huge earner for Apple Music Publishing.

Given the consistent success of Badfinger and all of the work generated by the ex-Beatles and Yoko Ono, Al Steckler could no longer continue to essentially run the production and operations side of the US Apple label on his own. To help manage the increased workload, he hired 22-year-old Glenn Friedman, an American who had recently returned to New York City after several years of working in London.

"Steckler hired me because I was kind of an up-and-coming A&R guy," says Friedman. "I had been a producer for Decca in England from early 1969 to 1971, and then I came back to the States. I interviewed with him in 1972, and he told me I would be great at Abkco/Apple and that I could take a lot of the mastering work off his shoulders. So he hired me and gave me an office right next to his. He was a great guy, a great boss and basically let me do what I wanted to do. In the other office next to me was a guy called Joel Silver who ran Abkco Music and administered Apple Publishing. Allen Klein was great to me. I was in meetings where I was just stunned by the way he reacted with people who crossed him, he was a monster. But with me, he had this paternal sort of vibe. He always liked me, because he'd stroll around at lunch and look in all the offices, and I was always there. I would always order a sandwich up, and he would sit across from me at my desk and ask me what was going on. The first time it happened I had no idea of what to say. He was really curious about what was going on in the street and what people thought of him. I would regurgitate whatever the prevailing attitudes were, and he would laugh. He would tell me about Cameo Parkway and his work with Neil Bogart. He went out of his way to tell Al Steckler to get me more active in the studio. It was just the two of us there having anything to do with Apple Records. I was answering the phones, 'Hello, publicity, hello promotions, hello A&R.' It was just the two of us doing anything related to A&R and mastering."

Apple had once again become busy, but now, they were actually starting to make some significant non-Beatles money. Apple's good fortune throughout the early months of 1972 proved that the company could indeed be successful independent of the Beatles. Yet that success was fragile, given that most of Apple's non-Beatles record and publishing revenue was generated by a single act, Badfinger. Given Apple's small roster of artists and the fact that little new music was issued by the ex-Beatles in 1972, Apple relied heavily on Badfinger to keep the label's momentum going. Fortunately for Apple, Badfinger were a very prolific band. Even before *Straight Up* had been released in England, the industrious group had already started work on what they hoped would be their next album.

Regrouping after the 1971 Christmas holiday, Badfinger had gone into the Apple Studio with Todd Rundgren on 17 January to start recording a follow-up to *Straight Up*. Given that most of the group had claimed to not have enjoyed working with Rundgren (they felt that Rundgren was too domineering and seemed to have little respect for their musical abilities – a common complaint amongst Rundgren's production clients), he was certainly an odd choice for producer. During the four sessions held at Apple, Badfinger completed two songs – "The Winner" and "I Can Love You" – before Rundgren pulled out of the project due to an ongoing dispute with Apple over the production credits for "Day After Day."

Further recordings – mostly self-produced by the band – were completed, but with Badfinger due to embark on their third American tour in February, work on the album was reluctantly put on hold as the band prepared to head out on another grueling tour. Joey Molland remembers that Badfinger were not particularly enthused to be recording at Apple Studios and that they hoped they would be able to resume recording at a different studio when they returned from their tour. "Apple Studios wasn't a great place to record," he explains. "It was much more comfortable to record at Olympic Studios or Abbey Road. The Apple Studio was a tiny basement room, it was L shaped and fifteen-feet-wide, but it wasn't right for us. We did "Piano Red" and "Timeless" there."

Badfinger's American tour would keep them out of a recording studio for several months. The tour opened in Boston on 3 February, and Badfinger were arguably at the peak of their powers. The highlight of this particular visit to America was certainly their triumphant performance at Carnegie Hall in New York City on 1 March. Badfinger were enthusiastically received by the audience, and the show attracted glowing reviews from the usually reserved New York City music press. During the concert, Al Steckler stepped out on stage to present Badfinger with a gold record award for "Day After Day." It was a nice gesture, despite the fact that the award presented to Badfinger that night was not "Day After Day" but rather another gold record hastily snatched off the wall at Abkco (Steckler remembers that the actual award for "Day After Day" had not arrived at Apple, so he used the first gold record he could find, which was George Harrison's "My Sweet Lord"). The only element missing from the event was Allen Klein. Although four seats had been reserved for Klein, the manager of Apple tellingly did not bother to attend this prestigious New York City performance – held only a few blocks away from the Abkco/Apple office – by one of the best-selling acts on the Apple label.

Glenn Friedman's recollection was that no one at Apple's New York office was even invited to attend the show. "I loved Badfinger and their singles and even saw them once before I worked for Apple," he recalls. "Abkco was more interested in the movies of Alejandro Jodorowsky than Badfinger. If it was the difference between seeing *Holy Mountain* or *El Topo* or going to see Badfinger at Carnegie Hall, the company would be told to see Jodorowsky. That was the priority of the company. Even if I had been invited to see Badfinger at Carnegie Hall, I don't think I could have found anyone at Akbko who would have wanted to go with me."

The lack of a show of support from their American record company notwithstanding, the tour was a great success, and Badfinger scored another US hit a few weeks into their American trek when Apple issued "Baby Blue" as a single on 6 March. The song – a soaring, bittersweet number written by Pete Ham – was a massive hit on American radio, and it eventually climbed to number 14 on the singles chart. "Baby Blue" was the second single taken from the *Straight Up* album, earning Badfinger the distinction of being the only Apple artist at that time, apart from George Harrison, to have two American hit singles taken from one album.

The decision to release "Baby Blue" as an American single had been made by Al Steckler, who was confident that the song would make an excellent follow-up to "Day After Day." Steckler's only reservation about issuing "Baby Blue" as a single was that he felt the mix featured on *Straight Up* did not do full justice to the song.

Steckler remembers that he initially attempted to get Todd Rundgren to do a remix, but when he was unable to secure Rundgren's services, he elected to remix the song himself. The resulting mix, as overseen by Steckler, was a dramatic improvement over the original. Steckler replaced the dull thud of the drums on the introduction with a crisp, echoed drum sound that greatly enhanced the vitality of the song. His mix also brought a brighter sound to the guitars, giving them a jangling quality that would later characterize the power pop movement of the late seventies.

Given the song's hit status in America, it seemed obvious that "Baby Blue" should have been issued as a single in the UK, yet for reasons no longer remembered by either Badfinger or Steckler, this never happened.

Released almost simultaneously with "Baby Blue" was the single "Sweet Music," which marked the Apple Records debut of Lon and Derrek Van Eaton. But where "Baby Blue" was embraced by American radio, "Sweet Music" never connected with radio programmers. "Sweet Music" – having been given a sublime production by George Harrison – was an uplifting rock ballad that had all the hallmarks of a hit, yet it received airplay in only a handful of radio markets across the United States. When it became apparent that "Sweet Music" was not getting added to radio station playlists, an exasperated George Harrison cabled Allen Klein, Al Steckler, and Pete Bennett at Apple's New York office, imploring, "For fuck sake, do something with "Sweet Music" by Lon and Derrek Van Eaton. It's a potential No.1 hit."

But it was too late. The moment had passed, and there was nothing that even Pete Bennett could do to get "Sweet Music" into the charts.

Apple's plan had been to quickly follow the release of "Sweet Music" with a Lon and Derrek Van Eaton album entitled *Brother*. The record was originally supposed to be a ten-song album, comprised – with the exception of "Warm Woman" – exclusively of tracks that the brothers had recorded in London between September and December 1971. The track listing was to have been:

Side1
"Warm Woman"
"Sun Song"
"Home Dear Home"
"The Sea"

Side 2
"Can't Wait"
"Maybe There Is Another"
"More Than Words"

"Sweet Music"
"Sunshine"
"Song of Songs"

The original version of *Brother* was absolutely superb, boasting a vaguely English feel that perfectly complemented the Van Eaton's songs. Had it been released, it would have been one of the best rock albums to be released by Apple. But when "Sweet Music" failed to chart, Apple decided to hold off on the proposed May/June release of *Brother*. Issuing a debut album by an unknown artist without the benefit of a hit single was deemed to be too much of a risk.

Klein summoned the brothers to the Apple office in New York for a meeting. "We went into his office, and he asked us what we needed. We could have anything," remembers Lon Van Eaton. "But we had no idea of how things worked, so we asked, 'Well, can we go back into the studio?'" As requested, Klein arranged for the Van Eaton brothers and Klaus Voormann to record new tracks at Bell Sound Studios in New York the following month, but nothing more in terms of promotion or tour support would be done on behalf of "Sweet Music."

Sporadic releases from new artists like Lon and Derrek Van Eaton confirmed that Apple knew that they needed to sign more artists if the company was to succeed beyond simply being an imprint for albums by the ex–Beatles and Badfinger. By 1972, the label's artist roster had almost completely turned over, leaving only Badfinger and Mary Hopkin left from the original 1968 artist roster.

Unlike Badfinger, Mary Hopkin had not managed to sustain her initial success. Newly married and having never been particularly enamored by the machinations of the music business, Hopkin decided that she would not renew her Apple contract. In March, it was announced that Hopkin would be parting ways with Apple.

Mary Hopkin had been Apple's one true international star, and she was strongly identified with both the Beatles and Apple. Since 1970, Hopkin had been desperately attempting to reshape her image from that of the wholesome pop singer of "Those Were The Days" into that of a more serious folk singer. *Earth Song/Ocean Song* had done much to burnish Hopkin's contemporary folk credentials, but Apple was simply not structured to nurture that sort of artist. By the spring of 1972, there were very few people left at Savile Row who were at Apple back when "Those Were The Days" had seduced the world. Hopkin's relationship with the label had been reduced to little more than her management dropping off tapes and Apple pressing those tapes into records. The music press predictably tried to frame Hopkin's departure as an end of an era for Apple, but Apple simply wished her well and then went back to work developing the careers of the ex-Beatles, Badfinger and a new generation of Apple artists.

Apple Records and Publishing were not the only Apple divisions to get a new lease on life in 1972. Throughout the year, Apple would devote substantial resources to re-launching Apple Films. Having essentially been dormant since Denis O'Dell left Apple, Ringo Starr had reactivated Apple Films to produce a movie featuring his new friend Marc Bolan. In 1971 and 1972, Bolan and his band, T-Rex, were perhaps the biggest pop act in England, and Starr was fascinated by the fan hysteria that he was now free to observe from the vantage point of a spectator. *Born To Boogie* was filmed in March and April, and it would mark Starr's debut as a film director.

Starr found film making to be unexpectedly time consuming, but in between days spent on the set and in dark editing suites, he would still show up at the Apple office to attend to Apple Records business. It was Starr who was responsible for signing British singer Chris Hodge to the label. Like Lon and Derrek Van Eaton, Chris Hodge's signing was almost straight out of Apple's original 1968 script for finding and developing new talent. Chris Hodge is still amazed by how easy it seemed to get a deal with Apple. "I was born in 1949 and was twenty-two when I signed to Apple," he explains. "I was living in Rome for three years working as a fashion photographer, writing poems and songs. When I left Italy, I came back to London and signed a music publishing deal with Robert Mellin Publishing; they gave me money to record some demos. After I got back from Rome, I tried all the record companies, and I kept getting turned down because they weren't into UFOs. One day in early 1972, I phoned up Apple and spoke to Apple's A&R man, Tony King. We had a nice chat and I told him I'd written a killer song about UFOs, and he said come on in. So, I met him and I played him my tape. I left my tape at Apple, and Tony played my music to Ringo, who then wanted to meet me, personally.

"I remember when I came to Savile Row to meet Ringo; he was lying on a couch and he had jeans on with a big rip at the knee," continues Hodge. "He said, 'Hey man, do you want to release your demo?' I said I wanted to do some changes to it. I wanted to polish it up and add an orchestra and a choir. He was ready to go with the demo. But Ringo really liked it, so they put me in the Apple Studio at Savile Row to record a new version. When they heard the first version of the demo, they realized that some of the lyrics had to be changed, because I said in the lyrics, 'The karma is gonna be heavy on all the Mafia men; the karma's gonna be heavy on all the Ku Klux Klan.' They told me I couldn't say that, so I had to take those lyrics out. I had told Ringo that I wanted to do it with a choir and a large orchestra, and Ringo gave me a free hand

and said, 'Just change those lyrics around a little bit and then go do what you want to do,' so then I recorded the track along with "Supersoul," which actually did better in Europe than "We're On Our Way." When I finally got the deal with Apple, I stumbled across Tony Cox, and he ended up producing "We're On Our Way." Apparently, Apple changed his mix in New York. It was done by friends of Phil Spector's people in New York. They asked us if we approved, and we said go with it, it sounded good."

Tony Cox – not to be confused with Yoko Ono's first husband – was an ex-pop star of sorts (he had been a member of the pop duo the Young Idea in the mid-sixties) and was now a highly regarded young producer and arranger, having worked with such critically acclaimed progressive acts as Caravan, Trees, and Magna Carta. "Chris was a typical kind of Kings Road, Chelsea kind of trendy character," remembers Cox. "His brother, Gavin Hodge, was a well-known society hairdresser, who used to cut my society hair at the time! Someone had recommended me to Chris Hodge as a producer, and Chris came to me one day with an idea for a record he wanted to make. He just wanted everything that was hip at the time – soulful girl singers, he wanted a sitar – everything that you could think of that might be in vogue at the time. I was skeptical because he was not any kind of musician, but his enthusiasm sort of swept me along. I told him, great, let me know when you have a record deal, and amazingly one day he came along and told me he had got a record deal and it was with Apple, and would I come and meet Ringo. So, we did, and Ringo said, 'Well as long as you don't do it like that George Martin crap,' which I thought was a bit ungenerous of him, to be honest.

"We cut the record at the Apple Studio, with a very good engineer, Phil McDonald, who was a pleasure to work with. But the guy (Hodge) had no talent, I have to tell you," says Cox almost apologetically. "All he had was a lot of nerve. He didn't really play anything and had no technical skills. He just had a lot of these really unoriginal ideas, but lots of them. He had a lot of front. I never had any belief in "We're On Our Way," because I just thought it was too mad. Because he wanted to put everything on it – everything that had been on other people's recordings over the previous two years – just to make sure that it would be a hit. But he was right! I don't remember who played on the session, except that the backing singer was P.P. Arnold, and the sitar player was Lyn Dobson. We took a few sessions to complete the single, and money was no object."

Like Tony Cox, Tony King was somewhat bemused by Chris Hodge and remembers that Hodge quickly became a regular visitor to the Apple offices. "Chris Hodge was such a nightmare," recalls King with a laugh. "He was a very, very gregarious, outgoing person. He charmed his way into Apple, and he came in wearing his silver boots with stars on. He used to wear lots of satin jackets and things. He played me the song, and I sort of liked it. I played it to Ringo, and he liked it, too, so we signed him. Chris was a bit of a headache, though. He just never stopped bugging me, but I guess that was his enthusiasm. He came in all the time! I think he got on everybody's nerves after a while, he was just a bit too persistent. I was shocked when "We're On Our Way" became a hit. It was very gratifying. Al Steckler called me up to tell me it was in the American charts, and I was thrilled. Ringo was really pleased, as it was Ringo who was behind Chris Hodge. George was very much behind the Sundown Playboys and Lon and Derrek."

Apple released "We're On Our Way" in the United States in May 1972. Though, as Tony Cox explained, totally overproduced, "We're On Our Way" is a great, silly pop record that was one of the most commercial singles that Apple ever issued.

Given their poor track record for breaking new acts, Apple was genuinely shocked to see "We're On Our Way" climb to number 43 on the American charts. Presumably because there were only a few Beatles-related projects to promote at the time "We're On Our Way" was released, Pete Bennett was able to devote at least some of his time to promoting Hodge's record. Hoping to emulate the success that Hodge enjoyed in America, the single was released in England in June, although it failed to get the same enthusiastic reception as it had in America. Still, encouraged by America's positive response to "We're On Our Way," Apple sent Hodge into the studio to work on new material.

Hodge remembers: "After "We're On Our Way" and "Supersoul," I cut a lot of other different tracks in Apple Studios, because I was planning to do an album. One of the tracks was called "The Year 2000," which was never released by Apple because they thought the lyrics were too heavy. It talks about, 'All revolution boys are dead, laser shots through their heads in the year 2000.' UFO activity and Stonehenge seemed to be a running theme in my writing at the time. I recorded around four or five other tracks that I was playing around with to use on an album. Another track was "Karma Is Going To Get You" with a giant orchestra of cellos and a big American Indian drum that I brought in. Tony Cox was still involved. I was doing some crazy stuff in those days. I recorded my second single, "Goodbye Sweet Lorraine," at Apple Studios, too. I remember that all the plug sockets were gold, and the floors were rainbow colours, they had all this soft rainbow lighting in there. It was unbelievable.

"One of the biggest mistakes of my career was that I never came to America. I never went to Apple's New York office. Apple's publicity in America was immense. They bought full-page ads in Billboard and

Cashbox. For some reason Europe favoured the B-side, "Supersoul," and Apple promoted "Supersoul" in England. There was one DJ in England who had "Supersoul" as the intro to his radio show."

The unanticipated success of an unknown artist such as Chris Hodge seemed to encapsulate the sudden sense of fresh potential from Apple. With a new recording studio, a manageable artist roster, and professional, highly respected staff members such as Tony King and Bernard Brown on the payroll, the Apple of 1972 had changed almost beyond recognition from its original incarnation. In fact, Apple appeared to have almost completely rebounded from the problems that had initially plagued the early days of the company. Had Paul McCartney still been actively involved with Apple – other than in his role as reluctant artist and owner in exile – he would have certainly been pleased.

Speaking to *NME* in May 1972, Badfinger's Joey Molland admitted that the Apple offices had changed greatly from how they were in 1969: "You'd never feel really comfortable. I never did when we went in there. It was like that from my first day until Apple sort of disintegrated and this new place opened up. I like it a lot more now. The bigness of it has gone. They're just trying to be a good record company now. They seem to be getting it together really well."

Part of their efforts to "get it together" involved Apple making a concerted effort to earn back some of the money that the label had invested in Billy Preston between 1969 and 1970. Having sat back and watched in amazement as Billy Preston scored several massive hits for A&M Records in 1972, Apple re-promoted Preston's *That's The Way God Planned It* album in the summer of 1972, and from June to August, Preston's initially overlooked Apple debut enjoyed renewed sales and spent several months in the American album charts.

One of the more arduous projects undertaken by Apple during the summer of 1972 was packing the entire contents of the Savile Row building into boxes and moving the company into a temporary office in order to enable renovations to be made to the Apple building. The renovations – which began the first week of July – were allegedly necessary to keep the entire building from collapsing. "Savile Row was unsafe to be in after a while," remembers Tony King, still amazed by how close the building came to literally falling to pieces. "I remember we had a Christmas party at Savile Row, and the next day the architects came and said, 'We wish you had told us you were having a Christmas party, because the whole building could have collapsed.' That could have ruined the whole party!"

Some of the structural problems at 3 Savile Row could be attributed to the advanced age of the building; others were self-inflicted. It has been alleged that during the attempted construction of the original recording studio in late 1968 and early 1969 that important structural supports were removed from the basement, which ultimately threatened the stability of the entire structure.

In order for the engineers to carry out the renovations, Apple was required to completely empty the upper floors. Apple decided that as long as they were going to be doing extensive construction on the Savile Row building, they might as well also use it as an opportunity to expand their facilities. To accommodate all of the business that Apple Studios was attracting as well as the apparent revival of Apple Films, Apple drew up plans to build a film editing suite and a second mixing studio on one of the upper floors. The recording studio in the basement was to remain open during the renovation, but all of the other Apple departments were moved to a temporary office at 54 St. James's Street.

Anticipating that the renovations to Savile Row would take only twelve to eighteen months, Apple appeared to have put little thought or effort into finding an appropriate temporary office. The St. James's Street building was conveniently located close to Savile Row, but that was really all that the location offered. Apple's new office had previously been a car showroom, and the space was hardly a traditional office setting for a record company. When the Apple staff moved in, they simply put up curtains in the large windows of the former showroom and resumed their business activities. In addition to the large, wide-open ground floor space, Apple also had the upper floor of the building. Tony King remembers: "Apple had the whole building. The upstairs floor was Ringo's office, my office was in the front where the cars are now, and then there was a basement. We had the basement, ground floor and first floor. It was a weird building, I don't know why they picked it."

Steve Brendell, who was now working as Neil Aspinall's assistant, confirms that none of the staff could figure out why Apple had selected the office on St. James's Street. "It was a huge change to move out of Savile Row to St. James's, which was just an old office over a car showroom. The car showroom became Bernard Brown's office." Brendell also remembers that the move to St. James's Street coincided with a renewed effort by Allen Klein to push Neil Aspinall out of Apple. "There was a time when Neil was at St. James's, and Allen Klein was trying to get rid of Neil. Neil – for a time – was barred from using his office, and he used to sit outside Ringo's office, which was incredibly embarrassing for the guy. I mean, he was like the MD of Apple and he had almost everything removed from him. I don't know what the ins and outs were as it was all behind closed doors, but he was more or less barred from his own office. I don't know how it happened, but I can remember him having to sit outside or use Ringo's office. It was at that time that he (Neil) literally took the *Long And Winding Road* film apart, because he was so worried that Allen Klein would get his hands on it. It then took all those years to finally complete it. Neil was really worried that Klein was going to get him out of the organization and steal it from him."

The abandoned upper floors of the Savile Row building were eerily quiet after the staff exodus to St. James's Street, but in the basement studio, there was round the clock activity, which included George Harrison and Ringo Starr coming in to record tracks for their *Living In The Material World* and *Ringo* albums. Apple Studios had remained in operation throughout the summer of 1972. The same week that workmen were moving furniture and shipping boxes out of the upstairs offices, down in the basement, Apple Studios Engineer Phil McDonald was recording an album for English singer Linda Lewis. McDonald had joined Apple in November 1971 as a senior balance engineer. Like so many of the Apple Studio staff, McDonald had started his career at EMI Studios, and at the age of twenty-five he had already engineered sessions for the Beatles, Roy Harper, the Shadows, as well as solo sessions by all four of the ex-Beatles.

The renovation work on 3 Savile Row began almost immediately after Apple moved its staff and files to St. James's Street. But work on the building appeared to stop in early 1973 after the upper floors of the building's interior had been totally gutted. From their vantage point in the Apple Studio, George Peckham and Nigel Oliver were bemused by what was going on above them. Nigel Oliver remembers: "It was surreal, because after 1972, you could go up the studio stairs to what had been the offices and there was just sky... all the floors had been knocked out. All the artists had to go up to the first floor to use the toilet and there was nothing there, just the walls and the bog. When the building was knocked down inside and only the studio was left at Savile Row, we weren't really aware of what was going on with the rest of Apple. I went over to St. James's once in a while, but when Apple moved there, the studio and the record company became very separate. It became a sort of them and us situation. Apple Records at St. James's Street was still Abkco dominated, and we went back to being more of a studio, and George and Ringo used to come in and it used to be like it was before Klein."

Between all of the record releases, recording sessions, and building renovations, there was always something happening at Apple, yet there was a conspicuous lack of new releases on the part of any of the four ex-Beatles in 1972. The only ex-Beatle to release an album that year was John Lennon, who released the decidedly unspectacular *Some Time In New York City* that summer. Pete Bennett remembers that he had a significant disagreement with Lennon about the commercial merit of *Some Time In New York City* and especially the album's single, "Woman Is The Nigger Of The World."

"John Lennon came to me with "Woman Is the Nigger Of The World," and he and Yoko wanted to put it out in America very badly," Bennett recalled. "They thought it was a number one record. I told him I hated it, I thought it was a piece of shit, and I told him that I wouldn't promote it. So John says to me, 'Well, you're our promotions man, you have to listen to us, we pay you, I'm the President of Apple.' I said, 'John, I don't care what the story is. I don't want the record, I'm not going to promote it. If I don't like it, I won't promote it.' So John says, 'I'll tell you what, I'll promote it, and if I make this record number one that means you're not the number one promotions man in the business.' I said, 'John, you got a deal, but if the record doesn't happen, I want you to kiss my butt and double my salary and expenses.' So he says, 'You got a deal, but I'm gonna make it number one.' But without John knowing, I checked out all the radio stations, and they said they weren't going to play it.

"So John called all of the stations himself, and he tried to do a promo job. He was so happy, and he came back to me and said, 'We still got that bet?,' and I said, 'John, god bless you, we still have that bet and you better kiss my butt if you lose, and if you win, you can tell me, 'Peter, you're shit,' and if you don't want me to work with you anymore, that's it.' 'Well, you're gonna lose,' he told me, because he had called Chicago, he called San Francisco, and he talked to the Program Directors and they were so nice to him, they took interviews with him. The thing was, the stations put him on tape, and while they played the record in the studio, they never put it on the air. What happened was that a few idiots played it on FM, but at that time FM was nothing, it couldn't sell two records, and all the top stations wouldn't play it. Apple sent out 30,000 records, and about 15,000 came back. The highest it went on the chart was like 68. And he did kiss my butt. He bowed to me, and Yoko said, 'You see, we have to listen to Peter.'"

In stark contrast to George Harrison – who used Apple as a means to develop new artists with genuine commercial appeal and to sharpen his skills as a record producer – John Lennon's commercial instincts were often overshadowed by his tendency to become obsessive – and lose his objectivity – when it came to particular projects that he held near to his heart. Lennon was officially the President of Apple Records and had been – to some extent – involved with Apple's business decisions since 1968. It would not be until 1972 that Lennon started to take an active role in finding and producing talent for Apple.

Lennon had always been interested in Apple but mainly as an outlet for releasing albums by himself and Yoko Ono. From 1969 to 1971, Lennon could often be found at 3 Savile Row, either working on his own projects or attending to various Apple matters. In recognition of the time he spent at Apple, in 1969 Lennon even had a promo photo created that showed his face with the caption "I am at 3 Savile Row most days."

Lennon would never again set foot in Apple's London office (or England, for that matter) after he moved to New York City in August 1971, but he would continue to be actively involved with Apple business. Once Lennon and Yoko Ono set up camp in New York City, the pair became regular visitors to Apple's New York office. It was not long before Lennon had signed several New York City artists to the Apple label. But unlike the artists that George Harrison brought to Apple, Lennon seemed to sign acts more as a personal favor to the artist involved, as opposed to them being a viable commercial prospect.

The first act Lennon signed to Apple was Elephant's Memory, a hard-rocking, denim and leather clad group that had been active on the New York City scene for several years. Lennon made contact with the group during his search for a backing band to work with while he and Ono were in the United States. Having settled into an apartment in New York's trendy Greenwich Village, Lennon and Ono were anxious to start playing live shows and recording new music. Drummer and founding member of Elephant's Memory Rick Frank remembered: "The hook-up with John Lennon was quite coincidental. We did a very high-energy radio show for WLIR in Long Island. It was a really good tape, and it was simulcast. Lennon heard it, or it was brought to his attention. He was looking for a band that could reproduce the sound of his last album, with sax and hard rock guitar, because every time he wanted to record, he would have to bring in Eric Clapton or Ringo Starr or Jim Keltner. So when he heard our tape he said, 'That's the sound I want.'

"So, Lennon got in touch with us through Jerry Rubin, and Rubin came to see me at my apartment on Bank Street. He put us in touch with Lennon, who asked me to bring over some photos and informational material. Within a day, I was in a studio auditioning for him on drums, he had me play on material that had no drum tracks recorded. I walked into the Record Plant and I saw an engineer we had worked with, so I connected with him right away. I was never a Beatles fan, so the awe-struck aspect of it, it was there, but it was not like I had some fanatical desire to meet John Lennon, or his lovely wife. But I connected with Lennon, and he asked me to put drums on these songs. The rest of the band was at this little eight-track studio in the Village called Magnographics.

"In the spring of 1972, Elephant's Memory were at a very confused point. We were either going to sign with this black music label, or we were going to break up. The band didn't believe that I was really going to meet John Lennon. I didn't brag about it, I just told the band that I was going to a very important business meeting and that their careers might depend on it, so why don't you hang out and rehearse a little? I kept them waiting for around four hours. John was very casual. After we played and recorded, we went to a tea house, had some tea and talked things over while the band was still waiting there for me in the studio. I finally called the band at the studio, and they thought I was bullshitting them. So Yoko, John, Phil Spector and I met up with the rest of the band, and we started jamming within minutes."

The first project that Elephant's Memory would undertake with John Lennon and Yoko Ono was to back them on the recording sessions for what would become the *Some Time In New York City* album. It was during these sessions that Lennon expressed an interest in producing an album for Elephant's Memory. The band's deal with Lennon stated that Elephant's Memory were free to sign to any label they wanted, although Lennon cautioned that if the group were to sign with a label other than Apple, it could create contractual problems that could ultimately jeopardize Elephant's Memory ability to do any more work with Lennon and Ono. Frank remembered that the band agonized about signing to Apple.

"We were signed to Apple," noted Frank, "but we had the right to play shows on our own, plus we had a relationship with John where he would give us money under the table because we weren't getting enough from Apple. When we signed to Apple, we were on salary, and it was taxable and all that; John gave us cash. Apple didn't pay us a hell of a lot, but John made up for it, so we were OK. I ended up negotiating the deal myself. We were signed to managers Leber and Krebs – they managed Aerosmith and the New York Dolls, too – and they figured they had a right to be in on the Apple deal. But having been in the business since 1967, I knew all the answers, so I did it myself. But I didn't know much about legal matters, so I hired John Eastman as our attorney, and he helped negotiate the deal. Eastman was suing the Beatles for Paul, but Eastman and Lennon didn't care, there was no conflict of interest. As John said, 'The more the merrier.'

"We signed a multi-album deal with Apple with a commitment to do the double album for John, several singles for John and Yoko, and a double album for Yoko. In return, John and Yoko would produce an album for Elephant's Memory. It was a great deal, except for that the business of Apple was folding and they were slowly going under. I only met Allen Klein once, and it was a scary experience. This was when May Pang worked at Abkco, and she still had nothing to do with John at the time. I knew her very well from other circles. May helped take care of business for us. There weren't that many people working for Apple, just Al Steckler and Dan Richter, who was helping out around Apple. We were also signed to do a tour with John and Yoko, but due to

Lennon's immigration problems he wasn't allowed to work in America."

By the time Elephant's Memory had signed to Apple, they were already music industry veterans. Formed as a jazz-influenced rock group in 1967, Elephant's Memory had gone through several line-up changes and had contributed to the soundtrack to *Midnight Cowboy*. They had already released albums on both Buddha and Metromedia Records prior to signing to Apple and had even come close to scoring a top 40 hit with their single "Mongoose" in 1970. Elephant's Memory had once been considered to be something along the lines of a "bubble gum" band through their early association with the Buddha label, but by 1972, the group had evolved into a dynamic hard rock-outfit.

Elephant's Memory were not the only New York City act to capture Lennon's attention. Lennon also signed David Peel, a "street singer" who had previously released several albums on Elektra Records. David Peel remembers: "I met John Lennon on a Friday in the spring of 1972. I met him on St. Marks Place at a hippy clothes store called Limbo. I had a friend named Howard Smith who brought John and Yoko to see me perform in Washington Square Park on Sunday. They liked my song "The Pope Smokes Dope." Then there was another time when I told Jerry Rubin that I wanted to audition a song for John Lennon. I wrote a song about them called "The Ballad Of New York City – John Lennon And Yoko Ono." I went to their house on Bank Street, and they liked the song, of course, it was about them. Then John and Yoko signed me to Apple."

Peel signed to Apple on 10 February 1972. The contract was for a single album, and Peel was given an advance of $10,000. Soon after the contract was finalized, Lennon took Peel into Record Plant Studios in New York City and produced a full album of Peel's ragged, enthusiastic street rock. The completed album – provocatively titled *The Pope Smokes Dope* – was issued in the United States in April 1972. Presumably due to the controversial nature of the title and the music, Peel's album was never issued in Europe. Lennon actively helped to promote the album in the United States, yet despite his involvement with the record and the fact that Peel was already somewhat established in the music industry, the album sold poorly, suggesting perhaps that "the people" were not interested in Peel's would-be street rock anthems like "I'm A Runaway," "Everybody's Smoking Marijuana" and "I'm Gonna Start Another Riot."

Peel admitted that his Apple album was not particularly well received and claimed that it was almost impossible to find the album in stores. He was also convinced that Lennon and Ono were the only people at Apple who thought that his album was even worthy of release. "I met George Harrison at Apple, and I shook his hand. He looked at my pictures, and then he turned around and left. The other Beatles didn't like me, but John didn't care, they didn't like Yoko either. They didn't like me singing about dope and pot and revolution. I was too radical for their image. Paul McCartney thought I was a troublemaker. As a matter a fact, I was given a quote from Paul McCartney. In 1972 McCartney played on a song called "God Bless California" on ESP Records, and I did a song on the same record, "To Err is Human," and he told Leslie Fradkin, the band director, 'I never thought that I would see the day that I was on the same record as David Peel.' I don't know what Paul thought about my music, but I got his attention."

John Lennon may have been initially entertained by Peel's antics, but Rick Frank of Elephant's Memory had a less charitable view of his radical label mate: "David Peel is a joke. He was a symbol of something that might have been if things had been the way John wanted, the ultimate hippie trip. David Peel was constantly asking us to play drums on records, and he was always in the wings. We had to physically restrain him from appearing with us a lot. David Peel and the Lower East Side was embarrassing. We usually brushed him off."

Unbowed by commercial and critical indifference to *The Pope Smokes Dope*, Lennon immediately threw himself into his next project, which was producing an album for Elephant's Memory. Rick Frank recalled that, "John Lennon was great in the studio. He was a lot of fun and very, very committed to an ongoing production value. There was a lot of jet-setting while we were recording our album, which John thought was funny for a while, but it wasn't in our best interest. We went to dinner at Jackie Onassis's house one night, and Rosie Greer came down to see Lennon and it cut into our recording time. It was not something that John wanted to get too involved with, and I felt the same because we were losing our impetus. We were losing the ability to have John Lennon as a producer because we were going to dinner with Jackie O. So, we finally cut some cords and made sure everyone left us alone while we finished our album.

"The sessions were endless. John wanted to release certain songs as singles that we didn't want. He really related to this song "Black Sheep Blues," and he sang double lead on it. We recorded a lot of songs that didn't come out. It was confusing, because John and Yoko had a drug problem and they were trying to cure it alternatively. They saved us from a major drug problem by keeping it apart from the studio and apart from the scene. We were more of a drinking band; we were never really into hard drugs. John was trying to tidy up his heroin problem and work very hard on our album. John was a very appreciative guy, and he appreciated how hard we worked on Yoko's album trying to make it sound good, and that was very hard because she had a difficult voice and was a difficult person to work with. With Yoko, we had an agreement that we were going to back each other to the hilt. I did interviews saying all these glamorous things about her."

The self-titled album that Elephant's Memory recorded for Apple came out in the United States in September 1972 and would be released in England in November. *Elephant's Memory* received mostly positive reviews, but sales were only average, despite the Lennon connection. The album, which featured everything from rocking boogie numbers like "Liberation Special" to melodic ballads like "Wind Ridge," was of its time and arguably deserved to do better than it did commercially.

Elephant's Memory bassist Gary Van Scyoc suggests that band politics resulted in several of the more commercial songs on the album being overlooked as potential singles. "One of the songs we recorded one night during the sessions was my song, "Forty-Two Down The Line." But John hated it, it was too country rock for him. But he inspired me, and I went home that night and wrote a song about my childhood called "Wind Ridge," and he picked it as a single, actually. He loved that one, and we spent a whole night on it, just myself, Tex Gabriel (Elephant's Memory guitarist), Jim Keltner, and John, who wrote some piano lines for the song. It was way more commercial than anything else we recorded, which is why John picked it. But Stan and Rick were the leaders of the band, so they picked their song "Liberation Special" as the single. They didn't want my song, because they didn't think it was representative of what the whole band sounded like. They might have been right, but it was our best shot at a single. John picked it as a single, they picked their song "Liberation Special," and Pete Bennett picked "Madness." It was a toss-up there for awhile, but Rick and Stan won out and "Liberation Special," the political song, won out as a single, unfortunately."

The lack of a hit single certainly hindered the commercial prospects of the *Elephant's Memory* album. Rick Frank also placed much of the blame on Allen Klein's attitude towards any Apple Records artists who were not former Beatles. "When our Apple record finally came out, it didn't happen, because Allen Klein only worked for the Beatles. He didn't push anything else. We needed promotion, our managers, Leber and Krebs, had failed us. In fact, they were going to sue us to get in on the Apple deal. And here I was doing all the work of a manager, and John was, too. I'm not going to slight his efforts; he was really our manager. He did all the work helping to package our record. It was a very expensive album. John was very proud of the album. He wanted to get a single out and wanted to get us on the road. Elephant's Memory needed the support of Apple to do promotional stuff, tie-ins with radio stations, and they weren't doing it. Allen Klein was not willing to spend money on outside projects besides the Lennons. John raised hell with Klein, but it didn't do any good. Klein was the kind of guy who was extremely paranoid; he sat in a bullet proof, sealed-off office with a shotgun next to him. When I met Klein, I was a pretty rough guy at the time, and he scared us. We only went up to Apple when we needed to."

Al Steckler feels that Elephant's Memory were not victims of Klein's indifference but rather that Apple simply had trouble promoting acts like Lon and Derrek Van Eaton and Elephant's Memory. "Pete Bennett couldn't promote an album like Lon and Derrek Van Eaton. He was a top 40 guy, and it was not that kind of album. Elephant's Memory was the same thing. Elephant's Memory was a project that no one was interested in other than John. They were a pretty good bar band but nothing more than that."

Glenn Friedman agrees with Steckler, adding: "Elephant's Memory were there because John liked them. They were like bikers, they were rough. Toby Mamis – who we hired to do freelance publicity – was the main guy with them. I don't remember seeing a manager, just one guy in the group who was sort of a big mouth. They weren't particularly well received at Apple, and the company didn't know what to do with them anyway. It wasn't the kind of music we were known for. I played their album in my office a couple times, and Joel Silver – this big guy who was around six foot two and who ran Abkco Publishing and was the Administrator for Apple Publishing in America – had the nerve to come into my office and tell me to turn it down. I told him, 'Hey, this is a record company,' and he just said, 'That's just god-awful music, I don't like that shit.' But I didn't really like the album that much, so I didn't play it that often anyway. But I could play ELO as loud as I wanted, because Al Steckler loved them. To his credit, Steckler liked other music besides what we had. In fact, most of the time he would never play anything from Apple. He was totally into ELO!"

Elephant's Memory may have been one of John Lennon's pet projects, but this did not result in the group receiving any special treatment from Apple. "They gave us token promotion, ads in *Billboard* and *Cashbox*, but it didn't last long," recalls Van Scyoc. "I remember we went up to Apple at 1700 Broadway one day, looking for the promotion department. It was hard to find; there wasn't any! We walked around the floor looking for the door that said "promotion," but it was nonexistent. It was very subdued and very sterile up there. There was no music being played in the office. We heard "Liberation Special" on the radio a few times, but it didn't last long either. We did play a few shows, including some with Billy Preston and Badfinger, but it was really just going out on the weekends for us. John and Yoko would call in and introduce us over the public address system which was kind of cool."

In conjunction with the release of the *Elephant's Memory* album, Apple issued Lon and Derrek Van Eaton's *Brother* in America that September. But the record that was shipped to record stores bore only a passing resemblance to the first version of *Brother* that Apple had come close to releasing several months earlier. Only six songs from the original album were retained, now joined by five tracks that had been recorded in New York City on which the brothers were backed by slick American session musicians. Lon Van Eaton had hoped that a single could be derived from the new recordings, but Apple rightly felt that none of the tracks were sufficiently commercial for a single. With the exception of the bluegrass-styled "Without The Lord," the other four tracks bore a strong soul influence, which totally changed the feel of the album.

Nevertheless, *Brother* garnered excellent reviews, with the 23 November edition of the then-influential *Rolling Stone* going so far as to proclaim that, "This staggeringly impressive first album by the Van Eaton brothers ... displays more energy, good feeling, and sheer musical talent than any debut rock record I've heard this year." But the positive press and even a radio ad that featured Ringo Starr extolling the virtues of *Brother* seemed unable to persuade record buyers to purchase the album.

"When the album came out, I was in New York by then, and the Abkco people really thought it was great and wanted to do something (with the album), but most of the time they were just interested in the Beatles and the rest was not important to them, so not much happened with the album," remembers Klaus Voormann.

Even in its altered form, *Brother* was far more commercial than the Elephant's Memory record, and it should have sold much better than it ultimately did. In addition to "Sweet Music," which had been issued as a single earlier in the year, the album showcased a wide variety of sounds, ranging from the fragile acoustic balladry of "More Than Words" to forceful melodic rock like "Sun Song," which Apple had considered – and ultimately decided against – issuing as an American single (possibly Apple 1860) in early 1973.

The Elephant's Memory and Lon and Derrek Van Eaton albums were not the only new Apple product issued in September. Late in the month, radio programmers and obscure record aficionados were treated to "Saturday Nite Special," a single by an American group called the Sundown Playboys. Released in England in November, the single consisted of two authentic Cajun songs, performed by a part-time band from Lake Charles, Louisiana. The band comprised several oil refinery workers, a grocer, a truck driver, and two students, including seventeen-year-old Pat Savant on accordion. Featuring two rousing Cajun stomps sung in Cajun French, the "Saturday Nite Special" single was a wonderful record that had no realistic chance of becoming a hit, yet Apple promoted it to the full extent of its abilities.

To this day, Tony King remains effusive in his praise for the Sundown Playboys. "I loved the Sundown Playboys; it was my favorite of all the things I did for Apple. I got this strange little 45 from Pat Savant, I played it, and it was wild; it sounded so fresh and real. I played it to Ringo and George and they loved it, and I told them I'd really love to put this out on Apple, and they said, 'Let's do it.' So I called up Pat Savant and told him we'd like to put it out on Apple, and he couldn't believe it, he was seventeen. I think the oldest member of the band was sixty-five or something! I did a really good press release for it, and it got loads of play in England. It was a turntable hit, but it didn't sell. People liked listening to it, but they didn't want to spend money on it. It was played all over the place. It really brought Cajun music to people's attention. It was such a wild sounding record that I decided to do a 78. It was kind of magic, that song."

Pat Savant, who was a high-school senior when he was signed to Apple, has especially vivid memories of his time as an Apple Records recording artist. "I started with the band in June 1971, and in December 1971 we got together the finances to have the two songs released as a single on the Swallow Records label. We recorded the single in December of 1971 at the Swallow Studio, and it came out in the first part of January 1972. At the time we made our record, there were a lot of groups out on the Apple label, I think Mary Hopkin and Badfinger. I loved Badfinger's music. So around March or April I was just wondering out loud to a friend in a record shop, 'You know, I wonder what they would think about our music,' so I sent a copy of the single we did on the Swallow label and an explanatory letter to Apple's London office. Two weeks to the day that I sent our record to Apple, I heard back from Tony King, Apple's A&R Manager, and the letter he sent me was to the effect that Apple was interested in the group and were we going to record any new material.

"So we sent them some information, the history of the group, brief bios of the band members and so forth. They were particularly interested in "Saturday Nite Special," so they wanted more copies of the Swallow record, which we sent them. This went back and forth until we signed a contract in August of 1972. The first letter I got from Apple was from Tony King, but after that I started hearing from his assistant, Margo Stevens. So we went to Floyd Swallow and asked him to come in on this. Of course, he wanted his percentage, but we knew that he had dealt with the big companies. The first time Apple issued us a contract, they wanted to pay us based on 90% of sales, but Floyd got them up to 100% and they redid the contract. Apple signed us to a single deal and wanted an option on all our material for five years. The contract was that if they didn't want to release a song, we had the right to release it locally or on some other label. I remember I had to have my father sign for me because I was under-age. I signed it, and he had to sign his name under my signature. So after he finished the contract, Floyd Swallow sent off the master tape to Al Steckler at Apple in New York, and it was released in September 1972." Apple also bought the English publishing rights to "Saturday Nite Special," which was originally published by Swallow's Flat Town Music.

"After we did "Saturday Nite Special" Apple wanted some more material, and we did something with a country and western flavour, a song called 'Back Home in Louisiane,' and we sent that to them along with some other material," recalls Savant, "but they didn't seem all that interested. I guess the sales weren't as good as Ringo Starr or some of the other records they had done before. I also think that Apple started going downhill around then."

"Saturday Nite Special" was not a hit, but Savant feels that being on Apple opened a lot of doors for the Sundown Playboys. Despite the fact that Paul McCartney and John Lennon had recently released such mediocre albums as *Wild Life* and *Some Time In New York City*, anything even remotely associated with a former Beatle and the Apple label still had an almost magical allure in 1972.

"The local reaction to "Saturday Nite Special" was unbelievable," remembers Savant. "We had a local radio station, KLOU, that called itself "the Rock of Lake Charles," and they would play nothing but top forty material. When we did "Saturday Nite Special" for Swallow, our guitarist, Darrel Higgenbothem, and I went to the radio station to talk to the Program Director and see if he would play our record on the rock station. He looked at our single and told us something to pacify us at the time, but it was never played. So a few months later, Darrel and I took another ride over to the radio station, and the Program Director remembered us. We asked him, 'Do you have any new Apple Records?' and he said, 'Well, we have some records that just came in, but I haven't had the chance to look at them yet.' He still had the old copy of our Swallow single, and he looked through the stack of new records and there was our Apple record. He said, 'I can't believe this, this is the same record on Apple?' Then they really got behind the record. We had pretty good record sales locally.

"I never met anyone from Apple. I talked to Chris Stone in Apple's London office on the phone, but that was it. Apple did this nice full-page ad for us in *Billboard*. I went to this record shop, and the owner of this record shop handed me a copy of the *Billboard* ad and said, 'Here, take it.' It was a really nice time for us. At that time Danny and I were kind of oddballs, because our music was kind of the music of the older generation. There weren't that many young people playing Cajun music at the time. We were few and far between back then. If nothing else, being on Apple made the people of my generation realize that maybe what was in the top forty was not the last word in music, maybe people somewhere else look at things differently, and that's what the people at Apple apparently thought. If nothing else, the Apple single did that."

The release of the Sundown Playboys' single neatly coincided with Apple's short-lived "Back To Mono" campaign. Though Tony King no longer recalls the motives behind this campaign, it was presumably initiated to create advance publicity for Apple's planned reissue of Phil Spector's 1963 Christmas album. It was a half-hearted gesture at best, as "Back To Mono" consisted of little more than a red "Back To Mono" pin that Apple distributed as a promotional item and issuing the Sundown Playboys "Saturday Nite Special" single only in mono. As an attention getting promotional item, Apple also had a limited number of 78rpm copies of the Sundown Playboys' single pressed up to distribute to select members of the press.

Savant recalls: "Apple sent us each copies of the 78 and the English version of the single with a small hole in the centre. They also sent us a kit with promo material about the band. I remember they had this 'Back To Mono' campaign going at the time, and they also sent each of us this 'Back To Mono' badge."

The "Liberation Special" single by Elephant's Memory – issued in November – was also given the mono-only treatment. Apple's "Back To Mono" campaign culminated with the international release of *The Phil Spector Christmas Album* in December 1972.

The release of such eclectic, adventurous records as those by the Sundown Playboys and Chris Hodge suggested that Apple had finally found its footing and was now establishing itself as a legitimate record company. Badfinger was making good money for both Apple Records and Publishing and it appeared that Apple had at long last been transformed into a well-run and even profitable business. At one point, Apple was looking so promising that in February 1972 Allen Klein had initiated talks with Lennon, Harrison, and Starr about the possibility of Abkco buying Apple from the ex-Beatles. David Peel remembers how he and a few other people "knew that Allen Klein wanted to buy Apple, and we thought that it was very un-revolutionary for someone like that to control Apple. So we told John that it would be a very bad idea to sell to Allen Klein and his people."

It will never be known if Lennon heeded Peel's advice, but due to the complicated issues involved with Apple's ownership and ongoing litigation with Paul McCartney, no deal was ever struck.

But any plans that Apple may have had of becoming a full-blown record label came crashing to a halt when Badfinger unexpectedly signed to Warner Brothers Records on 4 October 1972. With their Apple Records contract set to expire in July 1973 and their Apple Music Publishing contract ending in October 1973, Badfinger's business manager, Stan Polley, had been attempting to renegotiate a new contract with Apple at various times throughout the year. The members of Badfinger had always assumed that they would re-sign with Apple, and they had instructed their management to negotiate a new deal. But when Polley was unable to get Allen Klein to agree to a cash advance as part of a new deal, he started to shop Badfinger to other labels.

"Everybody in the office who were young loved Badfinger, but none of the suits got them. But there were other problems," says Glenn Friedman, who felt that Badfinger's American management had undermined Badfinger's relationship with both Apple and Abkco. "This guy kept showing up to meet with Steckler called Stan Poses. I was in one meeting where he was complaining about this and that, and that nothing was happening for Badfinger and he was really pissed off at the company and that he was catching so much shit from the members of the group. He went on and on, and when he left, everyone said what a dick he was. I think he really alienated people at the company, to tell you the truth. Klein would not meet with him, so he passed him on to Steckler."

Reflecting on Badfinger's split from Apple, Joey Molland later explained: "We tried to negotiate with Allen Klein; we wanted to stay with Apple. We wouldn't have wanted to stay with them if they had been screwing us around. Klein was in control, though, now at Abkco in New York City. We went to see him... we wanted a sixteen-track tape machine and a mixing console... What was ridiculous about the whole thing was that we had enough money in Chemical Bank in New York that we could've bought fifteen 16-track machines. But our business manager didn't want to spend the money. He wanted to keep it for himself. We left Apple because Klein wouldn't negotiate with us at all. We were the biggest band on Apple, bar none. We were selling more records than John Lennon, we were the biggest selling act on the label, and we were doing it quite regularly for them. I'm not trying to be egotistical. We didn't really make those kind of demands. I can say that now looking back on it, because it's a fact. But we went to Allen Klein and said, 'Look, we want to build a little studio. We'll buy ourselves a house, and we want to build a 16-track studio, will you give us the money?' It was about fifty grand, it was nothing. We made fifty grand in two weeks. And he [Klein] said, 'No. And from now on you're going to pay your own recording costs.' Klein would not negotiate with us, even though we were making money for the company."

On top of allegedly wanting Badfinger to start paying their own recording costs, Klein was said to have suggested that Badfinger take a royalty cut as well. Their original Apple contract, written in Apple's idealistic early days, gave Badfinger an artist royalty of 5% of the retail selling price of their records, but with Apple picking up all recording costs and any other expenses related to promoting Badfinger's records.

Recording contracts of the time gave a typical act an artist royalty rate that could range from anywhere between 5% to 15% of the retail selling price of a record. But with these contracts, the artist would not receive any royalty payments until all of the recording and marketing costs had been recouped by the record company. So Badfinger's royalty rate of 5%, which the group would earn off of every record sold, regardless of whether recording or marketing costs had been recouped, was actually quite a fair deal.

But securing a fair record deal for Badfinger was not the primary motivation of Stan Polley. Polley wanted a cash advance on future royalties, which was something Apple Records (with the notable exception of the David Peel deal) simply did not do. Warner Brothers offered what – on paper – appeared to be a substantial advance for Badfinger to sign to Warner Brothers Records. The Warner Brothers deal stipulated that Badfinger would deliver two albums per year for which they would be advanced $550,000 ($225,000 per album), and they would receive a 12% royalty rate. Badfinger also signed a contract with Warner Brothers Music Publishing at the same time, under which they would receive an advance on their publishing royalties of $100,000 per album.

Tony King believes that Badfinger leaving Apple for Warner Brothers was, indeed, the beginning of the end of Apple. "Badfinger were thought of very highly by the people at Apple," he recalls. "They were Apple's stars. I don't know why Badfinger didn't do better in England, perhaps they were a little bit too 'Beatley.' We did alright with the singles, but we did better with their albums in America.

"When Badfinger left Apple for Warners, everybody was a little bit hurt, because it was a very personal thing between Badfinger and Apple. Everybody had put themselves out a lot on behalf of Badfinger, and in a way Badfinger had ridden to success on the back of the Beatles, so it was natural that we were upset. But at the end of the day, when someone waves a big fat cheque at you, off you go. After Badfinger left, people started to lose interest in Apple, and it started winding down. The trouble is when you're an artist like George and Ringo and you have artists on your label, they take up a lot of time. In a funny kind of way, you have to be a businessman to deal with artists, it's no use you being an artist dealing with other artists, because they want a lot of time and you want a lot of time. George was really attentive to all the artists he worked with, but I think there's a limit for everybody. He still had to go off and make his own records and do his own tours, you're not always available to work with the artists."

Al Steckler agrees that when Badfinger left Apple, "It was a big nail in the coffin. George was not happy about it, but none of them ever did anything to keep them on Apple. Their manager was looking for big bucks and Apple just didn't do that, and Badfinger got something like a two-million-dollar advance from WB for something like six albums. After they signed, Bill Collins came up one day with Peter Ham and told me what the advance was, and I figured it out for them. When you deducted the costs of the albums that they had to pay for, deducted Polley's cut (Stan Polley, Badfinger's American business manager) and split the money between Collins and the four guys in the group, it came out to nothing, it was like $60,000 apiece per album. They really thought they were millionaires. They looked at each other and realized that I was right and that it was too late to do anything about it. Peter just had this horrible look on his face. That was the last time I saw Peter. They had a deal with Apple that was unheard of at the time. Apple would pay for all studio costs, and the band would get paid from record one. Most record deals at the time made the artists recoup all the costs for the album before they got paid. It was a very, very fair deal."

According to Steckler, George Harrison was extremely upset when he found out that Badfinger were leaving Apple. Joey Molland claimed that Harrison angrily confronted Badfinger manager Bill Collins, asking him, "Why the fuck didn't you tell us? You guys fucked us, after we did all that work for you." Collins told Harrison that the reason Badfinger left Apple was that Badfinger had been unable to talk to Harrison directly and that Klein was unwilling to work out a deal. Like the members of Badfinger, Harrison had assumed that Badfinger would simply re-sign to Apple, and he seemed to be unaware of Klein's actions.

Molland admits that it was a difficult decision to leave Apple. "We didn't come in and announce that we were leaving the company. It was all done in third person. There was never a time when we were in Apple and said, 'That's it, we're leaving.' The decisions were made by businessmen, by Stan Polley, Bill Collins, and Allen Klein. The deal with Warner Brothers was a spectacular record deal. Allen Klein, on the other hand, wanted to give us nothing. Klein was managing the Beatles, he didn't care about us. There was no one bigger than the Beatles. I think he might have liked us as another badge on his lapel, but the Beatles overshadowed everything for Allen Klein."

With still almost a year to go on their Apple Records and Publishing contracts, signing to Warner Brothers in the autumn of 1972 could have made for a very uncomfortable environment for Badfinger at Apple, but

Molland insists: "We never got a bad vibe from anybody when we left. I think maybe they were a bit puzzled. But when everybody looks back, there really wasn't any other way for Badfinger to react in the situation. We didn't have any options. It wasn't like we could go to Neil and he could sign us. That just wasn't going to happen. Once they handed over the company to Klein – it didn't matter that it was Klein, it could have been anybody – but once the company was handed over to someone else in the business sense, then all of the original relationships that the group had with Apple went out the window."

By late 1972, it was no longer just the Apple artists and the London office employees who were exasperated with being "an Abkco managed company." Several Apple employees recall that George Harrison and Ringo Starr also appeared to be growing weary of both Klein and Abkco. George Peckham remembers: "Right before Christmas 1972, Nigel Oliver and I went upstairs into Neil Aspinall's old office and designed an 'Abkco Brown Nose of the Year Award'. We always used to catch Malcolm Davies trying to be an Abkco company man, so we thought we'd go after him and also (Apple Studio engineer) John Mills. We made these badges with Abkco on it and put 'Brown Nose of the Year Award' around the edges. We also made this presentation box. We called it a Grummy award.

"So at the Christmas party, the whole office was there, and we awarded John Mills a Grummy award. It had a plaque on it for not making a fool of himself in public. John Mills threw it in the Thames later that night. It was a great party... Donovan, George Harrison, and Nilsson were there. Later that night, I was putting these 'brown nose' badges on Malcolm Davies's back, and George caught me. I thought, 'Oh shit, I've been caught,' but George pulled one off of Malcolm's back and said, 'Come here, give us some of these, they're great,' and he and Terry Doran put them all over their jackets. Just then, one of Klein's guys, Terry Mellis, comes over and says, 'I don't think this is funny at all,' and George gave him this look and told him, 'They're bloody marvelous!'"

George Harrison's wariness of Allen Klein was hardly a new development. "At the Apple Christmas party in 1971, I was sitting on a small couch with George drinking wine," remembers Robin Garb. "He was telling me how glad he was to be in the position to help nurture some new talent because when he started out it had been really rough before they (the Beatles) had been given a break. I told him how much I appreciated the opportunity, but I guess because I had already had a couple glasses of wine, I said I was curious – having worked with Nat Weiss and Nemperor and knowing Nat's relationship with Brian – why, when Brian died, had he picked Allen Klein over Nat Weiss or one of the other big players at the time. He said, 'Oh, I know, because of all the indictments and everything?' I said, 'Yeah,' and he said, 'I'll tell you why. I know that if we went with Nat Weiss, he would find money that we were supposed to be paid. I figure that he would find maybe five million dollars and not steal any of it. But we think that Allen Klein will find ten million dollars but only steal two.' I tried to close my mouth after hearing that, and I said, 'George, isn't stealing a progressive kind of thing?' and he laughed and said, 'We think we can keep an eye on him.' It was truly a decision to dance with the devil."

Apple would release two more albums in the closing months of 1972. Mary Hopkin's once idyllic association with Apple came to an end in November 1972 when Apple released *Those Were The Days*, a Mary Hopkin best-of collection. Apple was confident that this album, which contained most of Hopkin's non-LP singles, would be a big hit for the 1972 Christmas season, but it was not a big seller in either England or America. In conjunction with the American release of *Those Were The Days,* Apple issued Hopkin's two-year old recording of "Knock Knock, Who's There?" as her final Apple single. The song limped to a lowly number 92, which would be Hopkin's final appearance on the American pop charts.

Apple did enjoy an unexpected but welcome surprise with their December 1972 release of *The Phil Spector Christmas Album*. The album, which featured Christmas songs record by the Ronettes, Darlene Love, and other Phil Spector-produced acts, had originally been issued on Spector's Phillies label in 1963 but had been out of print since Spector had shut down Phillies Records in 1966. Al Steckler remembers that, "*The Phil Spector Christmas Album* did very well for us. I brought that album to Apple. I used to go out to the office in California, and I saw Phil a lot. One day I said to him, 'Phil, it's a shame that the Christmas album isn't out, can we have it for Apple?' and he said, 'Sure!' It was as simple as that. I went to Klein and said we wanted to put it out, and Klein worked it out with Phil."

To make the album more attractive to the modern music consumer (the original 1963 album cover showed the artists – all dressed in dated looking suits and dresses – popping out of oversized gift boxes), Apple engaged John Kosh to design a new cover. Kosh remembers that Spector was one of his most unusual subjects. "We shot the Phil Spector Christmas cover in New York. We started in London, and I remember I had to meet Phil in the bathroom of his hotel because he was worried about snipers. He was extremely paranoid. He was convinced that someone was trying to assassinate him, so we actually had to meet sitting on the bathroom floor. But he was very well behaved at the session."

Since being hired by John Lennon in 1969, Kosh had become Apple's favourite designer. After designing the *Let It Be* album and book in early 1970, almost every subsequent Apple album – with the notable exception of the Badfinger albums – had a cover designed by Kosh. He was also responsible for designing most of Apple's press advertisements, including the elaborate eight-page advertisement that Apple took out in the 1972 *Billboard Music Annual*.

For the *Phil Spector Christmas Album*, Kosh designed a colorful sleeve that was more in line with the times. The album sold well in the United States and did especially well in England, where it reached number 21 in the charts. This was Apple's highest charting non-Beatles album in England since Mary Hopkin went to number 3 with *Postcard* in 1969.

Klein had also wanted to put out *The Beatles Christmas Album* (a compilation of the Beatles' seven 1963-1969 Christmas flexi-discs that had been manufactured as an album by Apple and sent to fan club members for Christmas 1970) as a commercial release, but he ultimately did not get the support needed from the ex-Beatles to proceed with the project. "I loved the *Phil Spector Christmas Album*," enthuses Glenn Friedman. "We wanted to put out the *Beatles Christmas Album*, too, all those fan club records, but someone didn't want to do it. I don't know who stopped it, but it didn't stop with Klein."

Apple Films did some brisk business in England during Christmas 1972 with their T-Rex film, *Born To Boogie*. Released in December, just in time for the school holidays, the film proved to be very popular with Bolan's legion of young fans. *Born To Boogie* was packed with many exciting music sequences, but the overall film was a bit of a mess. Ringo Starr's first outing as a film director was somewhat reminiscent of *Magical Mystery Tour*, as it eschewed a coherent story line in favour of disjointed fantasy sequences such as a magic tea party and perplexing scenes of Ringo wearing an animal costume, behaving strangely.

It was the music – which included excellent live footage of T-Rex in concert and a jam session in Apple Studios featuring T-Rex, Ringo Starr, and Elton John – that ultimately made *Born To Boogie* a success. The film didn't garner much critical praise, but it made money for Apple and – more importantly – gave Ringo Starr a creative outlet at a time when it was still unclear whether he would be able to sustain a successful solo music career.

THE DREAM IS OVER

Despite the exodus of Badfinger and Mary Hopkin in 1972, Apple maintained the outward appearance of being an active record label well into the early months of 1973. George Harrison – the only Beatle other than Ringo Starr who remained interested in the original Apple concept of finding and developing new talent – had contemplated buying Apple from the other Beatles and re-launching the label. But after Apple lost Badfinger, Harrison decided that he would be better off starting a new label from scratch and began making plans to launch his own record label.

For the time being, Apple continued to issue new records. Apple even signed one final artist in 1973. Early in the year, American singer-guitarist John Beland was touring England as a member of Johnny Tillotson's band, performing on a package tour that featured Tillotson, Bobby Vee, and Del Shannon. Beland came to Apple's attention through a demo tape submitted to Tony King. "I recorded this tune out in L.A. called "Banjo Man," and it was kind of like a "New York Mining Disaster," Bee Gees kind of tune. I used a lot of Beatles effects on the drums, and it was very sort of Beatles/Bee Gee-ish," recalls Beland. "Midway through the demo sessions, I took the rough tracks with me to England. While we were on tour in England, Johnny (Tillotson) said he really liked what I cut, and he said, 'I have this friend over at Apple Records who used to do publicity for me, and his name is Tony King. Let me set up an appointment, and you can go into London on a day off and see Tony and play him your stuff.' So on my day off I went down to Apple and walked in. I remember that the office was very white, and there were a lot of gold records up all over the place. There was beautiful furniture in Tony's office, but from the outside it was just another little building. I also remember that I was nervous and freaking out because it was the Beatles' label.

"I went up and played the tape to Tony and he really liked it, so I left him the tape and that was the end of that, and I went back to Birmingham to do the rest of the tour. Then early one morning I got a call and I hear this heavy English accent saying, 'John, it's Ringo here,' and I thought it was one of the guys from our English band pulling my leg, so I said, 'Yeah, uh huh,' and he laughed. Then he said, 'Wake up, mate, this is Ringo,' and I made some comment like, 'Tell John and George that I said hello,' and he says, 'Wake up, mate, it *is* Ringo.' When I realized it was him my hands started to shake, because it was the real deal. He said, 'Tony gave me your tape, and I really like it. Why don't you come on down and we can talk about you joining the Apple family?' I called my manager, Downey (Morton Downey Jr. – who would become a notorious television talk show host in America in the late eighties), and told him to get over here because the Beatles wanted to sign me to Apple Records. But instead of being happy for me, he was real mad because he had already verbally agreed to a deal with Scepter Records. So he got on the plane, and the next day Tillotson, Downey, and I went down to Apple and signed a deal. It was a really fair deal. There was no advance, strictly recording the album and putting it out. I could go to any EMI studio where I wanted to record and they would pay for it. They seemed to be very pro artist. They had no problem at all with me producing and arranging the whole album. So we signed the deal, we got all the new pictures taken, and then we went out to a private club where the Beatles used to go to. It was a funny label. You didn't expect to be heard one day and actually signed two days later. It happened so fast that I thought someone had spun me through a revolving rock and roll door."

In New York, Glenn Friedman had also tried to get some new artists on the label, but nothing ever came of his efforts. "I tried to sign bands to Apple, but it didn't work," says Friedman. "I tried to get Klein and Al Steckler to sign this band that I was recording at night called Lugar, who featured Ivan Krall, who would later play guitar for Patti Smith. Ivan was, in fact, around the Apple office, I think he was working there, but I'm not sure what he did. He just bopped in and out of the office. It was a lot harder edged that anything Apple had dealt with before. It wasn't pop, it was kind of like underground New York sort of stuff, like the New York Dolls. They just didn't get it at Apple or Abkco. I sent a copy over to the office in London, and they sent it back to me. We also had a chance to sign the Kinks to a deal for North America. I think the Kinks' manager got in touch with Allen. He was trying to jack up the deal, and then RCA signed them."

Apple's first American release for 1973 was a new single by Ringo Starr's protégé, Chris Hodge, whose "Goodbye Sweet Lorraine" was issued in January. Presumably because Hodge's "We're On Our Way" had attracted little interest in England, the record was only released in the United States, Canada, and France. Unlike "We're On Our Way," "Goodbye Sweet Lorraine" failed to generate much interest (or sales) in America.

Chris Hodge believes that Apple didn't really get behind "Goodbye Sweet Lorraine" but also concedes that "Goodbye Sweet Lorraine" was probably not the best follow-up to "We're On Our Way." "I had a double single deal with Apple," he explains. "They were going to give me an LP deal, but then everything started falling apart at Apple. I should have followed up "We're On Our Way" with another hard rocker, and "Goodbye Sweet Loraine" was more like a laid-back Eagles song, but more spacey, of course. But I was twenty-two and had no manager or anyone to direct me. No one at Apple gave me any real guidance.

"The only people I ever dealt with were Tony King and Ringo Starr, and that was it. I never met any of the other Apple artists. George, Ringo, and Allen Klein signed my contract. I think you needed two Beatles to sign an artist. I popped into Savile Row every once in a while to see Ringo, have some coffee and shoot the shit. I remember Ringo telling me, 'Hey, man, you got a hit single with a bullet,' and I said, 'If it ain't in the top ten it doesn't mean shit to me,' and he couldn't believe I was so naive. For some reason, I figured that it had to be high up in the charts. Ringo said, 'No, this is great for a first single.' All I could think was, why wasn't it in the top ten!"

The first album issued by Apple in 1973 was *Approximately Infinite Universe*, the second consecutive two-record set by Yoko Ono that was issued in January in the United States and in February in England. Featuring excellent support from Elephant's Memory, the album was Ono's most consistent and almost-conventional outing to date. But as compelling as tracks like "Yang Yang" and "Move On Fast" may sound to twenty-first century listeners, in 1973, the album appealed to few outside of Ono's core group of admirers.

Apple issued another two-record set in January, which was a live album entitled *In Concert 1972* by Ravi Shankar and Ali Akbar Khan. "When the mentor of Ravi Shankar and Ali Akbar Khan died," explains Al Steckler, "the two of them decided that they wanted to play together as a tribute. I heard about it so I called George and told him that I wanted to record it, and he thought it was a great idea and told me to do it. So we recorded it live, and George mixed it. That's how things happened. And it sold pretty well, around 40,000 copies. It's a beautiful record." It would not be until April 1973 that *In Concert 1972* was issued in the United Kingdom.

In England, Apple finally got around to releasing Lon and Derrek Van Eaton's *Brother* in February 1973. The album was followed by the March release of the duo's first English single, "Warm Woman." Derrek Van Eaton admits that he has no idea why Apple chose to wait almost half a year to release their album in England, nor why Apple picked "Warm Woman" to be the English single. "Warm Woman" had been taken from the original demo tape that the Van Eaton brothers had submitted to Apple. It had been recorded in a primitive recording studio that the Van Eaton brothers had set up in their home and, as a result, had a lo-fi, murky sound that would have precluded the song from being played on radio. Derrek Van Eaton remembers: "Klaus Voormann had wanted "Sun Song" to be the single from the start, and there was talk of putting it out, but that never happened."

The same month that *Brother* was issued in England, Lon and Derrek Van Eaton went into the Record Plant in New York City with producer Tony Bongiovi to start work on a second album for Apple. There had also been several earlier sessions that were held at Media Sound Studios. "We did a few tracks, and George came and played a wonderful slide guitar on a track called "Where Are You,"" recalls Lon Van Eaton.

Prior to Tony Bongiovi being brought in to produce, Glenn Friedman had been asked to oversee the initial sessions. "One day, their manager, Robin Garb, came in and said he wanted us to book Media Sound Studio on 57th Street and that George Harrison was going to be on the session," recalls Friedman. "Robin wanted me to oversee the recording. I said I'd be glad to, and I invited a friend of mine and my brother, Don – which was a big mistake – to the session. So Lon and Derrek were in the studio recording for about an hour or two, and the session was going well until my brother, who was seventeen or so, pulled out a bag of Quaaludes. Everybody in the control room asked for one except for the engineer. Then George shows up, who came in with someone I don't remember, so I told myself that I had to pull it together. I went up to George and told him I took a Quaalude and that I was messed up. George told me that was cool and then sat down and asked the engineer for a playback. Lon and Derrek came in to listen to the playbacks, and Lon looks at me and says, "Boy, are you fucked up." But Lon and Derrek were happy that George was there and exchanged pleasantries, and then they went back into the studio to record more vocals.

"They were at it for about fifteen minutes and then my brother trips down the stairs and was telling me, 'Give this to George, give this to George.' George looks over and asks, 'What's going on over there?' and I told him, 'My brother is handing me a Quaalude, George, that's what we're up on.' And he says, 'Give me one of those.' So, George popped one, and his friend took two. Within thirty minutes it was bedlam, and we were going on midnight or one in the morning and that was the session. The next day I got a call from Al Steckler at home before I even left for the office, and he told me to get into the office right away. It was like eight in the morning, which was earlier than he usually came in to work. He told me that he got a call from Robin Garb and that Lon and Derrek complained that the session at Media Sound was a waste and that everyone was messed up. He was about to lay into me when the phone rang, and he told me to leave the office. Fifteen or twenty minutes later he came into my office with a big grin on his face and told me, "That was George, and he said that he had a great time last night. So I'll let you off the hook on this one."

It was not long after these preliminary sessions that it became apparent to the Van Eaton brothers that their future with Apple was, at best, an uncertain proposition. Derrek Van Eaton recalls: "I remember we had gone ahead and finished *Brother,* and George came up to us and said that the Apple thing was breaking up. He said that it wasn't any good and that they wouldn't be able to put the promotion into it anymore. He said, 'I'm going to talk to Richard Perry about you guys, because I don't think it's fair that we didn't promote the album like we should have,' and that's how we ended up with Richard. We had been back in New Jersey since coming back from England in December 1971, we never did go back to England after that. After George informed Richard Perry that Apple wasn't going to be able to promote our album, Richard sent us some money and said he'd get something going for us out in Los Angeles. So, we drove across the country, and the night we drove into L.A. we went right to the studio and played on the session for Ringo's "Photograph" after we had been driving all day."

On 31 March 1973, Abkco's management contract with the Beatles and Apple expired, and the three ex–Beatles who were managed by Abkco elected not to renew the deal. Neither Allen Klein nor the Beatles ever commented definitively on record about the split, though it has been intimated that Klein not being able to reach a settlement with Paul McCartney, and thus free Apple and the ex–Beatles from the confines of the receivership, was a considerable source of friction.

Effective 1 April, John Lennon, George Harrison, and Ringo Starr opted to have their individual managers and Apple assume management of their respective business affairs. Management of Apple Records and Publishing would be transitioned back to the Apple office in London.

With the decision made to not renew the Abkco contract, Apple found itself having to quickly vacate their office space in Abkco's headquarters at 1700 Broadway. May Pang remembers: "We took out Apple and all the paperwork from the Abkco offices, and we brought it over to the Dakota (the spacious Upper West Side apartment building in New York City where John Lennon and Yoko Ono had recently relocated) and that's where we left it. We never set up another proper Apple office until Tony King went out to L.A." Temporarily without an American office, the displaced Apple Records label listed the New York office of Capitol Records – 1370 Avenue of the Americas – as their new address. Apple never really did establish a new office in the United States, and more than two decades later, Apple Records master tapes were still in storage at the Dakota.

Apple's split with Abkco also led to the closure of the Apple office in Los Angeles. "We closed the L.A. Apple office when the Beatles split with Klein," recalls Charlie Nuccio. "I think we kept it open for two or three months as Abkco, but there wasn't enough to sustain it. When Allen was out of the management of the three ex–Beatles, that was the end of the relationship. I never even discussed the possibility of keeping the office open with Apple in London, the contract was over. We knew it was coming. Allen was trying to make it work, he tried to renew it, but I guess they didn't."

Across the Atlantic, little time was wasted in getting Klein's people out of Apple's London office. Tony King recalled in 1998: "I sort of remember that Peter Howard and Terry Mellis had to go. And I remember that was a bit of a thing. But because I liked Terry and Peter and Allen, I wasn't one of the gloating committee. There were a certain amount of people in the office that didn't mind seeing the back of them, but I wasn't one of them. They were all very good to me. I still have a very good relationship with Allen. Allen is still my friend. Peter and Terry didn't get along with the people in the office, but I liked them."

Reflecting on Allen Klein's stint as manager of the Beatles, Pete Bennett concludes: "It was a good thing, in that they got me to promote them. It was lucky for them because I was in the middle between them and Klein, but I don't think their association with Klein was a good thing for them. In my opinion, Klein was deadwood, it was luck. I think he got himself a fortune without doing anything. They wanted their records to be broken, and Klein told them, 'I got Pete Bennett, I got the accounting, and I'll run the whole label and the publishing for 20%.' In 1972, they decided that they wanted to have me run Apple. I said, 'Look, I couldn't do that to Klein, and we'll see what we can do.' They found out that Klein wasn't the guy for them.

"They found out that Klein wasn't worth 20%, he wasn't even worth 5%. They wanted the promotion, that's all they wanted. They didn't need Klein for that. You don't need an Allen Klein to negotiate a deal for Apple Records with Capitol. But at the time they signed with Klein, John didn't want to go with the Eastmans because of Paul and the fights that they were having. The Beatles could get any accountant they wanted. That's how John and Lee Eastman explained it to them. The Beatles would have been better off going with Lee Eastman and John Eastman, because they would have had a legal office, an accountant, and me to do promotion. I wasn't tied to Klein. They could have hired me independently."

Peter Brown concurs with Bennett's belief that the Beatles and Apple would have been much better off with Lee Eastman. "It would have been a good idea, because the Eastmans have proved now over the years, particularly John Eastman, to have been very successful dealing with artists like Billy Joel and David Bowie and being a very low-key and reliable attorney, accountant, etc. I think going with the Eastmans would have been a very successful route for the Beatles if they had gone that way. However, there was a problem in that Lee Eastman was a much

The Beatles/Mary Hopkin/
Billy Preston/Plastic Ono Band/
The Modern Jazz Quartet/
James Taylor/Jackie Lomax/
The Iveys/White Trash

APPLE RECORDS

Apple Records 3 Savile Row London W1
New York c/o Abkco Industries 1700 Broadway NY 10019

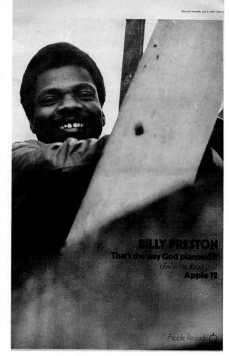

BILLY PRESTON
That's the way God planned it
b/w What about you
Apple 12

Apple Records

I am at 3 Savile Row, most days

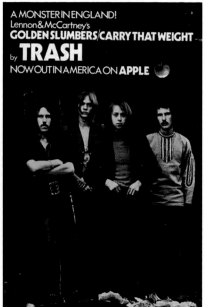

A MONSTER IN ENGLAND!
Lennon & McCartney's
GOLDEN SLUMBERS/CARRY THAT WEIGHT
by **TRASH**
NOW OUT IN AMERICA ON **APPLE**

RHADA KRISHNA TEMPLE

Apple Records **DORIS TROY** 3 Savile Row W1

JOHN & YOKO
with PLASTIC ONO BAND
and ELEPHANTS MEMORY

Apple Records · 1700 Broadway, New York, N.Y.

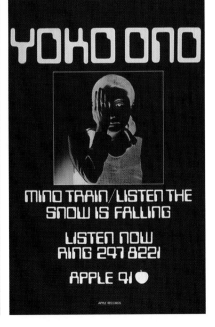

YOKO ONO

MIND TRAIN / LISTEN THE
SNOW IS FALLING

LISTEN NOW
RING 247 8221

APPLE 41

APPLE RECORDS

apple's back

featuring releases from
JAMES TAYLOR
BILLY PRESTON
JACKIE LOMAX
BADFINGER
MARY HOPKIN
and more coming from
GEORGE HARRISON
THE IVEYS
DORIS TROY

more dominating figure than his son, John. John Eastman is much quieter about the way he does things, so Lee Eastman was a bit of a problem. But the real problem would have been the fact that Lee Eastman was Paul's father-in-law, and the balance would not have been as good as it was. Paul was always the most noticeable of the Beatles, and he had the most drive and energy. Also, Paul had built Apple, and by the late sixties Paul had become the frontrunner within the Beatles, although John, George, and Ringo still regarded the Beatles as John's band."

"I can't honestly say why the three of them split from Klein. I was so caught up with just doing my job that I didn't get involved with the big problems," says Tony King. "Don't forget that by this time all of them had managers. Ringo had Hilary Gerrard, George had Denis O'Brien, and John was really looking after himself with Yoko, but he did have Harold Seider (Allen Klein's ex-attorney). So everybody had their own representatives so it kind of fragmented off at that time and Klein was given the elbow. Twenty percent was a lot, but at the same time, he renegotiated their contract with EMI. I think the problem with Allen is that he does a good job for people he represents, but he does a really good job for himself, too."

Al Steckler – perhaps the only person who saw the split from the perspective of both Apple and Abkco – noted that throughout 1972 and 1973, "the relationship was slightly eroding, though not with any really visible incidents. Klein had his own agenda, which wasn't always their agenda. I really think what happened was that when the contract was due to be up, George really believed that he could get the group back together. He was more unhappy with Klein than John. I don't really know to what extent Ringo was involved and how important a role he played. I don't think he played a big role. I think in those days, everything had to do with McCartney, John, and George. John was struggling with his career, George was starting to struggle with his career. George seriously thought about getting the Beatles back together, and I think George realized that he couldn't do that with Allen in the picture. What I recall having heard was that he called Ringo a day or two before the contract was up and said to Ringo, in essence, 'If we're ever going to get together as a group we can't re-sign with Abkco, so let's just not do it.' So Ringo called Klein and that was the end of it. John was very unhappy about the split with Klein. He and Klein had a very good relationship."

Throughout his tenure as manager of the Beatles and Apple, Klein had continued to hold out hope that the Beatles would one day reunite. "There was always a rumor that Paul and John were not liking each other at this point," says Glenn Friedman. "But I went down to Bank Street once where John lived, and John greeted me at the door. He invited me in and asked if I wanted a cup of tea, and we sat there talking. John was a really wonderful guy. He had about ten television sets hanging all over his apartment and none were on any stations, they were all flickering, all static and horizontal bars. I asked him what was wrong with his televisions and why they weren't working, and he said they were just having a little art show. My reason for being there was for Yoko Ono. Abkco wanted me to get her to approve the colors and the typeset for *Approximately Infinite Universe*. She was giving Steckler a hard time, so Steckler said fuck this and sent me. She had some ideas how things should be done, that the lettering needed to be different here and the credits were wrong there. I wasn't one of the older veterans of Abkco, so she approached me cautiously. She asked, 'Did Klein send you?' and I told her, 'No, Steckler sent me,' and she said that was ok. So the phone rings in the distance, and Yoko answers it and says, 'Ok, I'll get him.' She gave the phone to John, and then John walked off with a thirty-foot extension cord. Later I asked her, 'I heard you say to John that it was Paul on the phone….as in Paul McCartney?' And she just brushed it off and said, 'Yeah, they talk all the time.'

"So I went back to the office and told Steckler what had happened, and Steckler said, 'Really? Oh my god,' and he went right off to his private entrance into Klein's office to tell Allen that John and Paul were talking again. It was a big deal that they were talking to each other."

But that was of no consequence to Klein once the Beatles terminated his management agreement. Al Steckler remembers that Klein reacted quickly to the news that Apple would not be renewing his contract, demanding that Apple immediately vacate the Abkco office on 1700 Broadway. "It all had to be out," recalls Steckler. "They had like a week to move out. When it was over, it was over."

Breaking ties with Abkco more or less signaled the end of Apple as an active record label, not that Apple had any major artists left outside of the four ex-Beatles. By April 1973, the only non-Beatles artists still under contract were Yoko Ono, Ravi Shankar, Elephant's Memory, David Peel, Chris Hodge, John Beland, and Lon and Derrek Van Eaton, although George Harrison had already made it clear to the Van Eaton brothers that he would help them find a new record deal.

Free from Allen Klein and Abkco, the Beatles once again turned to Neil Aspinall to take control of Apple. Aspinall explained: "What happened was that John, George, and Ringo asked me if I'd run Apple. I said, 'OK, but as long as it's OK with Paul,' because I wasn't going to get into any three-on-one situation. I'd always been with the four of them. So I rung up Paul and said, 'Hey, the other three have asked me to do it, is that OK with you?' He said, 'Sure, that's fine,' so I was back. I'm working for the four of them... their individual battles might be going on between their individual advisors, if you like, but I was neutral to that."

Ironically, the Beatles split with Abkco just a week before the release of a record project that Klein and Abkco had been working on for several months. On 4 April, Apple issued the long-awaited Beatles double LP greatest hits collections, *1962-1966* and *1967-1970*.

"I did all the re-mastering for the Beatles *1962-1966* and *1967-1970* albums," says Glenn Friedman, adding, "I did both of those with one arm tied behind my back, in a sense. I asked Klein if he could get the stereo mixes of any of the early Beatles tunes, and he said no, just fake it, fake the stereo. I protested to Steckler, but he just told me to do what the boss wanted. Allen Klein then announced the release of the two albums by holding them up at a convention. He just held up the two covers, that I still had to get approved at Queens Litho. There was no press release or anything, he just lifted them up. The place went berserk, and the phones were ringing all over the place. Capitol went ape shit because they didn't know anything about it. Klein just sorta sprung it on everybody.

"I did the work at Sterling Sound. We had a few of the original tapes, but mostly copies. When I remastered the tracks, I noticed that George Martin had put the vocals on the left and the instruments on the right when he did stereo. Sometimes he had the drums in the middle, but invariably the instruments were on the right. What I did was alternate the vocals on the right and instruments on the left and bring up the mid-range and such. We had a big listening party at the office, and everybody loved it. So we sent the test pressings down to John to approve. About two days went by, and Steckler came in and told me that John wanted to talk to me. John thanked me for making them sound better than they ever had before. I asked him what he meant, and he noticed that I had shifted the vocals and instruments. 'We didn't do that, but it's good that you did, it sounds better.' I was flattered, no one else even noticed. We gave a copy to George and to Ringo and sent a copy over to Eastman, but no one else said anything."

Both albums became immediate worldwide best sellers, and they would – with their iconic photos of the fresh-faced 1962 Beatles looking over the staircase of EMI's Manchester Square London headquarters on one side of the album, and the long-haired 1969 Beatles posed the same way only seven years later on the other – be the gateway into the world of the Beatles for several generations of music fans who had been too young or not even born yet when the Beatles had been the undisputed rulers of the pop scene.

Both David Peel and Elephant's Memory recorded more material for Apple in 1973, but no further recordings by either artist were ever issued by Apple. "We did a song called "Amerika" for the soundtrack to a film, *Please Stand By*," recalled Peel. "Yoko wanted Apple to put out

"Amerika" as a single, but because of the problems with Apple, it didn't happen."

On 28 March 1973, Elephant's Memory went into Media Sound Studios in New York with producer Marty Thau to record a new single for Apple. Even though Apple assigned the resulting song, "Everglade Woman," a catalogue number and pressed up test copies of the single, it was never released. Still linked to Apple, Elephant's Memory next went over to England to play some shows to support their Apple album.

Rick Frank recalled how, "After the Apple album came out, we did a tour of England and played the Cavern in Liverpool. We ended up in Wales, where we did a spec album at Rockfield Studios. It ended up coming out on Polydor. Apple gave us no support when we were over there. We had no manager, and John was our only manager and he couldn't leave the country, so it was very difficult to communicate all the things we needed to communicate with Apple. Polydor eventually paid for the recording. Apple never even bothered to drop us, we were actually signed to John and Yoko, so we were free to sign to any label we wanted. I was sort of aware of Apple's problems when we got involved with them, but I was trying to play the optimistic side. But here we were playing with former Beatle John Lennon, and we had to make the most of it. And I pushed that aspect of it all the way, even though I was very angry at times."

The strained relationship that Elephant's Memory had with Apple was not helped by John Lennon wanting to distance himself from the radical excesses of the previous year. May Pang suggests that there came a point when John Lennon simply lost interest in Elephant's Memory and David Peel. "John liked David Peel in the beginning," she recalls. "He thought he was different and very New York. But when John's own political album came out, which was *Some Time In New York City*, he couldn't handle that he didn't get a good review. So he withdrew, and he didn't record anything for a long time. He was depressed, part of his ego couldn't handle it. So after that he didn't want to hear about the politics. Even Elephant's Memory was too radical for him after a while. John also got upset at David for saying that nothing was done for him. John did a lot for him at Apple. John saw him on TV one day talking about how Apple didn't help him, so John got really annoyed and never wanted to speak to him again."

Even with the diminished support of John Lennon, Elephant's Memory and David Peel had both been allowed to record new material for Apple. Badfinger were also working up new songs for Apple. In April, Badfinger and former Beatles engineer Chris Thomas went into Manor Studios in Oxford to complete the last album that Badfinger owed Apple under their original contract. One of the new songs recorded at the Manor was a Pete Ham composition entitled "Apple Of My Eye," a bittersweet ballad that perfectly summed up the end of the Apple era and Badfinger's association with the label. According to his friends and band mates, Pete Ham was genuinely sad to leave Apple, as he cherished the family atmosphere he felt there.

"The words were true," says Joey Molland. "'I'm sorry but it's time for us to go (sic), inside my heart I really want to stay,' and it was really true. We didn't want to go anywhere. Apple treated us well. They paid us on time, they didn't screw us for money. They used all the weight they could to break us, spent loads of money in America promoting the band, with full-page ads, posters and billboards."

Once Badfinger and Thomas wrapped up work on the album and submitted the tapes to Apple, there was little non-Beatles label-related activity in the Apple office. Given that none of Apple's early 1973 releases enjoyed any real success, the label started scaling back operations. With the exception of Yoko Ono, all of the Apple artists would be released from their contracts by the end of the year.

Unlike the other non-Beatles artists on Apple, Yoko Ono would continue to release records on the label throughout 1973. In England, Yoko Ono's "Death Of Samantha" was released in May, but as had been the case with all of Ono's previous singles, it failed to stir up much commercial interest.

Pete Bennett believed that, "Apple could have been a full-scale label, but there was too much work with the Beatles. You have to understand what it was like to have four recording artists who owned the label. If they saw new artists breaking like mad and their records weren't breaking, they'd say fuck the other artists. So Apple was never gonna happen. We could have signed a lot of people, but they didn't want to, they didn't give a shit. They had the resources to do it. They never expressed any concerns to me about the other artists not happening. The only one was George, who asked me to see if I could get Badfinger a hit, and he sat down with me to discuss Lon and Derrek Van Eaton, but that album didn't have it, but they were nice guys."

May Pang agrees that the former Beatles were generally too involved with their own music and careers to be much concerned with the other artists on Apple. She remembers a discussion she had with John Lennon about Badfinger, when she told him: "Don't you realize that we have "Without You"? That's an Apple Publishing song,' and he was like, 'It is?' John was oblivious to a lot of this stuff. For all of them, when they were involved with themselves, they were involved with themselves. The four owners were not going to turn around and say that I'm really interested on a day-to-day basis in somebody else. George Harrison was involved to a certain degree. When he had his first solo album coming out, he was very protective about it. After that release he did a lot of production for the other artists like Badfinger and Ravi Shankar, so he spent a lot of time at the Apple offices at Savile Row."

Back at Savile Row, all was not well at Apple Studios either. Once it became clear that something was amiss at Apple, many key Apple Studio staff members began to leave the company. In mid-1973, both Geoff Emerick and George Peckham resigned. George Peckham recalls: "The studio staff was pretty stable. Once you started, everyone wanted to stay. There was no reason not to. The Apple Studio had a staff of around twenty. There were a lot of junior tape ops and trainee engineers. I finally left in 1973. I felt I was working very hard but getting nowhere fast. I wanted to update equipment and things like that, and nothing was being done. I was still upset about the *Let It Be* album. On the bloody *Let It Be* album, it says engineer Malcolm Davies... he never even touched the tapes. I did all the edits, all the acetates and the masters, and it has his name on it! I said to Malcolm, 'What the fuck is this?' He was like, 'I don't know, it must have been Phil who put that on there.' It made me laugh, because Mal was round the pub all the time getting pissed with the lads, and I was busy working away on the records. All that work and then someone else got the credit for the job I did... all these little secrets between Malcolm and Paul... so I decided to go elsewhere."

The departure of Geoff Emerick and George Peckham presumably should have meant an increased workload for the remaining Apple Studio staff. But Nigel Oliver remembers that by mid-1973, there was often very little to do at the studio. "After George Peckham left, I was left there with just Malcolm Davies – who had been appointed studio manager – and he had to cut everything, and he didn't like that at all. I used to drop acid and take drugs during sessions. When I started at Apple, I was very anti-drug, and Apple used to send me out in a taxi to buy dope for John Lennon. It was a maintenance engineer at Apple, Paul Leighton, who turned me on to drugs. I took acid because I thought, 'Well, the Beatles took it, I should take it.'

"I had done three years as an office boy upstairs, and then I went into the studio around 1972. I set up the tape library with Malcolm Davies. But for the two years after Geoff Emerick left in 1973, Phil McDonald didn't like me very much, so I didn't get any sessions. I just sat in the tape library and did nothing; there was nothing to do. There were three engineers – John Mills, Geoff Emerick, and Phil McDonald – and three tape operators, but there was only one studio, so only one pair could be working at any time, the other pair would be doing nothing. The engineers wouldn't have to come in, but the tape operators would have to be there. And we'd just sit around and take LSD and smoke dope and do nothing. It was wild. I had another job for part of the time in a shirt factory, because there was absolutely nothing to do. I left in September 1974 because it was just so boring in the end. I had worked for the Beatles for six years."

It was not long after the split from Allen Klein and Abkco that Neil Aspinall and the three ex-Beatles who were still actively involved with Apple made the decision to extract Apple from as much non-Beatles related business as possible. Once this course of action had been agreed upon, the only outstanding project left to see through to completion was the release of Badfinger's final Apple album. Given the success of *Straight Up* in 1972, Apple assumed that the new Badfinger album would be a decent money-maker for the label. Badfinger's manager, Stan Polley, and his attorney, Walter Hoffer, met Neil Aspinall and Bernard Brown on 9 May and tentatively agreed to issue Badfinger's new album, entitled *Ass*, in the summer of 1973.

There were several significant legal issues that would hinder Apple's plans to release the *Ass* album. Due to Joey Molland never having actually signed a contract with Apple Music Publishing, Stan Polley was trying to use this issue to bargain for concessions from Apple. Since Apple Publishing did not "officially" own the rights to Molland's new songs (Molland had previously assigned Apple Music Publishing the rights to his songs on an album to album basis), Apple needed to be granted the rights to Molland's songs before they could issue a new Badfinger album.

Complicating the negotiations was the fact that Apple was overdue in paying Badfinger £20,000 in back royalties. Due to the receiver having been appointed to oversee Apple's finances as a result of Paul McCartney's 1971 lawsuit, any Apple expenditure – including paying royalties to Apple artists – had to be cleared by the court-appointed receiver. Getting the receiver to release large sums of money was a time-consuming effort.

Apple had every intention of paying Badfinger's royalties, but they were having difficulty getting the funds released from the receiver. During the 9 May meeting with Apple's Brown and Aspinall, Polley negotiated a deal where Molland's songs would be assigned to Apple Publishing if Badfinger's royalties were paid out immediately and if Apple let Badfinger out of their record and publishing contracts in May as opposed to the respective July and October termination dates of Badfinger's original contracts with Apple. Aspinall and Brown allegedly agreed to this deal and to a tentative summer release date for *Ass*, but they also told Polley that formal approval of the deal would have to come from either John Lennon or George Harrison.

Joey Molland believes that Apple may have even tried to sell the *Ass* album to Warner Brothers. "I think Apple tried to sell us to Warners... I've got an acetate... it's got an Apple on it. It says Badfinger *Ass*, and then it says at the top of it, Warner Brothers. So, I think a deal was started to be made there. I think Apple made some acetates and sent them to Warners 'cause they knew that Warners was sniffing, and Klein wasn't negotiating... maybe they decided, 'What the hell, why don't we just sell the Badfinger product off to Warners and, you know, wash our hands of it.' I think maybe that's what happened there. Of course, it was never released on Warners... it was released on Apple... at exactly the same time as our first Warners record."

Even though Apple had scaled back its involvement with any non-Beatles artists, Tony King maintains that Apple remained as busy as ever during this period. "There was always something going on, especially from '73 to '75 because there were all these solo albums; there was *Goodnight Vienna*, there was *Ringo*, there was *Mind Games*, there was the *Rock And Roll* album, there was *Walls And Bridges*, there was *Living In The Material World*. There was lots and lots going on, especially with John. John kept me really busy. Once I went to America, I was always busy doing stuff for John.

"I moved to America in 1974. I had gone over to America in the spring of 1973 to help Capitol put the art together for the *Ringo* album. Capitol was having a lot of problems with getting the artwork together, so they asked if someone from Apple could come out to California to help, so I went out. I was working out of the Capitol tower for three or four weeks, and I was just about to go home when John called me up and said, 'I'm coming to L.A. tomorrow, can you hang on? Because I got an album, and I'd like you to help me put it out.' By this time he had left Yoko and was living with May. He came out with May Pang and brought with him the *Mind Games* album.

"So I started working on the *Mind Games* album, the promotion, fixing John up to do interviews with *Record World* and *Billboard*, getting him out to meet people, getting him to do stuff I thought he should be doing because he hadn't been doing these things. While he had been with Yoko he had been involved with all these semi-subversive activities, which had not given him a great reputation in America. He said to me at the time, 'Look, I've got this album, what do you think I should do?' I said, 'Honestly, you've just got to go out and make a few friends, because you've lost a bit of support because you've been involved with things of a controversial nature.' So he said, 'Fine, you organize it, I'll do it,' and he did. At the same time, John started to make an album in Los Angles, the *Rock And Roll* album, and then things got a bit mad. There was a lot of lunacy going on.

"One night when we were at the Whiskey, John turned to me and told me that he wanted me to come and work in America. I said, 'Oh, really?' and he said, 'Yeah, I'd like you to come over here and be Apple's person in America. George and Ringo have people in London, but I don't have anybody over here, so I'd like you to come over.' I told him I'd have to think about it. I was kind of undecided about it, but then in the end he kind of persuaded me. At Christmas in 1973, I went to Ringo and George and told them about John's wishes, and they were OK with it. I had a lot of fuss and bother getting myself over to America, because Capitol was a bit resistant to me being over there all the time, and they said, 'We'll only agree to do it if all four Beatles agree,' thinking it would never happen because of Paul's separation from the other three. But I went to Paul and asked if he would help me out with this. He said, 'Yeah, I won't sign anything myself, but I'll get my manager to do it.' So I went out to work for Apple at the Capitol tower in July of 1974."

In stark contrast to the now diminished record division, Apple Films – under the direction of Ringo Starr – was still operating much as it had before the split with Abkco, with several projects in production. Throughout 1973, Apple Films had been working on two feature films, *Son Of Dracula* and *Little Malcolm And His Struggle Against The Eunuchs*.

Little Malcolm was George Harrison's first attempt at being an executive producer of a feature-film. (Harrison would enjoy great success as a film producer in the 1980s and 1990s with his production company, Handmade Films.) The film – a dark drama starring English actor John Hurt – prominently featured the song "Lonely Man," written by Mal Evans and Bob Purvis (former guitarist and songwriter for the group Half Breed).

Bob Purvis had left Half Breed after Mal Evans had been unable to get the group a deal with Apple. Bill Elliot stayed with the group for a few months after the departure of Purvis, but he too would resign from the band towards the end of the summer of 1971. Purvis and Elliot would join forces again in new group called the Truth – who were by all accounts a much better band than Half Breed – but Purvis grew restless once again and left the Truth in the spring of 1972. Purvis next decided to try his luck as a singer/songwriter and moved to London, where he secured the services of Mal Evans as his manager.

But outside of writing some songs with Mike Gibbins of Badfinger and playing a few odd sessions, not much happened for Purvis until his former manager, Rob Hill, convinced him to give his partnership with Bill Elliot one more try. That summer, they formed a duo that would be known as Splinter.

Once again, the hapless Mal Evans found himself in a situation that was excruciatingly similar to his experience with Badfinger several years earlier, where he had been poised to become actively involved with a promising pop group, only to be pushed aside at the last moment. Even though Evans had been managing Bob Purvis for several months and had been largely responsible for getting Purvis to London, it was Rob Hill who would be selected to manage Splinter. Evans was bitterly disappointed, yet he remained willing to help the duo, and it was through Evans that Splinter first came to George Harrison's attention. Harrison had been looking for a song to use for the soundtrack of *Little Malcolm*, and he agreed with Evans that Splinter's "Lonely Man" would work well in the film. Harrison – aided by Badfinger's Pete Ham – recorded a rough version of "Lonely Man" with Splinter at Apple Studios that was utilized for the film's soundtrack.

Harrison explained to the press when Splinter's debut album was released on Harrison's Dark Horse Records label in 1974: "While making the film *Little Malcolm And His Struggle Against The Eunuchs*, Big Malcolm Evans materialized with the ideal group song required for a certain part of said film and, thinking it was a potential hit that may help to get the film noticed by the controllers of the film industry, I thought I would try to produce a hit single by Splinter."

"Lonely Man" never did become a hit (it was never even issued as a single), although a new Harrison-produced version of the song was a highlight of Splinter's *Harder To Live* album, which was issued on Harrison's Dark Horse label in 1975.

Son Of Dracula was a far more elaborate – and eccentric – production than *Little Malcolm*. The feature-length film starred Harry Nilsson (who had no previous acting experience) as a vampire who no longer wanted to be a vampire. In an effort to boost the film's commercial prospects and perhaps help get Beatles fans into the theatres, Ringo Starr – who was the film's producer – took a supporting role as Merlin the magician. Starr invited several of his friends to join in on the fun and both Keith Moon and Led Zeppelin's John Bonham were given parts in a musical sequence in the film. Starr, who is said to have disliked having the responsibility associated with producing a movie, allegedly had great difficulty completing the film. Harry Nilsson later claimed that copious alcohol consumption on and off the set greatly slowed progress, although he noted that he, Ringo, and Mal Evans took great pleasure in going out to London clubs at night while still in costume.

With George Harrison and Ringo Starr engrossed in their respective film projects, the responsibility for resolving several ongoing Beatles-related business issues fell to Neil Aspinall. In November 1973, Apple initiated its first lawsuit against Allen Klein for "mismanagement." Named as plaintiffs in the suit against Allen Klein were John Lennon, George Harrison, and Ringo Starr, as well as the English companies Apple Publishing; Apple Films; Subafilms; Harrisongs; Startling Music; Python Music; Singsong Music; and Ono Music. The American companies involved in the lawsuit were Apple Records Inc. of New

York; Apple Records Inc. of California; Apple Music Publishing Co Inc.; Apple Films Inc. and Apple Music Inc..

November 1973 also saw the release of the final Yoko Ono material to be issued by Apple, which was the *Feeling The Space* album and its accompanying single, "Run Run Run." John Lennon was now living in Los Angeles with May Pang, but he was still apparently very committed to Yoko Ono and her art. Many of Apple's remaining staff assumed that once Lennon had shifted his affections to May Pang, that would be the end of Yoko Ono's career as an Apple Records artist. It came as quite a surprise then that not only was Apple issuing Ono's *Feeling The Space* album, but that they were also giving it ample promotional support in America.

Tony King explains: "John absolutely adored Yoko. He respected her and thought she was a great lady. When he split up with Yoko, he said to me, 'I want you to go to the Dakota when you are in New York, and I want you to meet Yoko, she's a great lady.' It was a great love. She's a rather remarkable person. If John laughed at Yoko, it would have been in a sweet rather than malicious way. John used to laugh at her a lot. When I first got to know her, I used to say to John, 'God, she's such a funny character,' and he'd say, 'I know, tell me about it.' They were fabulous together. John had a nice time with May, too, but Yoko was his great love."

Only weeks after issuing *Feeling The Space*, Apple finally released Badfinger's *Ass* album in the United States on 26 November 1973. *Ass* was the last non–Beatles album to be issued on the Apple label. The final Badfinger single for Apple, "Apple Of My Eye," would be released a few weeks later, on 17 December.

Ever since the meeting between Neil Aspinall, Bernard Brown, and Stan Polley in May, the release of *Ass* had been pushed back several times due to intense wrangling on the part of Badfinger's management. Having been originally scheduled for release in America during the first week of September 1973, the album was delayed until November after Polley boldly requested that Apple assign the rights to the *Ass* album to Warner Brothers. Polley was allegedly frustrated by not being able to get at the Badfinger royalties that Apple was holding, yet the only reason that Apple was holding onto Badfinger's royalties was that it was difficult for Apple to get the receiver to clear the payment. Apple attorney David Braun had informed Polley of this problem and even suggested that Apple could take out a loan to pay Badfinger, but Polley was unwilling to give Apple the time needed to get a loan together.

Apple and Capitol finally grew tired of Polley's antics and issued *Ass* without securing the mechanical license rights to Joey Molland's songs. To protect themselves legally, Apple simply credited the songs to "Badfinger" instead of the individual writers. Since Badfinger were under contact to Apple Publishing, it would now be difficult for Polley to sue Apple for unauthorized use of Molland's songs. Polley, however, was not deterred by Apple's admittedly clever move. The company that he controlled, Badfinger Enterprises, sued Apple in New York City District Court on 5 December for copyright infringement.

Ultimately, all the legal action was done for little gain after *Ass* failed to breach the top 100 of the American charts. The commercial failure of *Ass* was devastating to Badfinger and disappointing to Apple, considering that Badfinger's previous album, *Straight Up*, had made the top forty and had spawned several hit singles. But with little incentive to further develop Badfinger's career and no longer having access to dedicated promotions and sales staff, Apple did little to promote the *Ass* album. Without Pete Bennett in their corner, Apple found out that it was difficult to get records played on American radio. But by the time Apple had made that discovery, it no longer really mattered.

Ass was also a very different record than previous Badfinger albums. On *Ass*, the majority of the songs were written and sung by Joey Molland, rather than Pete Ham, who had composed all of Badfinger's hits except for "Come And Get It." *Ass* was an excellent album, but it was clearly not as commercial as either *No Dice* or *Straight Up*. Due to rivalries within the group, there were only two Pete Ham songs featured on the album, and even Ham's "Apple Of My Eye" – a poignant farewell to Apple which Apple had ironically decided to issue as a single – was not in the same league as Badfinger hits like "No Matter What" and "Day After Day." In fact, the most distinctive feature of *Ass* was its cover, which at first glance appeared to represent a bitter attack on Apple.

The striking colour cover painting depicts a donkey wearing headphones looking up at a giant hand extending a carrot from out of the clouds. Joey Molland refutes that the group had any intention to slight Apple, insisting that the cover was their view of the music business in general. "We were the donkey," he explains. "The group was the ass being tempted. It wasn't about Apple or Warner Brothers, it was about the business. There was never any intention to brand Apple as some sort of business assholes. It wasn't a malicious feeling. We were very pleased to be associated with Apple and loved the people there dearly. Apple wasn't a bad thing at all. It was a great thing. At the bottom of it all, everybody wanted Apple to be a perfectly normal place of business, and they got damn close to achieving that."

The release of Badfinger's *Ass* album would be Apple's final act as a full-fledged record label, and all of the artists still under contract were officially cut free from Apple in December. Chris Hodge clearly remembers how: "On my birthday, 22 December 1973, I got a letter from Apple saying that the Beatles' company was making changes or coming to a close and that they were going to release me from the second part of my contract and that I was free to find another record deal. I was surprised, because I had no idea that Apple was in trouble." Released from his Apple contract, Hodge went on to record singles for both RCA and DJM Records, before emigrating to America to work in the film industry.

John Beland, who had been signed to Apple only months earlier, claims that he was never informed by either Ringo Starr or Tony King that there were problems at Apple. Upon completing the tour of England with Johnny Tillotson's band, Beland recalls that he immediately returned to America to start recording his debut album for Apple. "I went back to America with my contract in my hand, and I did the string session for *Banjo Man*. It was an Apple session," he recalls. "And then Downey called me and said that he had got a telegram from Tony King saying that, because of litigation, everything at Apple was frozen. I was devastated, I had told all my friends in Hollywood. Apple said they would put out the album once the litigation was over, or we could have our contract back and take the tracks with us, which is just what we did. I had no idea that Apple was in trouble. Downey was able to go back to New York and salvage his deal with Scepter who eventually released the album."

1974: NOBODY LOVES YOU WHEN YOU'RE DOWN AND OUT

With all non-Beatles Apple artists now released from their respective contracts, the remaining fifteen-person staff of Apple were transformed into what was essentially a management, album production, and accounting office for Lennon, McCartney, Harrison, Starr, and the Beatles' back catalog.

For the Apple staff whose interest was working for a record company, Apple's transition into an accounting office was not an entirely welcome development. Shirley Natanson recalled: "I was originally in the International Department with Jack Oliver and Tony Bramwell. I was at Apple for six years until the end, and I ended up being the liaison between Apple and EMI. I was hired in April 1969, and I was the first person hired after Allen Klein had gotten rid of all those people. My job was working as the secretary in the International Department, communicating with all of the international companies around the world what was going on with Apple. As time went on, I was the person who communicated with EMI because people left, and I sort of became the label manager. Towards the end there weren't a lot of people left, and we did everything. When I wasn't busy, I helped other people, like Ringo and his assistant when he was making a couple of movies. It was a very small office. I never considered Bernard Brown to be my boss, but he wanted everybody typing up all these long statements of royalties. I tried to do it, but I hated it. I remember complaining to Ringo, and he told me, 'You don't have to do that, you don't work for him," and I didn't do it after that. Because that was really all there was left to do. It got sort of depressing towards the end, as by then it was mostly administration."

With no new non-Beatles product to work with, Apple had started to tentatively consider options for exploiting the Apple catalog. Early in the year, Bernard Brown and Tony King negotiated a licensing deal with Seymour Stein's Sire Records to feature Mary Hopkin's "Those Were The Days" and Badfinger's "Come And Get It" and "Day After Day" on *The History Of British Rock* series of double albums that Sire had compiled for the American market. It was the first time that an Apple master recording was to appear on a label other than Apple.

Acknowledging that Apple's time had passed, George Harrison announced the formation of his own label, Dark Horse, in May 1974. One of Dark Horse's first releases would be Ravi Shankar's *Shankar Family And Friends*, an album that Harrison had produced in April 1973 and had originally planned to release on Apple.

Early 1974 also saw the curtain abruptly come down on Apple Films, whose *Son Of Dracula* was premiered in Atlanta, Georgia on 19 April. The film was a critical and commercial disaster, and Apple Films became dormant once again after *Son Of Dracula* failed to gain national distribution. The soundtrack album – issued on the custom "Rapple" label (presumably a joint venture between Apple and Nilsson's label, RCA) – was also a commercial disappointment.

The other Apple Films project, *Little Malcolm And His Struggle Against The Eunuchs*, fared even worse than *Son Of Dracula*. After being shown at several international film festivals and garnering significant critical praise, the film seemed to literally vanish from the face of the earth, and it would not be seen again until being reissued on DVD in 2011. Director Stuart Cooper claimed that the theatrical release of the film had become ensnared in a funding dispute with the Beatles' court-appointed receiver and that Apple Films was unable to secure the funds needed to properly launch the film.

Apple Records issued its final non-Beatles releases in England in March, which were Badfinger's *Ass* album, and the accompanying "Apple Of My Eye" single. Seven years after the Iveys had helped launch Apple, it seemed only fitting that Badfinger had the honour of being the final non-Beatles artist to release a record on the Apple label. But even during the best of times, Badfinger's records had not sold particularly well in England. Now, given almost no promotion by Apple, neither record charted.

The ongoing lawsuit against Apple by Badfinger's management certainly did little to encourage Apple to invest more than the most basic level of support to promote *Ass* and "Apple Of My Eye." Badfinger's claim against Apple would be resolved in June when the court decreed that Joey Molland was indeed bound by Badfinger's 1968 Apple Music Publishing contract. The court also ruled that Apple was required to pay Badfinger their back royalties within two weeks of the settlement, which gave Apple's receiver a justifiable reason to release the frozen funds.

The Badfinger litigation now resolved, Neil Aspinall assumed that Apple would now be free from having to deal with any non-Beatles business. He was, therefore, quite surprised to receive calls from Tom Evans and Joey Molland shortly after the settlement. Molland and Evans told Aspinall that Badfinger had started to suspect that their manager, Stan Polley, was embezzling money from the group.

Evans and Molland were concerned that the Apple royalties that Aspinall had recently released to the group were in danger of being misappropriated by Polley. Due to Badfinger's tangled business affairs, the group would be powerless to stop the loss of their royalties unless they were able to keep Polley away from the money. Desperate to avoid losing any more money to their management, Molland and Evans pleaded with Aspinall to have Apple hold on to Badfinger's publishing and record royalties until the group had found a way to protect the funds from their business manager. A sympathetic Aspinall agreed to their request, and Apple cancelled the original cheque they had cut several weeks earlier and awaited further instruction from Badfinger.

The release of *Ass* had marked the end of Apple as a label for anything other than records by the ex-Beatles, but Apple Records did contemplate several further non-Beatles record projects in 1974. The first was to have been a double album compilation that would feature highlights from Apple's first five years. A track listing was compiled, but no album was ever released. Initial work on this album had been started by Al Steckler several years earlier. "I remember seeing artwork in Al's office, back in the day, an illustration of a parade featuring all the non-Beatle artists," recalled Toby Mamis. "The album was to include some of their tracks as a kind of promo for all their stuff. Doris Troy, Jackie Lomax, Chris Hodge, Mary Hopkin, of course, and others."

The second project was to have been a fifth album by Yoko Ono. Ono did indeed record a new album for Apple at the Record Plant Studios in New York City in 1974, but the album was not issued until 1992, when it appeared as part of a Yoko Ono box set.

No longer having to attend to the needs of any non-Beatles artists, Bernard Brown and Tony King now had ample bandwidth to handle any work associated with the solo albums that the ex-Beatles issued through Apple. Freed from the day-to-day demands of running a record label, Neil Aspinall could now devote himself to trying to broker a deal that would end the Beatles' partnership.

Once Lennon, Harrison, Starr, and Apple had terminated their relationship with Allen Klein, Paul McCartney's lawyers had been able to make some progress in negotiating an agreement that would formally end the partnership. A tentative agreement was finally reached in November, and McCartney, Harrison, and Lennon made plans to meet – either on 19 or 20 December – at the Plaza Hotel in New York City after a George Harrison concert at Madison Square Garden. (Starr was trying to avoid being served with court papers by Allen Klein, so he arranged to sign the agreement in London). The decision was made to meet on Friday 19 December to sign the agreement. Both Paul McCartney and George Harrison arrived as planned to sign the small mountain of papers, but John Lennon apparently had second thoughts at the last moment and failed to show up. May Pang remembers that Lennon "got so freaked out, he locked himself in the room. I called up Yoko and asked her, 'What should I do?' Finally, he opened the door, and he was in tears, he was in bits. He was afraid that he would be responsible for paying so much money in taxes to the United States. A lot of people don't realize that they were paper rich and cash poor. John was nervous to be liable for one or two million dollars worth of tax. He was freaked out. He didn't want to be left poor."

The agreement had been structured to be fair to all parties, but it would require Lennon – who had lived in the United States since 1971 – to personally pay approximately one million dollars in tax to the United States. Pang speculates that Lennon's reluctance to sign may have also had something to do with his realization that signing the agreement would mean the official end of the Beatles.

Lennon – along with May Pang and Neil Aspinall, who had come over from London for the signing of the agreement – met with Lee Eastman the next day on 20 December to discuss proposed changes to the agreement, but little came of the meeting. Lennon, Pang, and Aspinall would join George Harrison later that evening at a party to celebrate the merciful end of Harrison's American concert tour, before Lennon and Pang departed New York City for Florida, where they would spend the Christmas holiday with Julian Lennon.

May Pang believes that it was Paul McCartney who finally convinced Lennon to sign the agreement. "When John didn't sign the agreement, Paul called up and said, 'OK, we're brothers, I'm here, what is it that we can do to work this out?' Paul jumped in." A revised agreement was sent to Lennon in Florida, and Lennon signed the papers in his suite at Disney World on 29 December, bringing the formal end of the Beatles one step closer to fruition.

1975: And In The End....

By early 1975, the Apple staff knew that it was only a matter of time before the company would cease to exist. Apple was still involved with coordinating the releases of solo albums by the former Beatles, but there was less to do with each passing week. When Dee Meehan (who had joined Apple Publishing at Baker Street as a secretary in 1967) left the company to have a baby, Neil Aspinall was the sole remaining staff member to have been with Apple since its inception.

Since the moribund Apple had plenty of unused space in its office at 54 St. James's Street, Ringo Starr had started operating a new record label, Ring O' Records, out of the Apple office. Following Harrison's lead, Starr had elected to start an entirely new label, rather than try to resuscitate Apple Records.

No one at Apple really had any idea of what was going to happen in the coming months, although the end of the company became much more likely on 9 January 1975, when the Beatles partnership was formally dissolved "at a private hearing before a high court judge."

The four ex-Beatles were now legally free from their partnership and were no longer required to put their individual royalties into a shared Apple account. But they still remained co-owners of Apple, which would – for the time being – remain open to administer their joint interests and to work on resolving several lawsuits that all four ex-Beatles had an interest in settling.

Within weeks of the Beatles' partnership agreement being terminated, McCartney – who had already satisfied the number of albums he was required to deliver under the original Apple/EMI contract – signed a spectacular new solo deal with Capitol/EMI that not only gave him a higher royalty on the sale of Beatles records than the other ex-Beatles (an increase that came out of the Capitol/EMI share, not the "Beatles" share of royalties) but also full ownership of the five solo albums that he had released since 1970. From this point on, Apple would only be involved with the Beatles catalog and the solo work of Lennon, Harrison, and Starr.

In the wake of the legal dissolution of the Beatles' partnership, Apple lingered for a few more months before an announcement was made on 6 May that Apple Records was officially ceasing operations. Neil Aspinall would retain a small staff of some half a dozen employees to assist with accounting and other related matters, but apart from that core group of business affairs staff, all of the remaining Apple employees were let go by the end of the month.

Steve Brendell recounts the day that Neil Aspinall informed the staff that Apple was closing: "Everyone was made redundant, except for Ishmael, Brian (Brian Capocciama and Ishmael Kassan were Apple's in-house accountants) and a couple of others. Neil went through the whole office. Everybody was asked to go into his office, and he made everyone redundant on the same day. When he got around to me, he said, 'Oh well, Steve, you probably know what's going on,' and I said, 'Yeah, I got an idea,' and he said, 'I'm making you redundant, and you'll get a couple weeks pay.' Although the announcement came from out of the blue, it wasn't that much of a surprise when Apple closed. It (Apple) wasn't boring so much as it wasn't really doing anything. By that time, I wasn't doing much more than driving Neil around in his Jaguar.

I used to pick him up in the morning, drive him around a bit and then hang around Apple."

Bernard Brown, Apple's General Manager of Records and Publishing, left the company at the end of May, explaining: "To me and other people, this was inevitable. Now that the Beatles have gone their own way and have their own set-ups, what future was there for Apple? There was no point in keeping the organization going at its present level."

Tony King remembers that as late as 1975, the general public still considered Apple to be an ongoing concern. "We used to get an endless amount of tapes. I remember once when we did this thing in the newspaper about looking for new artists that we had so many people coming around to the building and so many phone calls that the switchboard girl lost her voice after three days. This was around 1970 and 1971. Towards the end we would still get tapes and such, but nothing ever came of it. To be honest, Apple was all a bit amateurish. I don't know if the music business at the time was as business-like as it is today. It was more of a family affair at that time. It was part business and part family, and people were signed because people liked them and stuff like that. It would be quite different if it was around today. I mean, nobody would sign the Sundown Playboys today. They would say, 'What a joke, there's no album behind it.' It was done on a whim.

"That's what the joy of it all was, and that's what Apple represented, and when Apple closed its doors, it was the last of all that, really. It was rather a wonderful thing. I must say I'm rather proud of my association with Apple, and I'm particularly proud of the Sundown Playboys. I was very proud to be involved with putting out something that was completely out of the ordinary and bringing people's attention to a sort of music that people hadn't heard of over here. It was a real thrill, and I think Apple at that time represented that to a lot of people. It couldn't exist like that now."

The decision to wind down the Apple Records label was a sound one; the closure of Apple Studios was somewhat less understandable. Since opening for business in late 1971, Apple Studios had remained constantly busy and had developed a highly respected staff, even after the departure of key personnel in 1973. The studio was making money for Apple, yet in the end, Apple simply cancelled any remaining projects that had booked studio time, locked the doors, and walked away from 3 Savile Row. After announcing the shutdown of the Apple label, Apple seemed to have no immediate plans for the future of the studio, with studio manager Malcolm Davies admitting: "It's going into mothballs as far as I know... and I only hope that the facilities and the reputation that we built up do not go to waste."

Apple's prodigal sons, Badfinger, had been among the final acts to record at Apple Studios. In December 1974, the group went into the studio with engineer Phil McDonald to record their third album for Warner Brothers. Despite there being a feeling at Apple that Badfinger had deserted the label, few of Apple's staff blamed them for leaving and they were pleased to hear that Badfinger were back recording at Savile Row. Even after the group had departed Apple for Warner Brothers, the Apple staff remained fond of the group, and it came as a horrible shock to everyone at Apple when – less than four months after Badfinger completed their sessions at Apple Studios – Badfinger leader Pete Ham committed suicide on 24 April 1975.

May Pang, who spent a week in Apple's London office that April, met Pete Ham and Tom Evans a few days before Ham's death. "I was always Badfinger's biggest supporter, because they were good people," she recalls. "So I called them up when I was in London. I remember that Tommy said, 'Oh my god, I can't believe you would talk to us,' and I said, 'Why? We're friends,' and he replied, 'Well, you know, you're kind of famous.' I felt that they had a very low self-esteem just by saying that to me. So I offered to take them out to dinner. I asked them to please meet me at Apple, and that was the first time they had set foot in Apple since they split. Laurie McCaffrey said to me later that she didn't realize that it was Pete who came with Tommy, they looked different, especially Pete. The look of worry changed their look. Everyone was surprised to see them. I guess I was the only one who brought them in. I know that Tommy and Pete enjoyed the visit, and everyone who knew them was genuinely happy to see them."

Paul McCartney, who received news of Ham's suicide while he was in Los Angeles finishing his *Venus And Mars* album claimed that, "It upset me, because he was so good. It was one of those horrible things where you think, 'What if... what if I called him a week ago? Would that maybe have stopped him doing it?' You always wonder."

Having already released two unsuccessful Badfinger albums and now involved in their own management-related litigation with Badfinger, Warner Brothers had decided not to release the album that Badfinger recorded at Apple Studios. Their decision to shelve *Head First* was surprising, given that Badfinger had so many allies at Warner Brothers. Since 1970, Warner Brothers' London office had become home to several former Apple employees and artists. After leaving Apple, Derek Taylor had become Director of Special Projects, and Ron Kass later joined Taylor, becoming Manager of Warner Brothers' London office. In addition to Badfinger, both James Taylor and Jackie Lomax had been signed to the Warner Brothers label.

The album that Badfinger had recorded during the final days of Apple Studios may have gone unissued for many years, but there had never been any shortage of artists wanting to record at Apple. Apple Studios could have remained a lucrative investment for the ex-Beatles, but given the increasingly complex web of legal problems that haunted the former Beatles and Apple, Apple presumably thought it best to be involved with as few activities as possible, and they made no plans to re-open or even sell the studio.

Tony King feels that there came a point when the ex-Beatles simply wanted to be free of Apple. "I think John was quite relieved when Apple was shut down," he says. "I think that everyone was quite relieved at the time. I don't remember anyone being particularly upset about it. It was a bit of a headache that was got rid of. By the time Apple closed its doors, I was only involved with Ringo and George. When Apple closed their doors, I got paid off. They gave me my Mercedes and some money, and then I went to work for Elton John at Rocket Records. Apple to me was the turning point in my career. It was a fabulous time for me. I loved working for Apple. Probably some of the happiest years of my life were spent working at Apple."

"I was happy when they closed down Apple, because I thought it was silly," says Klaus Voormann. "The three of them (Lennon, Harrison, Starr) were also happy to close Apple. Apple was very disorganized, and in retrospect, I think it was ridiculous what they did. The idea of treating artists differently than they were normally treated, it just doesn't work. You have to have a strong hand. The way that Paul did Mary Hopkin, that was good. But you can't just make a record with Billy Preston or Doris Troy, you have to follow up on it. You need to arrange the tour and do the promotion, and all this was just haywire at Apple. Neil and Peter Brown couldn't do that work. Derek Taylor could write stories and do a little promotion, but he couldn't possibly build up a promotional scheme for a band. There was no one at Apple who was able to really do a professional job. Once the band folded, all they needed to have organized was sort of what Neil is doing now, keeping the Beatles projects together. And the rest, everybody could do on their own. That was my opinion."

The ex-Beatles may have felt a sense of relief when Apple Records was closed, yet even Paul McCartney was proud of what had ultimately been achieved with Apple, noting that, "Apple was together in a lot of ways...I still think all the records that came out of it, Billy Preston and James Taylor, Badfinger, Mary Hopkin, all the people we did take on all had very good records. George, even with the Radha Krishna Temple, I think that's great stuff. I don't think you can fault any of the artistic decisions. Looking back on it, I think it was a very successful thing."

Since the pared-down Apple organization no longer needed a large office, the company moved across the street to a smaller office at 29-30 St. James's Street. Occupying a simple front office on the first floor of an anonymous looking building, Aspinall and the small Apple staff he had retained put the past behind them and focused on looking after the remaining shared affairs of Lennon, McCartney, Harrison, and Starr and re-structuring the Apple organization to operate in a world without Beatles.

Though Apple Records had "officially" ceased operations, Apple would continue to coordinate the production and promotion of solo albums by Lennon, Harrison, and Starr until the expiry of the Beatles' contract with EMI and Capitol. Since the three ex-Beatles were signed to EMI until February 1976, the Apple imprint would be kept alive until that time and would be looked after by Shirley Natanson. "When I left Apple in 1975, EMI offered me a job and I became a label manager at EMI, and I still looked after the Beatles and Apple at EMI."

In October 1975, Apple released a John Lennon greatest hits collection entitled *Shaved Fish* and George Harrison's *Extra Texture* album. *Extra Texture* was the last album of new music to be released on the Apple label. Having worked so hard to keep Apple viable in the early 1970s, it's not surprising that Harrison was the only Beatle to acknowledge Apple's passing. To signify the end of Apple, the record label on Harrison's album featured an Apple logo on which the Apple had been eaten to the core.

In addition to those two albums, Apple finally released John Lennon's "Imagine" as a single in England, where it effortlessly found its way into the top 10. In December, Ringo Starr's *Blast From Your Past,* a greatest hits collection, became the final album to be released on the original Apple Records label.

APPLE AFTER APPLE

Upon vacating the 54 St. James's Street office, Apple appeared to have been quickly forgotten by both the music press and apparently most of the English record buying public. Two final Apple singles were issued in the UK in early 1976, but neither garnered much press coverage and both failed to chart. The first single, released in January, was Ringo Starr's "Oh My My," a three-year old, disco-friendly track taken from the *Ringo* album. It was followed by George Harrison's "This Guitar Can't Keep From Crying," a gloomy song lifted from Harrison's poorly-received *Extra Texture* album from the previous year. Receiving only cursory promotion from Apple and EMI, both records did little more than signal that the Apple label had indeed reached the end of the line. With the expiration of Apple's deal with EMI, the distinctive Granny Smith Apple label was retired, and all future pressings of Beatles albums and solo albums by Lennon, Harrison, and Starr that had originally appeared with Apple labels reverted to Parlophone/EMI in the UK and Capitol in the United States. The expiration of the Capitol/EMI deal also resulted in Apple's entire catalogue of non-Beatles recordings going out of print.

Apple's business affairs had certainly become more complicated in the wake of splitting with Allen Klein in 1973 and the formal end of the Beatles partnership in 1975, but it was an unusual and arguably unnecessary step for Apple to delete its entire non-Beatles catalogue. The Apple albums of James Taylor, Billy Preston, and Badfinger would have certainly continued to sell had Apple bothered to work out a deal with Capitol/EMI to keep them in print. Instead, all of the non-Beatles Apple albums were remaindered and consigned to record store cut-out bins. Within a few years, it would be almost impossible to purchase new copies of *James Taylor* or Badfinger's *Straight Up* and both albums became sought-after collector's items.

Not only had the Apple albums gone out of print, but the rights to the non-Beatles material were more or less frozen due to the end of the EMI deal and several ongoing lawsuits. Peter Asher approached Apple in 1976 to license the Apple masters for James Taylor's "Carolina In My Mind" and "Something In The Way She Moves" for James Taylor's *Greatest Hits* album, only to learn that Apple was unable to license the master recordings to Taylor's label, Warner Brothers. "We made enquiries but wanted to avoid the muddle of all the legal stuff," explains Asher. "It became clear that it would be a slow and annoying process. So we said forget it and re-recorded the songs in the style that James was playing them on stage at the time."

Taylor's album went on to sell in excess of eleven million copies. Had Apple been in a position to license the songs to Warner Brothers for a modest two cents per track – a four cent royalty per album sold – Apple would have earned more than $400,000 in royalties.

George Harrison apparently had tentative plans to reissue at least three albums from the Apple catalog – Ravi Shankar's *Raga,* the two-LP *In Concert 1972* set, and the Radha Krishna Temple album – on his Dark Horse label. On 29 December 1974, Harrison's Ganga Distributors (the corporate parent of his Dark Horse label) gave Apple Records £100 for the rights to all three albums. Apple retained the right to sell off any unsold inventory, although Harrison was given the first option to purchase any surplus inventory at cost. Harrison ultimately must have had second thoughts about investing his money in reissuing albums that would be easily found in the remainder bins of record stores for the next decade, and none of the three albums would ever be issued on Dark Horse.

The Apple era had ended and, for the ex-Beatles, probably not a moment too soon. Change was thick in the air, and several new musical genres – disco on one end of the spectrum, and punk at the other – would soon be the new sound of the seventies. By ceasing to operate as a record label, Apple was spared the indignity of becoming an inconsequential relic of the sixties and would not be relegated to coasting on past glories and the increasingly hard-to-market talents of four middle-aged musicians.

Of course, the decision to shut down the Apple label had been made long before 1976. Paul McCartney had signed a lucrative new solo deal with EMI/Capitol in early 1975. George Harrison had also secured a new record deal when he signed his Dark Horse label to A&M Records the previous year. Indeed, A&M had agreed to fund and distribute Dark Horse with the expectation that Harrison would record for the label when he completed his contractual obligations to Apple and EMI.

With McCartney and Harrison contracted to other companies, only John Lennon and Ringo Starr were free to continue with Apple should either of them have elected to keep the company going as an active record label.

But John Lennon had no intention to sign with any label after the expiration of the Beatles' Capitol/EMI contract in 1976. Retiring from the music business altogether to raise his new son, Sean, Lennon would not record again until 1980. As for Ringo Starr, even though his *Ringo* and *Goodnight Vienna* albums had been big hits, his subsequent records would prove to be a commercial liability to the labels that had signed him, Atlantic (US) and Polydor (International), after his Capitol/EMI deal expired.

The mid-seventies would be a difficult time for all but one of the ex-Beatles. George Harrison continued to possess some of the commercial appeal that he had experienced earlier in the decade, but sales of his excellent 1976 album, *33 And 1/3,* could hardly compare to the glory days of *All Things Must Pass* and *Living In The Material World.*

The Dark Horse label – despite switching from A&M to Warner Brothers for distribution – was underperforming and having trouble establishing itself as anything more than an outlet for George Harrison records. The label's main act, Splinter, had been unable to follow-up the minor success of their debut single, "Costafine Town." Worse still, in the space of three years, none of the albums released by Dark Horse artists – including Splinter, the American rock band Jiva, the R&B band Stairsteps, former Wings guitarist Henry McCulloch, Ravi Shankar, or Attitudes (a band featuring session men Jim Keltner, Paul Stallworth, David Foster and Danny Kortchmar) – sold many records. Harrison would allow the label to limp on for another year before finally letting go of all the Dark Horse artists (other than himself) in 1977.

Harrison's decision to shut down the Dark Horse label surprisingly coincided with an uptick in the fortunes of his music publishing business. Soon after the Dark Horse artists were released from their contracts, "Honey Don't Leave L.A.," a failed Dark Horse single by Attitudes, was covered by James Taylor on his *JT* album in 1977. *JT* sold more than three-and-a-half million copies and earned the song's publisher, Harrison's Ganga Publishing, some unexpected and very welcome royalties.

The following year, another Attitudes song, "In A Stranger's Arms," would bring further revenue to Ganga, when it was covered on Yvonne Elliman's top 40 album, *Night Flight.* Harrison scored another coup in 1978, when he secured the publishing rights to the soundtrack for *Monty Python's Life Of Brian.* The film was a big hit, and one of the songs, "Always Look On The Bright Side Of Life," took on a life of its own and even became a top five single in the UK when reissued in 1991.

Ringo Starr's Ring O' Records would experience even less success than Dark Horse, and unlike Harrison, Starr's music publishing ventures did nothing to offset the losses generated by the label. During the three years that the company existed, Ring O' would issue an odd collection of records that ranged from an album of recording engineer David Hentschel interpreting the entire *Ringo* album on synthesizer, to a reissue of John Tavener's Apple album, *The Whale.* The only artist of consequence to sign to Ring O' was Graham Bonnet (a former member of the late 60s band the Marbles). Bonnet's 1977 album for Ring O' and several singles were moderate hits in Bonnet's native Australia, but he and Ring O' were unable to export that success into other territories. Starr eventually gave up on the label and shut it down in December 1978, explaining to journalist John Blake that, "If you don't sell records, then it costs you money. You have to look at it straight and say, 'What's going on?' and you either turn it around or you do as I did yet again (and say) that it is time for it to end."

Paul McCartney was the only former Beatle who would be able to keep pace with the evolving music scene of the mid-seventies. Whether undertaking a massive tour of American stadiums or serving up catchy disco-pop hits like "Silly Love Songs," McCartney retained much of his Beatles-era ability to give the public exactly what they wanted. As a result, his career thrived as his former partners struggled to come to terms with the latest developments in pop music.

McCartney – ably mentored by Lee Eastman – also proved to be a far more astute businessman than his former colleagues. After disassociating himself from Apple – to the extent that he could – McCartney had been advised by Eastman to invest in music publishing. McCartney slowly began to build a catalogue of music copyrights, comprised of his own compositions as well as those of such famed writers as Buddy Holly, Harold Arlen, and others. McCartney's publishing company, MPL, went from strength to strength and is now among the largest and most successful independent music publishing companies in the world.

Of the ex-Beatles, only McCartney maintained his commercial standing in the years that immediately followed the dissolution of the Beatles and Apple. Both Harrison and Starr now found themselves in an unfamiliar place, where their new music was no longer guaranteed to find a receptive audience. They had to quickly adapt to this new post-Beatles reality, as did several of their former Apple associates. Mal Evans, in particular, had become increasingly lost without Apple or the Beatles in his life. Since 1963, Evans had served the Beatles on what amounted to a 24-hour a day, seven days a week basis. Even after the Beatles split in 1970, Evans had continued to road manage the recording sessions of Lennon, Harrison, and Starr and worked on various projects at Apple. But as Apple wound up operations and there was little work to be had at what was left of the company, Evans had relocated to Los Angeles where he hoped to find work as a record producer.

"Mal wasn't a producer, really," reflects Steve Brendell. "He was looking for work. He more or less didn't have a job. There weren't any Beatles tours to do. There was nothing to do other than occasionally a Beatle would call him up and say, can you do this for us? Mal didn't really have an office. His main thing was when the Beatles were recording, and then he would be there full-time every minute they were in there, and he would be there with them, looking after them."

In Los Angeles, Evans had been involved in an unsuccessful attempt to produce a solo album by Keith Moon of the Who. Relieved of his production duties by Moon's label, MCA, Evans spent the final months of 1975 working on demo tapes for Natural Gas, a new band formed by former Badfinger guitarist Joey Molland. Reunited with Molland for the first time in several years and finding the band receptive to his production ideas, Evans was in good spirits and was (by all accounts) looking forward to starting work on Natural Gas's debut album on 5 January 1976.

During the Natural Gas sessions, Evans seemed to be the same old "Mal" to Joey Molland, yet many of Evans's friends from this period claim that he often seemed depressed. Evans's troubled emotional state finally caught up with him on the night of 4 January 1976, when officers of the Los Angeles Police Department were summoned to an apartment that the 40-year-old Evans shared with his girlfriend, Fran Hughes, and her young child. Evans had allegedly been drinking heavily and, in a drug and alcohol-fuelled stupor, had been wandering around the apartment, yelling and waving a Winchester rifle. "It was a proper Winchester rifle. I had the Winchester in my hand five or six weeks before he died," remembers Bill Elliot of Splinter. "When Mal went to the desert with Ringo to film *Blindman,* Mal got right into guns. Mal had his pistols, his Smith and Wessons and Colts, all in racks going up the stairs."

Frightened by Evans's behavior, Hughes called the police to request help. When the officers arrived at the scene, they broke down the door, saw Evans standing in the middle of the room holding a gun, and they opened fire, instantly ending the life of Mal Evans in a hail of bullets.

Harry Nilsson – who received a call from Fran Hughes within hours of the shooting – later recounted to *Record Collector* journalist Ken Sharp that he had to go down to the Los Angeles jail to get Hughes out of jail (she was being held as a material witness) while Nilsson's wife and another friend went to clean the apartment. The cleaning job was presumably not done to the satisfaction of the building owner, who later presented Hughes with a bill to cover the cost of cleaning the carpet in the room where Evans had been gunned down. Hughes promptly sent the bill to Apple, which Peter Brown claimed Neil Aspinall refused to pay.

The ex-Beatles were reportedly very shaken by Evans's death, although that didn't stop John Lennon from making a final joke at the expense of his old friend. Upon learning that Evans's cremated remains had been lost in the mail while being shipped back to England, Lennon is alleged to have suggested that Mal had probably ended up in the dead letter office. Nilsson later confirmed that this is exactly what had happened.

It had been Nilsson's suggestion to cremate Evans, as it would cost less for his family to ship his remains back to England. Nilsson arranged for Evans's ashes to be shipped to Apple, only to receive a call from Neil Aspinall a few days later, telling him that Evans's mother and wife had come to Apple to collect Mal's ashes but that the ashes had never arrived. The ashes eventually turned up at the airport, where – according to Nilsson – they had indeed been found in the dead letter office. Once the remains were recovered, Evans's family would hold a memorial service for the man who was warmly remembered as a gentle giant by almost everyone who had known him. None of the ex-Beatles attended.

The death of Mal Evans was but one of several links to Apple's past that was permanently severed during 1976. In October, Apple finally sold the freehold of what remained of its former headquarters at 3 Savile Row. Due to the poor condition of the building after Apple's attempted "renovations," the once stately townhouse would remain derelict for the next five years. Ringo Starr paid final tribute to the Apple era when he put a photo of the graffiti-scrawled door of the abandoned Savile Row building on the back cover of his 1976 album, *Rotogravure*.

Given that the ex-Beatles were no longer contractually bound together, former associates were surprised when the group did not totally dissolve Apple in 1976. It appears that even though the individual ex-Beatles were no longer forced to pool all of their earnings into one central company, they grudgingly realized that Apple could actually serve a vital purpose of looking after their shared business interests. Despite Paul McCartney having spent a good deal of time and money in the early seventies trying to completely extract himself from Apple, as the tensions associated with the Beatles' break-up began to subside, it became apparent that a single organization was in a much better position to look after the Beatles legacy than four individual companies.

From 1977 onwards, Apple – which was now little more than Neil Aspinall, a small accounts office headed by Brian Capocciama, and a battery of retained lawyers on both sides of the Atlantic – reconfigured itself to be the sole caretaker of the Beatles legacy and to represent the Beatles in ongoing lawsuits with Capitol/EMI, Allen Klein, and any other party that they deemed to be a threat to the Beatles' legacy. "There was a lot going on," claimed Aspinall in an interview with *Mojo*. "First of all, when I started running Apple again there was still the internal lawsuits between Paul and the other three. The second thing that had to be done was Allen Klein. That lawsuit with him had to be dealt with. After that, I was looking at various contractual commitments. Trying to sort out the legalities of what was going on with our record company, that took from '78 to '89. Sorting out what happened with *Yellow Submarine*. What happened to those thirty-nine cartoons that had been made? What was the deal? There was a lot of stuff. So the hiatus period was really pulling as many strings together as you could, so we had an idea what was going on. A lot of it was establishing what you owned and what you didn't own."

One thing that Apple was certain that they didn't own were the royalties that they had been holding on behalf of Badfinger since 1974. Three years after agreeing to temporarily hold Badfinger's royalties until the group could get their managerial difficulties sorted, Apple was no longer comfortable with holding on to this increasingly large sum of money. In 1977, Apple went to court to have the money turned over to a court-appointed receiver. The court complied with Apple's request, and from then on, Apple paid Badfinger's publishing royalties directly into a court supervised account and would do so until the surviving members of Badfinger managed to reach an agreement on how to divide the royalties in September 1985.

Sadly, the agreement would be reached too late for Badfinger's Tom Evans, who took his own life by hanging on 19 November 1983. Evans, who friends and family claim to have never fully recovered from the shock of Pete Ham's suicide in 1975, had allegedly been despondent over career setbacks and frustrated by not being able to get his share of the Apple royalties.

Between 1975 and 1977, Apple spent a good deal of time and resources trying to resolve their long-standing dispute with Allen Klein. On 10 January 1977, Apple finally reached an out-of-court settlement with Klein and Abkco, paying the former Beatles manager $5,009,200 to settle his claim, which had been whittled down from the original $63 million dollars that Klein had originally claimed he was owed for the work he did on behalf of Apple. As part of the settlement, Abkco would then pay $800,000 to Apple, which would be divided amongst Harrisongs, Ringo Starr, Apple Films, and Apple Records (California). In comments made after the settlement, Allen Klein attributed the success of the deal to Yoko Ono's "Kissinger-like negotiating brilliance."

Even though Paul McCartney maintained a 25% stake in Apple, neither McCartney nor Lee or John Eastman were involved in the negotiations with Abkco, though Lee Eastman told *Billboard* that McCartney was "delighted to see his friends end this problem." McCartney had originally been targeted by Abkco for $34 million in damages, but Abkco's claim against McCartney had been dismissed by the appellate division of the New York Supreme Court in June 1976.

Allen Klein's good fortune turned out to be short-lived. In April 1977, the United States Internal Revenue Service indicted Klein on tax evasion charges. Working with information provided by Pete Bennett, who himself had been indicted on 6 December 1976, the Internal Revenue Service claimed that Klein was guilty of selling close to a quarter of a million dollars worth of records by the Beatles and several unnamed Apple artists without disclosing the sales to the United States tax authorities.

The government attorney prosecuting the case claimed that for a three-year period between 1970 and 1972, Klein had instructed Capitol Records to send promotional copies of Apple albums directly to Abkco, requesting that the albums not be marked as promotional goods. The government's case detailed how an Abkco employee – Pete Bennett – then sold the albums to record stores and distributors in the New York City area as new product. Since Abkco had received the records at no cost, a tidy sum was earned from selling the records at wholesale prices to record stores. In the course of their investigation, the Internal Revenue Service concluded that through the illegal sale of promotional records, Klein had earned $118,022.43 in 1970, $55,045.80 in 1971 and $42,974.38 in 1972.

Klein and his attorneys did not contest that Abkco had received the promotional albums, but they were adamant that they had not received money from the sale of those albums. The government was able to prove that Bennett – who was cooperating with the prosecutors – had, in fact, pocketed money from the sales, but they were able to find only circumstantial evidence that Klein had directly profited from the scheme. In the end, Klein was never found guilty of selling the albums but, rather, was charged with the misdemeanor of making a false claim on a tax return.

In addition to violating United States tax laws, this unfortunate scheme had deprived Apple of sales of approximately 84,000 albums. Had these records been purchased through legitimate means, they would have certainly helped secure stronger chart performances for the albums. Abkco's actions had deprived Apple Records of more than a quarter of a million dollars of revenue, but Apple received no compensation from Klein as part of the court action, other than the satisfaction of knowing that Klein was to spend several months in jail as part of his sentence. Though sentenced in 1978, Klein would not serve his jail term until 1980.

Upon settling with Klein, Apple appeared to drift into an extended period of limited activity. Aspinall kept himself busy sorting out the details of ancient contracts and tending to various legal disputes, yet he also had enough time on his hands to enable him to attempt to launch a second career in artist management. Working with John Gilbert – a close friend and the former manager of the English rock band Family – Aspinall set up a management company called G&A Productions in 1977.

The company's principal artist was Charlie Ainley, a competent vocalist and songwriter who had enjoyed minor notoriety during the brief "pub rock" boom that swept through London in 1974 and 1975. Aspinall used his decade-old business relationship with Nat Weiss to secure Ainley a contract with Weiss's Nemperor Records, and two albums by Ainley were issued by Nemperor. Neither album sold particularly well, and it was not long before Aspinall gave up on artist management to return to devoting his full attention to Apple.

By the early eighties, there were few traces of Apple visible to the general public; Apple had been effectively transformed into what was little more than a holding company. Even the old Apple office at Savile Row had changed beyond recognition. The new owners of 3 Savile Row had basically purchased the foundation, basement, and façade (as Apple had gutted the upper floors several years prior in anticipation of their never realized studio renovations) and had to create an entirely new interior. On a nostalgic visit back to Savile Row in the early eighties, Derek Taylor had a look around the newly remodelled building and was saddened to find that the building's once grand interior bore almost no resemblance to how it had looked during the Apple years.

Since divesting itself of Apple Records and the Apple Studio, Apple – now pared down to Aspinall and approximately three staff members – had evolved into little more than an anonymous business office, handling contractual matters and initiating lawsuits with increasing efficiency. Few visitors, including the company's owners, ventured into Apple's first floor office on St. James's Street.

One unexpected but very welcome visitor to the office was Derek Taylor, who spent the afternoon of 11 December 1980 ensconced in the office with Aspinall, reminiscing about the past and fielding the many phone calls that were coming into the usually quiet Apple office. On this cold, sunny day, it was 1969 all over again, with Taylor and Aspinall discussing the Beatles and attending to Apple business, except this time John Lennon was dead and the two old friends were trying to make sense of Lennon's murder in New York City the previous evening. And for a brief moment later that day, Taylor was once again asked to serve as Apple's press officer, advising George Harrison on the wording and tone of Harrison's press statement about Lennon's death.

Apart from the profound personal loss experienced by the three surviving Beatles, Lennon's death would fundamentally change the structure of Apple. It could not have been long before the remaining Beatles realized that Yoko Ono was now an equal partner in Apple Corps. Considering the tension and ill-will that had existed between the three Beatles and Ono in the sixties, becoming business partners with their former nemesis could have been a major challenge. But Ono's elevation to partner status did not turn out to be as dramatic as it could have been, especially given that Ono had already been representing Lennon on the Apple board for four years, ever since he had elected to stay at home and raise the couple's son.

Ono's sudden transformation from board member to owner had little direct impact on the day-to-day activities of Apple. After Lennon's death, Aspinall and Apple's lawyers resumed their vigilant watch over the Beatles' empire and continued to work towards reaching a settlement to an ongoing dispute with Capitol and EMI. Curiously, one of the most consequential legal matters addressed by Apple in 1981 had nothing to do with Capitol Records or even the Beatles, but rather with the Apple name itself.

In the late seventies, it had come to Apple's attention that an American computer company in California had been trading under the name "Apple Computers" for several years. Lawyers for Apple Corps took immediate action to protect the trademark that Apple had held since 1968. A settlement was quickly reached, where Apple Computers is believed to have paid Apple $80,000 (the terms of the agreement were never officially disclosed) and agreed not to use the Apple name to manufacture computers capable of making music. In exchange, they would be allowed to share the "Apple" name.

The Apple name had been safely secured, and little more was heard from Apple Corps until 1983, when the company left the 29-30 St. James's Street office they had occupied since 1975 to move to new premises at 48 Charles Street. Similar to the most recent St. James's Street office, Apple's new location on Charles Street was a far cry from the elegant office at Savile Row.

Former Apple artist Pat Savant of the Sundown Playboys remembers visiting Apple in the early eighties: "The first time I visited England was in June of 1983 and I went to Apple Records when they had this small, insignificant office on Charles Street. I talked to Neil Aspinall's secretary, Chris. I just wanted to talk to Neil, that's all. I went back three or four times, and she kept saying that he was out and the last time she said that he was on vacation. I guess I shouldn't have been as forward, but I said, 'Before you can go on vacation, you should work first,' and she got a big laugh out of that. I never was able to make contact with him."

Aspinall may very well have been on holiday when Savant visited the Apple office, but he would spend a considerable amount of time away from Apple after reportedly suffering a heart attack in late 1983. Thankfully, Aspinall recovered and was able resume his duties – although working a shorter work week than he had done previously – as head of Apple.

Upon his return to Apple, Aspinall maintained the low profile that he had cultivated since 1975, and little was heard from Apple for the next few years. There were no major new Beatles projects being developed that Apple was directly involved with, and neither Aspinall nor the Beatles had any interest in doing anything with the Apple Records catalog. Apple still owned the Boston Place building – identifiable only by the small "Apple" name plate under the doorbell – which they had continued to use for storage. But inside, film cans and master tapes were exposed to water seeping in from damage to the structure that had not been repaired, which suggested that at this date, Apple had yet to truly appreciate the value of their archive.

But there were others in the music industry who felt certain that there was value in the Apple legacy. It was during this time that several members of Apple's sixties-era management team began formulating an ambitious plan to re-launch the Apple Records label. Former Apple Records head Ron Kass had long felt that Apple could have been a successful record label, had it not been for Allen Klein. Perhaps in an attempt to reclaim past glories, or maybe simply just to give Apple Records the chance he felt it deserved, in early 1986 he contacted former members of Apple's 1968-69 management team to discuss the possibility of a re-launch of Apple.

Ken Mansfield remembers: "Ron Kass called me in Nashville, where I was living at the time, and told me that he had just got back from London and asked, 'If we put Apple back together, would you come back?' We'd had some conversations in London about putting Apple together. We wouldn't reconstruct the label, but we'd re-do Apple with the original people. He said what he wanted to do was to not have the Beatles fund it, but rather fund it through someone else. I had a friend, Ted Solomon, who was a big financier, and he committed ten million dollars to the venture. So Ron, Ted, and I went to London and met with Neil Aspinall and Tony Bramwell, and Kass had already talked to Ringo and George about it. He thought it could happen as long as the Beatles didn't have to dip into their own pockets again. Ron had even made the concession that Apple's home office could be in Nashville, Tennessee, because I had had my fill of New York and L.A. When we got back from London, we all had specific tasks we had to do, but I suddenly couldn't get a hold of Ron Kass. While we were in London, we had noticed that Ron Kass seemed unwell. When he got back to the States, he went to the doctor, found out he had colon cancer and died six months later."

With the death of Ron Kass, the idea of re-launching Apple was quietly put to rest.

Having spent most of the eighties operating in relative obscurity, Apple burst back into the public view in February 1989, when Apple's lawyers emerged from the shadows to once again take on the now-giant Apple Computers, arguing that Apple Computers had violated the terms of the

1981 agreement with Apple Corps. In less than a decade since the original trademark sharing agreement was forged between the two Apples, Apple Computers' desktop computers had evolved into powerful machines that could be used to create sophisticated music via their midi capabilities. Apple's case against Apple Computers, which ultimately became a benchmark case for trademark law, would now require significant legal and business resources from Apple Corps. Fortunately for Apple, just as they were launching their lawsuit against Apple Computers, they finally managed to reach an out-of-court settlement with Capitol Records.

Apple had sued Capitol Records in 1979, claiming that between 1969 and 1979, Capitol had classified $19 million worth of Beatles records as having been scrapped or destroyed, and thus had paid Apple and the Beatles no royalties on these records, when, in fact, many of these albums had been sold. The audit of Capitol that Apple had undertaken also found that Capitol had used an excessive number of Beatles promotional albums (for which the Beatles received no royalties) to help promote the records of other Capitol Records recording artists.

The Capitol settlement, which paved the way for the original Beatles albums to be issued on CD, granted Apple an increased royalty rate and creative control over the Beatles catalogue. Capitol would also be required to add a small Apple logo to all of the Beatles albums, as well as any reissued 1970-1975 solo albums by John Lennon, George Harrison, and Ringo Starr. Finally, Capitol also agreed to a comprehensive reissue program of the non-Beatles Apple catalog. Unlike the fanciful plan that Ron Kass had envisaged of re-launching the Apple label by re-issuing the back catalogue and signing new artists to Apple, Capitol and Apple would focus solely on reissuing the original Apple albums that had been out of print for more than a decade.

The resolution of the Capitol lawsuit set the stage for a new surge of activity from Apple. Perhaps in anticipation, Apple moved their offices from the Charles Street location to new offices at 6 Stratton Street.

THE NINETIES: APPLE'S BACK

No "new" Apple products came out in 1990, but it was a busy year as the company worked on several projects that were scheduled to hit the market in 1991. In preparation for the reissues of the original Apple albums, Apple began searching through their tape and photo archive to find previously unutilized photos and music to be used for the reissue series. At Abbey Road, producer Ron Furmanek and several engineers began dusting off and re-mixing tapes that had been sitting in Boston Place since the early seventies. Aspinall even brought Derek Taylor back to Apple to create a press kit for the reissue project and to write the liner notes for the reissue of George Harrison's *Wonderwall Music*. Apple appeared to be fully committed to developing a high-quality reissue program, and as Taylor optimistically noted in an interview that came with the press kit he created, "It's about progress and a little bit of respect for the past... no money spared on it... just make a good job on it. And it will sell!"

The reissue program commenced in October 1991, when Apple Records issued its first "new" non-Beatles product since 1974. The inaugural release was a four-song vinyl and CD single (both released only in England) that featured a track apiece by Badfinger, Mary Hopkin, Billy Preston, and Jackie Lomax. To everyone's surprise and delight, the record even charted for a week, reaching #60 in the pop charts on 2 November 1991.

In conjunction with the resurrection of the Apple Records label, the Apple Films entity was reactivated to develop and produce a documentary film about the Beatles' first visit to America in February 1964. *The Beatles First US Visit* was the first new Apple Films project since the 1974 *Son Of Dracula* debacle. Issued on VHS and laserdisc in November 1991, *The Beatles First US Visit* enjoyed healthy sales and set the stage for a far more ambitious undertaking that would dominate Apple's efforts for the next five years.

Apple set up a new subsidiary company called Apple Productions for the sole purpose of producing a definitive video history of the Beatles. The project – which was ultimately dubbed *The Beatles Anthology* – was essentially an expanded update of the *Long And Winding Road* film that Neil Aspinall had originally compiled in 1970 and 1971. Given the limited space available at Apple's Stratton Street office, Apple Productions set up shop in a building at 5 Wendell Road, a then-scruffy residential neighbourhood in West London. Apple Productions soon employed eleven people, including producer "Chips" Chipperfield, director Geoff

Wonfor, and writer Bob Smeaton.

Given all of the work that went into getting the Apple Records reissues project off the ground and the development of *The Beatles First US Visit*, 1991 had been a busy year at Apple. It was also a highly lucrative year for the company on the legal front. On 11 October, Apple's London attorney, Gordon Pollock (known in legal circles in England as "the Bruiser"), announced to a high court judge that, after 116 days in court, Apple Corps had reached an "amicable" out-of-court settlement with Apple Computers. The settlement stipulated that Apple Computers would pay Apple Corps $26,400,000 for the right to continue to use the Apple name on their computers.

It was a stunning legal victory. Apple had returned with a vengeance, and a month after the resolution of the Apple Computer trademark action, Apple Records reissued five long out-of-print albums on CD (all would also be made available on vinyl and cassette). The November 1991 releases included Billy Preston's *That's The Way God Planned It*, Jackie Lomax's *Is This What You Want?*, Badfinger's *Magic Christian Music*, Mary Hopkin's *Postcard* and James Taylor's self-titled Apple album. Each release was bolstered by the inclusion of unreleased tracks or non-lp singles, with the exception of *James Taylor*, which featured just the original twelve songs as Taylor vetoed adding any unreleased material to the reissued album.

There were certainly a few thousand people around the world who were delighted to finally get Jackie Lomax's 1969 album on CD. Nevertheless, a few questions were raised about the timing and motivation behind Apple's decision to reissue the original Apple albums. Though never officially confirmed, it was suggested that Apple reissued the Apple Records catalogue primarily to prove ongoing international use of the famous Apple logo as part of their dispute with Apple Computers. Capitol's limited promotion of the Apple reissue series – consisting of a single poster and tee-shirt proclaiming "Apple's Back!" and a handful of Apple tracks being featured on a Capitol Records sampler – certainly does lend some support to this theory.

The Apple reissue campaign would continue in waves, culminating in 1993 with the long-awaited release of Badfinger's *Straight Up* album on CD. Later that year, Badfinger would earn Apple more than a million pounds when red-hot pop vocalist Mariah Carey's internationally successful remake of "Without You" became one of the biggest selling records of the decade. Although the revenue generated by "Without You" was now shared with Warner Chappell Music Publishing – the company that Apple had contracted to administer the Apple Music Publishing catalogue – Apple still earned an enormous sum of money from Carey's impassioned rendition of the twenty-year-old

Badfinger song.

Having re-entered the record business via the reissues of the non-Beatles Apple albums, Apple began to give serious consideration to issuing new albums of previously unreleased Beatles recordings. Granted creative control of the Beatles' EMI recordings as a condition of the 1989 settlement of their lawsuit against Capitol, Apple was now free to develop albums comprised of archival Beatles material. The ex-Beatles had long maintained that there was little music of merit that remained unreleased, but Apple would prove them wrong by releasing no less than four collections of previously unreleased Beatles music between 1994 and 1997.

The first album comprised of previously unreleased Beatles recordings (discounting *Live At The Hollywood Bowl,* which had been issued by EMI in 1977) was a two-disc set entitled *Beatles Live At the BBC,* featuring performances that had been taped live for BBC Radio between 1962 and 1965, including unique recordings of songs that had appeared on Beatles records as well as many songs that the Beatles had only performed for these BBC sessions. Issued in November 1994, *Beatles Live At the BBC* quickly sold over three million copies in America and nine million copies worldwide. Particularly notable about this release was that it was the first Beatles album to feature the iconic Apple Records label since the seventies.

In the midst of coordinating new record projects and overseeing the completion of *Anthology,* Apple once again moved offices. The new Apple building – an impressive four-storey townhouse at 27 Ovington Square – is the largest office that Apple has occupied since 1975. George Harrison's Harrisongs publishing company also moved into the building.

For many years, the only indication of Apple's presence in Ovington Square was a hand-lettered note (since replaced by a proper brass name plate) over the front doorbell that read "Apple." The interior of the building, however, was an entirely different matter.

Writer Robert Sandall, who was given an audience with Neil Aspinall (though not allowed to tape the conversation) for a 1996 profile on Apple in the English magazine *Arena,* suggested that Apple's new office reflected the company's re-emergence as a full-service music and entertainment company. "Concert posters line a foyer wall that leads into the office, with its two-storey wall of gold and platinum records and its reception area dominated by Richard Avedon's 1968 psychedelic portraits... the odd thing about the place, though, is the noise. There isn't any. Aside from the discreet chirruping of phones, Apple feels almost deserted. Apple today is a reluctant employer. On the two days a week that he's in the office, Derek Taylor spreads his papers over the table in the ground floor boardroom. There is a small phone-answering, photocopying, coffee making secretariat which includes Ringo's son Jason."

Sandall's article was one of the first published accounts of life at Apple since the early seventies, and several similar interviews soon followed. Given Aspinall's celebrated reclusive nature, the music press were perplexed by the sudden accessibility of Neil Aspinall and Apple. But as soon as journalists sat down to speak with Aspinall in his first-floor office in the Ovington Square building, it was clear that Apple had big plans for 1995 and that the company was willing to do whatever was necessary to gear up the publicity machine.

Apple's first project of the year was the release of the long-awaited greatest hits album by Badfinger, the first "new" album to be issued by Apple Records in almost two decades. The album was issued in May 1995, and it became Apple's best-selling non-Beatles release since the reissue of Badfinger's *Straight Up*. In conjunction with the Badfinger album, Apple also released an expanded version of *Those Were The Days*, the Mary Hopkin singles compilation that had originally been issued in 1972. *Those Were The Days* was released on compact disc in England at the same time as the Badfinger album (which was also released as a 2 LP vinyl record) and was scheduled for release in America, but for reasons unknown, Apple and Capitol ultimately decided to not issue Hopkin's album in the United States.

In the UK, Apple promoted the two releases by purchasing ads in several British music magazines that showed the covers of both albums under a cryptic headline that could have been lifted straight from the original Apple advertisements of the late sixties. The ad copy – almost certainly written by Derek Taylor – simply stated: "The stars are so big, the earth is so small, stay as you are." Whether or not this ad stimulated sales of the Badfinger or Mary Hopkin albums is open to debate, yet its appearance represented a welcome, albeit small, return to form for Apple.

The release of the Badfinger and Mary Hopkin CDs, however, was insignificant when compared to Apple's big project for 1995: *The Beatles Anthology* – the definitive film history of the Beatles that Apple Productions had been meticulously crafting since 1991. The first stage of the *Anthology* project would be the international release of the film, which would be broadcast over several nights as a television mini-series. Although Apple had originally envisaged *Anthology* as a home video, they wisely changed their mind and elected to sell worldwide broadcast rights for the series.

In America, the ABC television network bought the rights for nearly $20 million, while in England, ITV outbid the BBC with an offer of almost £5 million. And to the surprise of many television industry insiders who thought that the series could not generate enough interest and capture the amount of viewers needed to justify such an outlay, ABC announced that almost all of the advertising time for *Anthology* had sold within days of being offered.

Starting on the evening of Sunday, 19 November, *Anthology* was broadcast for three successive nights, and it touched off a mini wave of Beatlemania. Reacquainting old fans with the group and introducing the band to a new generation of music buyers, *Anthology* was an unequivocal creative and marketing triumph. Featuring pristine versions of rarely seen films and promo clips, *Anthology* was, indeed, the definitive history of the Beatles. The only real criticism of the film was that it tended to downplay the more difficult periods of the group's career, instead offering a somewhat sanitized version of the Beatles' story.

Due to the tendency of *Anthology* to gloss over anything that made Yoko One or the three surviving Beatles uncomfortable (as owners of Apple, they had final say over what made it into the finished product and what remained on the cutting-room floor), the story of Apple was given only minimal consideration in the film. The Apple era was represented by a brief montage of filmed performances by the Iveys, James Taylor, Jackie Lomax, Badfinger, and Mary Hopkin, followed by some perfunctory remarks by Aspinall and the ex-Beatles. Many former Apple employees were surprised at how easily Apple was dismissed in *Anthology*. After viewing the film, former Apple Records President Jack Oliver remarked: "It was a real downer. I felt let down by the *Anthology* video. I liked the first one, it was quite good, but when they got to the Apple years, basically they skipped most of it. I was sort of depressed when it was over. I never felt that when I was there. It never felt as depressing as they depicted. A lot of people say how bad it was, but it wasn't that bad. I think it was pretty crazy, but it wasn't overly crazy. Everybody was having a good time working, and you weren't supposed to have a good time working. We sort of invented having a good time and having a job at the same time."

Fortunately for fans, while the Beatles may have elected to keep certain elements of the group's history "off limits," they were less inhibited about sharing their music. As a result of the Beatles' decision to fully open the vaults, *Anthology* featured a bounty of rare music that ranged from the Quarrymen's 1958 recording of Buddy Holly's "That'll Be The Day" to "What's The New Mary Jane," a meandering, drug-inspired "song" from 1968 that Lennon had recorded with the assistance of George Harrison, Yoko Ono, and Mal Evans.

The most critical component of the *Anthology* campaign would be the albums that would accompany the film. The project ultimately spawned three double CDs worth of previously unreleased tracks, alternative versions, and a host of live recordings. On 21 November, Apple/Capitol/EMI released the first two–CD (and three–LP) set in the *Anthology* series. It entered the American charts at number 1 and stayed there for three weeks, a highly impressive feat for a group that had not performed together for close to a quarter of a century.

The entire *Anthology* campaign had exceeded all expectations. By late 1995 and well into 1996, the Beatles were once again on the covers of countless magazines, were regularly featured on television, and were even back on top 40 radio. In December 1995, Apple Records released the new Beatles single, "Free As A Bird" (which featured the three surviving Beatles completing an unreleased John Lennon demo from 1977), and it quickly became a top ten hit in both England and the United States. It was the first Beatles single of "new" material to be released since 1970, and "Free As A Bird" was also the first Beatles single to be fully owned by the group.

Capitol and EMI owned all of the Beatles and solo material of Lennon, Harrison, and Starr issued prior to 1976. But since Lennon was no longer under contract to EMI when he wrote "Free As A Bird," ownership of the song was retained by the Lennon Estate, Harrison, Starr, and McCartney, and the Beatles licensed the rights to "Free As A Bird" to Capitol and EMI via Apple Records.

Anthology would be followed by *Anthology 2* in March 1996 and by *Anthology 3* in October 1996. Like *Anthology*, both collections were two–CD, three–LP sets and both reached number one on the American charts. *Anthology 2* also included a "new" Beatles single, "Real Love," which was another late seventies John Lennon demo that the surviving Beatles had completed. It was slightly less successful than "Free As A Bird," though it still earned the Beatles a gold record in the United States for sales in excess of 500,000 copies.

Looking to augment and leverage the sales of the *Anthology* CDs, Apple ventured into merchandising by launching a mail-order clothing line called Apple Organics. Operated in conjunction with EMI Merchandising, Apple Organics offered a collection of Beatles hats, backpacks and several shirts emblazoned with an Apple logo. All of the products offered were manufactured from environmentally friendly organic fibres, and order forms for the products were included in every *Anthology* album.

Due to all of the activity surrounding the *Anthology* project, little notice was given to two Apple Records reissues (on CD and vinyl) that were released in the UK in the summer of 1996, Badfinger's *Ass* and Ravi Shankar and Ali Akbar Khan's *In Concert 1972*. The lack of attention given to the *Ass* and *In Concert 1972* releases once again illustrated the problem that had plagued Apple since its inception, where any non–

Beatles releases were almost always overshadowed by Beatles projects. The decision to not reissue *Ass* in the United States was particularly odd, given that Badfinger were far more popular in the United States than they were in England, but Apple and Capitol were both focusing all of their effort on *Anthology* and the American CD release of *Ass* – Badfinger's poorest selling Apple album in the seventies – was simply not a priority for either company.

The final stage of the *Anthology* campaign was launched on 5 September 1996, when Apple released the *Anthology* home video, which consisted of eight videos packaged together in a custom slip case. Despite many consumers having taped the *Anthology* series at home when it had been broadcast, it quickly became one of the best-selling music videos of the year.

By 1997, thirty years since the Beatles had launched the company, Apple was once again active and thriving. Like its four owners, Apple had travelled a long and winding road since its inception. Even at this late date, a number of familiar faces from the old days could still be found at the Apple office. Neil Aspinall was still in charge, and Apple's loyal accountant, Brian Capocciama, remained a fixture in the accounts department. Even Derek Taylor was back at Apple, coming into London from his Surrey home a few times a week to work on several projects. As Taylor explained to *Request* magazine in 1997, the new Apple, "certainly isn't the philanthropic organization it was in the late sixties, but in some surreal way it does quite resemble the sixties again, with the Beatles all back together again, making decisions in the same room."

Sadly, just as the activity at Apple was reaching fever pitch with the *Anthology* campaign, Derek Taylor had been hospitalized for cancer surgery in March 1996. Taylor made a modest recovery and was able to contribute to the ongoing publicity campaign, but he relapsed in early 1997 and died on 7 September 1997.

For many former Apple employees and Beatles fans, Derek Taylor encapsulated the true spirit of Apple. In some ways, his passing brought the company's fleeting return to a new golden age of Apple to an abrupt and definitive end. Taylor's wit, intense sincerity, and warmth seemed to touch everyone who met him, and more than any other Apple employee, Taylor was a true champion of the Apple dream. In the press handout that accompanied the first wave of reissued Apple albums, Taylor wrote: "...and in a wonderful loop of time suspended, the Apple singles and albums are newly out and about and we find ourselves again approving the same artwork and liner notes and worrying anew in case we aren't honouring our old pledges to give everyone their best shot... so, really, *these* are the days."

The timing may have been coincidental, but soon after Taylor's passing, Apple suspended the reissue schedule of the Apple catalogue (leaving Lon and Derrek Van Eaton, Elephant's Memory, David Peel, and a promised Apple rarities album unissued) and several of the already reissued Apple titles slipped quietly out of print. With Taylor no longer Apple's spokesperson, little more than product emerged from Apple's Ovington Square office. Paul McCartney's longtime publicist, Geoff Baker, who worked under Taylor during the *Anthology* promotion, would occasionally assume the role of "Apple spokesman," but the genial Baker had little of the style and panache that made Derek Taylor such an ideal representative for Apple and the Beatles.

ROCK OF ALL AGES

It would not be until the twentieth century ticked over into the new millennium that Apple would unveil any significant new products. First out of the gate in September 2000 would be *The Very Best Of Badfinger*. Combining the highlights of Badfinger's Apple output with four tracks taken from the two albums that the group had released on Warner Brothers in 1974, this project would mark the first time that Apple licensed material from another record company for an Apple Records release.

The Badfinger CD would be followed in November 2000 by *1*, a single CD collection (also issued on cassette and double vinyl) of the Beatles' number one singles. Taken at face value, it was difficult to discern the appeal of this collection. The main selling point was presumably the enhanced sound quality of the tracks, but other than that, it was a set of very well-known songs that were readily available on multiple Beatles compilation albums. The most recent song featured on the album had been recorded more than forty years earlier, but to everyone's amazement, the album shot to number one in the charts in both the United States and United Kingdom and it would sell in excess of 30 million copies worldwide over the next decade.

The unfathomable success of *1* took the music industry – and even Apple – by surprise. It would have been easy for Apple to become complacent after enjoying such an unexpected windfall, but to their credit, they stuck to the tried and true formula that they had perfected over the previous decade, methodically overseeing the development of multiple projects but being careful not to take on too many at any one time. These ongoing endeavors ranged from getting movies from the Apple Films catalogue restored and issued on DVD to the creation of a "new" Beatles album, *Let It Be... Naked*. During this period, Apple would also venture into previously uncharted territory, co-creating with Cirque du Soleil, *Love,* an acclaimed Las Vegas theatrical show based on the music and iconography of the Beatles.

There was much work to be done, and additional personnel had been brought in to bolster the thinly staffed Apple organization. The most visible addition to the Apple team was Jonathan Clyde, an experienced executive (and brother of Jeremy Clyde of the sixties pop group Chad and Jeremy) who had worked for several English record labels since starting his music industry career in the early seventies. The affable Clyde had been orbiting the Beatles' inner circle for several decades, having been hired by George Harrison in 1974 to manage the UK office of his ill-fated Dark Horse label. Clyde – who, like all Apple staff at the time, was given no official job title – was initially brought in to oversee DVD projects but later saw his role expand into other areas. He would become one of the most high-profile employees at Apple, regularly being made available to the press to promote various Apple ventures. Paul McCartney's longtime publicist, Geoff Baker, had been acting as Apple's informal spokesman since the death of Derek Taylor, but in the wake of Baker's strange and acrimonious split with McCartney in 2004, Clyde found himself frequently pressed into service to fill that role.

The remarkable success of the *Anthology* and *1* projects may not have had much impact on how Neil Aspinall viewed Apple's mission, but it appeared to have had a transformative effect on others at Apple. The once sacrosanct Beatles catalogue was now – quite rightly – viewed as a source of substantial revenue by Apple's Board of Directors. *Anthology* and *1* had proved that there remained a receptive market for thoughtfully repackaged Beatles material, and Apple responded to this demand by digging even deeper into their tape and film vault to develop new products.

It was George Harrison who was the catalyst for one of the most intriguing ventures that Apple would ever undertake. In 2000, Harrison had been discussing the possibility of a Beatles themed Cirque du Soleil show with his friend, Guy Laliberte, one of the founders of the troupe. Both men agreed that it was certainly an interesting proposition, and a concept slowly evolved as negotiations began between Apple and Cirque du Soleil. It would take several years of negotiations before all of the ex-Beatles were fully behind the concept, but an agreement was ultimately reached and work on this ambitious project was able to begin in earnest.

Tragically, George Harrison would not see the project come to fruition. On 29 November 2001, he would succumb to brain cancer, having been battling different manifestations of the disease since the start of the year. Just over a month before his passing, Harrison had resigned from the board of Apple Corps on 26 October 2001, with his wife, Olivia, being appointed to the board in his place.

Harrison had re-joined Apple's board in February 1993, after he split from his long-time manager, Denis O'Brien, who had previously been Harrison's representative on the board. Harrison and O'Brien fell out over – among other issues – massive losses incurred by Handmade Films, which had left Harrison in a precarious financial situation in the mid-nineties, until his finances were restored by the success of *Anthology*.

Though he was not involved with any of the studio work undertaken for the next Apple album project, Harrison did apparently sign-off on the concept of *Let It Be... Naked*, which was issued in November 2003. Essentially a reimagined version of the *Let It Be* album, *Let It Be... Naked* was championed by Paul McCartney, who had long been aggrieved by the orchestration and mix that Phil Spector had given the original 1970 release. Comprised of cleaned up, remixed versions of most of the tracks found on *Let It Be* (several lesser tracks were dropped, and two alternate versions were utilized for good measure), *Let It Be... Naked* featured none of the controversial orchestral overdubs or studio chatter that had distinguished the original album. Though not radically different from the 1970 LP, *Let It Be... Naked* was a worthwhile effort and sold well, making the top ten in most international markets.

Apple being Apple also meant that the company remained active on the legal front, becoming immersed in several major court cases. In 2003, Apple was back in the news as they prepared to face off against Apple Computers (now Apple Inc.) for a third time. With the April 2003 launch of Apple Inc.'s iTunes service, which sold MP3 music files directly to consumers via the Apple online store, it appeared obvious to Aspinall and Apple's retinue of lawyers that Apple Inc. had clearly breached the agreement that had been previously reached between Apple Inc. and Apple Corps, wherein Apple Inc. agreed not to use the "Apple" name for products or services that pertained directly to music.

On 4 July 2003, Apple Corps initiated legal proceedings in England against Apple Inc., claiming that the iTunes service was a direct violation of the 1991 settlement between the two Apples. The case wound its way through the court system for several years before the actual trial commenced on 29 March 2006.

Apple Corps and their legal team were confident that they would prevail and were genuinely shocked when, on 8 May 2006, the court ruled that Apple Inc. was, in fact, not in breach of the 1991 agreement. The trial judge, Martin Mann, reasoned that Apple Inc.'s use of the Apple logo was limited to their online store and not to the music sold by the store. In his written decision, Judge Mann noted that "the use of the Apple logo is a fair and reasonable use of the mark in connection with the service, which does not go further and unfairly or unreasonably suggest an additional association with the creative works themselves."

In the press release issued by Apple Corps after the decision was handed down, a disappointed Neil Aspinall noted, "With great respect to the trial judge, we consider he has reached the wrong conclusion. We felt that during the course of the trial we clearly demonstrated just how extensively Apple Computer had broken the agreement. We will accordingly be filing an appeal and putting the case again to the Court of Appeal. We have been advised by our legal team, including two eminent specialist QCs and our solicitors, Eversheds, that we have every prospect of reversing this decision on appeal."

It was an impressive show of bravado from Aspinall, but the stakes for Apple Corps were now exponentially higher. If the appeal was not successful, Apple Corps would be on the hook for close to £5,000,000 in legal costs, which represented the legal fees incurred by Apple Corps as well as those of Apple Inc. (under very sensible English law, the plaintiff needs to pay the defendant's court costs if the plaintiff does not prevail in court).

But no appeal was ever filed. The Apple vs. Apple saga took yet another unexpected twist when, on 5 February 2007, Apple Corps and Apple Inc. issued a joint press release stating that the two companies had entered into a new deal that would replace and supersede the original 1991 agreement.

Under the new agreement, Apple Inc. would pay Apple Corps $500 million and, in exchange, would assume global ownership of all of the trademarks related to "Apple." Apple Inc. would then license certain trademarks, such as the Apple Corps Granny Smith Apple logo, back to Apple Corps for use in their music, film, and Beatles-related licensing ventures. The agreement would end the trademark lawsuit initiated by Apple Corps in 2003, and both companies would be responsible for their own – and not insubstantial – legal costs.

In the Apple Corps press release, Neil Aspinall offered only a simple and to the point quote: "It is great to put this dispute behind us and move on. The years ahead are going to be very exciting times for us. We wish Apple Inc. every success and look forward to many years of peaceful co-operation with them."

Apple Inc. was not the only corporation to tangle with Apple Corps lawyers during this period. In late 2005 Apple Corps opened a second legal front, taking longtime Beatles record label EMI to court. On 15 December 2005, Apple initiated legal proceedings against EMI, claiming that EMI owed Apple more than $52.9 million in unpaid royalties. "We have tried to reach a settlement through good faith negotiations and regret that our efforts have been in vain," Neil Aspinall proclaimed in an Apple press release. "Despite very clear provision in our contracts, EMI persist in ignoring their obligations and duty to account fairly and with transparency. Apple and the Beatles are, once again, left with no choice but to sue EMI."

The case meandered through the US court system for over a year before being settled out of court in April 2007. Terms of the settlement were not made public and no comment was issued by either Apple or EMI, except for a brief statement by an EMI spokesperson that Apple and EMI had reached a "mutually acceptable agreement."

Neil Aspinall was a thoroughly seasoned plaintiff, having initiated dozens of lawsuits on behalf of the Beatles and Apple. But during the summer of 2006, he had found himself in court and in a much different role. This time he was acting as a prosecution witness for a music trade group that was taking action against music bootleggers. This particular case resulted from a law enforcement operation that spanned from 2002 to 2003, in which police recovered 504 tapes – approximately eighty hours of Beatles music – that had been used to produce bootleg CDs. The tapes – which were sound recordings made by the film cameras recording the *Get Back/Let It Be* sessions in January 1969 – had gone missing from Apple storage in the 1970s and had been presumed lost.

The police recovered the tapes in Amsterdam and charged two individuals who were in possession of the tapes. A key figure in the case was none other than Nigel Oliver, who had worked at Apple between 1969 and 1974. Oliver had brokered the deal (which was actually a police sting operation) for the tapes and was apprehended on 10 January 2003 in a forest near Slough, where he was waiting to receive his proceeds from the sale. Oliver was looking at several years in prison for his role in the scheme, but at his sentencing in July 2006 he was found "unfit to plead" and was put into supervised mental health care. The undercover operation had been initiated by the International Federation of the Phonographic Industry after Oliver had advertised Beatles memorabilia in the classified ads of his local newspaper. Apple gained control of the tapes, which they would one day put to good use.

The legal maneuvers of Apple Corps may have grabbed the headlines, but whilst Apple's lawyers waged war on Apple Inc. and EMI, the creative team at Ovington Square had been working diligently on several projects. One of the most eagerly anticipated was the development of the definitive DVD edition of the 1971 Apple Films production, *The Concert For Bangladesh*. Work on the project had been initiated while George Harrison was still alive but was suspended after Harrison's passing and not resumed until several years later. The lavishly packaged DVD (which included an Apple logo decal) and CD were finally issued in October 2005.

Born To Boogie – another vintage Apple Films production – was restored for DVD by Sanctuary Music around the same time and was issued in June 2005. But unlike *The Concert For Bangladesh*, which had been an Apple project, *Born To Boogie* had been licensed to a third party. In addition, the film had been licensed not from Apple Films, but rather from Ringo Starr's Startling Music company. This policy of allowing Apple's Board of Directors to take ownership of pet projects that had originally been produced by Apple followed a precedent that appears to have been established by Yoko Ono in 1997, where she assumed control of the rights to her Apple albums and licensed them to Rykodisc Music (although small Apple logos did appear on the CDs), through her company, Ono Music.

The Harrison estate was particularly enthusiastic in securing the rights to Apple-era projects that had been championed by George Harrison. Their Umlaut Corporation took control of the rights to the *Raga* film as well as the two Billy Preston albums that had originally been issued by Apple. They also had the publishing rights to the Radha Krishna Temple songs transferred from Apple Publishing to Harrisongs.

Given Apple's need to focus on lucrative Beatles projects, the company devoted only minimal resources towards any business matter or creative project that did not directly involve one or all of the Beatles. Since the September 2000 release of *The Very Best Of Badfinger*, Apple had done nothing with their non-Beatles catalogue. Possibly in an effort to once again bolster its case against Apple Inc., between March 2003 and May 2004, Apple reissued several CDs that had been out of print since the late 90s, including Doris Troy's self-titled album, the 1972 concert album by Ravi Shankar & Ali Akbar Khan as well as the Apple albums of Billy Preston and the Modern Jazz Quartet.

Apple Music Publishing was another line of non-Beatles business that was generally allowed to languish. At the time, Apple Publishing owned the copyrights to over four hundred songs – among them some of the most celebrated songs of the English psychedelic rock scene of the late sixties – yet it appears that many of those songs are now little more than titles on a sheet of paper in a file cabinet at Ovington Square.

In 2004, Paul Tennant of Focal Point contacted Apple to enquire about his Apple published songs. "I wrote to Apple asking for a full list of our songs that they own the copyright for. They sent me a list of about twenty-five songs," recalled Tennant. "I also asked for copies of the demo tapes, we made tapes of all these songs, every single one of them. I got a letter saying they did not have any. I then wrote again asking for lyrics and the top line of all the songs. I wrote about six times, sent emails, and eventually phoned asking why they had not answered any of my letters. I pointed out to them that I had a right to the lyrics and top line, as they were the publishers and if they do not have the lyrics, demos etc., they were not protecting my copyright. Indeed, how can they protect a copyright if they don't know what they are protecting? I got a letter saying, 'Sorry, we don't have any copies of lyrics.' Goodbye!"

After Bernard Brown left Apple in 1975, Apple Publishing had been administered by Warner Chappell Music Publishing, who took a portion of the royalties that were earned by Apple in exchange for handling the collection of royalties, bookkeeping, payment of royalties to the songwriters, and other administrative tasks that had once been handled by the staff of Apple Publishing. Thanks to the copyrights of songs such as "Without You," "No Matter What," and "Day After Day," Apple Publishing continued to generate a reliable revenue stream, with little effort being required of Apple.

That comfortable arrangement was to change, however, when Apple lost the US publishing rights to the songs of Pete Ham and Tom Evans. In August 2005, the estates of the two deceased members of Badfinger signed an agreement with the US-based music publisher, Bug Music, to administer the rights to the songs written by Ham and Evans. Copyright law in the United States for songs published prior to 1978 stipulates that if a songwriter dies during the initial 28-year term of a copyright, the heirs can reassign the publishing rights to any songs composed during that period.

When informed of the intention of the Ham and Evans estates to reassign the rights to a new publisher in the United States, Neil Aspinall expressed interest in retaining the songs as global Apple copyrights and met with the representative of the estates to negotiate a new deal. Apple's final offer was to continue to administer the songs as before, though with a higher royalty rate going to the songwriters. But Apple – unlike Bug Music – did not offer a cash advance on royalties, and as a result, the estates elected to have the US copyrights for the songs of Pete Ham and Tom Evans administered by Bug as opposed to Apple Publishing.

Apple Publishing retains control of the 1968-1973 Ham and Evans songs for all non-US territories, and worldwide ownership of the songs of Mike Gibbins and Joey Molland, but in losing the American rights to the Ham and Evans copyrights, Apple lost a valuable source of non-Beatles revenue that had earned the company millions of dollars over the past several decades.

But Apple was certainly not hurting for money, and several new lucrative projects were nearing completion. The most ambitious Beatles project developed post-*Anthology* would be the staging of *Love*, a surrealistic, multi-media show put together by Apple and Le Cirque Du Soleil. In 2006, after several years in development, the show was finally ready to open. Apple was given a good measure of creative input, but their main contribution would be to provide images and sounds for the production. The show debuted on Friday, 30 June 2006 at the Mirage Hotel in Las Vegas, with Paul McCartney, Ringo Starr, Yoko Ono, Olivia Harrison, and George Martin attending the gala premier. *Love* opened to very positive reviews and, as of this writing, is still playing to packed houses.

The *Love* soundtrack album – comprised of remixes and mashups of Beatles songs – was issued in December 2006 and reached the top ten in several markets around the world. A year and a half (May 2007) after release, worldwide sales were at a respectable 4.6 million copies.

A NEW DAY DAWNING

Love would be the last major creative project undertaken during Neil Aspinall's tenure as head of Apple. On Tuesday, 10 April 2007, a press release from Apple announced that Aspinall was leaving the company. The news came as a total surprise and shocked the music industry, as Aspinall, the Beatles, and Apple had been so deeply intertwined for decades. It was obvious that Aspinall's departure had been in the works for some time, as his replacement was named the same day. In the statement released to the press, Apple announced that Jeff Jones, a former executive vice president at Sony BMG, had been appointed to replace Aspinall. Jones, a 51-year-old American, had been EVP of Sony Legacy, the Sony business group tasked with exploiting the Sony Music back catalogue. The Apple press release added:

Apple also announces the departure of Neil Aspinall, who had been with John, Paul, George and Ringo for a spectacular 40 plus years, during which he played an indispensable role for the four. He was there since the inception of the band in Liverpool and has meant so much to the Beatles' family for all these years and still does. However, he has decided to move on. Apple as a whole, and each member of this company, wishes him great success in whatever endeavor he chooses to pursue in the future.

In the weeks that followed Aspinall's departure from Apple, rumors regarding the circumstances of the split began to circulate, ranging from his having resigned in response to health concerns, to his leaving due to business differences with Apple's Board of Directors. Phillip Norman, in the 26 March 2008 issue of *The Independent*, recalled a meeting he had with Aspinall a few weeks after Aspinall had resigned from Apple. He noted that Aspinall had told him that it had been "by mutual agreement and quite amicable" and that upon leaving he had been given a gold watch by Paul McCartney, simply inscribed "Ta, la."

Apple board member Yoko Ono provided some additional detail in a 2008 interview with journalist Bill DeYoung. When asked how things were at Apple after Aspinall's departure, Ono replied: "I think that Jeff Jones, obviously, brought in some fresh air, and it's all very exciting. But it doesn't mean that Neil did a bad job – Neil was part of the whole history, and he was doing a brilliant job. It's just that sometimes it's good to go through some changes, and we decided to do that."

Aspinall's departure from Apple took many by surprise, and it would soon be followed by an even more shocking development. Less than one year after his resignation from Apple Corps in April 2007, Aspinall succumbed to lung cancer on Sunday, 23 March 2008. In a statement issued by Geoff Baker, the Aspinall family divulged that the 66-year-old Aspinall had been battling the disease for two months.

With Aspinall's passing, the two surviving Beatles lost not only a close friend and trusted associate, but also one of the last living links to their fabled past. Aspinall had been at their side since 1961, and now he, too, was gone. Several months after he left Apple, the legendarily secretive Aspinall had reached out to author Mark Lewisohn, who was deep in the development of *Tune In*, the first of his definitive three installment history of the Beatles. Aspinall told Lewisohn that as he was no longer employed by Apple, he now felt free to discuss the Beatles and was ready to break the silence that he had maintained for so many years.

Lewisohn was able to meet with Aspinall several times before the sudden onset of Aspinall's illness brought their discussions to an end. Sadly, the majority of Aspinall's memories of the Beatles and Apple had not been addressed at the time he took ill, and these stories are now lost forever.

Neil Aspinall would be a hard act to follow. Any executive brought in by the Apple board would have had to find their place in Aspinall's long shadow. The appointment of Jeff Jones, who had extensive experience in merchandising vintage music, suggested that the Apple board was looking to get serious about exploiting the Beatles catalogue. As early as 2001, George Harrison had shared with Klaus Voormann that he wanted to make "necessary changes at Apple." Voormann recounted Harrison stating that, "It annoys me to see that the whole world makes money with our heads, and we can't manage to get a decent merchandising concept together."

During his tenure at Sony, Jones had overseen critically acclaimed reissue campaigns for such major artists as Bob Dylan and Miles Davis, and the Apple board clearly wanted a comparable treatment for the Beatles.

In addition to his music merchandising acumen, Jeff Jones would bring with him a more traditional corporate approach to Apple. Titles were soon given to Apple employees, with Jones being named CEO and Jonathan Clyde becoming Director of Production and Marketing.

Upon relocating to London from New York, Jones inherited responsibility for Apple's small staff as well as several projects in various stages of completion that had been initiated under Neil Aspinall. The first order of business would be to complete the development and marketing plan for the remastered Beatles albums, which had not been upgraded since their initial transfer to CD in 1987. Jones was also expected to develop a comprehensive digital strategy for Apple.

Jones's first foray into the digital realm on behalf of Apple was to revamp the Beatles.com web site. In late 2008, the e-commerce portion of the site was expanded and even included an "Apple Boutique" section where customers could purchase reproductions of vintage Apple promotional items such as an Apple Records dart board and the Apple Zippo lighter. Apple clothes and posters of artwork by the Fool were also made available, although the lion's share of the site was dedicated to Beatles products.

It would not be until almost two years into Jones's leadership that Apple would bring any significant new products to market. But on 9 September 2009, the new Apple emerged with great fanfare, releasing spectacularly remastered versions of the entire Beatles catalogue as well as box sets comprised of the stereo and mono Beatles albums. It was assumed by many industry observers that the 2007 settlement with Apple Inc. would have laid the groundwork for digital downloads of the Beatles music being made available, but downloads were conspicuously absent from the reissue campaign.

But the lack of downloads did not mean that Apple was ignoring new technologies. Released the same day as the remastered Beatles albums was the *Beatles Rock Band* video game. Developed in conjunction with Harmonix Music Systems, the game enabled users to "play along" with forty-five Beatles songs. *Beatles Rock Band* received generally positive reviews from the gaming community and according to Harmonix had sold approximately three million copies worldwide by the end of 2009.

The long-anticipated digital downloads of Beatles material may not have been part of the reissue campaign, but Apple did make a concession to digital technology several months later with a limited-edition release (30,000 copies worldwide) in December of an Apple-shaped 16GB USB drive featuring the 14 re-mastered stereo Beatles albums.

Jones's next undertaking would be to revamp the non-Beatles Apple catalogue, a project that had decidedly less commercial potential than the Beatles reissues, but one which Apple would undertake with admirable enthusiasm. For the new reissues, Apple went deep into their tape vault for bonus material, finding several previously overlooked or misplaced tapes that contained unheard material by Jackie Lomax, Billy Preston, and other Apple artists.

On 25 October (26 October in the US) 2010, Apple issued fourteen CDs of albums that had been released by Apple Records between 1968 and 1973. Several artists – John Tavener and the Modern Jazz Quartet – had the two albums they had each recorded for Apple combined onto a single CD. The Modern Jazz Quartet CD was further enhanced by the inclusion of a bonus track, on which they paid tribute to the Beatles with an excellent rendition of "Yesterday" that was recorded during the 1969 sessions for *Space* but remained unissued at the time. Freshly remastered and featuring new liner notes, photos, and – where possible – new bonus tracks, the CDs were a significant upgrade from the original 1990s reissues. The new Apple reissues also marked Apple's entry into the world of digital downloads, with all of the albums – as well as additional material that was only offered as downloads – available online.

Joining the fourteen CDs of previously issued Apple albums was the first ever Apple Records best-of collection, entitled *Come And Get It* (the original working title of the compilation, *Those Were The Days*, was deemed to be too maudlin). Given the catalogue number Sapcor 29, the CD compiled twenty-one tracks that had originally appeared as singles on the Apple label (including the long awaited "official" Apple release of Brute Force's "King Of Fuh," which had to be licensed from Brute Force as Apple had relinquished the rights back to Brute Force in 1969). Space considerations meant that there were a few noticeable omissions – specifically Badfinger's "No Matter What" – but the CD perfectly captured the eclectic nature and consistent quality of the Apple label as well as could be expected from a single disc.

Notably missing from the 2010 reissues was the "Apple Rarities" CD, which had been compiled as part of the original 1992 reissue program but never issued.

The fifteen CDs were available individually and were also packaged together in a somewhat flimsy cardboard box and sold as an "Apple Records box set." Exclusive to the box was a two-CD set assigned the catalogue number Sapcor 30 and apparently entitled *Apple Records Extra*. Packaged in a sleeve cleverly designed to look like an old Apple Studios tape box, this collection gathered the download-only tracks by Badfinger, Jackie Lomax, and Mary Hopkin onto CD.

To promote the new reissue program, Apple produced an eighteen minute *The Story Of Apple Records* film hosted by Peter Asher. The highlight of the film was a previously unseen colour clip from the summer of 1968 of James Taylor performing a solo live version of "Something In The Way She Moves" at Trident Studios. In the United States, Apple also issued *Ten Green Apples*, which was a limited box set featuring a ten-song CD of highlights from the reissue series, packaged with an Apple Records tee-shirt.

Under Jones's direction, the project had taken on a much different tone than previous reissue efforts, particularly when it came to the bonus material used for the CDs. Where Neil Aspinall had previously vetoed including the rather good unreleased Badfinger track "Baby Please" from *The Very Best Of Badfinger* simply because he, personally, did not like the song, Jones had no qualms with including it and several other unissued masters as bonus tracks on the new reissue of Badfinger's *Straight Up*.

For the 2010 reissue series, Apple tried to include as much previously unreleased material as possible to enhance the sales potential of the CDs, which is pretty much a standard practice for music reissue projects.

Unfortunately, not all of the former Apple artists shared that vision. James Taylor once again refused to sanction the release of the excellent – and very different – Apple version of "Fire And Rain," which remains in the Apple tape vault, although he did finally agree to allow the inclusion of several 1968 acoustic demos and two tracks from the 1969 recording session for his aborted second Apple album. Peter Asher – who had previously worked with Jeff Jones at Sony – had been engaged to work on *The Story Of Apple Records* film, and he recalls that, "They thought I might want to get involved with trying to talk James into using whatever other track that they had that he didn't want to use, but I said no, I'll leave that to you guys! That was all discussed with me, and I knew what was happening. I have no objections to outtakes and early attempts and all that, I think it's interesting. James is from the other school of thought, which also totally makes sense, which is that you finally made the version that you meant to make and it's better than the others, so that's the one that should be out. I can see it both ways."

Mary Hopkin was another artist who was allegedly not particularly enthusiastic about the prospect of adding unreleased material to the reissues of her two albums, and therefore, none of the outtakes languishing in the Apple vault were included on the new CDs. Hopkin had allowed "When I Am Old One Day," an exquisite outtake from the *Earth Song/Ocean Song* sessions to be included on the 1996 reissue of *Those Were The Days*. But "When I Am Old One Day" really belonged on *Earth Song/Ocean Song* and the song was featured as a bonus track on the 2010 CD.

Given that none of the original Apple contracts gave artists the right to veto the release of material recorded for the label, Apple should at least be credited for adhering to the artist friendly ethos of the original label, even if that policy undermined the commercial appeal of several of the reissued albums.

Not labouring under the forty years of Apple history that framed many of Neil Aspinall's decisions, Jeff Jones appears to take a more pragmatic view than did Aspinall of Apple's non-Beatles assets. Where Aspinall had been very protective of any and all Apple property, Jones was willing to relinquish control of copyrights that were likely to generate little or no income for Apple. In 2008, Apple Publishing returned the copyrights to all of the songs written by Focal Point to Paul Tennant. Gallagher and Lyle were also able to secure the copyrights to the dozen or so of their songs that Apple Publishing had continued to publish, including "Sparrow" and "International," which are both featured on

Mary Hopkin albums. Jones was even open to returning the rights to certain unreleased sound recordings back to the artists. In 2007, Trevor Bannister of Contact was given the rights to the three tracks Contact recorded for Apple in 1968.

In the post-Aspinall era, Apple also started to license Apple masters to third parties, such as the two songs from Doris Troy's 1970 Apple album that were licensed to Ace Records for a career-spanning Doris Troy compilation. And for the first time ever, Apple licensed a complete album to a third party, with Lon and Derrek Van Eaton's *Brother* album being reissued by the English label RPM/Cherry Red in 2012. RPM was granted access to all the Van Eaton tapes still held in the Apple tape library and was able to include the tracks from the unreleased first version of *Brother* and other unissued material as bonus tracks on their CD reissue.

Apple's association with RPM later resulted in several other notable releases, including a compilation of Grapefruit recordings from 1967-1968 (all owned by Apple) and Mortimer's never-before issued *On Our Way Home* album, which was released on both CD and vinyl in 2017.

Apple's primary business is – and always has been – the Beatles. But Jeff Jones and the staff of Apple do seem to genuinely appreciate and value the Apple legacy. For the non-Beatles reissues, Apple was keen to involve as many of the former Apple artists as possible, to drive home the artist-friendly legacy of Apple, as well as help promote the reissue campaign. Joey Molland of Badfinger was particularly active in this role. Finding himself back at the Apple office on several occasions in 2010, Molland was pleasantly surprised to find that the modern Apple was in some ways still similar to the Apple he knew forty years earlier. "Apple has the same vibe today. I get the same vibe when I go in there. It's the Beatles place, and it's got a great atmosphere to it, kind of awe inspiring, if you like," he explains. "The posters are all there, the gold and platinum records are all over the place, and I guess the charity offices are there that the Beatles are all involved with separately and together. The whole thing is pretty much like it was, except it is not wide open like it was. In our time there were people walking in and out of the offices all day and doing whatever they liked."

Molland suggests that the appointment of Jeff Jones as Apple CEO was a significant factor in the renewed interest from Apple in the non-Beatles aspect of the Apple legacy. "At Apple, Neil was much more involved with the Beatles, because he was their roadie and that was his natural bent," offers Molland. "Jeff Jones is a record company man; he's worked with plenty of labels. And he's ambitious in that sense, he's ambitious for Apple. I think they actually approached Paul to see if he was interested in actually revitalizing the record label in terms of getting new artists and new people on the label or even getting catalogues of old projects and getting them on the label. But I don't think that Paul was very much interested, or that the Beatles, as a whole, weren't really into it."

The Apple catalogue titles sold reasonably well upon release, but they were quickly relegated to yesterday's news by Apple's next project. Only three weeks after the Apple Records CDs and downloads hit the market, Apple Corps announced that the entire Beatles catalogue would be available as downloads via Apple Inc.'s iTunes service starting on Tuesday, 16 November.

Driven by an extensive television, print, and online advertising campaign funded by iTunes, initial sales were very positive in the US with sales in the UK being somewhat less robust though still respectable. In January 2011 – after two months of sales – iTunes announced that worldwide sales for the Beatles downloads had been more than five million individual songs and one million albums. Considering that in 2010 many Beatles fans had already created digital files from their CDs or had secured illegal downloads, the download sales numbers were quite impressive and confirmed that the Beatles were still a commercial force to be reckoned with in the digital era. Legal digital downloads had been the last barrier that remained for the Beatles to cross. With the iTunes deal, the Beatles had fully entered into the 21st century, and there would be no turning back.

In May 2012, Apple would embrace yet another new technology, when they issued a restored version of the *Yellow Submarine* movie on Blu-ray (in addition to the standard DVD format and via iTunes). After the rights to *Yellow Submarine* had reverted to Apple/Subafilms, Apple invested in having the film restored literally frame by frame to a standard that rivaled the vibrancy of the original 1969 prints.

The restored *Yellow Submarine* film was quickly followed by a restored and expanded edition of *Magical Mystery Tour*. Since the mid-eighties, Apple had licensed *Magical Mystery Tour* to several third parties for release on VHS and DVD, but this would be the first attempt at restoring the film and issuing it – since its 1967 television broadcast – as an official Apple product. George Martin had previously remixed the music tracks for a 1988 release of the film on VHS and LaserDisc, but for this new 2012 edition, the music would be given a fresh update by Giles Martin.

Produced by Jonathan Clyde, the film was painstakingly restored to deliver picture and sound quality that exceeded that of the original 1967 production. The updated film also included additional material sourced from the Apple tape vault, including a scene of Ivor Cutler ("courier" Buster Bloodvessel) performing his song, "I'm Going In A Field," and a sequence of Steve Winwood and Traffic frolicking on a hillside to their 1967 hit "Here We Go Round The Mulberry Bush" that was funded and filmed by Apple and was – bizarrely – at one point considered for inclusion in the original *Magical Mystery Tour* film.

To promote the re-release of the film, Jonathan Clyde and Apple Films produced a one-hour documentary, *Magical Mystery Tour Revisited*, that was shown – along with the restored film – in the UK on BBC Arena and on PBS in the United States. The DVD and Blu-ray editions of the restored film were issued on 8 October (one day later in the United States) as was a deluxe box set that featured the DVD and the Blu-ray discs as well as a 55-page book, a replica of the double seven inch *Magical Mystery Tour* EP, and a few other odds and ends.

The *Magical Mystery Tour* film would be the final Beatles project to go through EMI, which had been the Beatles' home for four decades. In the wake of a disastrous 2007 sale of EMI to a private equity group, Terra Firma, much of what remained of EMI – including the Beatles catalog – was sold off to Universal Music in September 2012. In November, Universal established a subsidiary company, Calderstone Productions, to oversee any projects related to the catalogs of the Beatles and the 1970-1975 output of John Lennon, George Harrison, and Ringo Starr that came through the Universal system.

On a less momentous, though still poignant note, during a year when Apple was severing a business relationship with EMI that had been in place since the company was formed in 1968, in October, long-serving accountant Brian Capocciama retired at the age of sixty-five. Capocciama was the last remaining Apple employee to have worked at Savile Row, and it was truly an end of an era when he walked out the front door of the Ovington Square office after having worked his last day at Apple.

Following the release of *Magical Mystery Tour*, no major projects would emanate from Ovington Square for several years. Apple had now successfully brought both the Beatles and the non-Beatles catalogue into the digital age, and the music of the Beatles had connected with a new, younger fan base who did not typically consume music via physical media such as CDs and vinyl LPs.

For Apple's non-Beatles artists, having their material available as digital downloads at least offered an opportunity to have their music exposed to a new generation of music consumers, but digital sales for the non-Beatles Apple catalogue were generally modest. It was not until September 2013 that Apple experienced the full commercial potential of the digital ecosystem.

Badfinger's "Baby Blue" had been selected to be used in the closing scene of the finale of the immensely popular American television series *Breaking Bad*. A very respectable sync license had been negotiated, but neither Apple nor the Ham estate expected what ensued after the show aired. The placement of "Baby Blue" in a broadcast that was seen by more than ten million people exposed Badfinger to an audience who were largely unaware of the group or the song. Within days of the episode airing, "Baby Blue" was suddenly back in rotation on FM radio, the song topped the Amazon digital download sales chart, and *The Very Best Of Badfinger* CD enjoyed renewed sales.

Due to the sudden and wholly unforeseen resurgence of interest in Badfinger, Apple dusted off a project that had been prepared for release in 2011 but never issued. *Timeless…The Musical Legacy* was given the catalogue number Sapcor 31 and was issued as a budget priced CD in December 2013. The compilation featured fourteen highlights from Badfinger's Apple catalogue, as well as several licensed tracks; one song taken from their 1974 Warner Brothers album, *Wish You Were Here*, and one more from Badfinger's 1979 reunion album (which featured Joey Molland and Tom Evans only), *Airwaves*. A sticker was affixed to the CD wrapping that plugged the *Breaking Bad* connection, and the album sold well over the Christmas season.

The remarkable success of "Baby Blue" appeared to have led Apple to reconsider the value of the Apple Music Publishing copyrights and how that catalogue was handled. In July 2015, Apple severed Apple Publishing's decades-long administration deal with Warner Chappell Publishing and signed instead with Imagem Music, a smaller, hungrier company that Apple hoped would generate increased revenue from the songs in the Apple Publishing catalogue.

Another notable event in 2015 was the departure of a long-term member of Apple's Board of Directors, Hilary Gerrard, who resigned on 24 August. To replace the eighty-two-year-old Gerrard, Bruce Grakal, an American attorney who has worked with Ringo Starr since the mid-seventies, joined the Apple board to represent Starr's interests.

Once the Beatles' music catalogue had been given its long overdue digital upgrade, Apple next turned its attention to the vast film archive that they had been amassing. The crown jewels of Apple's film holdings were the many Beatles promotional videos that had been produced by Subafilms and later Apple Films. These films – excerpts of which had been utilized for *Anthology* – had been mostly unseen in their entirety since the sixties, and they would form the basis of *1+*, a repackaging of Apple's blockbuster CD from 2000 that combined a remastered version of *1* along with a DVD (or Blu-ray disc) featuring the corresponding music videos of the twenty-seven songs on the music CD. There was also a deluxe version issued that featured a second DVD of alternate videos and rare performance clips, most in pristine quality.

Issued in November 2015, *1+* was another sales success and confirmed yet again that the Beatles catalogue remained as commercially potent as ever, forty-five years since the group disbanded.

But with each passing year, the sales numbers for music products issued on physical media – specifically CDs, DVDs and Blu-ray discs – continues to dwindle. Sales of vinyl records have been increasing, but those resurgent vinyl LPs sell only a fraction of the copies that were sold during the heyday of vinyl records in the seventies. Conceding the obvious, Apple negotiated deals to have the music of the Beatles made available on multiple streaming services in December 2015. This would be followed in May 2017 by the launch of an all-Beatles channel on Sirius XM satellite radio.

Now more than a decade since he replaced Neil Aspinall as head of Apple, Jeff Jones has transformed the company into a very different organization than it had been throughout the preceding four decades. Jones – certainly with the blessing of Apple's board – has accelerated the pace of project development at Apple and appears to be far less cautious than his predecessor in seeking out new opportunities to sell and market the music and likenesses of the Beatles.

Despite the increasing popularity of music streaming, there remains a market for thoughtfully produced music reissue projects, though these reissues sell considerably fewer copies than they would have only a decade earlier. Starting with the 2017 release of the remixed and expanded edition of *Sergeant Pepper*, Apple has gone into overdrive with their Beatles projects. The following year saw the 50th anniversary reissue of *The Beatles* (aka "the White Album"), which was followed in 2019 by the 50th anniversary reissue of *Abbey Road*, both albums having been – like *Sergeant Pepper* – given the remix treatment by Giles Martin and released as stand-alone CDs and vinyl LPs, as well as deluxe box sets.

Nothing more has been done with the non-Beatles Apple catalog since Apple licensed Mortimer's *On Our Way Home* to RPM/Cherry Red for release in 2017. In 2017, Apple did reissue the *James Taylor* album on vinyl in the United States. Unfortunately, the initial pressing of this particular release was marred by one of the songs, "Brighten Your Night With My Day," being accidentally left off of side two of the record, even though the song was listed on both the record label and the sleeve.

What the future holds for Apple is really anyone's guess. Originally due in September 2020 – though delayed until 2021 by the COVID-19 pandemic – is the theatrical release of director Peter Jackson's fresh look at the 1969 *Get Back* sessions, which may or may not later be released with the restored version of the 1970 *Let It Be* movie.

The "Get Back/Let It Be" project will be the last "50th Anniversary" for a Beatles album. Jeff Jones and the Apple board - now including Sean Lennon who was appointed to the board on 5 October 2020 - presumably have a few ideas they are entertaining, though, at this point, there is not much more material, barring reissues of the pre-*Sergeant Pepper* albums, still left in the vaults that is suitable for exploitation.

But what is all but certain is that the music and likenesses of the Beatles will continue to be leveraged for commercial ventures that were never comprehended – or certainly never entertained – when the four Beatles, Neil Aspinall, and a handful of new friends and long-standing confidantes got together for meetings in a drab post-war office block on Wigmore Street in London to dream up the fascinating adventure that would be Apple.

APPLE RECORDS US SINGLES DISCOGRAPHY

(In the United States, solo records by the four ex-Beatles were issued
with Apple catalog numbers)

US Cat #	Release date	Title
1800	(Aug 1968)	**John Foster and Sons Ltd. Black Dyke Mills Band:** Thingumybob/Yellow Submarine
1801	(Aug 1968)	**Mary Hopkin:** Those Were The Days/Turn, Turn, Turn
1802	(Aug 1968)	**Jackie Lomax:** Sour Milk Sea/The Eagle Laughs At You
1803	(Jan 1969)	**The Iveys:** Maybe Tomorrow/And Her Daddy's A Millionaire
1804	(Mar 1969)	**Trash:** Road To Nowhere/Illusions
1805	(Mar 1969)	**James Taylor:** Carolina In My Mind/Takin' It In
1806	(Apr 1969)	**Mary Hopkin:** Goodbye/Sparrow
1807	(May 1969)	**Jackie Lomax:** New Day/Fall Inside Your Eyes
1808	(Jul 1969)	**Billy Preston:** That's The Way God Planned It/What About You
1809	(Jul 1969)	**Plastic One Band:** Give Peace A Chance/Remember Love
1810	(Aug 1969)	**Radha Krishna Temple (London):** Hare Krishna Mantra/Prayer To The Spiritual Masters
1811	(Sept 1969)	**Trash:** Golden Slumbers/Trash Can
1812	(Oct 1969)	**Hot Chocolate:** Give Peace A Chance/Living Without Tomorrow
1813	(Oct 1969)	**Plastic Ono Band:** Cold Turkey/Don't Worry Kyoko
1814	(Oct 1969)	**Billy Preston:** Everything's Alright/I Want To Thank You
1815	(Jan 1970)	**Badfinger:** Come And Get It/Rock Of All Ages
1816	(Jan 1970)	**Mary Hopkin:** Temma Harbour/Lontano Dagli Occhi
1817	(Feb 1970)	**Billy Preston:** All That I've Got/As I Get Older
1818	(Jan 1970)	**John Ono Lennon:** Instant Karma/Yoko Ono Lennon: Who Has Seen The Wind?
1819	(Mar 1970)	**Jackie Lomax:** How The Web Was Woven/Thumbing A Ride
1820	(Mar 1970)	**Doris Troy:** Ain't That Cute/Vaya Con Dios
1821	(Mar 1970)	**Radha Krishna Temple (London):** Govinda/Govinda Jai Jai
1822	(Oct 1970)	**Badfinger:** No Matter What/Carry On Till Tomorrow (edit)
1823	(Jun 1970)	**Mary Hopkin:** Que Sera, Sera/Fields Of St. Etienne
1824	(Sept 1970)	**Doris Troy:** Jacob's Ladder/Get Back

1825	(Oct 1970)	**Mary Hopkin:** Think About Your Children/Heritage
1826	(Dec 1970)	**Billy Preston:** My Sweet Lord/Little Girl
1827	(Dec 1970)	**John Lennon Plastic Ono Band:** Mother/Yoko Ono Plastic Ono Band: Why
1828	(Feb 1971)	**George Harrison:** What Is Life/Apple Scruffs
1829	(Feb 1971)	**Paul McCartney:** Another Day/Oh Woman, Oh Why
1830	(Mar 1971)	**John Lennon Plastic Ono Band:** Power To The People/Yoko Ono Plastic Ono Band: Touch Me
1831	(Mar 1971)	**Ringo Starr:** It Don't Come Easy/Early 1970
1832	(Apr 1971)	**Ronnie Spector:** Try Some, Buy Some/Tandori Chicken
1833	(not issued)	**Name of the Game** (single edit) by Badfinger
1834	(Jun 1971)	**Jackie Lomax:** Sour Milk Sea/(I) Fall Inside Your Eyes
1835	(Jul 1971)	**Bill Elliot and the Elastic Oz Band:** God Save Us/Do The Oz
1836	(Jul 1971)	**George Harrison:** Bangla-Desh/Deep Blue
1837	(Aug 1971)	**Paul and Linda McCartney:** Uncle Albert/Admiral Halsey/ Too Many People
1838	(Aug 1971)	**Ravi Shankar:** Joi Bangla/Oh Bhaugowan/Raga Mishra-Jhinjhoti
1839	(Sept 1971)	**Yoko Ono:** Mrs. Lennon/Midsummer New York
1840	(Oct 1971)	**John Lennon:** Imagine/It's So Hard
1841	(Nov 1971)	**Badfinger:** Day After Day/Money
1842	(Dec 1971)	**John Lennon:** Happy Xmas (War Is Over)/Yoko Ono: Listen, The Snow Is Falling
1843	(Dec 1971)	**Mary Hopkin:** Water, Paper & Clay/Streets Of London
1844	(Mar 1972)	**Badfinger:** Baby Blue/Flying
1845	(Mar 1972)	**Lon and Derrek Van Eaton:** Sweet Music/Song Of Songs
1846	(not used)	
1847	(Mar 1972)	**Wings:** Give Ireland Back To The Irish/Give Ireland Back To The Irish (Version)
1848	(Apr 1972)	**John Lennon:** Woman Is The Nigger Of The World/Yoko Ono: Sisters O Sisters
1849	(Mar 1972)	**Ringo Starr:** Back Off Boogaloo/Blindman
1850	(May 1972)	**Chris Hodge:** We're On Our Way/Supersoul
1851	(May 1972)	**Wings:** Mary Had A Little Lamb/Little Woman Love
1852	(Sept 1972)	**The Sundown Playboys:** Saturday Nite Special/Valse De Soleil Coucher (Sundown Waltz)
1853	(Nov 1972)	**Yoko Ono Plastic Ono Band:** Now Or Never/Move On Fast
1854	(Dec 1972)	**Elephant's Memory:** Liberation Special/Power Boogie

1855	(Nov 1972)	**Mary Hopkin:** Knock Knock Who's There/International
1856	(not issued)	
1857	(Dec 1972)	**Wings:** Hi. Hi, Hi/C Moon
1858	(Jan 1973)	**Chris Hodge:** Goodbye Sweet Lorraine/Contact Love
1859	(Feb 1973)	**Yoko Ono:** Death Of Samantha/Yang Yang
1860	(not issued)	
1861	(Apr 1973)	**Paul McCartney and Wings:** My Love/The Mess
1862	(May 1973)	**George Harrison:** Give Me Love (Give Me Peace On Earth)/ Miss O'Dell
1863	(Jun 1973)	**Paul McCartney and Wings:** Live And Let Die/I Lie Around
1864	(Dec 1973)	**Badfinger:** Apple Of My Eye/Blind Owl
1865	(Sept 1973)	**Ringo Starr:** Photograph/Down And Out
1866	(Not used)	
1867	(Sept 1973)	**Yoko Ono:** Woman Power/Men, Men, Men
1868	(Oct 1973)	**John Lennon:** Mind Games/Meat City
1869	(Nov 1973)	**Paul McCartney and Wings:** Helen Wheels/Country Dreamer
1870	(Dec 1973)	**Ringo Starr:** You're Sixteen/Devil Woman
1871	(Feb 1974)	**Paul McCartney and Wings:** Jet/Mamunia
1872	(Feb 1974)	**Ringo Starr:** Oh My My/Step Lightly
1873	(Apr 1974)	**Paul McCartney and Wings:** Band On The Run/Nineteen Hundred And Eighty-Five
1874	(Sept 1974)	**John Lennon with the Plastic Ono Nuclear Band:** Whatever Gets You Thru The Night/Beef Jerky
1875	(Nov 1974)	**Paul McCartney and Wings:** Junior's Farm/Sally G.
1876	(Nov 1974)	**Ringo Starr:** Only You/Call Me
1877	(Nov 1974)	**George Harrison:** Dark Horse/I Don't Care Anymore
1878	(Dec 1974)	**John Lennon:** #9 Dream/What You Got
1879	(Dec 1974)	**George Harrison:** Ding Dong/Hari's On Tour (Express)
1880	(Jan 1975)	**Ringo Starr:** No No Song/Snookeroo
1881	(Mar 1975)	**John Lennon:** Stand By Me/Move Over Ms. L
1882	(Jun 1975)	**Ringo Starr:** It's All Down To Goodnight Vienna/Oo-Wee
1883	(not used)	Promo copies of **John Lennon's Slippin' and Slidin'** were issued to radio stations with the catalog # P-1883
1884	(Sept 1975)	**George Harrison:** You/World Of Stone
1885	(Dec 1975)	**George Harrison:** This Guitar (Can't Keep From Crying/Maya Love

APPLE RECORDS UK SINGLES DISCOGRAPHY

UK Cat #	Release date	Title
APPLE 2	(Aug 1968)	**Mary Hopkin:** Those Were The Days/Turn, Turn, Turn
APPLE 3	(Aug 1968)	**Jackie Lomax:** Sour Milk Sea/The Eagle Laughs At You
APPLE 4	(Aug 1968)	**John Foster & Son Ltd. Black Dyke Mills Band:** Thingumybob/Yellow Submarine
APPLE 5	(Nov 1968)	**The Iveys:** Maybe Tomorrow/And Her Daddy's A Millionaire
APPLE 6	(Jan 1969)	**White Trash:** Road To Nowhere/Illusions
APPLE 7	(Not used)	
APPLE 8	(Feb 1968)	**Brute Force:** King of Fuh/Nobody Knows
APPLE 9	(Not used)	
APPLE 10	(Mar 1969)	**Mary Hopkin:** Goodbye/Sparrow
APPLE 11	(May 1969)	**Jackie Lomax:** New Day/Fall Inside Your Eyes
APPLE 12	(Jun 1969)	**Billy Preston:** That's The Way God Planned It/What About You
APPLE 13	(Jul 1969)	**Plastic One Band:** Give Peace A Chance/Remember Love
APPLE 14	(Not used)	
CT 1	(Jul 1969)	**Wall's Ice Cream EP:** The Iveys: Storm In A Teacup, James Taylor: Something's Wrong, Jackie Lomax: Little Yellow Pill, Mary Hopkin: Pebble And The Man
APPLE 15	(Aug 1969)	**Radha Krishna Temple (London):** Hare Krishna Mantra/Prayer To The Spiritual Masters
APPLE 16	(Not used)	
APPLE 17	(Sep 1969)	**Trash:** Golden Slumbers/Trash Can
APPLE 18	(Oct 1969)	**Hot Chocolate:** Give Peace A Chance/Living Without Tomorrow
APPLE 19	(Oct 1969)	**Billy Preston:** Everything's Alright/I Want To Thank You
APPLE 20	(Dec 1969)	**Badfinger:** Come And Get It/Rock Of All Ages
APPLE 21	(Jan 1970)	**Billy Preston:** All That I've Got/As I Get Older
APPLE 22	(Jan 1970)	**Mary Hopkin:** Temma Harbour/Lontano Dagli Occhi
APPLE 23	(Feb 1970)	**Jackie Lomax:** How The Web Was Woven/Thumbing A Ride
APPLE 24	(Feb 1970)	**Doris Troy:** Ain't That Cute/Vaya Con Dios
APPLE 25	(Mar 1970)	**Radha Krishna Temple (London):** Govinda/Govinda Jai Jai
APPLE 26	(Mar 1970)	**Mary Hopkin:** Knock, Knock, Who's There?/I'm Going To Fall In Love Again

APPLE 27	(not used)	
APPLE 28	(Aug 1970)	**Doris Troy:** Jacob's Ladder/Get Back
APPLE 29	(not used)	
APPLE 30	(Oct 1970)	**Mary Hopkin:** Think About Your Children/Heritage
APPLE 31	(Nov 1970)	**Badfinger:** No Matter What/Better Days (single edit)
APPLE 32	(Nov 1970)	**James Taylor:** Carolina In My Mind/Something's Wrong
APPLE 33	(Apr 1971)	**Ronnie Spector:** Try Some, Buy Some/Tandori Chicken
APPLE 34	(Jun 1971)	**Mary Hopkin:** Let My Name Be Sorrow/Kew Gardens
APPLE 35	(not released)	**Badfinger:** Name Of The Game (single edit)/Suitcase
APPLE 36	(Jul 1971)	**Bill Elliot and the Elastic Oz Band:** God Save Us/Do The Oz
APPLE 37	(Aug 1971)	**Ravi Shankar:** Joi Bangla/Oh Bhaugowan/Raga Mishra-Jhinjhoti
APPLE 38	(Oct 1971)	**Yoko Ono:** Mrs. Lennon/Midsummer New York
APPLE 39	(Nov 1971)	**Mary Hopkin:** Water, Paper & Clay/Jefferson
APPLE 40	(Jan 1972)	**Badfinger:** Day After Day/Sweet Tuesday Morning
APPLE 41	(Jan 1972)	**Yoko Ono:** Mind Train/Listen, The Snow Is Falling
APPLE 42	(Not used)	
APPLE 43	(Jun 1972)	**Chris Hodge:** We're On Our Way/Supersoul
APPLE 44	(Nov 1972)	**The Sundown Playboys:** Saturday Nite Special/Valse De Soleil Coucher (Sundown Waltz)
APPLE 45	(Dec 1972)	**Elephant's Memory:** Power Boogie/Liberation Special
APPLE 46	(Mar 1973)	**Lon and Derrek Van Eaton:** Warm Woman/More Than Words
APPLE 47	(Apr 1973)	**Yoko Ono:** Death Of Samantha/Yang Yang
APPLE 48	(Nov 1973)	**Yoko Ono:** Run, Run, Run/Men, Men, Men
APPLE 49	(Mar 1974)	**Badfinger:** Apple Of My Eye/Blind Owl
APP 1	(Oct 1991)	Apple E.P." Mary Hopkin: Those Were The Days, Billy Preston: That's The Way God Planned It, Jackie Lomax: Sour Milk Sea, Badfinger: Come And Get It

APPLE RECORDS US LP DISCOGRAPHY

(In the United States, solo records by the four ex–Beatles were issued
with Apple catalog numbers)

US Cat #	Release date	Title
ST 3350	(Dec 1968)	**George Harrison** – Wonderwall Music
T 5001	(Jan 1969)	**John Lennon/Yoko Ono** – Two Virgins
ST 3351	(Mar 1969)	**Mary Hopkin** – Postcard
SKAO 3352	(Feb 1969)	**James Taylor** – James Taylor
ST 3353	(Feb 1969)	**Modern Jazz Quartet** – Under The Jasmin Tree
ST 3354	(Mar 1969)	**Jackie Lomax** – Is This What You Want?
ST 3355	(Unreleased)	**The Iveys** – Maybe Tomorrow
ST 3357	(May 1969)	**John Lennon/Yoko Ono** – Life with the Lions (Zapple Records)
ST 3358	(May 1969)	**George Harrison** – Electronic Sound (Zapple Records)
ST 3359	(Sept 1969)	**Billy Preston** – That's The Way God Planned It
STAO 3360	(Nov 1969)	**Modern Jazz Quartet** – Space
SMAX 3361	(Oct 1969)	**John Lennon/Yoko Ono** – Wedding Album
SMAX 3362	(Dec 1969)	**Plastic Ono Band** – Live Peace in Toronto
SMAS 3363	(Apr 1970)	**Paul McCartney** – McCartney
ST 3364	(Feb 1970)	**Badfinger** – Magic Christian Music
SW 3365	(Apr 1970)	**Ringo Starr** – Sentimental Journey
SKAO 3367	(Oct 1970)	**Badfinger** – No Dice
SMAS 3368	(Sep 1970)	**Ringo Starr** – Beaucoups of Blues
SMAS 3369	(Oct 1970)	**John Tavener** – The Whale
ST 3370	(Sept 1970)	**Billy Preston** – Encouraging Words
ST 3371	(Sept 1970)	**Doris Troy** – Doris Troy
SW 3372	(Dec 1970)	**John Lennon** – Plastic Ono Band
SW 3373	(Dec 1970)	**Yoko Ono** – Plastic Ono Band
STCH 639	(Nov 1970)	**George Harrison** – All Things Must Pass
SMAS 3375	(May 1971)	**Paul & Linda McCartney** – Ram
SKAO 3376	(May 1971)	**Radha Krishna Temple** – Radha Krishna Temple
SW 3377	(Sept 1971)	**Soundtrack** – Come Together

SW 3379	(Sept 1971)	**John Lennon** – Imagine
SVBB 3380	(Sept 1971)	**Yoko Ono** – Fly
SMAS 3381	(Nov 1971)	**Mary Hopkin** – Earth Song Ocean Song
SWAO 3384	(Dec 1971)	**Soundtrack** – Raga
STCX 3385	(Dec 1971)	**George Harrison** – Concert for Bangladesh
SW 3386	(Dec 1971)	**Wings** – Wild Life
SW 3387	(Dec 1971)	**Badfinger** – Straight Up
SW 3388	(Dec 1971)	**Soundtrack** – El Topo
SMAS 3389	(Sept 1972)	**Elephant's Memory** – Elephant's Memory
SMAS 3390	(Sept 1972)	**Lon and Derrek Van Eaton** – Brother
SW 3391	(April 1972)	**David Peel** – The Pope Smokes Dope
SVBB 3392	(Jun 1972)	**John & Yoko/Plastic Ono Band** – Some Time In New York City
SW 3395	(Sept 1972)	**Mary Hopkin** – Those Were The Days
SVBB 3396	(April 1973)	**Ravi Shankar/Ali Akbar Khan** – In Concert 1972
SVBB 3399	(Jan 1973)	**Yoko Ono** – Approximately Infinite Universe
SW 3400	(Dec 1972)	**The Phil Spector Christmas Album**
SKBO 3403	(Apr 1973)	**The Beatles** – 1962-1966
SKBO 3404	(Apr 1973)	**The Beatles** – 1967-1970
SMAL 3409	(Apr 1973)	**Paul McCartney & Wings:** Red Rose Speedway
SMAS 3410	(May 1973)	**George Harrison** – Living In The Material World
SW 3411	(Nov 1973)	**Badfinger** – Ass
SW 3412	(Nov 1973)	**Yoko Ono** – Feeling The Space
SWAL 3413	(Nov 1973)	**Ringo Starr** - Ringo
SW 3414	(Nov 1973)	**John Lennon** – Mind Games
SO 3415	(Dec 1973)	**Paul McCartney & Wings** – Band On The Run
SW 3416	(Nov 1974)	**John Lennon** – Walls And Bridges
SW 3417	(Nov 1974)	**Ringo Starr** – Goodnight Vienna
SW 3418	(Dec 1974)	**George Harrison** – Dark Horse
SK 3419	(Feb 1975)	**John Lennon** – Rock And Roll
SW 3420	(Sept 1975)	**George Harrison** – Extra Texture
SW 3421	(Oct 1975)	**John Lennon** – Shaved Fish
SW 3422	(Nov 1975)	**Ringo Starr** – Blast From Your Past
7243 8 30129 23	(Apr 1995)	**Badfinger** – The Best Of
7243 5 26974 27	(Sept 2000)	**Badfinger** – The Very Best Of
5099964639727	(Oct 2010)	**Various:** Come And Get It: The Best Of Apple Records

Sapcor 30	(Oct 2010)	**Various** – Apple Records Extra
5099991906434	(Oct 2010)	**Various** – Ten Green Apples (CD and t-shirt box set)
50999 9 18373 2 5	(Dec 2013)	**Badfinger** – Timeless…The Musical Legacy

APPLE RECORDS UK LP DISCOGRAPHY

UK Cat #	Release date	Title
SAPCOR 1	(Nov 1968)	**George Harrison** – Wonderwall Music
SAPCOR 2	(Nov 1968)	**John Lennon/Yoko Ono** – Two Virgins
SAPCOR 3	(Dec 1968)	**James Taylor** – James Taylor
SAPCOR 4	(Dec 1968)	**Modern Jazz Quartet** – Under The Jasmin Tree
SAPCOR 5	(Feb 1969)	**Mary Hopkin** – Postcard
SAPCOR 6	(Mar 1969)	**Jackie Lomax** – Is This What You Want?
ZAPPLE 01	(May 1969)	**John Lennon/Yoko Ono** – Life with the Lions (Zapple Records)
ZAPPLE 02	(May 1969)	**George Harrison** – Electronic Sound (Zapple Records)
SAPCOR 7	(Unreleased)	**Delaney & Bonnie** – The Original
SAPCOR 8	(Unreleased)	**The Iveys** – Maybe Tomorrow
SAPCOR 9	(Aug 1969)	**Billy Preston** – That's The Way God Planned It
SAPCOR 10	(Oct 1969)	**Modern Jazz Quartet** – Space
SAPCOR 11	(Nov 1969)	**John Lennon/Yoko Ono** – Wedding Album
SAPCOR 12	(Jan 1970)	**Badfinger** – Magic Christian Music
SAPCOR 13	(Sept 1970)	**Doris Troy** – Doris Troy
SAPCOR 14	(Sept 1970)	**Billy Preston** – Encouraging Words
SAPCOR 15	(Sept 1970)	**John Tavener** – The Whale
SAPCOR 16	(Oct 1970)	**Badfinger** – No Dice
SAPCOR 17	(Dec 1970)	**Yoko Ono** – Plastic Ono Band
SAPCOR 18	(May 1971)	**Radha Krishna Temple** – Radha Krishna Temple
SAPCOR 19	(Feb 1972)	**Badfinger** – Straight Up

SAPCOR 20	(May 1971)	**John Tavener** – Celtic Requiem
SAPCOR 21	(Nov 1971)	**Mary Hopkin** – Earth Song Ocean Song
SAPTU 101/102	(Dec 1971)	**Yoko Ono** – Fly
SAPCOR 22	(Nov 1972)	**Elephant's Memory** – Elephant's Memory
SAPCOR 23	(Nov 1972)	**Mary Hopkin** – Those Were The Days
APCOR 24	(Dec 1972)	**The Phil Spector Christmas Album**
SAPCOR 25	(Feb 1973)	**Lon and Derrek Van Eaton** – Brother
SAPDO 1001	(Feb 1973)	**Yoko Ono** – Approximately Infinite Universe
SAPDO 1002	(Apr 1973)	**Ravi Shankar/Ali Akbar Khan** – In Concert 1972
SAPCOR 26	(Nov 1973)	**Yoko Ono** – Feeling The Space
SAPCOR 27	(Mar 1974)	**Badfinger** – Ass
SAPCOR 28	(Apr 1995)	**Badfinger** – The Best Of
7243 5 26974 27	(Sept 2000)	**Badfinger** – The Very Best Of
SAPCOR 29	(Oct 2010)	**Various:** Come And Get It: The Best Of Apple Records
SAPCOR 30	(Oct 2010)	**Various** – Apple Records Extra
5099991837226	(Oct 2010)	**Various** – Apple Records Box Set
SAPCOR 31	(Dec 2013)	**Badfinger** – Timeless…The Musical Legacy

END NOTES & BIBLIOGRAPHY

All quotes are taken from interviews with the author (1996-2020) unless otherwise attributed or mentioned below:

1967: The NEMS Years

"Paul came up with the idea of calling it Apple..."
Apple press release 1992

"We tried to form Apple with Clive Epstein..."
Melody Maker 1971

"A lot of people were nominated or put themselves forward..."
Paul Du Noyer *Mojo Magazine* October 1996

"We didn't have a single piece of paper. No contracts..."
Paul Du Noyer *Mojo Magazine* October 1996

"Customers seemed to be there only to shoplift..."
Peter Brown *The Love You Make*

1968: Something New Every Day

"Everything collected dust in the corner, we just couldn't cope..."
Geoffrey Giuliano, *Dark Horse*

"It was the first time I'd seen 'SA'..."
Jonathan Green *Days In The Life*

"We owe it to Mal for getting us..."
Peter Skiera *Good Day Sunshine*

"Twiggy saw the show...."
Bill DeYoung *Goldmine*

"I sang a few songs for him..."
Bill DeYoung *Goldmine*

"Apple was a funny old place..."
Matt Hurwitz *Good Day Sunshine*

"We worked for about three months..."
Timothy Crouse *Rolling Stone* 18 Feb 1971

"I went to the premier of Yellow Submarine…"
Mark Lewisohn, *Record Collector* August 1988

"Give it away, you are not a Jewish rag merchant..."
Paolo Hewitt *Fab Gear*

"At the Wigmore Street office in the early days…"
Jonathan Green *Days In The Life*

1968: The Revolution Begins

"When people heard I was on Apple…"
Tony Wilson *Melody Maker Sept 1968*

What we are trying to create …" Alan Walsh Melody
Maker 1 June 1968

"It was all too much for him… What we are trying to create"
Jonathan Green *Days In The Life*

"The pity of it was that it would have run better…"
Jonathan Green *Days In The Life*

'Well, you moving all your stuff out of here tonight? …'
Richard Dilello, *The Longest Cocktail Party*

"What we want to do now…"
Chris Welch *Melody Maker* 30 November 1968

"Your personal finances are in a mess…"
Stephen Maltz *The Beatles, Apple and Me*

"We are now more or less …"
Alan Walsh Nov 1968 *Melody Maker*

"£40,000 at its disposal..."
Denis O' Dell *At The Apple's Core*

1969: The Pre-Klein Era:

"Alex's recording studio at Apple was the biggest disaster of all time…"
Barry Miles *Many Years From Now*

"One night we were sitting in the Cromwellian Club, totally depressed…"
Jim Wilkie *Blue Suede Brogans*

"Songs that have been my favorites…"
Ann Nightingale *The Daily Sketch* 18 October 1968

"There were days when I went into Capitol…"
Ezra Bookstein *The Smith Tapes: Lost Interviews With Rock Stars And Icons 1969-1972.*

"Needs a new broom…:"
Ray Coleman *Disc And Music Echo* 1969

"The weirdness was not controlled at the start…"
Peter Doggett *Record Collector* August 1988

"The Beatles weren't together; they didn't know what they wanted out of Apple…"
Peter Doggett *Record Collector* August 1988

"He was so foul-mouthed and abusive…"
Peter Brown *The Love You Make*

"He [Lennon] made it clear..."
Craig Vetter *Playboy*

"Paul was pretty cool..."
Craig Vetter *Playboy*

"Loaded the offer…."
Peter McCabe and Robert Schonfeld *Apple To The Core*

1969: Life After Klein:

"I don't see why I should work for a company …."
Peter Brown *The Love You Make*

"I think that Apple must have given out a considerable amount of money…" Jonathan Green *Days In The Life*

"It isn't easy being nice…"
unknown press clipping

"Apple has been changing a great deal recently …"
Billboard 14 June 1969

"When I joined Apple…"
Disc And Music Echo 1969

"Nothing was happening…"
Jerry Hopkins *Rolling Stone* 23 Aug 1969

"In '69, in all that chaos, the traumas…"
Paul Du Noyer *Mojo Magazine* October 1996

"It was very difficult, …"
Tony Norman *NME* 3 June 1972

"We do feel a bit neglected…."
Disc And Music Echo 1969

"Oh wise one, oh sage, show us the light."
Dan Matovina *Without You: The Tragic Story Of Badfinger,*

"We were just making album tracks…"
Phil Symes *Disc And Music Echo* 24 Jan 1970

"Just one of Pauls' fun ideas…"
Bill DeYoung *Goldmine*

"Apple was a manifestation of Beatle naivety…"
Barry Miles *Mojo* 1995

"We invited George Harrison over to listen…"
Dave Zimmer *Crosby, Stills And Nash: The Authorized Biography*

"George told me he heard us on tape…"
Dave Zimmer *Crosby, Stills And Nash: The Authorized Biography*

"They were no fucking good…"
Richard Dilello, *The Longest Cocktail Party* Playboy Press 1972

"Derek was happy, but the Beatles had to be consulted…"
Jim Wilke *Blue Suede Brogans*

"That's a good imitation of us… it's going out."
Richard DiLello *The Longest Cocktail Party*

"They were not awfully friendly…"
Peter Doggett *Record Collector* August 1988

"Branson kept coming in to see…"
Derek Taylor *Fifty Years Adrift*

"Retrospectively hilarious listening session…"
Derek Taylor *Fifty Years Adrift*

1970: And Then There Were Three

"A couple of months after "Come And Get It"….Willie G. Moseley *Vintage Guitar Magazine*

"The reason I worked with Mickie…"
Bill DeYoung *Goldmine*

"Allen Klein was not going to spend any more money…"
Peter Skiera *Good Day Sunshine*

"He [Klein] came in and put a stop…" Bob Greenfield *Rolling Stone*

"Jackie was given all the shots..." Peter Doggett *Record Collector* August 1988

"The middle of the road..."
Peter Doggett *Record Collector* August 1988

"I remember hiring them..."
Apple press release 1992

"Spring is here and Leeds play..." *Apple* press release 1992

"The day after Paul's statement...."
Jan Holdenfield *Rolling Stone*

"When my office closed..."
Derek Taylor *As Time Goes By*

"...one of the great deals..." Geoffrey Haydon *John Tavener: Glimpses of Paradise*

"We didn't promote it; we really couldn't..."
Peter Doggett *Record Collector* August 1988

"No credits or liners...." *Rolling Stone*

"I'm about halfway through..."
Alan Smith *NME* 1970

"I was producing her album...."
George Harrison press conference 1975

"There wasn't much promotion..."
Gillian Saich *NME* 27 Feb *1971*

"Hello everybody..." Janis Schacht *Circus Magazine* 1971

"You'll stay on the..." Barry Miles *Many Years From Now*

1971: It Don't Come Easy

"Billy who?..." Michael Watts *Melody Maker* 1972

"It was traumatic for everybody..."
Paul Du Noyer *Mojo Magazine* October 1996

"They had to get their thing together..."
Ben Fong-Torres *Rolling Stone* September 1971

"When I was at Apple..."
Michael Watts *Melody Maker* 1972

"The only thing they [Apple] are doing now...."
Michael Watts *Melody Maker* July 1971

"Well, it's only just beginning…"
Richard DiLello *The Longest Cocktail Party*

"George was there doing a couple of mixes…"
NME 1974

"I guess at first, my involvement with Badfinger…"
Loraine Alterman *Melody Maker* 1972

"It's a bit sad now that Apple is in the position…"
Keith Badman *The Beatles Diary Volume 2*

"A bit for some pop record…" *The Daily Express* 1972

"The Beatles had split up by then…"
Paul Du Noyer *Mojo Magazine* October 1996

1972: They Seem To Be Getting It Together Really Well

"You'd never feel really comfortable…."
Tony Norman *NME* 1972

"This staggeringly impressive first album…."
Stephen Holden *Rolling Stone* 1972

"I met George Harrison at Apple…" unknown press cutting

"We tried to negotiate with Allen Klein…."
Jon E. Johnson *Discoveries Magazine* February 1991

"Why the fuck didn't you tell us…."
Bill King *Beatlefan Magazine*

1973: The Dream Is Over

"What happened was that John…"
Paul Du Noyer *Mojo Magazine* October 1996

"The words were true…"
Jon E. Johnson *Discoveries Magazine* February 1991

"I think Apple tried to sell us to Warners…"
Bill Last, *Good Day Sunshine* 1992

1975: And In The End...

"At a private hearing before a high court judge..."
AP *The New York Times* Jan 1975

"To me and other people, this was inevitable..."
Adam White & Brian Mulligan *Billboard* March 1975

"It's going into mothballs as far as I know..."
Adam White & Brian Mulligan *Billboard* March 1975

"It upset me because he was so good..."
Paul Gambaccini *Paul McCartney: In His Own Words* Putnam 1983

"Apple was together in a lot of ways..."
Paul Gambaccini *Rolling Stone* 31 January 1974

Apple After Apple

"If you don't sell records then it costs you money..."
John Blake *The Beatles After The Beatles*

"There was a lot going on..." Paul Du Noyer *Mojo Magazine* October 1996

The Nineties: Apple's Back

"It's about progress..." *Apple* press release 1992

"Concert posters line..."
Robert Sandall *Arena* November 1995

"Certainly isn't the philanthropic organization ..."
Sylvie Simmons *Request Magazine* 1996

"...and in a wonderful loop of time suspended..."
Apple press release 1992

Rock Of All Ages

"With great respect to the trial judge..." Apple press release 2006

"It is great to put this dispute..." Apple Press Release 2007

"We have tried to reach ..." Apple Press Release 2005

A New Day Dawning

"Apple also announces the departure of Neil Aspinall..."
Apple press release *2007*

"By mutual agreement..."
Philip Norman *The Guardian* 2008

"I think that Jeff Jones..."
Bill DeYoung *TC Palm* 2008

"Necessary changes at Apple...."
Klaus Voormann *Warum Spielst Du Imagine Nicht Auf Dem Weissen Klavier, John?* Heyne Verlag 2006

BIBLIOGRAPHY (BOOKS)

Badman, Keith *The Beatles Diary Vol 2: The Beatles After The Breakup, 1970-2001* (Omnibus UK 2000)

Beatles, The *The Beatles Anthology* (Chronicle Books 2000)

Blake, John *The Beatles After The Beatles* (Perigee Books 1981)

Bookstein, Ezra *The Smith Tapes: Lost Interviews With Rock Stars And Icons 1969-1972.* (Princeton Architectural Press) 2015

Brown, Peter and Gaines, Steven *The Love You Make: An Insider's Story Of The Beatles* (Macmillan 1983)

Castleman, Harry and Podrazik, Walter *All Together Now: The First Complete Beatles Discography 1961-1975* (Ann Arbor: Pierian Press 1976)

Clayson, Alan *Ringo Starr: Straight Man Or Joker?* (Sidgwick and Jackson 1991)

Coleman, Ray *Lennon* (McGraw Hill 1984)

Dilello, Richard *The Longest Cocktail Party* (Playboy Press 1972)

Doggett, Peter *You Never Give Me Your Money* (It Books/Harper Collins 2010)

Emerick, Geoff and Massey, Howard *Here, There And Everywhere* (Gotham Books 2006)

Engelhardt, Kristofer *The Beatles Undercover* (Collector's Guide Publishing 1998)

Fletcher, Tony *Moon: The Life And Death Of A Rock Legend* (Harper Entertainment 2000)

Goodman, Fred *Allen Klein* (Houghton Mifflin 2015)

Giuliano, Geoffrey *Dark Horse* (DeCapo 1997)

Green, Jonathon *Days in the Life: Voices From The English Underground 1961-1971* (Pimlico 1988)

Haydon, Geoffrey *John Tavener: Glimpses Of Paradise* (Gollancz 1995)

Hewitt, Paolo *Fab Gear: The Beatles And Fashion* (Prestel 2011)

Isaacson, Walter *Steve Jobs* (Simon and Schuster 2011)

Jackson, Tim *The Virgin King* (Harper Collins 1995)

Lewisohn, Mark *The Complete Beatles Chronicle* (Harmony Books 1992)

Lewisohn, Mark *Tune In* (Crown Archetype 2013)

Levy, Jeff *Apple Log IV* (MonhunProd Media Group 1990)

Maltz, Stephen *The Beatles, Apple And Me* Self-published/Amazon 2015

Mansfield, Ken *The Beatles, The Bible And Bodega Bay* (Broadman & Holman 2000)

Matovina, Dan *Without You: The Tragic Story Of Badfinger* Frances Glover Books

McCabe, Peter and Schonfeld, Robert D. *Apple To The Core* (Pocket Book 1972)

Miles, Barry *Many Years From Now* (Secker & Warburg 1997)

Neaverson, Bob *The Beatles Movies* (Cassell 1997)

Norman, Philip *Shout* (Simon and Schuster 1981)

O'Dell, Denis and Neaverson, Bob *At Apple's Core: The Beatles From The Inside* (Peter Owen 2002)

Pang, May *Loving John* (Warner Books 1983)

Schaeffner, Nicholas *The Beatles Forever* (McGraw Hill 1978)

Southhall, Brian *Northern Songs* (Omnibus Press 2007)

Taylor, Derek *As Time Goes By* (Pierian Press 1983)

Taylor, Derek *Fifty Years Adrift* (Genesis Publications 1984)

Voormann, Klaus *Warum Spielst Du Imagine Nicht Auf Dem Weissen Klavier, John?* (Heyne Verlag 2006)

Wilke, Jim *Blue Suede Brogans* (Trafalgar Square 1992)

Zimmer, Dave *Crosby, Stills And Nash: The Authorized Biography* (St. Martin's Press 1984)

(MAGAZINES)

Alterman, Loraine "The Ballad Of Todd Rundgren" *Melody Maker* 25 March 1972

Bruno, Antony "Games Beatles Play: How The Fab Four Went Digital" *Billboard* 12 September 2009

Bruno, Antony "Briefs" *Billboard* 10 December 2009

Charlesworth, Chris "What Happened To Sweet Little Mary?" *Melody Maker* 26 June 1972

Dallas, Karl "The Real Mary" *Melody Maker* 22 January 1972

Davis, Andy "Apple Records Beyond The Beatles" *Record Collector*

DeYoung, Bill "She's A Joan Baez Type, But We'll Soon Alter That" *Goldmine* 14 April 1995

Doggett, Peter "Apple Records: The Beatles Great Experiment" *Record Collector* August 1988

Du Noyer, Paul "Just Out Of Shot" *Mojo* October 1996

Fong-Torres, Ben "That's The Way He Planned It" *Rolling Stone* 16 September 1971

Greenfield, Bob "Jackie Lomax Is Leaving London" *Rolling Stone* 26 November 1970

Hennessey, Mike "Apple Plans To Invade U.S." *Billboard* 11 January 1969

Holdenfield, Jan "Ethel? It's Me, Yeah Doreen" *Rolling Stone* 11 June 1970

Hopkins, Jerry "James Taylor On Apple: The Same Old Craperoo" *Rolling Stone* 23 August 1969

Horide, Rosemary "Fickle Fate Of 'Finger" *Disc* 1 Dec 1973

Hurwitz, Matt "Meet The Real Percy Thrillington" *Good Day Sunshine*

Irwin, Collin "Harrison's Dark Horses" *Melody Maker* August 1974

Johnson, John "Death And Taxes: An Interview With Badfinger's Joey Molland" *DISCoveries* February 1991

King, Bill "Beatlefan"

Lubasch, Arnold "Ex-Beatles Manager Is Indicted On Taxes" *New York Times* 4 July 1977

McCallister, Bill "Badfinger & Bangla Desh" *Record Mirror* 26 Feb 1972

Miles, Barry "My Blue Period" *Mojo* November 1995

Moseley, Willie "Golden Apple Days" *Vintage Guitar* 1996

Newcomb, Peter and Lafranco, Robert "All You Need Is Love And Royalties" *Forbes* 25 September 1995

Norman, Phillip "The Circus Has Left Town , But We Still Own The Lot" *Show Magazine* January 1970

Norman, Tony "Beating A Bad Image" *NME* 3 June 1972

"Our Staff" "The Beatles: You Never Give Me Your Money" *Rolling Stone* 15 November 1969

Pearson, Paul "Paul's Shout Up At Shipley" *Melody Maker* 13 July 1968

Quinn, Jennifer "Beatles Lose Suit Against Apple Computers" *Associated Press* 8 May 2006

Saich, Gillian "Badfinger: To Americans A Substitute For The Beatles" *NME* 27 February 1971

Sandell, Robert "Beatlemania '95" *Arena Magazine*

Schwartz, Francie "Memories Of An Apple Girl" *Rolling Stone* 15 November 1969

Simmons, Sylvie "The Fall And Rise Of Apple" *Request* 1996

Smith, Alan "My Life's Not A Sham...." *NME* 28 November 1970

Skiera, Peter "Listening To Lomax" *Good Day Sunshine*

Tiegel, Elliot "Beatles Apple Firm Picking US Core Of Staffers, Artist Roster." *Billboard* 11 June 1968

Vetter, Craig "Playboy Interview: Allen Klein" *Playboy* November 1971

Walsh, Alan "Has Apple Gone Sour?" *Melody Maker* November 1968

Watts, Michael "Preston Power" *Melody Maker* 5 February 1972

Watts, Michael "Ringo" *Melody Maker* 24 July 1971

Welch, Chris "Why Grapefruit Squeezed Out Of Apple" *Melody Maker* 30 November 1968'

White, Adam and Mulligan, Brian "A Dead Apple In London: Apple's Staff Gets Pared" *Billboard* 10 May 1975

Williams, Richard "Doris Troy And The Marriage Of Music" *Melody Maker* 7 March 1970

Wilson, Tony "George, The A&R Man With A New Discovery." *Melody Maker* June 1968

(Liner Notes)

Badfinger: *Ass* (Apple Records/Universal) Andy Davis

Badfinger: *No Dice* (Apple Records/Universal) Andy Davis

Badfinger: *Magic Christian Music* (Apple Records/Universal) Andy Davis

Badfinger: *Straight Up* (Apple Records/Universal) Andy Davis

Alan Ginsberg: Holy Soul Jelly Roll: Poems and Songs 1949-1993 (Rhino) Hal Willner

Mary Hopkin: *Earth Song/Ocean Song* (Apple Records/Universal) Andy Davis

Mary Hopkin: *Earth Song/Ocean Song* (Apple Records/EMI) Derek Taylor

Mary Hopkin: *Postcard* (Apple Records/Universal) Andy Davis

Mary Hopkin: *Those Were The Days* (Apple Records/EMI) Andy Davis

Jackie Lomax: *Jackie Lomax* (Apple Records/Universal) Andy Davis

Yoko Ono: *Ono Box* (Ryko) Robert Palmer

Billy Preston: *Encouraging Words* (Apple Records/Universal) Andy Davis

Billy Preston: *Encouraging Words* (Apple/EMI) Peter Doggett

Billy Preston: *That's The Way God Planned It* (Apple Records/Universal) Andy Davis

Radha Krsna Temple: *Radha Krsna Temple* (Apple Records/Universal) Andy Davis and Derek Taylor

John Tavener: *The Whale/Celtic Requiem* (Apple Records/Universal) Andy Davis

James Taylor: *James Taylor* (Apple Records/EMI) Steve Kolanjian

James Taylor: *James Taylor* (Apple Records/Universal) Andy Davis

Doris Troy: *Doris Troy* (Apple Records/Universal) Andy Davis

Various Artists: *Come and Get It: The Best of Apple Records* (Apple Records/Universal) Andy Davis

ACKNOWLEDGEMENTS

It has been close to two decades since Iain McNay, MD of Cherry Red, took a chance on publishing a book about Apple Records. I would like to extend my sincere thanks to Iain for publishing *Those Were The Days* and setting into motion a chain of events that now brings us to *Those Were The Days 2.0*.

During the course of writing the first edition of *Those Were The Days,* I became aware of the existence of unissued Apple-era recordings by the Iveys, Grapefruit, Focal Point, and other artists. I found myself wondering if there was anything that could be done with these tapes and acetates of unreleased music, and it was Iain who put me in touch with Mark Stratford of RPM Records. Over the next fifteen years, I would develop and produce a number of CD projects for RPM. It was a great run, and I'd like to thank Mark for his partnership and for sharing with me his immense music business expertise.

In 2002, I pitched Mark the idea of a CD that explored the copyrights of Apple Music Publishing. There had never been a compilation album that focused on a music publisher, but Mark was game and we created *94 Baker Street*, the first in a series of Apple Publishing CDs that would eventually comprise five volumes, the last being *94 Baker Street Revisited* in 2013. The Apple Publishing CD series would ultimately lead to Mark and I working directly with Apple on several projects. These included the CD reissue of the Lon and Derrek Van Eaton *Brother* album, as well as *Yesterday's Sunshine*, a compilation of superb tracks from 1967-1968 (many unreleased) that Grapefruit had recorded for Apple Publishing. But the culmination of RPM's association with Apple was certainly the long-awaited release of Mortimer's never issued and almost mythical 1969 Apple album, *On Our Way Home*, which RPM released on both CD and vinyl in 2017.

In my youthful naivete when I first met Mortimer's Tom Smith and Guy Masson in the mid-nineties, I told them that I — at the time a low level Sony/BMG employee — would try to locate the tapes of their unreleased Apple album and one day get the album released. Truthfully, I thought the chance of that happening was somewhat remote to say the least, but then, you have to have hope, don't you? But with the support of RPM and Cherry Red, I was finally able to track the master tapes back to Apple and negotiate the release of Mortimer's absolutely wonderful album, though, sadly, Tom and Guy were no longer with us to see the dream that they had both held in their hearts for decades become a reality. Thankfully, Mortimer's Tony Van Benschoten is in top form and I thank him for his friendship and encouragement.

A hearty thank you also needs to be extended to Garth Tweedale and Aaron Bremner at Apple for all of the support that they have provided for these projects.

Those Were The Days 2.0 has been in development – in one form or another – for several decades. I'd especially like to thank the many Apple people who shared their stories with me, particularly Ken Mansfield, who provided the forward to this new edition of the book and who has been a friend and amazing source of Apple knowledge and positivity for many years. Special thanks also go to Steve Brendell for the support and enthusiasm that he has shown for this project.

This book would simply not have been possible without the time and generosity of spirit of the many wonderful individuals who shared their brilliant memories of Apple, including Peter Asher, Trevor Bannister (Contact), Wayne Bardell, John Barham, John Beland, Barbara (Bennett) O'Donnell, Pete Bennett, Mike Berry, Joe Bower (Fourmost) Tony Bramwell, Steve Brendell, Peter Brown, Leslie Cavendish, Louis Cennamo, Robert Couldry, Tony Cox, David Creech (Joker) Richard Dilello, Pete Dymond (Drew and Dy), Tymon Dogg, Terry Doran, Bill Elliot (Splinter), Terry Finning (Peter Cooper Band), Rick Frank (Elephant's Memory), Stephen Friedland (Brute Force), Glenn Friedman, Benny Gallagher, Robin Garb, Mike Gibbins (Badfinger), Geoffrey Glover-Wright (Buddy Britten), Ron Griffiths (Iveys), Stefan Grossman, John Hewlett, Richard Hewson, Chris Hodge, Richard Imrie, Tony King, Kosh (John Kosh), Dave Lambert (Fire), Ronnie Leahy (Trash), Derek Lepper, John Lewis (MJQ), Jackie Lomax, Graham Lyle, Toby Mamis, Ken Mansfield, Guy Masson (Mortimer), Mike McCartney, Joey Molland (Badfinger), Alan Morgan (Felius Andromeda), Lionel Morton, Shirley Natanson, Jean Nesbit, Charlie Nuccio, Mike O'Connor, Mike O'Donnell, Bill Oakes, Jack Oliver, Nigel Oliver, May Pang, George Peckham, David Peel, John Perry (Grapefruit), Jeff Peters (Turquoise), Dave Rhodes (Focal Point), Pat Savant (Sundown Playboys), Dave Slater (Focal Point), Tom Smith (Mortimer), Al Steckler, Roger Swallow (Denis Couldry's Smile), Geoff Swettenham (Grapefruit), Pete Swettenham (Grapefruit), Paul Tennant (Focal Point), Yannis Tsamplakos (The Perishers), Doris Troy, Lon Van Eaton, Derrek Van Eaton, Tony Van Benschoten (Mortimer), Gary Van Scyoc (Elephant's Memory), Klaus Voormann, Fraser Watson (Trash), Steve Webber, Debbie Wellum, George Young (Easybeats) and Monika Young

There are so many others who also went above and beyond, and they include: Richard Anderson, Christina Bolio, Matt Bristow, Mrs. Daphne Brown, Andy Davis, Neil Dell, Ed Dieckmann, Dhiraj,

Nathan Eighty, Kris Engelhardt, Joe Foster, Ron Furmanek, Guy Hayden, Paolo Hewitt, Matt Ingham, Tom Jenner, Graham Johnston, Axel Korinth, Andrew Lauder, Nigel Lees, Jeff Levy, John Lyndon, Dan Matovina, Jon Mills (*Shindig*), Jon Roberts, Andy Morten (*Shindig*), Simon Murphy, Jim Phaelen, John Reed, Ken Richards, Pat Richmond, Nick Robbins, Paul Robinson, Andrew Sandoval, Paul Sexton, Phil Smee, Neil Smithies, Dave Timperley, Adam Velasco, Natasha Wells, Paul Widger, and Richard Younger. Thank you all.

And finally, thanks and gratitude must go to my wife, Maggie, and our son, Will, for putting up with me during the creation of both *Those Were The Days* and the many CD reissue projects. Will was particularly accommodating as I endlessly auditioned Apple Publishing CDs during long car rides when he was a toddler. I confess to reacting with a combination of horror and pride, when, in a quiet moment, Will, at the age of four, proceeded to sing Denis Couldry's "James In The Basement" almost word for word. I will surely pay for my sins.

PHOTO CREDITS:

1) 1968 bookmark from the Apple Boutique

2) 1968 post card from the Apple Boutique

3) 1968 Grapefruit promo picture (courtesy John Perry)

4) 1968 Focal Point press clipping

5) 1968 Grapefruit music trade paper ad

6) 1970 Apple Post Card feat. 3 Savile Row

7) 1969 Apple Records press handout for James Taylor

8) 1969 Apple Records press handout for the Modern Jazz Quartet

9) 1968 insert that came with the Wonderwall Music album

10) Drew and Dy 1968 (courtesy Pete Dymond)

11) 1969 Iveys fan club card (courtesy Dan Matovina)

12) Jackie Lomax 1969 (courtesy the estate of Jackie Lomax)

13) Derek Taylor and Mary Hopkin in the Apple Press office 1969 (copyright Tom Hanley)

14) Apple Records President Ron Kass in his office at 3 Savile Row, 1969 (copyright Tom Hanley)

15) Mal Evans and Ken Mansfield 1969 (courtesy Ken Mansfield)

16) Neil Aspinall in his office at 3 Savile Row, 1969 (copyright Tom Hanley)

17) Paul McCartney and Mavis Smith in the Apple Press office 1969 (copyright Tom Hanley)

18) Derek Taylor and Peter Brown in the Apple Press office 1969 (copyright Tom Hanley)

19) John Hewlett in the Apple Publishing office (courtesy John Hewlett)

20) Tony Bramwell and Apple Doorman Jimmy Clark, 1969 (copyright Tom Hanley)

21) Mortimer 1969 (courtesy the estate of Tom Smith)

22) Peter Asher and Richard Hewson working on arrangements for Mortimer, 1969 (courtesy the estate of Tom Smith)

23) Barry Sheffield and Peter Asher in Trident Studios, recording Mortimer, 1969 (courtesy the estate of Tom Smith)

24) Allen Klein leaving 3 Saville Row, 1969 (copyright Tom Hanley)

25) Alan Pariser, Mal Evans and George Harrison in Harrison's office at 3 Savile Row, 1969 (copyright Tom Hanley)

26) 1969 Apple Records music trade paper ad

27) 1969 Billy Preston music trade paper ad

28) 1969 Apple Records post card

29) 1969 White Trash music trade paper ad

30) 1970 Radha Krishna Temple card from Germany

31) 1970 Apple Records press handout for Doris Troy

32) Al Steckler presents Badfinger (Pete Ham and Joey Molland) with a gold record at Carnegie Hall, 1972 (courtesy Al Steckler)

33) George Harrison, John Lennon and Yoko Ono at Apple, 1971 (courtesy Al Steckler).

34) Pete Ham and Tom Evans presented with a gold disc for "Without You" at Apple, 1972. L-R Tony King, Bernard Brown, Harry Nilsson, Tom Evans, Pete Ham and Ringo Starr (courtesy Tony King)

35) Derrek Van Eaton at Ringo Starr in Apple Studios, 1971 (courtesy and copyright Robin Garb)

36) Derrek Van Eaton, Pete Bennett, Lon Van Eaton, Al Steckler and Robin Garb at Brother release reception, 1972. (courtesy and copyright Robin Garb).

37) Ringo Starr, Klaus Voormann and Lon Van Eaton in Apple Studios, 1971. (courtesy and copyright Robin Garb).

38) 1972 Chris Hodge music trade paper ad

39) 1972 David Peel music trade paper ad

40) 1972 Phil Spector promo poster

41) 1972 Sundown Playboys music trade paper ad

42) 1972 Elephants Memory (with John Lennon and Yoko Ono) Apple Records press handout

43) Badfinger 1973 (Photo by Tony Beresford-Cooke, copyright Dan Matovina)

44) Yoko Ono promo advertisement

45) 1992 Apple Records promo poster

INDEX:

Other titles available from

A Plugged In State Of Mind: The
History of Electronic Music
Dave Henderson

All The Young Dudes: Mott The
Hoople & Ian Hunter
Campbell Devine

Arguments Yard – 35 Years Of
Ranting Verse And Thrash Mandola
Atilla The Stockbroker

Best Seat In The House: A Cock
Sparrer Story
Steve Bruce

Bittersweet: The Clifford T Ward
Story
David Cartwright

Block Buster! – The True Story of The
Sweet
Dave Thompson

Burning Britain: A History Of UK
Punk 1980 To 1984
Ian Glasper

Celebration Day: A Led Zeppelin
Encyclopedia
Malcolm Dome and Jerry Ewing

Children of the Revolution: The
Glam Rock Encyclopedia
Dave Thompson

Death To Trad Rock: The Post-Punk
fanzine scene 1982-87
John Robb

Deathrow: The Chronicles Of
Psychobilly
Alan Wilson

Embryo:- A Pink Floyd Chronology
1966-1971
Nick Hodges And Ian Priston

Fucked By Rock (Revised and
Expanded)
**Mark Manning (aka Zodiac
Mindwarp)**

Goodnight Jim Bob:On The Road
With Carter USM
Jim Bob

Good Times Bad Times - The Rolling
Stones 1960-69
**Terry Rawlings and Keith
Badman**

Hells Bent On Rockin: A History Of
Psychobilly
Craig Brackenbridge

Independence Days - The Story Of
UK Independent Record Labels
Alex Ogg

Indie Hits 1980 – 1989
Barry Lazell

Irish Folk, Trad And Blues: A Secret
History
Colin Harper and Trevor Hodgett

Johnny Thunders: In Cold Blood
Nina Antonia

Please visit **www.cherryredbooks.co.uk** for further info and mail order

Here at Cherry Red Books we're always interested to hear of interesting titles looking for a publisher. Whether it's a new manuscript or an out of print or deleted title, please feel free to get in touch if you have something you think we should know about.

books@cherryred.co.uk

www.cherryredbooks.co.uk
www.cherryred.co.uk

CHERRY RED BOOKS
A division of Cherry Red Records Ltd,
Power Road Studios
114 Power Road
London
W4 5PY